LIVING WITH COLOR

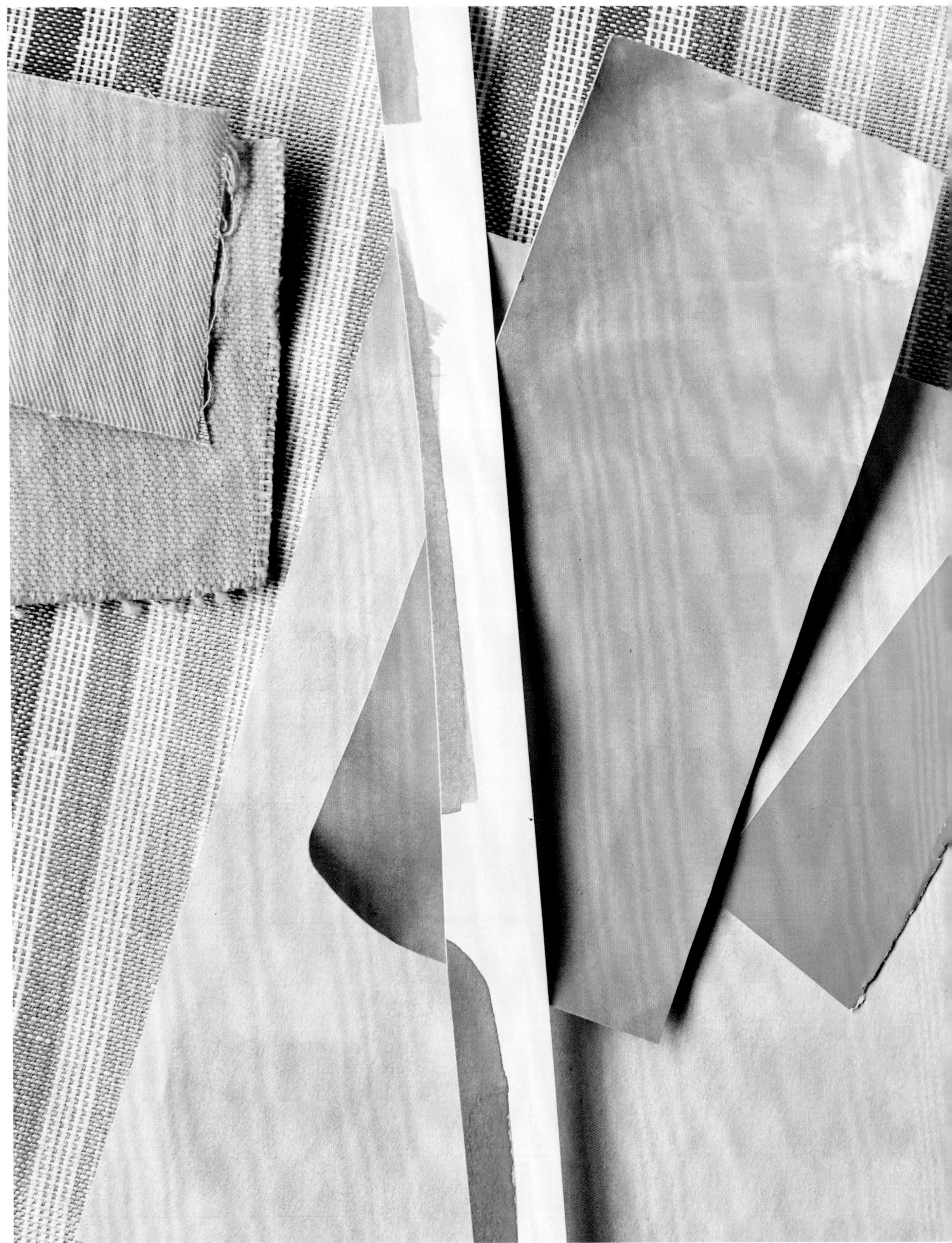

REBECCA ATWOOD

LIVING WITH COLOR

Inspiration and How-Tos to Brighten Up Your Home

Photographs by
SHARON RADISCH

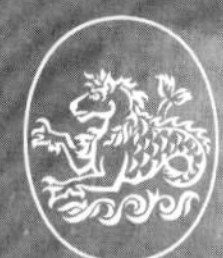

CLARKSON POTTER/PUBLISHERS
New York

Published in the United States by Clarkson Potter/Publishers,
an imprint of Random House, a division of
Penguin Random House LLC, New York.
clarksonpotter.com

CLARKSON POTTER is a trademark and POTTER with colophon
is a registered trademark of Penguin Random House LLC.

Library of Congress Cataloging-in-Publication Data
Names: Atwood, Rebecca, author. | Radisch, Sharon, photographer (expression)
Title: Living with color : inspiration and how-tos to brighten up your home /
Rebecca Atwood ; photographs by Sharon Radisch. Description: First edition.
| New York : Clarkson Potter, [2019] Identifiers: LCCN 2018050820 (print)
| LCCN 2018061531 (ebook) | ISBN 9781524763466 (ebook) | ISBN
9781524763459 (hardcover) Subjects: LCSH: Color in interior decoration.
Classification: LCC NK2115.5.C6 (ebook) | LCC NK2115.5.C6 A854 2019
(print) | DDC 747/.94—dc23
LC record available at https://lccn.loc.gov/2018050820

ISBN 978-1-5247-6345-9
Ebook ISBN 978-1-5247-6346-6

Printed in China

Book and cover design by Mia Johnson
Cover artwork (pattern) by Rebecca Atwood
Cover photography by Sharon Radisch
Illustrations by Rebecca Atwood

5 7 9 10 8 6 4

First Edition

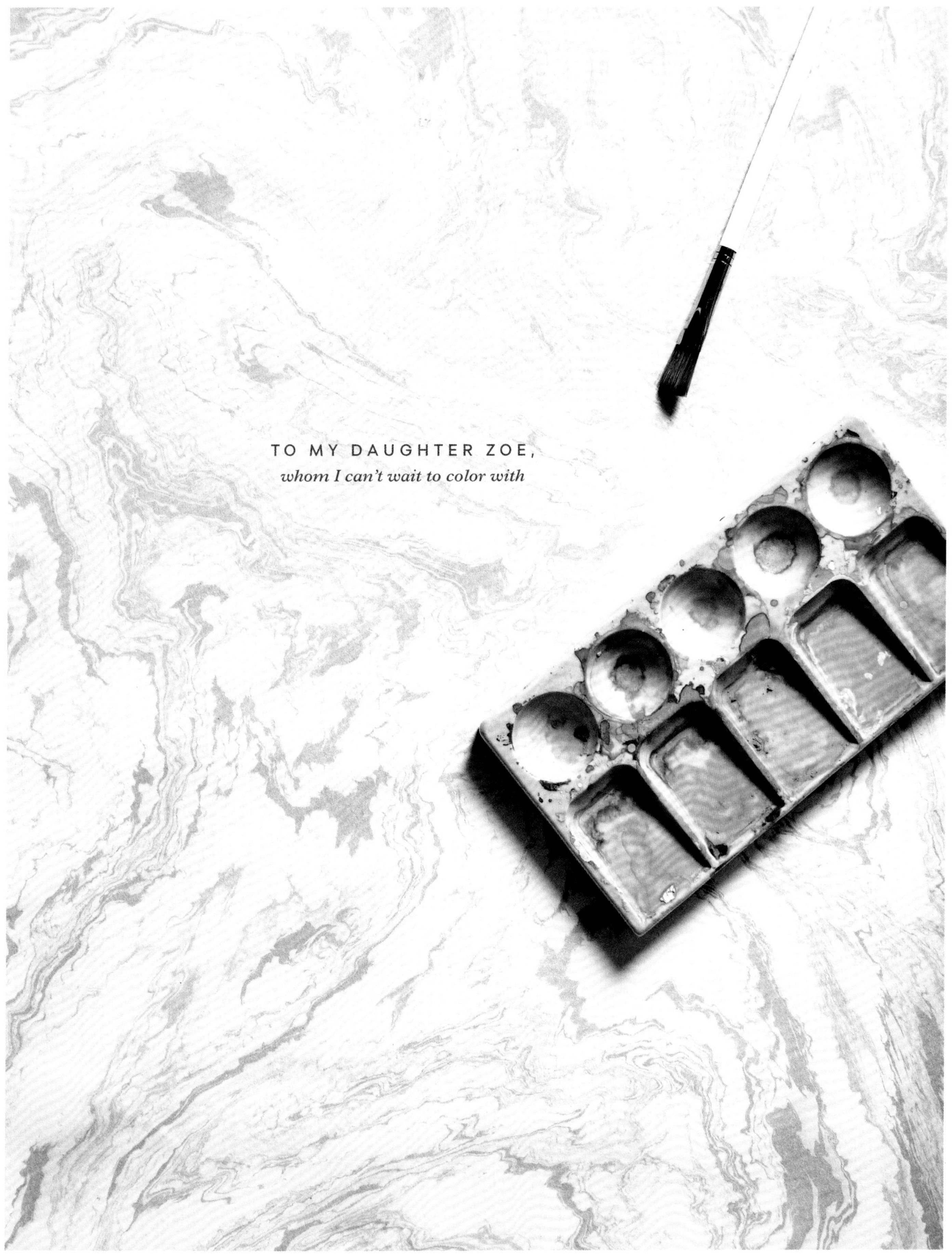

TO MY DAUGHTER ZOE,

whom I can't wait to color with

CONTENTS

PART FOUR

Living Color 122

PART FIVE

Finding Color 232

INTRODUCTION

MY COLOR STORY

I've always been drawn to color, and my parents encouraged my love of art at an early age. At just five years old, I had books on Monet and Renoir, and my earliest memories are of drawing with my two sisters. We would lie on the floor and color for hours, with the sunlight streaming in through the big glass door and our crayons, pencils, watercolors, and giant pieces of paper splayed out around us. At some point, our grandfather gave us a professional set of Pentel markers, and they seemed like a rainbow in a box compared to the simple primary colors we'd used up until then. Housed in a golden case, they were a beautiful object unto themselves, and the most fascinating thing about this rainbow was the multiple versions of the same colors—warm blue and cool blue, a true red and a burgundy. The marker set expanded my color palette, and with all these tools at my fingertips, I became hooked.

As I got older, my color story expanded. Growing up on Cape Cod, I was drawn to the beach in the off-season: the quieter time of year when the individual softer, muted tones of the natural landscape are highlighted because of the limited color palette. This is where I learned to see the beauty of neutrals—not your typical desaturated gray or tan but rather multicolored, chromatic neutrals, which I will teach you all about in this book.

Artists have long been drawn to the Cape because of its serenity, juxtaposed with dramatic light. In the course of one day, the sand shifts from a soft, pale caramel to a bright cream at midday and, finally, to an ethereal glowing pink before the sun sets. There are infinite hues within these colors of sand, and within all of nature—the sky, the sea, a field, or trees in the distance. There is always tonal variation, with the light picking up and highlighting the different textures in the landscape. I would sit on the beach, looking for these transformations and watching the waves coming in and going out, studying how the sky and water met at the horizon. I realized that this calm but colorful world was where I wanted to live.

Over time, my childhood predilection for drawing gave way to painting and making things with my hands. Painting became my greatest form of expression, and it's how I learned to understand color. I now recognize that I was attempting to mirror the beauty I saw in nature and the world around me. In middle school, I took a watercolor course where, in preparation for the class, we were given a shopping list of the "basic" colors we would need. We had a warm red and a cool red, as well as neutral hues like ochre and burnt sienna. I remember thinking, "Who would want these bland, boring hues when there's blue and yellow?" But through this class, and subsequent art lessons, I realized that these earth pigments are primers for creating a world that mimics nature and are building blocks for mixing hues. I was taught that when you're painting a landscape or a still life, you're re-creating how the light looks at a particular moment in time, and it subsequently shaped the way I think about color, art, and design.

I was so enamored with these concepts that studying fine art in college seemed like the natural next step, so after high school, I enrolled in Rhode Island School of Design as a painting major. I remember thinking that perhaps I should study something more "practical," like business, but I had faith that I would be able to bring art into everyday life. Over time I've realized that designing rooms and home goods was just like painting landscapes. With a room, you're making something out of nothing; you have to figure out which colors to use to achieve the feeling you want, and, just as in painting, neutrals are your base from which to build.

I graduated from RISD and began designing products for different companies, but with time I yearned to create art pieces for the home that felt like the landscapes from my childhood and that made it easy to layer livable color. I wanted to make palettes that captured the subdued tones of the Cape and to allow customers to bring the beauty of nature into their homes. I believed the product should feel personal, and I liked the idea of controlling how it was being made. I spent a lot of time thinking about my personal story, collecting inspiration and focusing on the creative process, dreaming up pieces that felt different from anything I'd seen. Instead of producing pieces in response to trends, I wanted to create home goods that could be paired together to make beautiful environments unto themselves. I studied color and never stopped being a student of nature and art, and I want to share all that I've learned with you in this book.

ABOUT THIS BOOK

I begin Living with Color *with the concept that color is alive.* In Part One: Understanding Color, I'll introduce you to the world of color through a scientific lens because, before you can decide which paint color is right for your bedroom, it's important to know that color is about perception. It is constantly changing, and we all experience it differently. This is why colors are so open to interpretation and deeply associated with feelings. Part One also explains how colors interact with one another and why certain colors make us feel cool and others warm. In this section, we'll consider what feelings you want to perceive in different rooms of your home. There is fascinating science behind why a room makes you feel cozy or calm!

Once you understand that color isn't static, you open up to the idea that there are infinite tones of colors that change with the season and time of day. In Part Two: Feeling Color, we'll explore these connections as well as the relationships between color and the senses. Color is so visceral—you can almost taste, touch, and smell it—and here I'll allow space for your mind to wander, for your mouth to water, and for you to draw free associations with the color world.

In Part Three: Seeing Color, I'll share my personal color memories with you and invite you to wash yourself in each color of the rainbow, soak in its rich history, and use it in a palette with other colors. We'll end this part with tips for how to incorporate each color into your home in thoughtful, organic ways.

In Part Four: Living Color, we'll tour! I'll take you inside the homes and lives of those who are living with color and using it in breathtaking ways. From chromatic neutrals to bright bursts, we'll see color stories in action, alive in the homes of artists and friends.

Lastly, we'll connect with color on a personal level. Color and meaning are complicated but also inspiring and captivating. In Part Five: Finding Color, I'll ask you to create your own distinct color wheel using your knowledge, personal exploration, and inspiration to design a rainbow that tells your unique color story. In the final pages of the book, we'll explore the kind of landscape in which you want to live. We'll dive into your own color memories and swim around in your color world. We'll go on a color hunt, looking for magic in the mundane, and open our eyes to the infinite color that surrounds us each day in exciting ways. Noticing the beauty in the myriad greens in your neighbor's front lawn or the variations in the grays on the sidewalk will make you feel more engaged in life and appreciative on your morning commute.

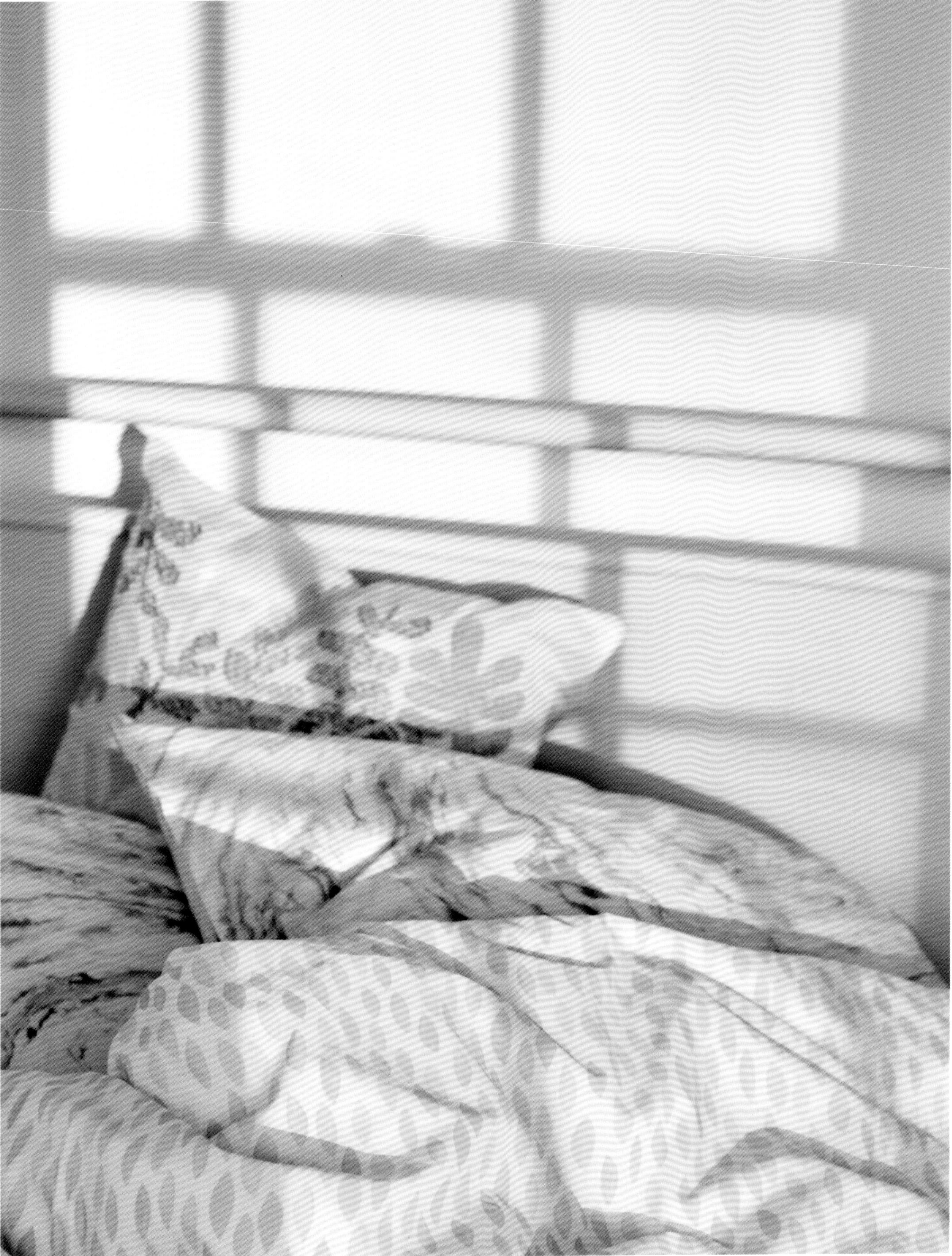

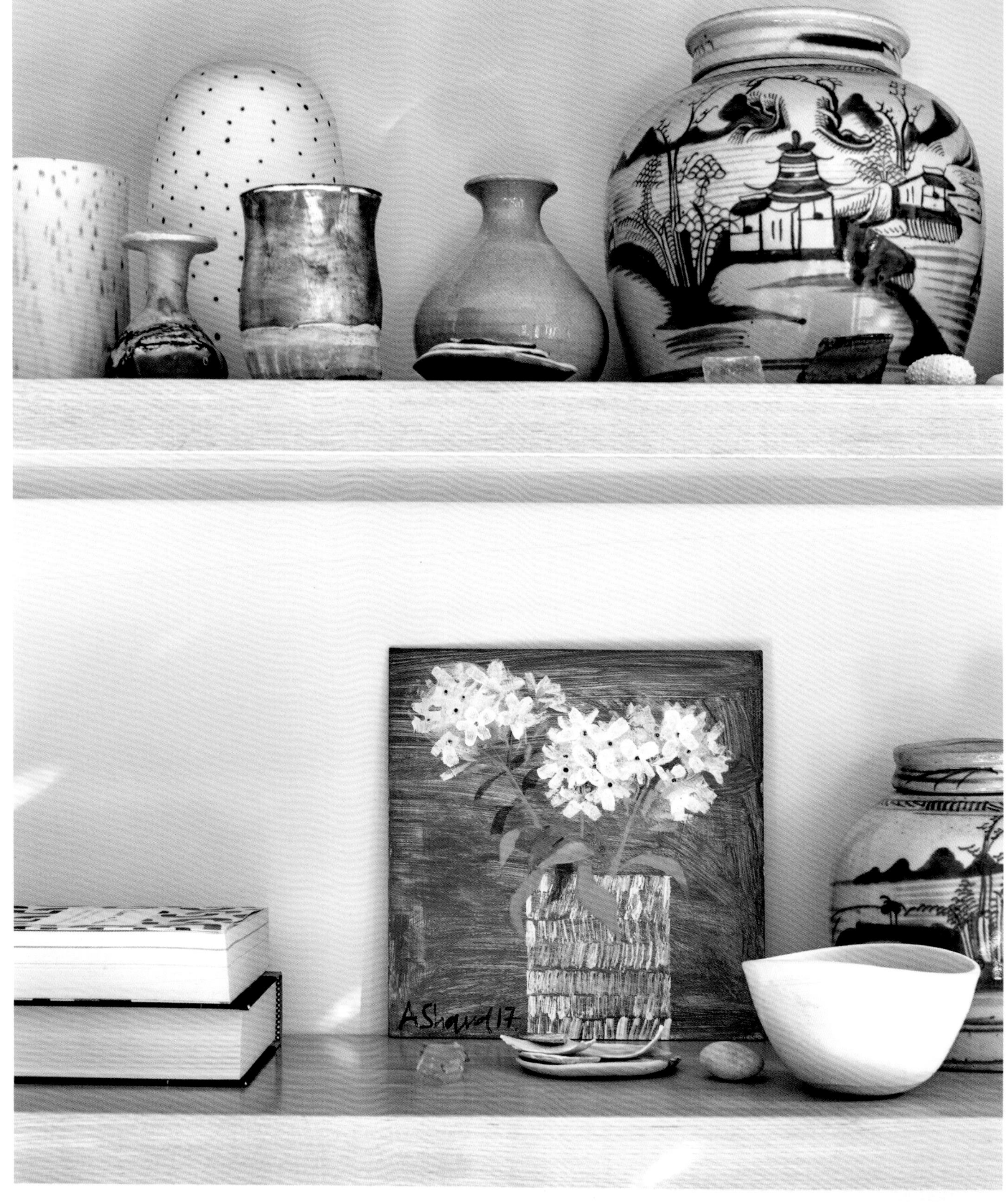
AShand17.

COLOR IS MAGIC

When you open your eyes to the color all around us, you realize that color is the stuff of life. Even now, I still find color magical. I was recently visiting my painter friend Michelle Armas in her studio in Atlanta, and I fell in love with two paintings filled with beautiful green hues and hints of lilac. They reminded me of dusk on summer evenings under the trees near my childhood home. I could feel it in my chest—and we both laughed about how physical that draw of color can be. "It's a thing!" we cried. I still get excited when I see something out in the world and the light hits it in this dreamlike way (what is referred to as the magic hour in filmmaking). Color is what makes walking the same route to work every single day interesting. It's never truly the same because of the variations in light. I live in Brooklyn, and the tower on Atlantic Avenue is the perfect example. It's a not-very-exciting taupe-gray building, but at a certain hour, it glows an otherworldly pink and looks dreamlike against the blue sky. If you explore how to utilize, layer, and wield color, you can create something breathtaking. Color can make you feel anew, and that's my hope for you after you read this book.

Our approach to decorating with color will be to channel the same ease you felt when you were a kid coloring. Building out a space can feel overwhelming, especially when it comes to questions and decisions about colors, but learning to trust your instincts and to play is so important. When I think of adding color in a space, I imagine how a pink colored pencil can feel soft and hazy like a sunset, while the same hue in a marker could be bright and shiny like a dewy flower from my mom's garden. Allowing yourself to enjoy color with this kind of delight, and to incorporate such memories, will translate into an intentional, beautiful, and realized space.

I hope you will read the pages ahead with the understanding that color is not a solid, serious entity but a changing, spirited use of light. Imagine that scene in *The Wizard of Oz* when Dorothy opens the door to her own dream and walks out of her black-and-white world into delicious, vivid Technicolor. I want to help you rediscover the freedom you felt picking flowers or finger painting and weave the entirety of that personal color story you've been writing all your life seamlessly into your home. I can't wait!

Welcome to the world in color.

PART ONE

understanding COLOR

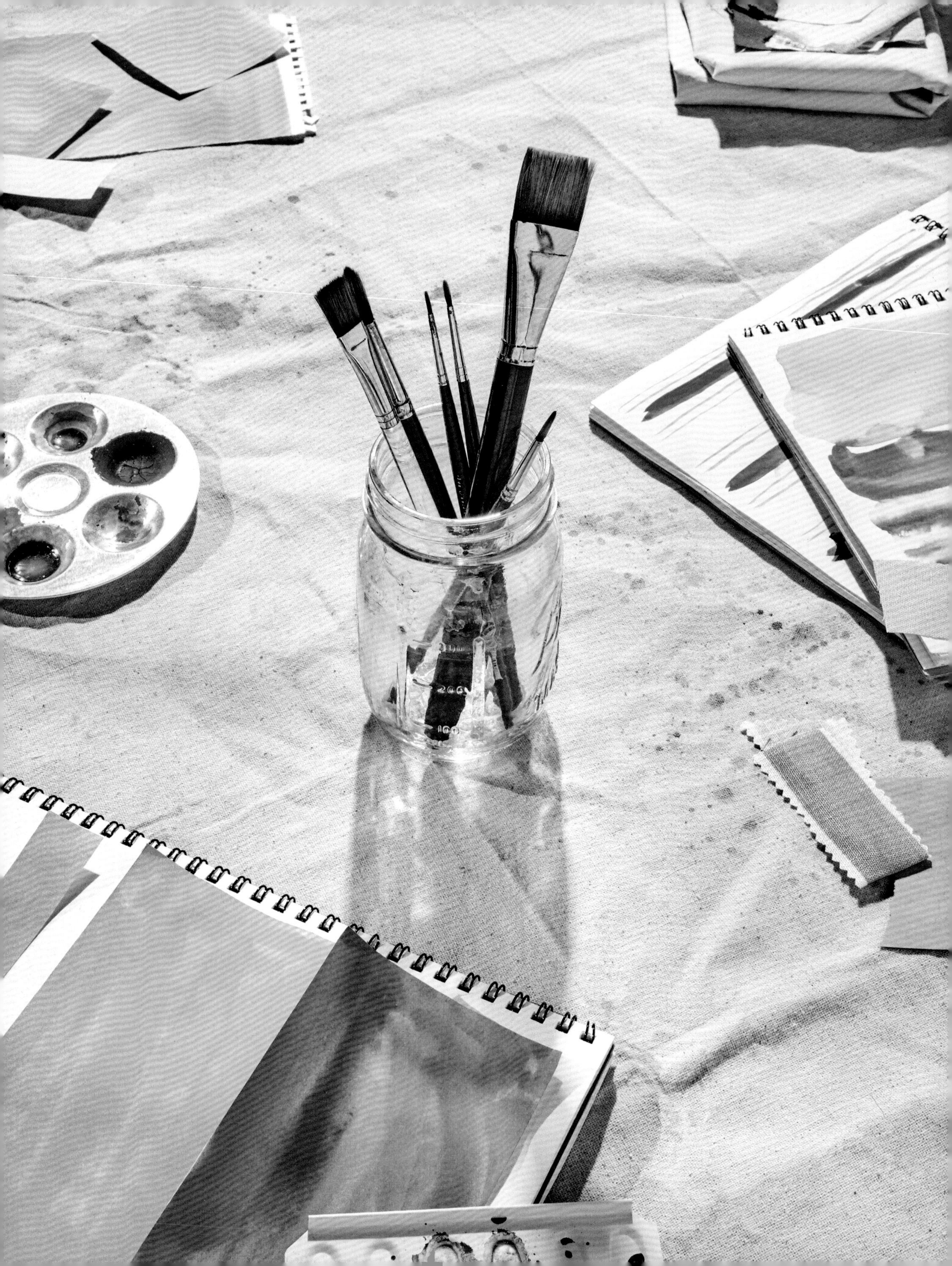

WHAT IS COLOR?

THE ELECTROMAGNETIC SPECTRUM

As a child, I loved looking for rainbows after a storm. I thought they were like something out of a fairy tale. I didn't understand exactly what they were, but they felt otherworldly.

To wield color properly and make it look beautiful in our homes, we must first understand exactly what color is. Is it even real? Or is it just a perception? Well, that depends on your definition of *real.* Color is not a solid entity but rather, as rainbows eventually taught me, a physical property of light. Each color travels along different wavelengths of light, creating a whole spectrum, and the portion of this spectrum that we can see with our eyes, and register with our brains, is visible light. Each of these colors, or wavelengths, operates at different frequencies. Yellows, reds, and oranges have the longest wavelengths, and we think of them as warm colors, while green, blue, and purple have shorter wavelengths, and we regard them as cooler colors. Later, we'll connect the idea of warm and cool colors to your home, but for now this helps explain that colors aren't static or fixed; they change depending on the light (which is affected by time of day and the seasons) and what other colors surround them.

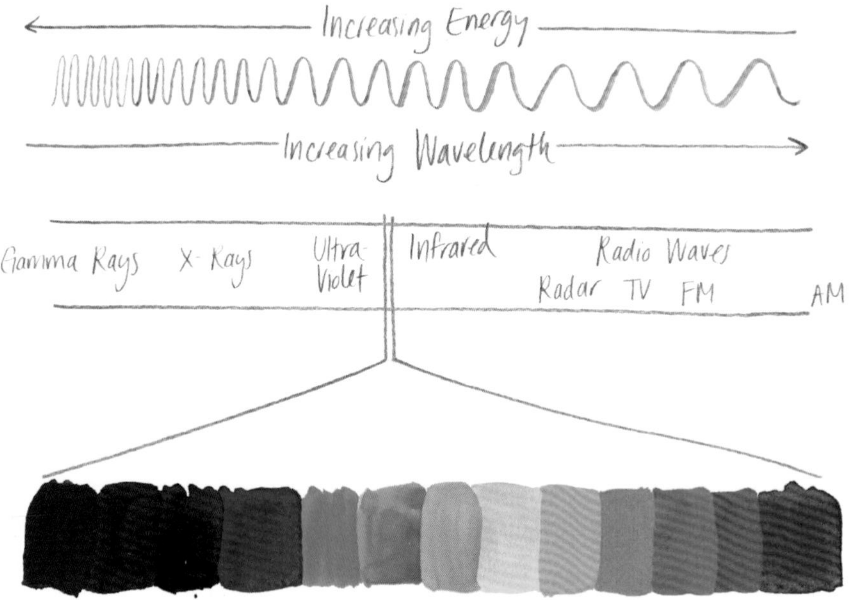

HOW WE SEE COLOR

To understand how we see color, let's look at a simple example, like an apple. The apple appears red, right? Well, the apple looks red because it is reflecting back the red color wavelength to our eye. All of the other color wavelengths (orange, yellow, green, blue, purple) hit the apple and are absorbed by it. The red bounces back, so red is what you see and what your brain perceives. But technically, the apple is actually every color *except* red. Wild, right? This is why I like to think of objects as *doing a color* rather than *being a color.*

Perception of color starts when light hits your retina, which is located in the back of your eye where there are different types of photoreceptors called rods and cones. The rods let us see in low-light conditions, but they do not help us see color. The cones operate on a more refined level and allow us to recognize specific colors. There are three types of cones, and they correspond to the colors red, green, and blue. So when we see that apple, our "red cone" picks up on this and sends a signal to the brain that this object is red.

Now take yellow, for example. When we look at a banana, there's no yellow cone to send the signal to our brain. The light hits our retina, and the red and green cones are activated because they are the closest to the color yellow, and the brain combines them to register yellow. Just by combining red, green, and blue, the human brain helps us see infinite colors. Scientists use this knowledge for technology like the television. Screens produce only red, green, and blue light, but because of how our brain processes color, we are able to see all of the colors we see on television screens. So when we see yellow on screen, the television is actually using just red and green light. Understanding how our brain sees color helps with our understanding of why people may perceive colors differently—or feel them differently.

Knowing that our minds are utilizing just three colors to interpret and create every other color is important because it expands our awareness as to why color is so complex and personal. It's not fixed—how one person perceives and reacts to a color will be different from how another person does. We have different sensitivities, brain chemistries, and associations.

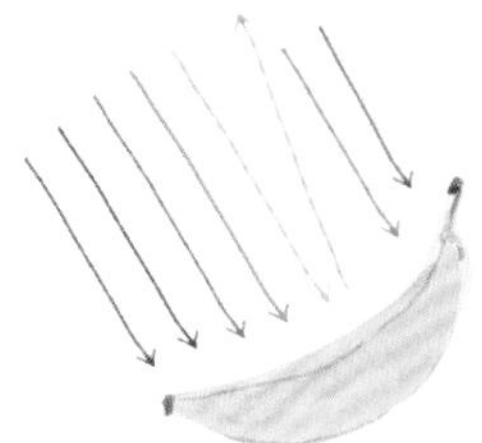

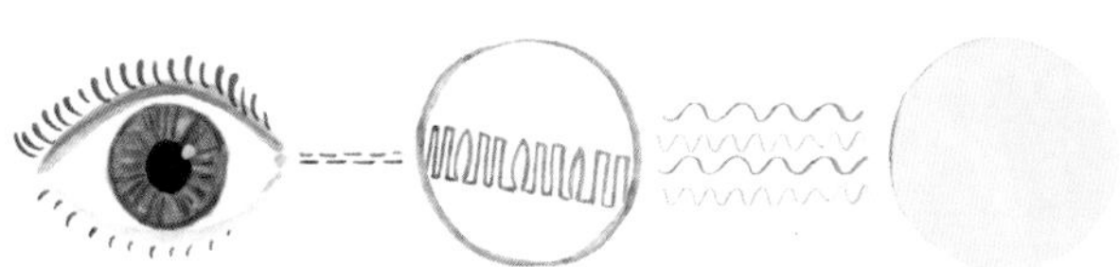

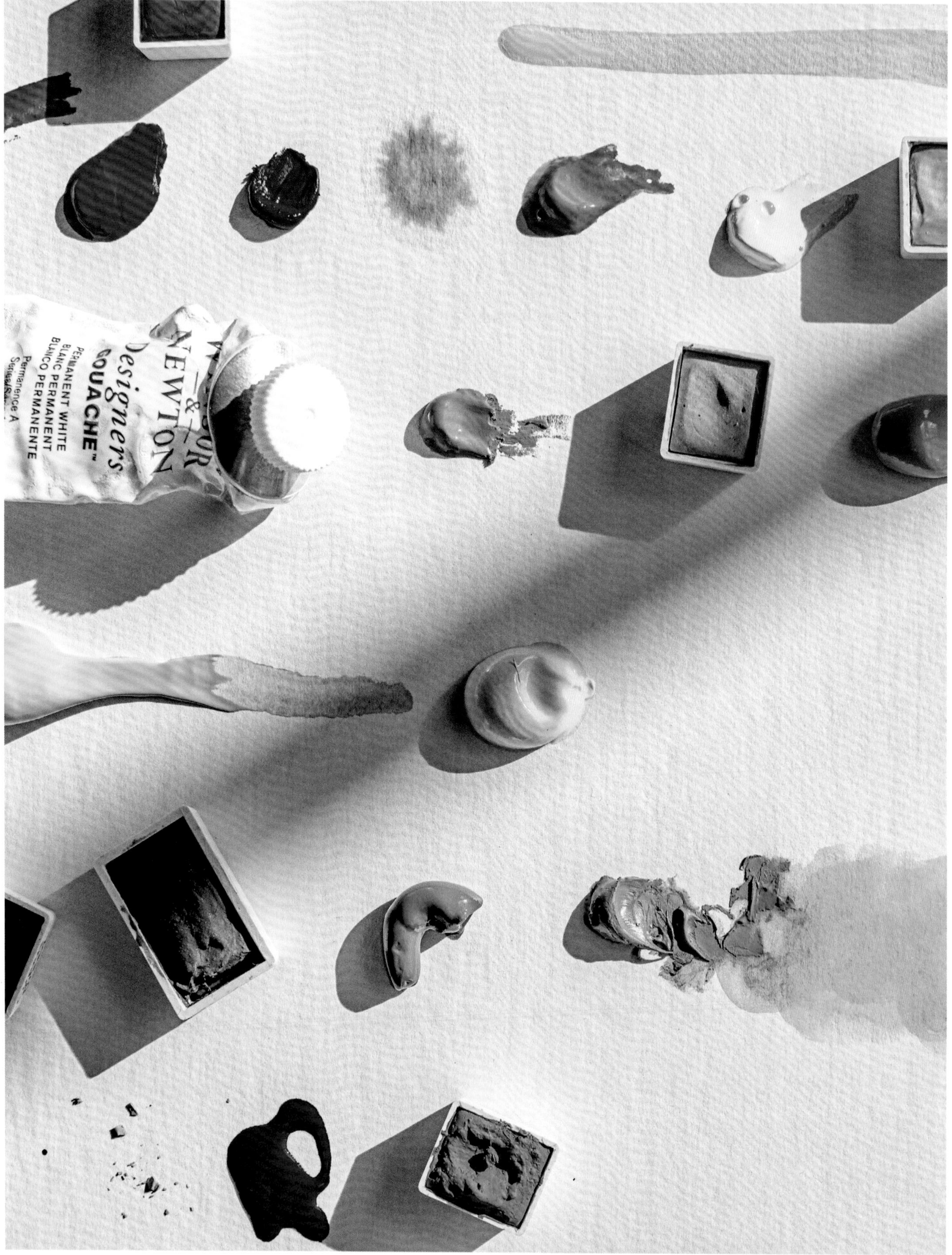
NEWTON
Designers
GOUACHE™
PERMANENT WHITE
BLANC PERMANENT
BLANCO PERMANENTE
Permanence A

THE COLOR WHEEL

With this basic foundation of color science, you're ready to experience the power of the color wheel. Do you ever wonder if certain colors will look good together in your home? The color wheel is your tool to answer that question, because it's a visual representation of each color's chromatic relationship to another. It's made up of primary, secondary, and tertiary colors. For centuries, the color wheel has been studied by artists, scientists, psychologists, and philosophers to understand the nuanced and varied effects of color on our minds, bodies, and souls. For our purposes here, we'll be looking at a color wheel based on subtractive color. Let's take a closer look.

PRIMARY

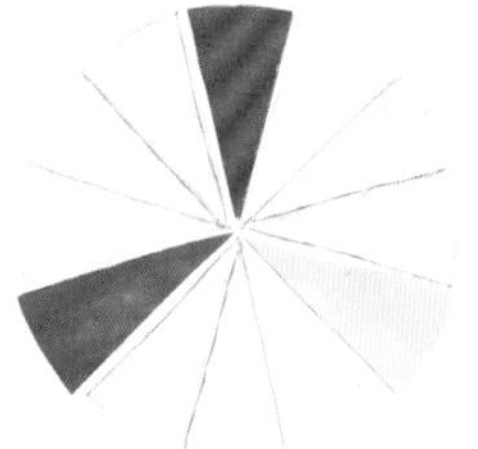

The primary colors are placed equidistant from one another. These colors cannot be created from mixing other colors—they are red, yellow, and blue.

SECONDARY

The secondary colors result from mixing two primary colors together. For example, mixing red and yellow creates orange, blue and yellow creates green, and blue and red creates purple.

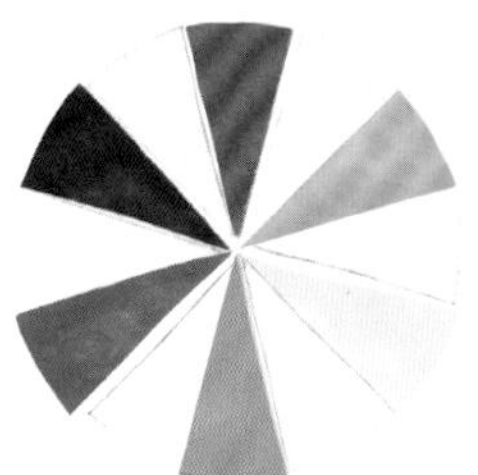

TERTIARY

The tertiary colors are the combinations of the nearest secondary and primary colors. For example, mixing red and orange creates red-orange, and mixing green and blue together will create green-blue.

With the wheel, you can go on mixing colors infinitely. When it comes to light, white is actually the presence of all colors—but with painting, if you mix all of the primary colors together you'll get black, or the absence of light.

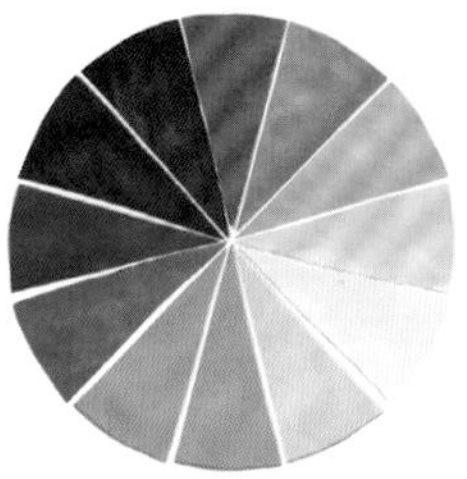

WARM COLORS AND COOL COLORS

The rainbow is broken up into warm and cool colors. If you know how these colors work, it can help you control the mood of a room.

The warm colors are red, orange, yellow, and all the colors in between. These colors advance in space, which means they come toward you and can make a big room feel smaller. They remind us of heat, sunshine, and warmth, and they make a space feel cozier. In some instances, we may feel warmer just by looking at them; you might even perceive a room to be a higher temperature if it's painted in one of these colors. Typically, they're thought of as stimulating colors, so they are used to energize and promote movement.

The cool colors are green, blue, purple, and all the colors in between. These colors recede in space when compared to warm colors. They are expansive and appear to push the walls of a room outward. They can make a space feel breezier, larger, and cooler. These colors remind us of water, sky, ice, snow, and cooler temperatures. Typically, they're thought of as calming colors, so they're used to help us soothe ourselves and unwind.

Every individual color has both warm and cool shades. For example, while red is a warm color, a cool red will have more blue in it, while a warm red will have more yellow. Think back to your crayon box—remember yellow-green and green-yellow? The difference may be subtle, but it's there. Both are actually warm greens, but one is edging warmer since it's more yellow. After we look at colors together, your eye will be trained to see the subtle difference between a cooler and a warmer version of a color.

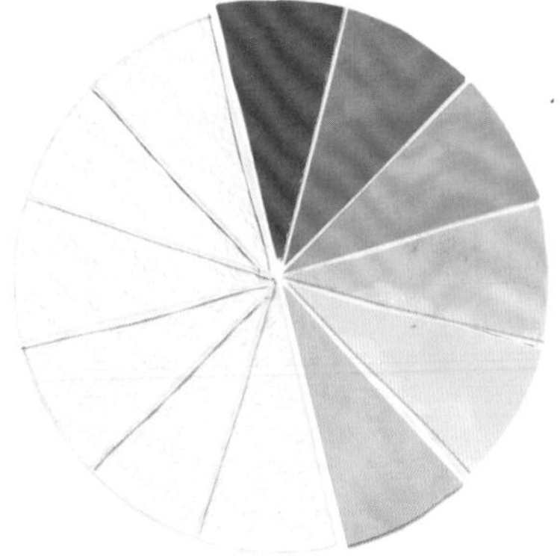

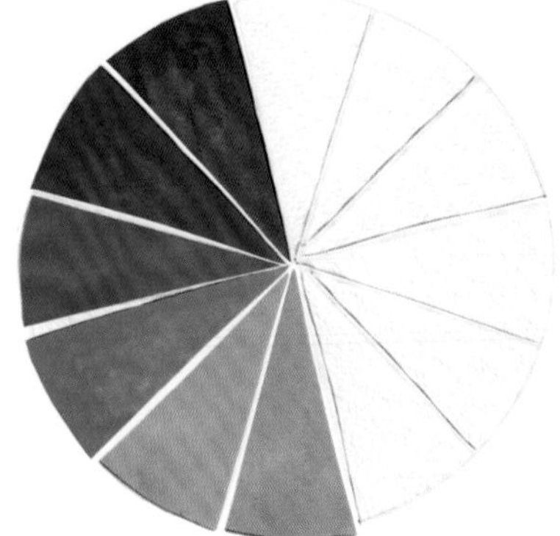

WARM NEUTRALS AND COOL NEUTRALS

Neutrals are versatile, subdued versions of brighter colors, which may not be how you're used to thinking about them. I want to break the habit many of us have of choosing any old gray sofa or oatmeal-colored paint and then throwing in bright "pops of color." Instead, I want you to slow down and think *thoughtfully, layered,* and *intentionally* when you approach a room. The oversimplified approach is to talk about neutrals being devoid of color, but the reality is quite the opposite.

Neutrals might *appear* to be without color, but most of the time, these hues have undertones, making them subtle versions of colors, which is how you should look at them. *White* is a blanket term for shades like cream and ivory, for example, but there are many different shades of white, and they can lean toward any color in the rainbow. You can have a blue-white or a red-white. If you go to the paint store and look at all the versions of white they offer, you'll see what I mean. Or, try this exercise I learned in college: paint a white egg on a white cloth—you'll find green, purple, the palest peach, and even more colors in that "white" egg.

Look for the undertones of a neutral, as this will help you understand what other colors it will look good with. For instance, if you're decorating with the color blue, pair it with a gray with a bit of blue in it to make it subtler, or if you want to accentuate the blueness, pair it with warmer neutrals and orange (think terra-cotta or natural leather) to bring it out. Recognizing and utilizing these variances gives you the utmost control over the palette of your room.

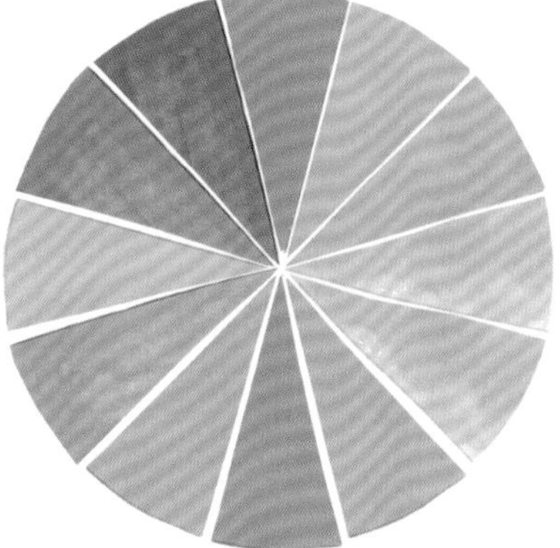

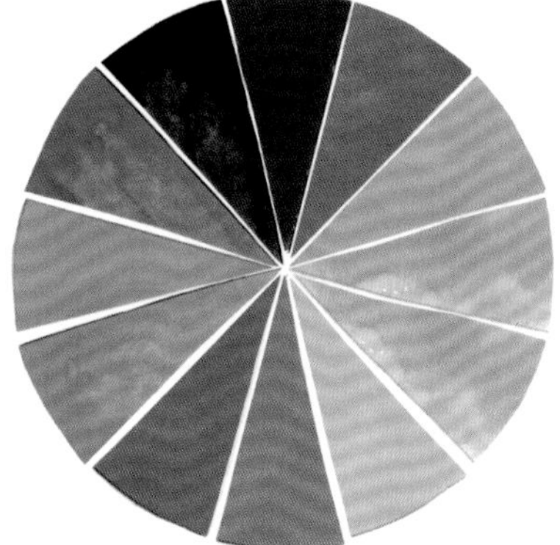

COMPLEMENTARY COLORS

Complementary colors are colors that are opposite each other on the color wheel. They intensify each other when placed in the same room. Creating these little vignettes is a great way to play with color and start a room.

RED & GREEN

When you think about red and green in a color palette, Christmas might come to mind, or the kelly green and bright pink that evoke Lilly Pulitzer, but there are so many other ways to use these colors. Imagine everything from mossy greens to deeper hunter greens.

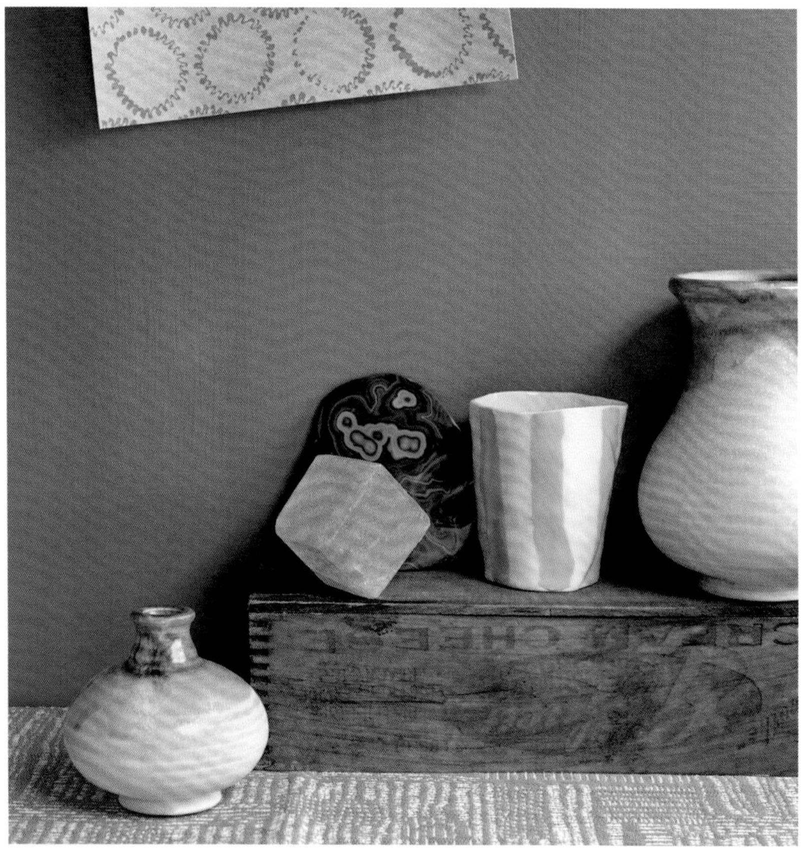

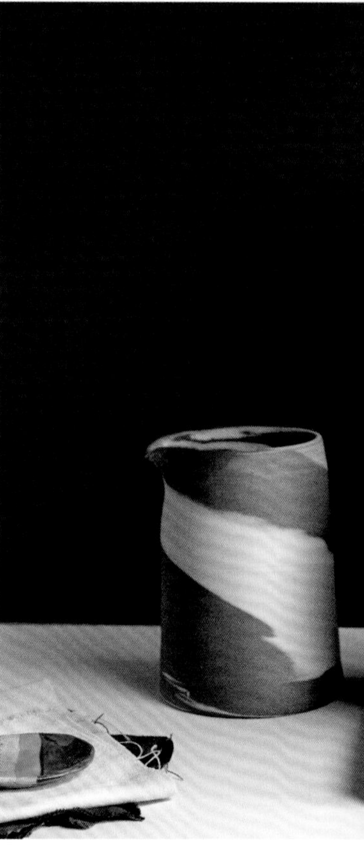

BLUE & ORANGE

With these hues, you might think of a sports team, like the New York Mets, but they can be a beautiful palette for an interior. Try a deep navy and a burnt rust–orange. Consider terra-cotta instead of orange; sometimes a natural material's color is easier to use than a flat painted version. Use bright versions of these colors, such as cobalt, as an accent.

YELLOW & PURPLE

Yellow and purple might seem like a wacky combination, but play with different saturations to create an unexpected pairing. Buttery yellows and golden neutrals make a great base for a room. Consider complex purples—like the color of a purple heart plant (*Tradescantia pallida*), with hints of green and red to accentuate the yellow.

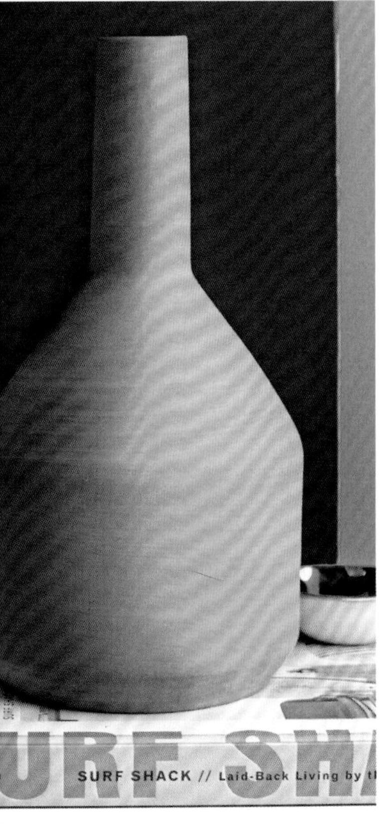

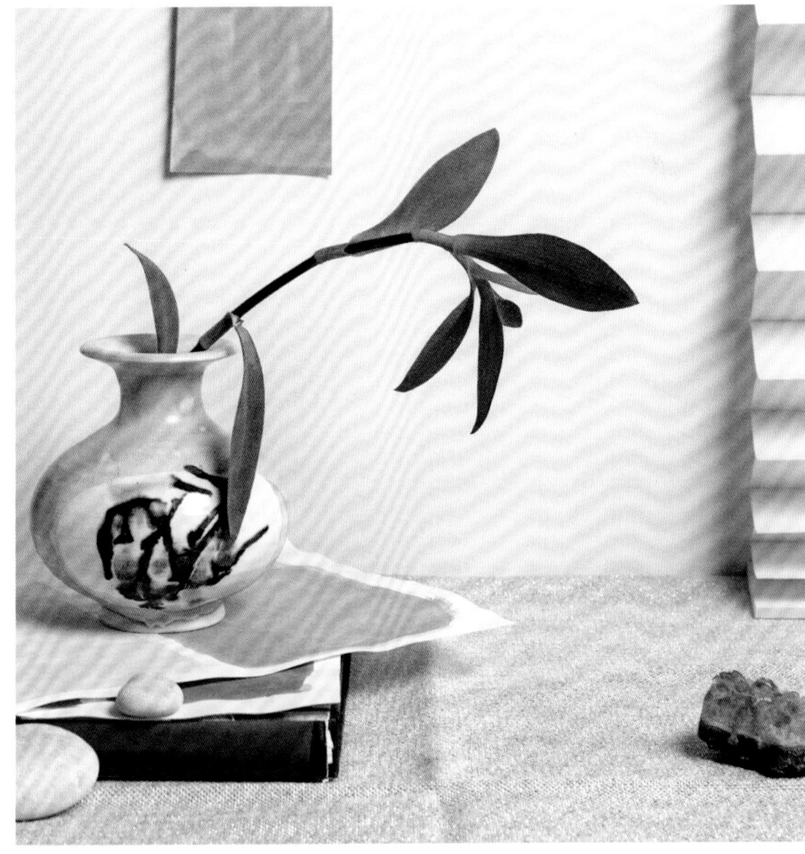

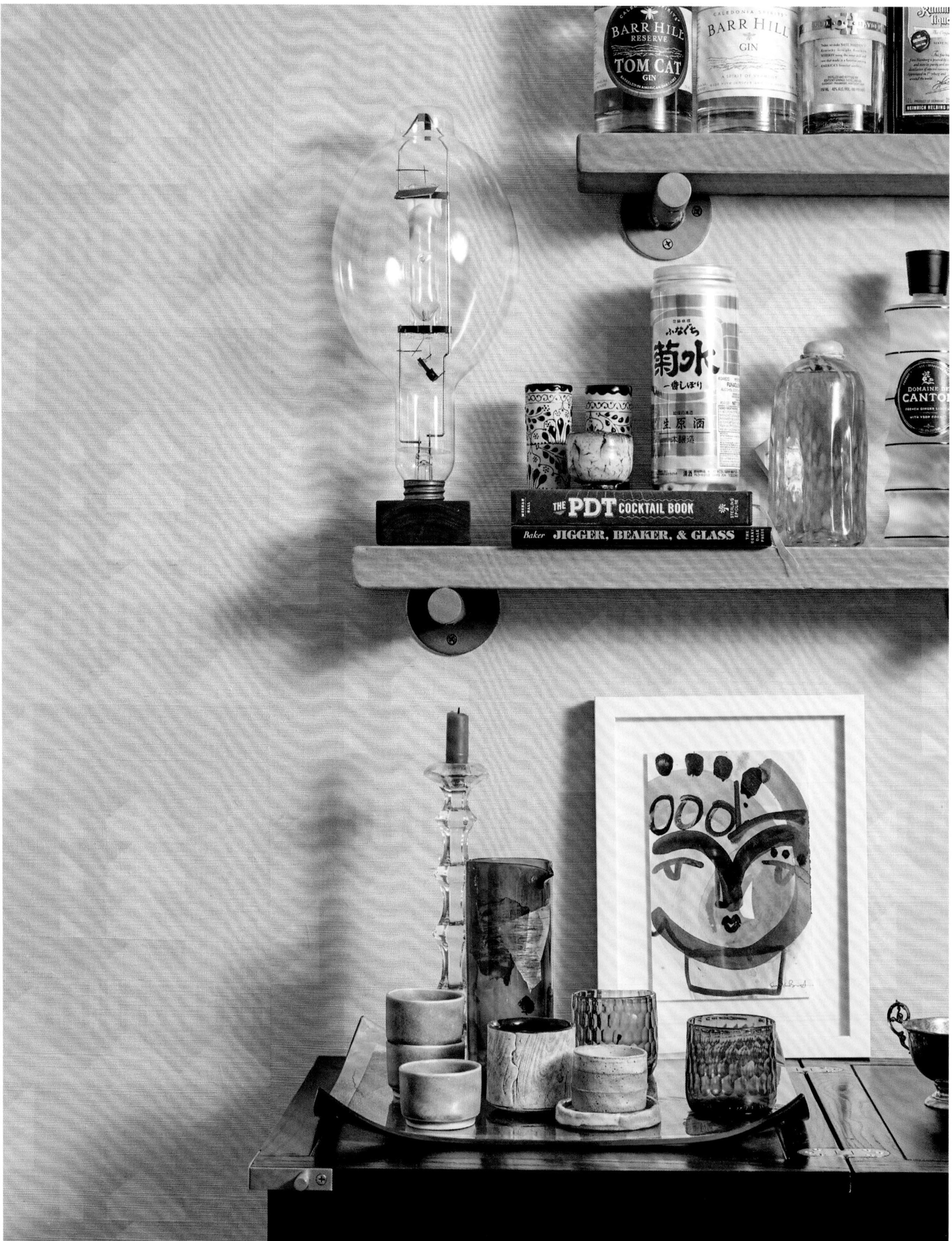
BARR HILL
RESERVE
TOM CAT
GIN
BARR HILL
GIN
菊水
THE PDT COCKTAIL BOOK
Baker JIGGER, BEAKER, & GLASS

FINISHES

Pigment is always a major factor if you're aiming for a rich, deep color or a minimalist vibe that is all about the simplicity and quality of the materials. I remember going to Dia:Beacon museum in Beacon, New York, and seeing Robert Ryman's white paintings. You might think, "How can all-white paintings be interesting?" Well, they are. They're luminous. The paintings glow and are quite mesmerizing because of their intensity. The materials here mattered and were integral to the process of creating the paintings. You can do more with less when the materials are carefully considered.

Whether something is glossy or dry and clay-like, or made up of synthetic versus natural materials, affects how we see color and how we use it. I took a class all about materials in art school where we learned about the quality of a paint, as well as how applying it to various surfaces makes it look different. The makeup and finish are important parts of how a color looks, as well as how the light interacts with the object. Does it absorb? Does it reflect? Is the color matte or shiny? Translucent or opaque?

Think about a shiny red versus a matte red. The matte red is going to feel more relaxed and casual, whereas the shiny red is going to be more luxe—or if it's not well made, it may look cheaper than a matte version. Shine attracts more attention—a glossy version of a hue allows you to dive in, and it can feel deeper and more reflective, so if you're a bit unsure about using a certain hue, a matte finish may be preferable. Either way, it's best to have a variety of finishes in a room to keep it visually interesting, especially when you're working with a neutral or monochromatic color palette.

COLOR TERMS

It's time to learn how to speak color. Color has its own vocabulary that allows us to best describe the endless variations of any one in particular. These words describe how much light, dark, depth, and richness a color can have. A true color expert is armed with these terms, because being fluent in color is part of feeling comfortable adding more of it to your life.

When we're decorating our homes, it's helpful to manipulate color to find the perfect look for a room, and these terms will allow you to use language to do so.

HUE / A color in its pure form. This is the most basic color term, because it determines the color we would like to use and sets the foundation for a color concept—for example, "orange," "blue," or "red."

PIGMENT / The material used to make a color. For instance, lapis lazuli is a stone used to make that specific blue. Pigment is where color price differences come into play—the difference between an expensive red paint and an inexpensive one is the pigment used to create it.

VALUE / The lightness or darkness of a color, which indicates the amount of light reflected.

SATURATION / The luminosity and intensity of a color. Saturation describes the purity of the hue. You can have two colors that are the same value, but one will feel brighter and more vibrant if it has a higher saturation. Imagine two different versions of blue: a bright cobalt and a blue-gray. The bright cobalt has a higher saturation and, therefore, appears more vivid and luminous than the blue-gray.

TINT / Mixing a color with white. An easy example of this is pink as a tint of red. Imagine tints as if they were hues bleached by the sun.

SHADE / Mixing a color with black. An easy example of this is navy as a shade of blue. Imagine how a hue darkens in the shade of a tree or at night.

TONE / Mixing a color with gray, which creates a duller version of a hue that falls in between a tint and shade, but with less saturation. Tone connects intrinsically with saturation.

CONNECTOR COLOR / While not a technical term, this is a label that I use throughout this book. When you're building a color palette, you often need a connector color—a tint, tone, or shade of a more saturated hue—to help you bridge the difference between an accent color and a neutral base. The connector color relates to other colors in the room so that, for example, the "pop" of an accent color feels less like a surprise that doesn't seem to fit in the space.

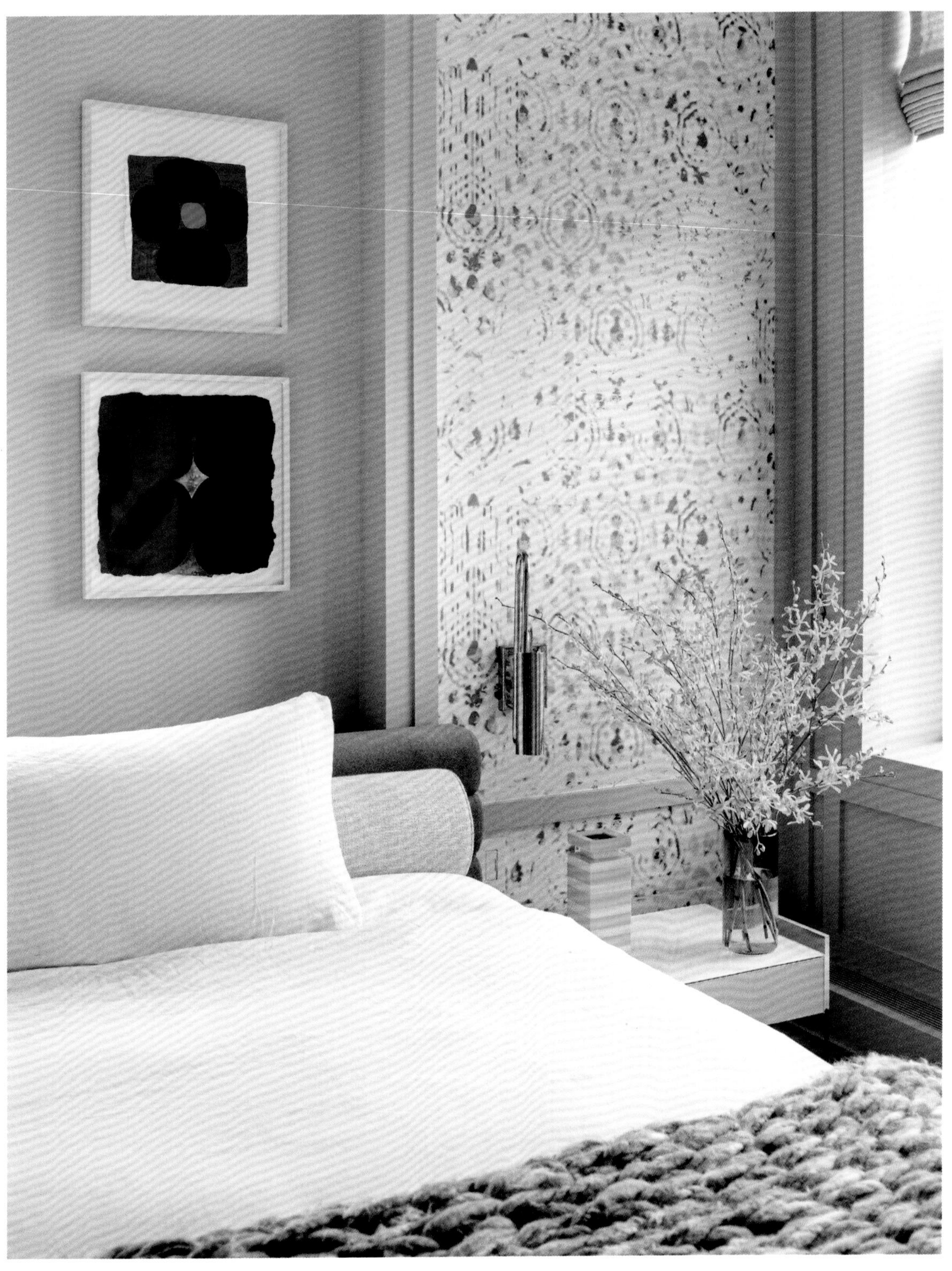

アルミ箔密封包装
熱湯を注ぎますと、日本茶独特の
香りがただよい、おいしいお茶が
召しあがれます。
Packed by
YAMAMOTOYAMA® of America
122 Voyager St. Pomona, CA 91768
Monterrey

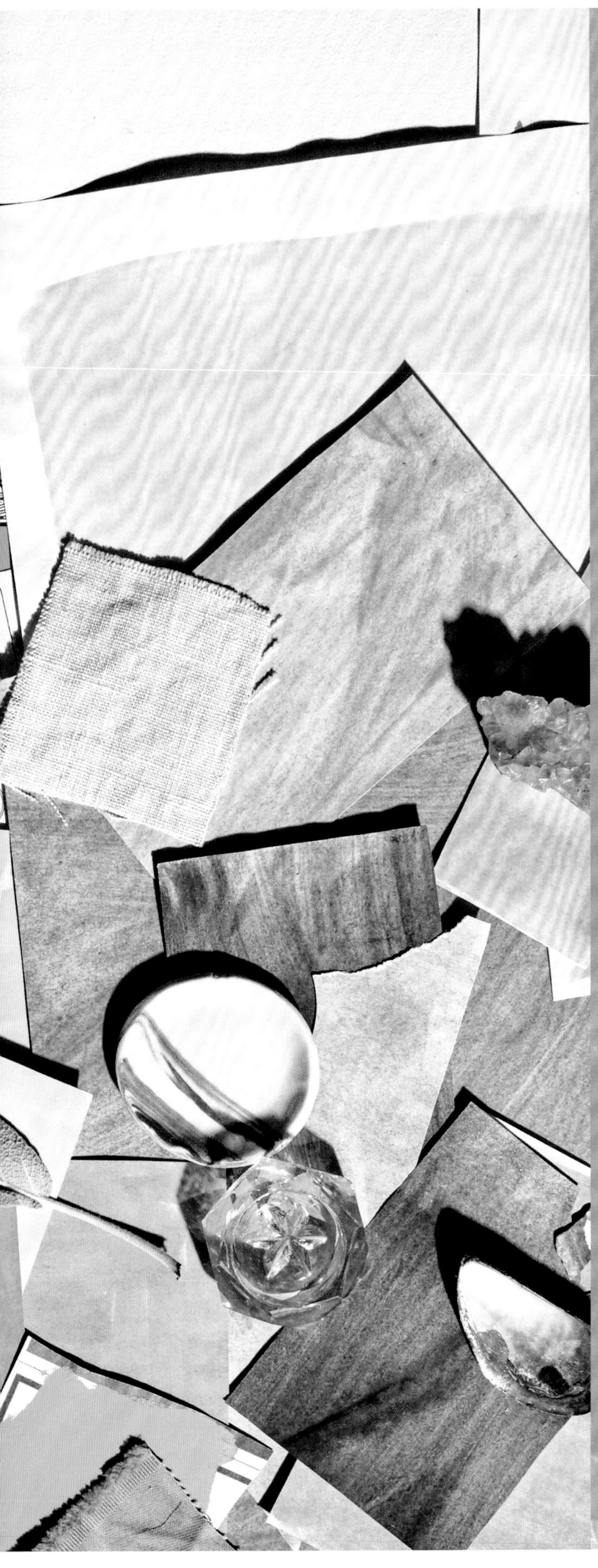

Color Basics

1 Color is light.

2 The color wheel is your foundation for understanding how colors relate to one another.

3 Warm colors advance in space and feel cozier, while cool colors recede in space and feel airier.

4 Expand your perception of neutrals and consider tints, tones, and shades of a hue.

5 Complementary colors accentuate one another through contrast.

6 Finish affects how a color *feels.*

PART TWO

feeling COLOR

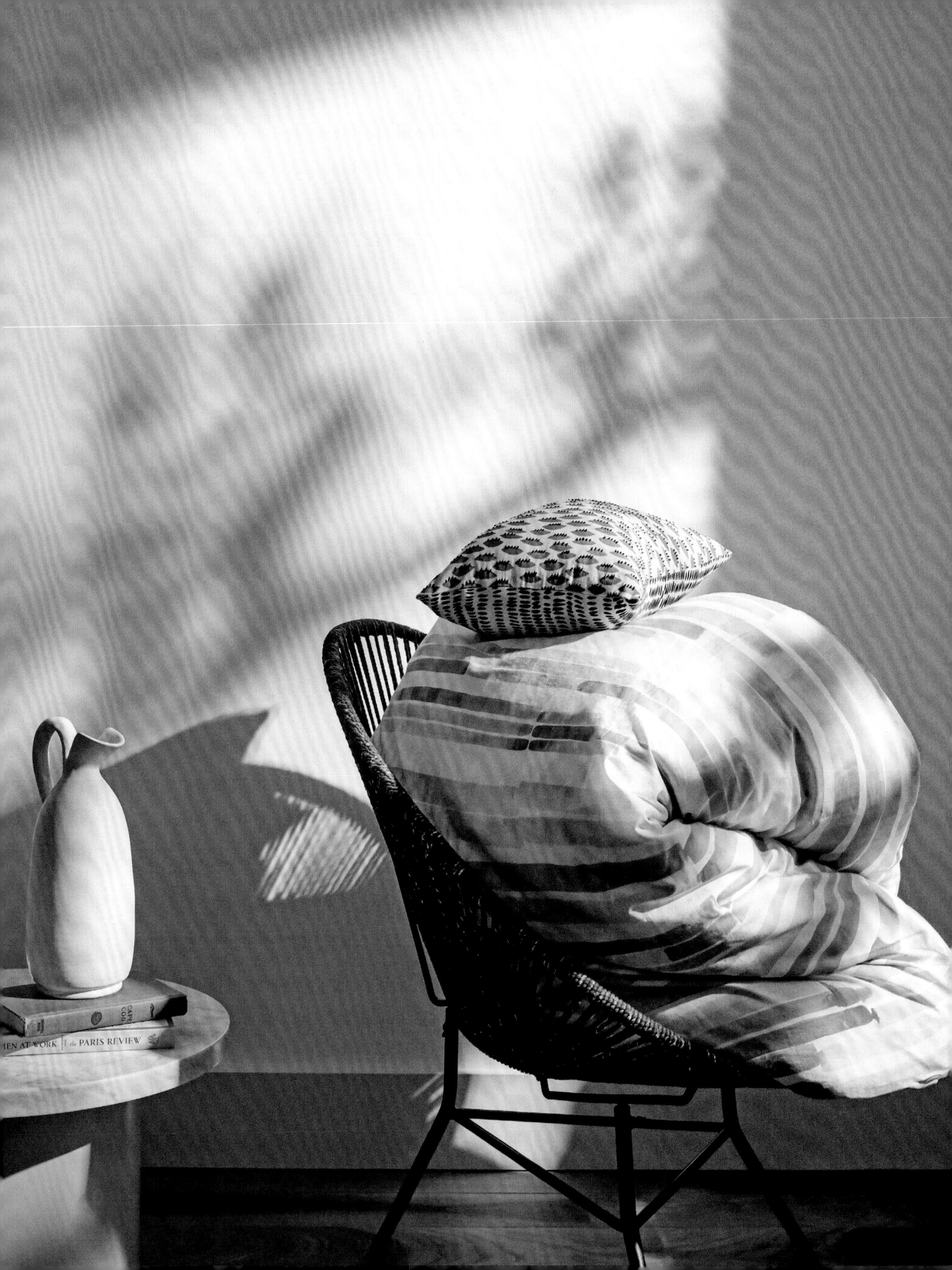
AT WORK
the PARIS REVIEW

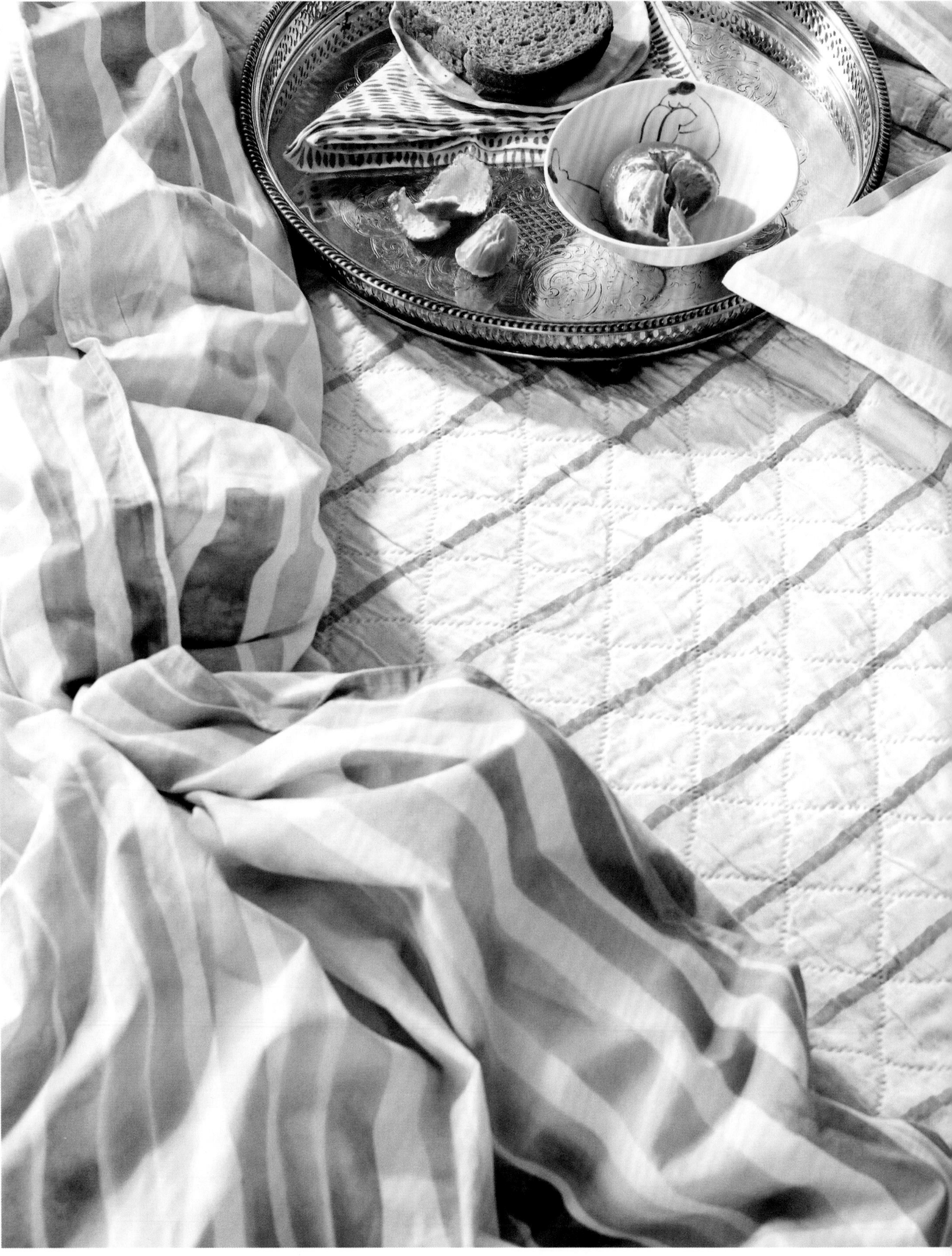

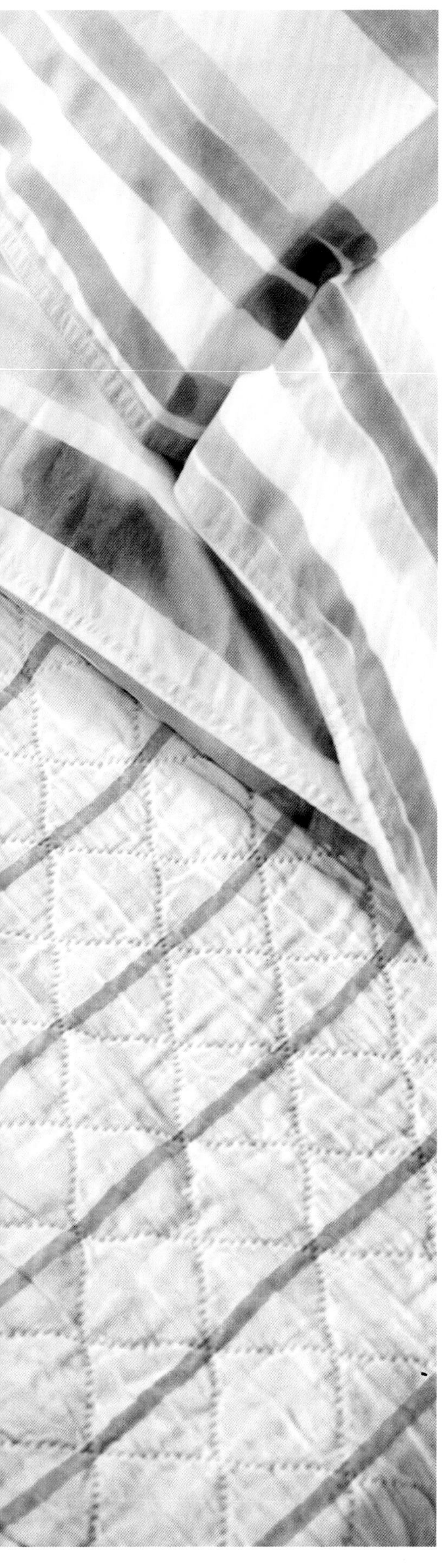

We experience color with senses beyond our sight. It's something you can touch, taste, smell, and remember. You can feel it deeply. Exploring how color makes *you* feel is an important part of making a room come alive and seem personal. We all have personal memories and associations with color, whether it's the color of the leaves on your grandmother's maple tree that makes you feel at home or the particular shade of green on the door to your parents' house that makes you feel happy. Some of us like yellow because we like lemon and brightness, while others shy away from it. We might crave color in a bleak winter, or we might want to bring nature colors into our homes to offset the city concrete. Because color is light. How we feel about colors can change with the seasons, as well as with the time of day. In the coming pages, I invite you to slow down and take the time to experience color in all its spicy, intense, calm, and fragrant variations.

COLOR
& SENSES

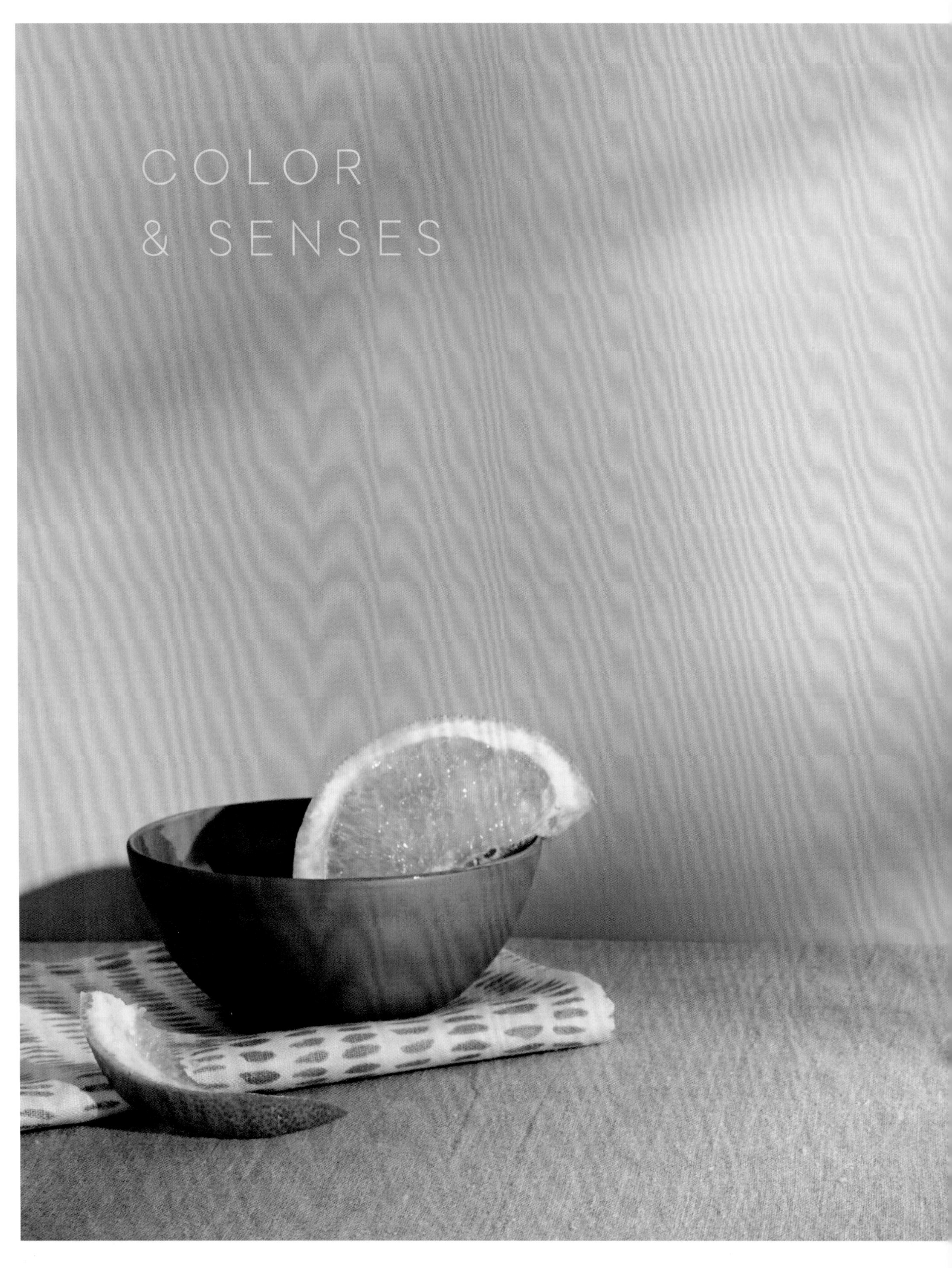

YELLOW + CITRUS

Unpeel a citrus fruit, and its scent fills the room. There's something amazing about this sweet, tart olfactory experience. In cooking, a lemon is said to add "brightness" to a dish. Lemons both look and taste like being awake. Citrus is strong, and that same sentiment can be applied to how you use these sunny colors. Too much acid and it's overpowering; not enough and it's dull or boring. Bright citrus hues, from poppy yellow to saturated grapefruit, infuse a space with a shot of energy. They're happy colors that evoke sunshine and warmth, so they're great for kitchens, living rooms, and children's rooms.

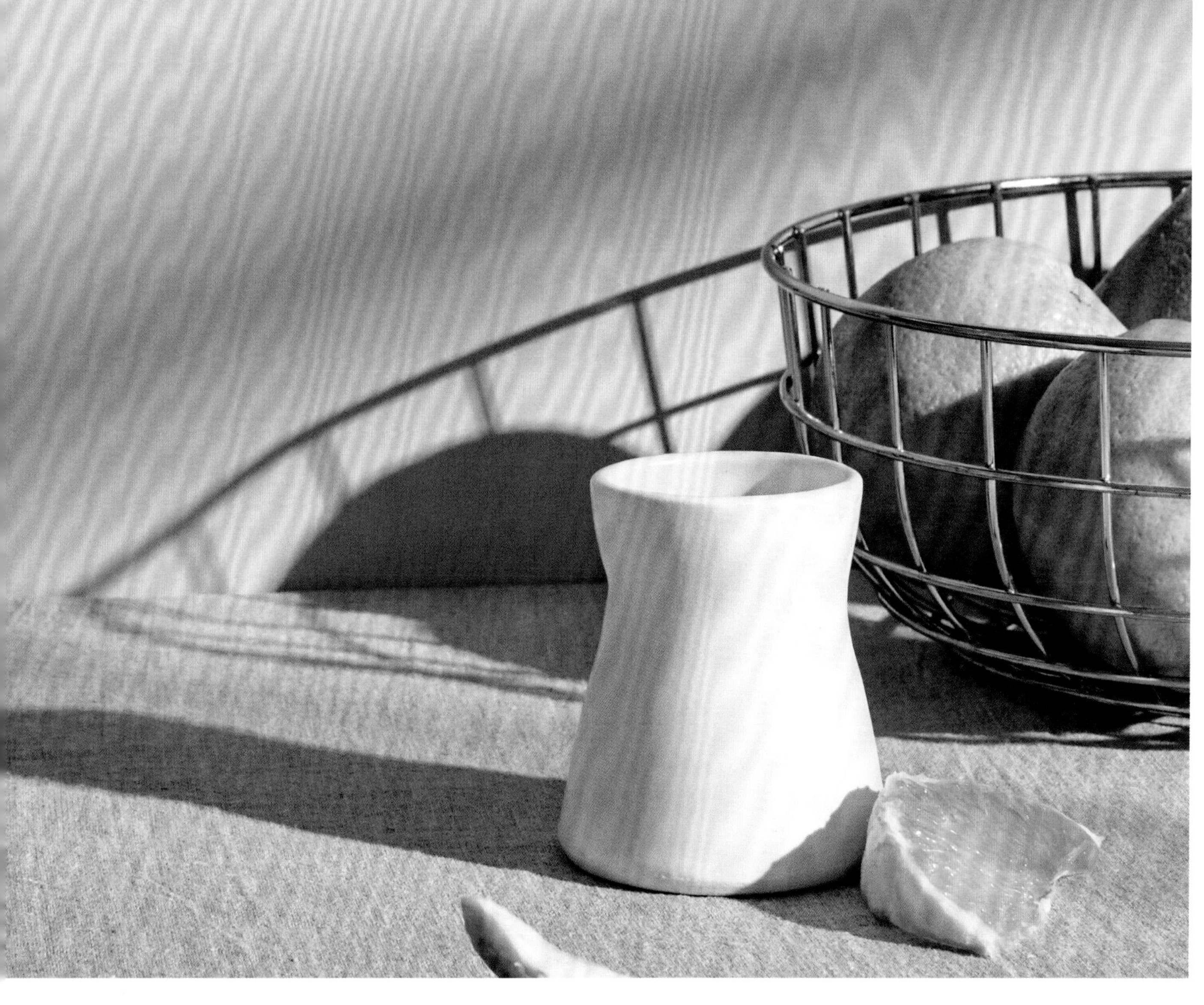

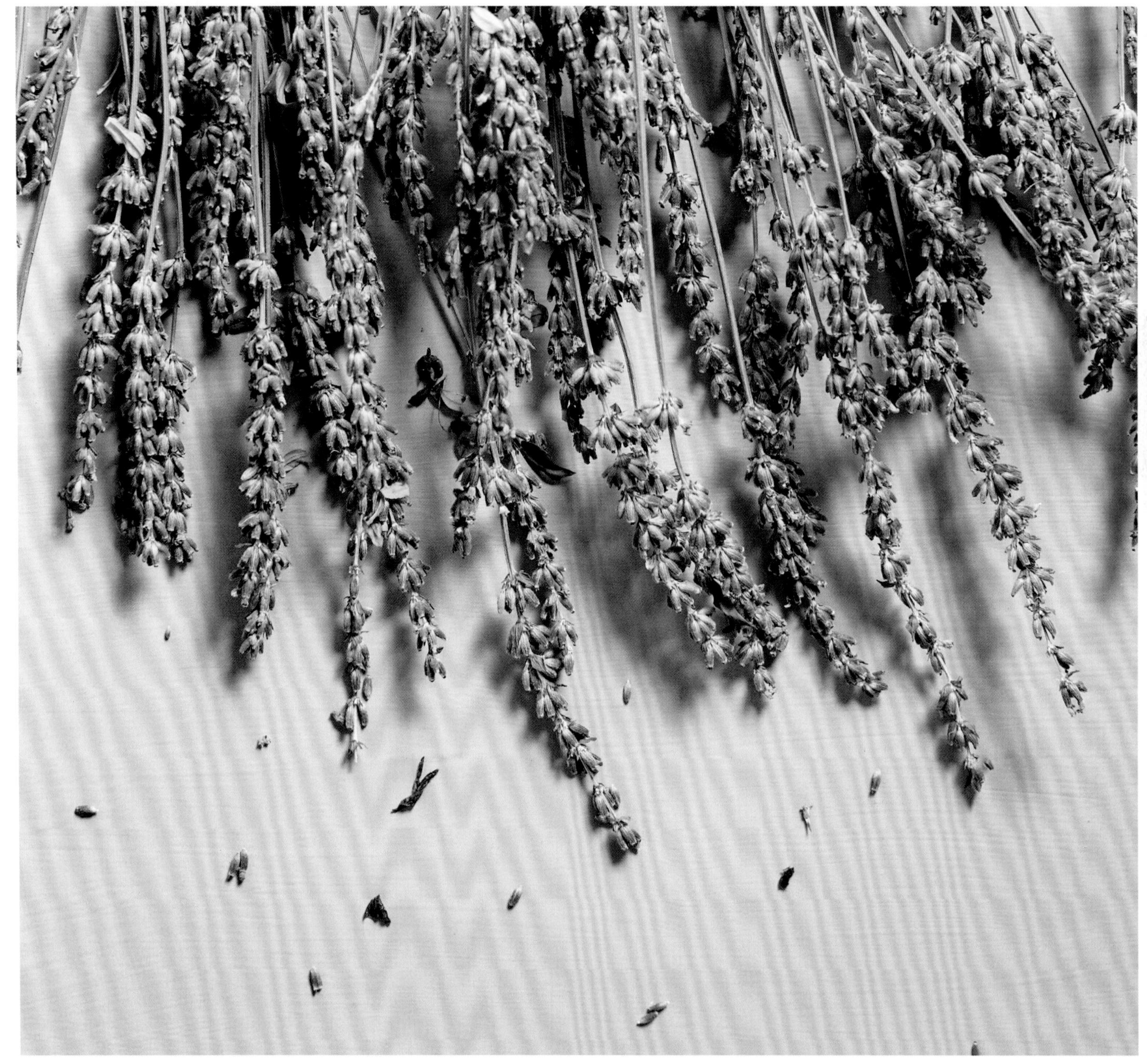

PURPLE + LAVENDER

Depending on how it's used, purple can give off the thick sweetness of grapes or a light, ethereal feel. The most engaging sensory purple to me is lavender. Its scent is calming, and the look of lavender-purple is soft and romantic. When dried, lavender is less saturated and becomes that dreamy purple hue Monet spoke of—the color of the atmosphere, mist, dusk. With this color, the scent, taste, and feel tend to be deeply personal and visceral.

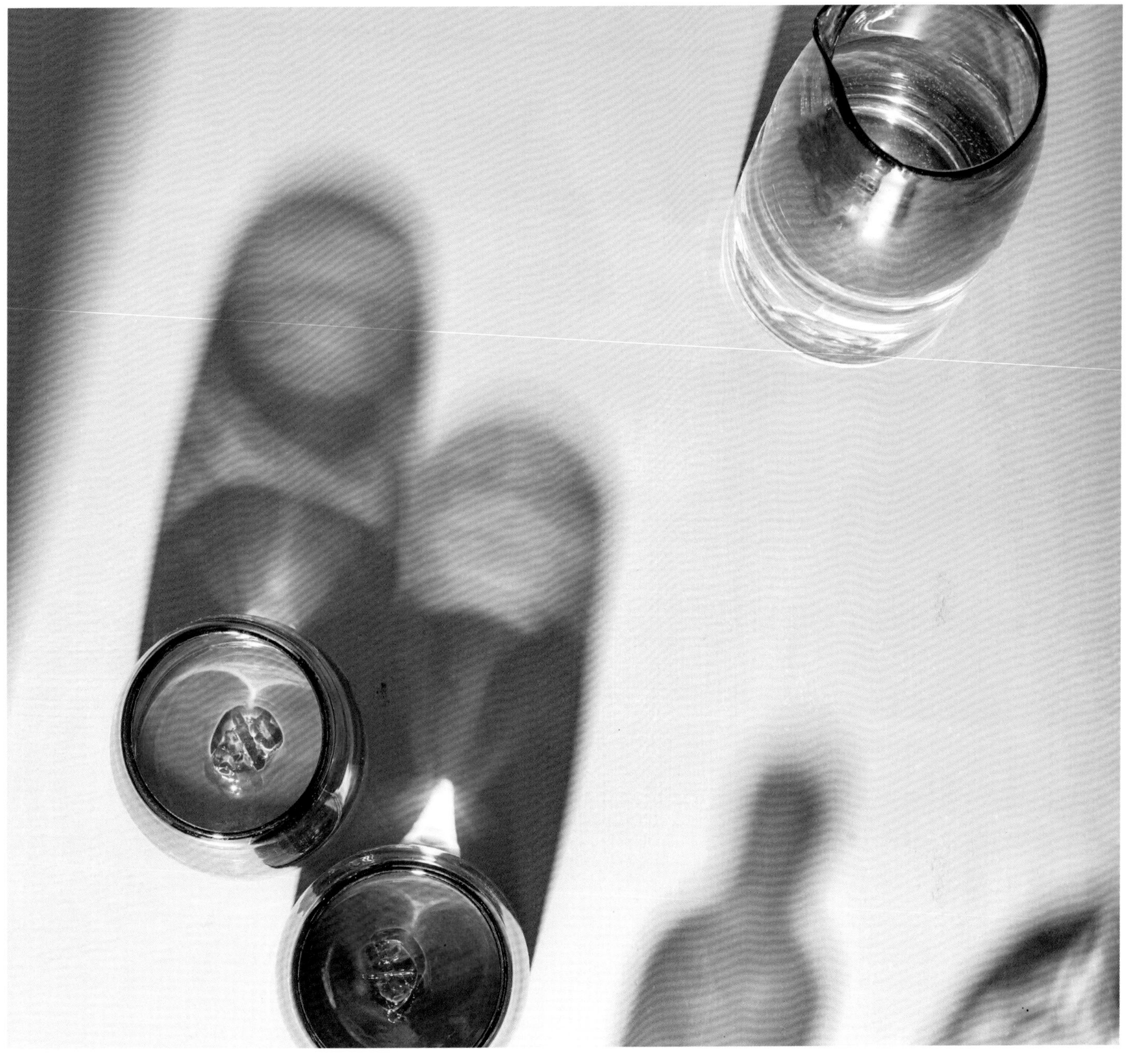

BLUE + WATER

Nothing is more refreshing than diving into a body of water on a hot humid day, or a cold glass of water when you're parched. Water is a sensory experience. It's therapeutic. It's deep and satiating. While water isn't actually blue, you feel the coolness of blue with this experience. Blue is so closely tied to water that the color itself almost evokes the lapping of the ocean. It can also remind us of the sky, a cool breeze, and the smell of clean air.

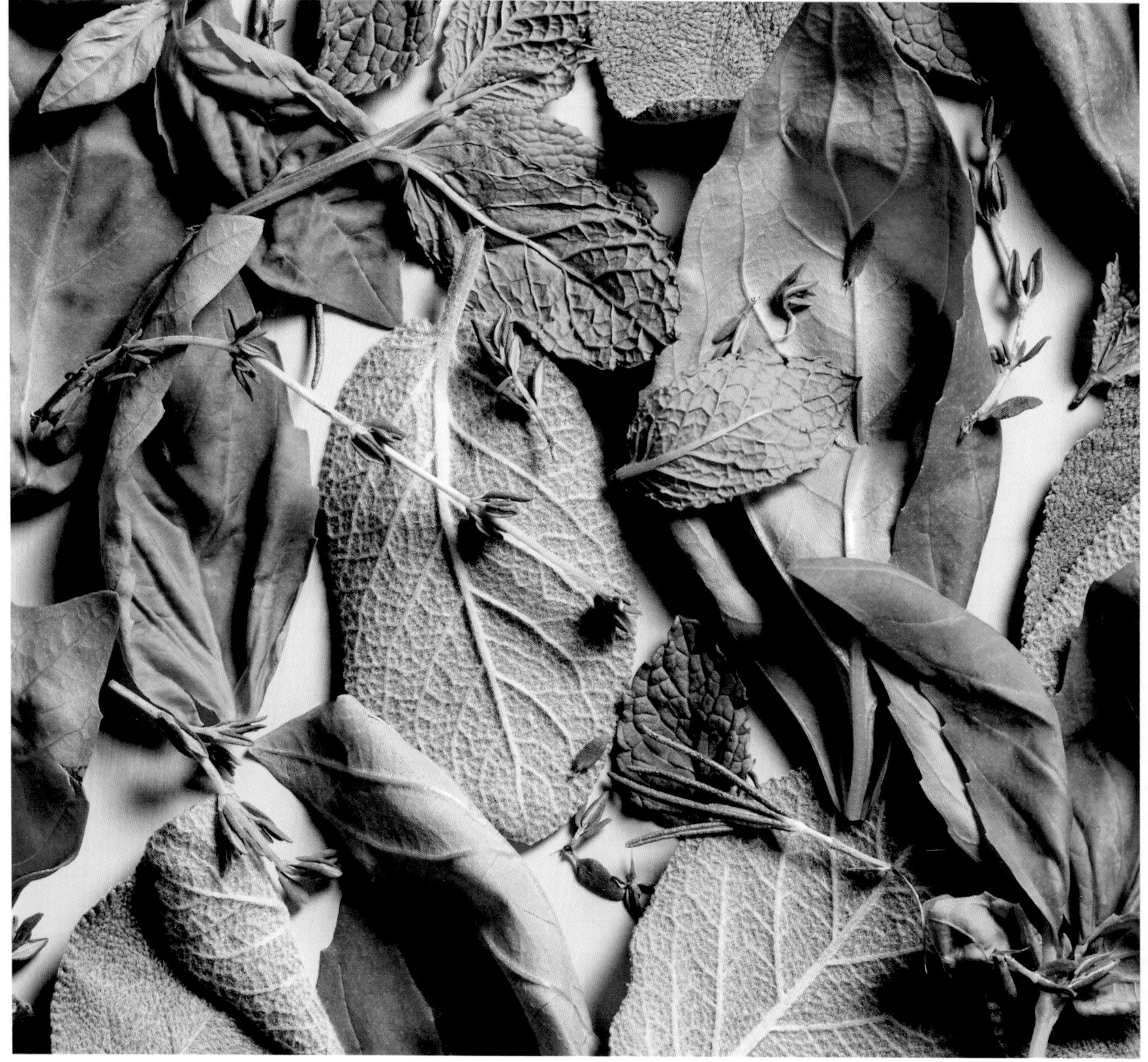

GREEN + NATURE

Green feels like growth and smells like the earth. It can be a muted, textured neutral, like the softness of a fuzzy sage plant, or cooling and colorful, like a mint leaf. It evokes the smell of freshly cut grass or the strong flavor of green herbs like cilantro and chives. Green is versatile and layered in its sensory associations, and that's the beauty of this verdant color.

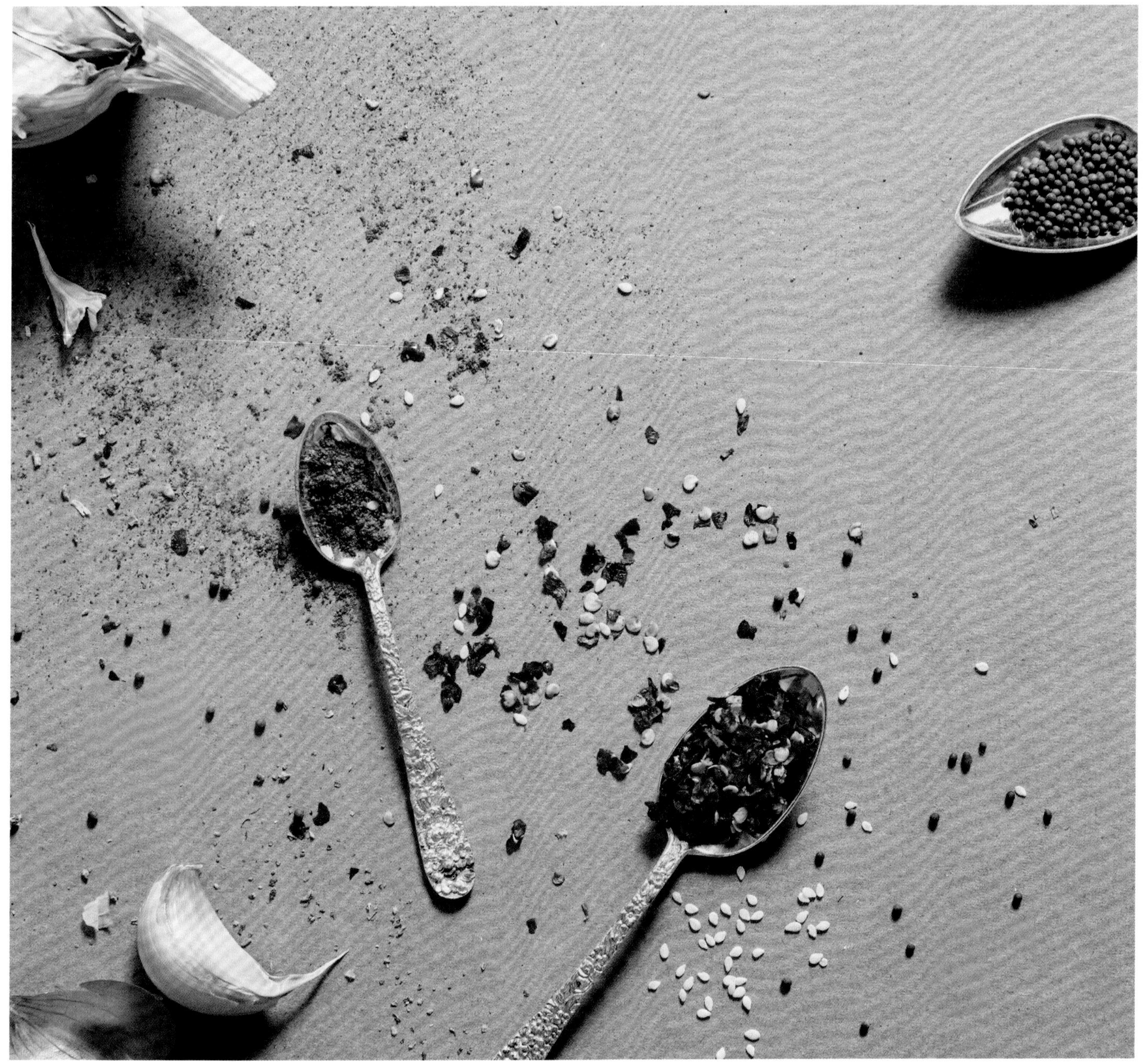

NEUTRALS + SPICE

In cooking, spices are your building blocks. Think about how a dish often starts with sautéing garlic and onions. Neutrals are your building blocks in decorating. If you carefully consider the tones you're using, it makes the room look better in the same way spices make your meal taste richer and more flavorful. Think about the colors of spices—mustard seeds, nutmeg, dried orange peel, black pepper, cracked red peppers, sesame seeds. Nuanced and sensory, neutrals create the foundation for a rich and beautiful room.

COLOR & THE SEASONS

If you're looking to evoke a certain feeling using color, the seasons are a great place to start. You're not going to redecorate your home as frequently as the seasons change, but we do reset our tables often, making this the perfect spot in your house to evoke the time of year. Plus, the table is traditionally a signifier of what's in season, so it's fitting to let nature and landscape inspire your dining experience. There are certainly other ways to incorporate the seasons into your home, but let's take a closer look at the dining table.

WINTER

I think of winter as a starting point. The new year is fresh, and the color palette of the world has become narrower, quieter, and calmer. It's muted and austere, almost dormant. The days are shorter, and the light quickly fades. When I imagine that landscape, I see soft grays, icy blues, silver, and even the softest hint of purple. Bring this concept to your table with white and blue plates, blue glasses, marbled textures, and silver accents.

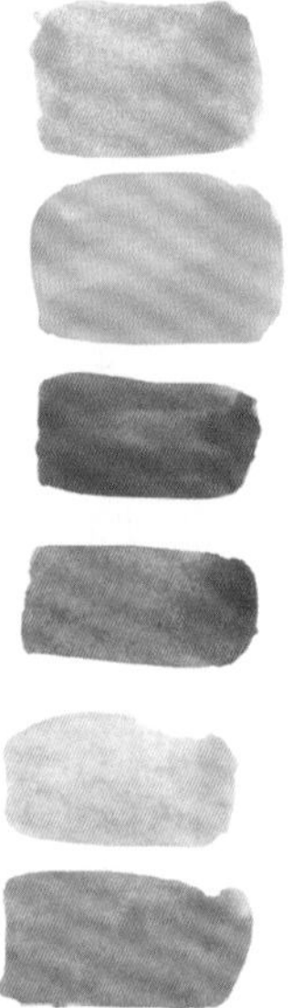

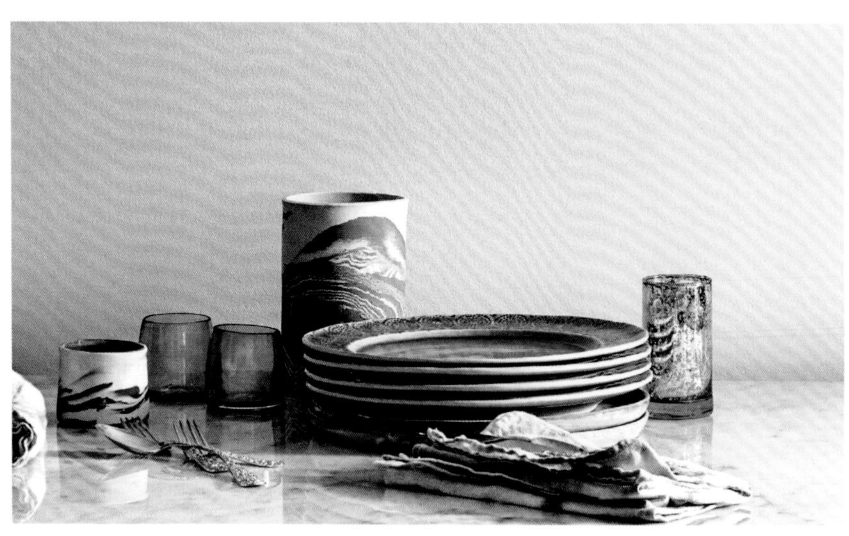

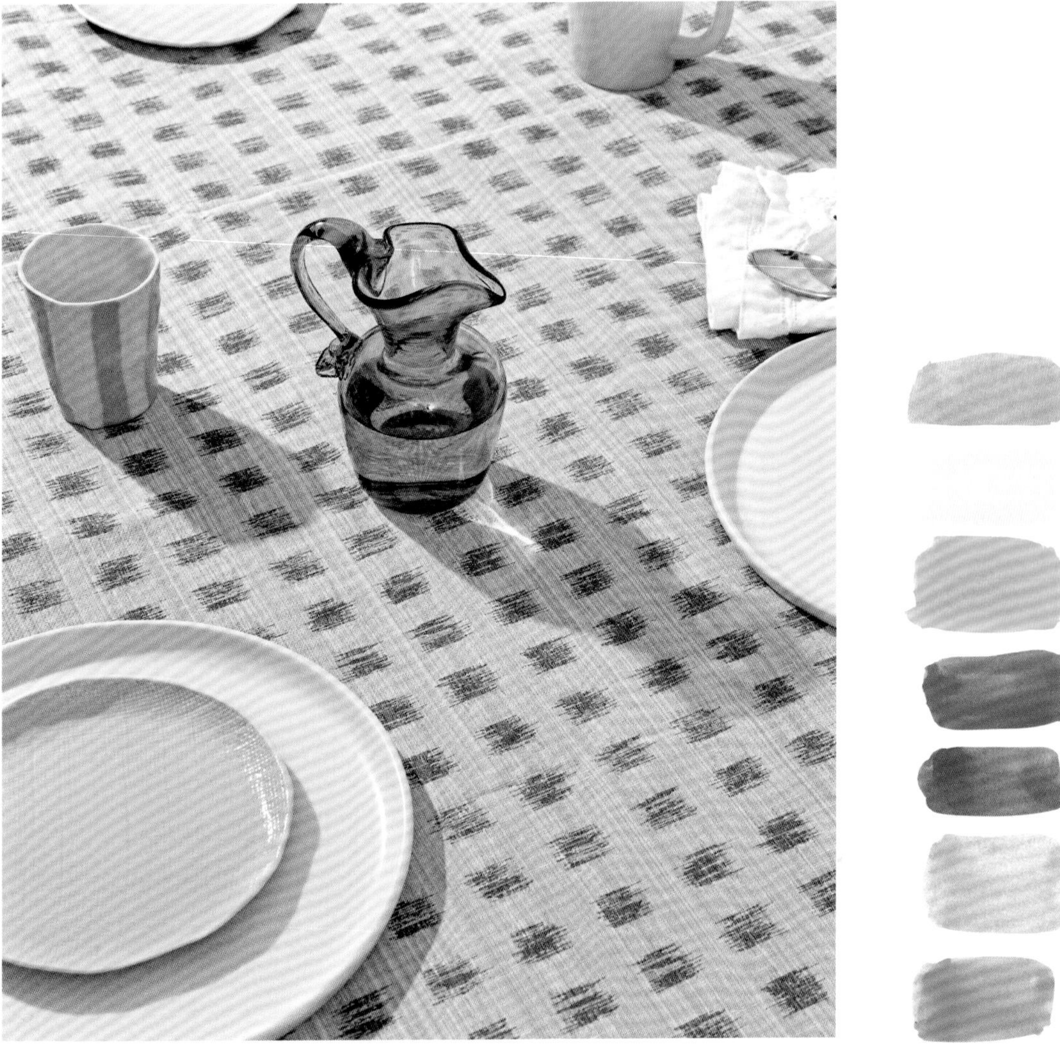

SPRING

Spring is all about renewed energy, growth, and hope. I love the small bursts of soft color and, most of all, how good it feels to see green. Bring soft shades of varying greens to the table, and layer them with creamy and cool whites. Consider minty-green textiles, bottle-green glass, and fresh sprigs of greenery.

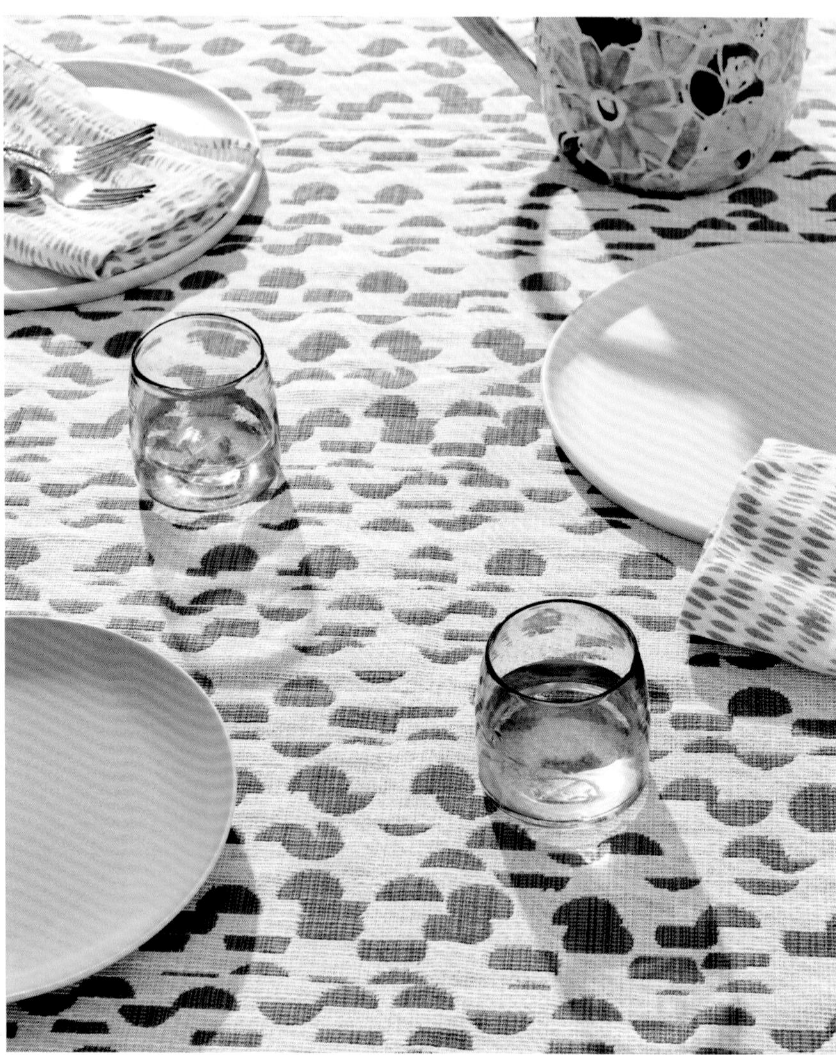

SUMMER

Summer is vibrant, and colors intensify during this time. It's characterized by bright, light, happy colors and a cheerful vibe. Use a multicolored palette of blue, tangerine, and egg-yolk yellow. Just one serving piece in a bright color can make the look. You don't need to be too serious about setting the table, so have fun and play with color here.

FALL

Fall is a time of change. The colors are warm and transitional, but not as bright as in summer. For me, fall is seeing the beauty in all of those cozy neutral hues. Look to the changing leaves as a cue for your palette. Bring in mixed metals, wood, speckled clay, the softest pink, varying shades of beeswax candles, and natural materials for an elegant table.

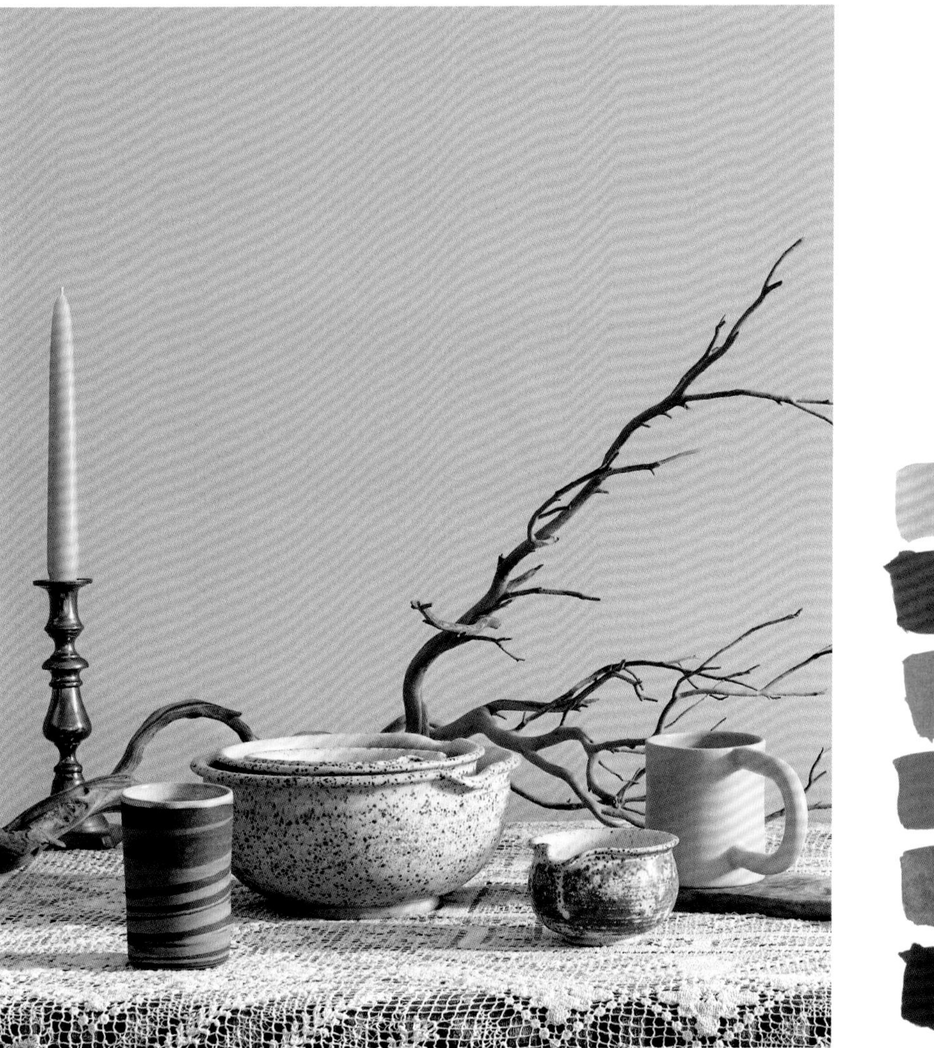

COLOR & TIME OF DAY

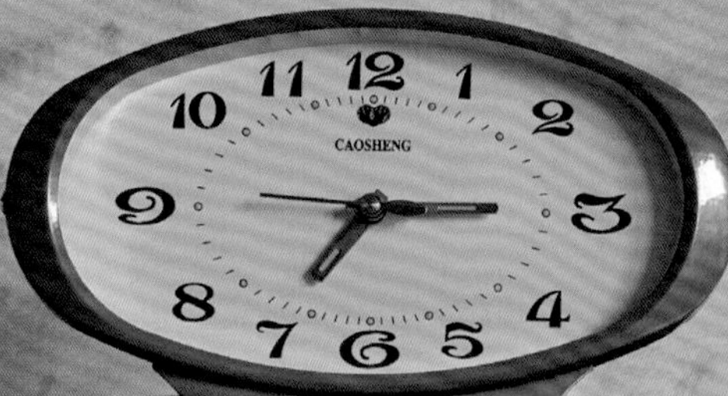

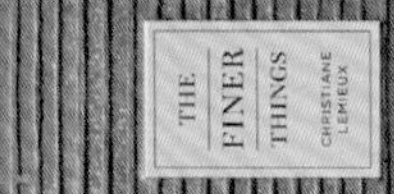

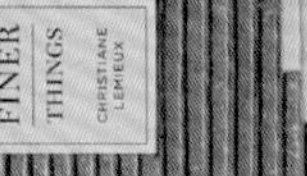

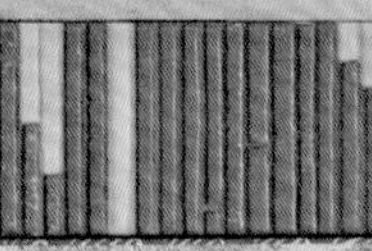

The rising and setting sun can make a big difference in how you see the colors of your home. Imagine which rooms you spend time in at each part of the day. For instance, do you tend to spend more time in the kitchen during the morning and more time in your bedroom at night? Look at the colors in that space during the time of day when you spend the most time there, since that's how you'll be experiencing them. Put a vase or a painting in those rooms and watch them at different hours to see if you're able to tell how the light is changing. Notice the subtle differences that happen and how the light can feel warmer, cooler, or brighter as the time passes. We photographed a still life in the morning and the afternoon to show you how the light changes.

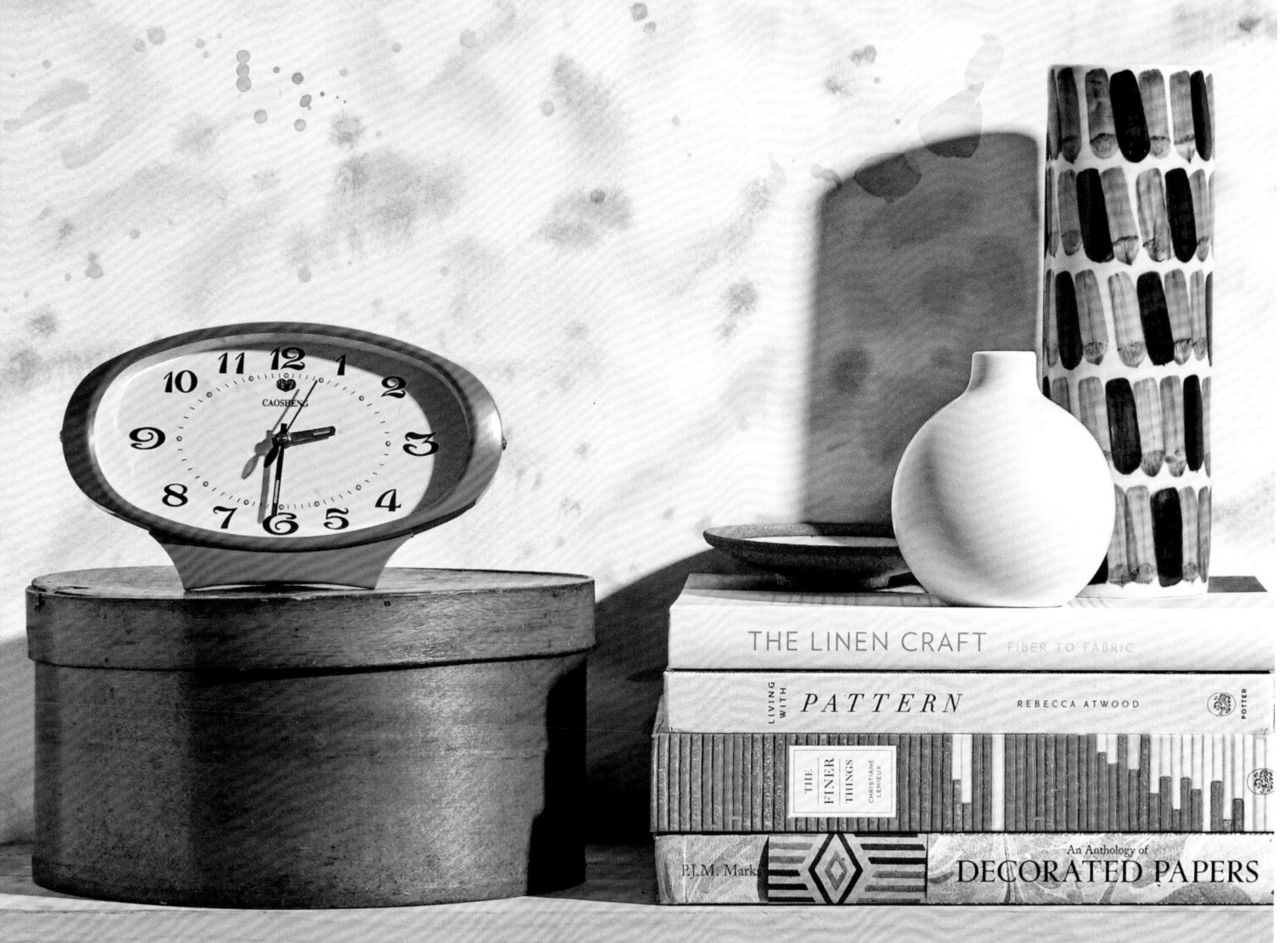

PART THREE

seeing COLOR

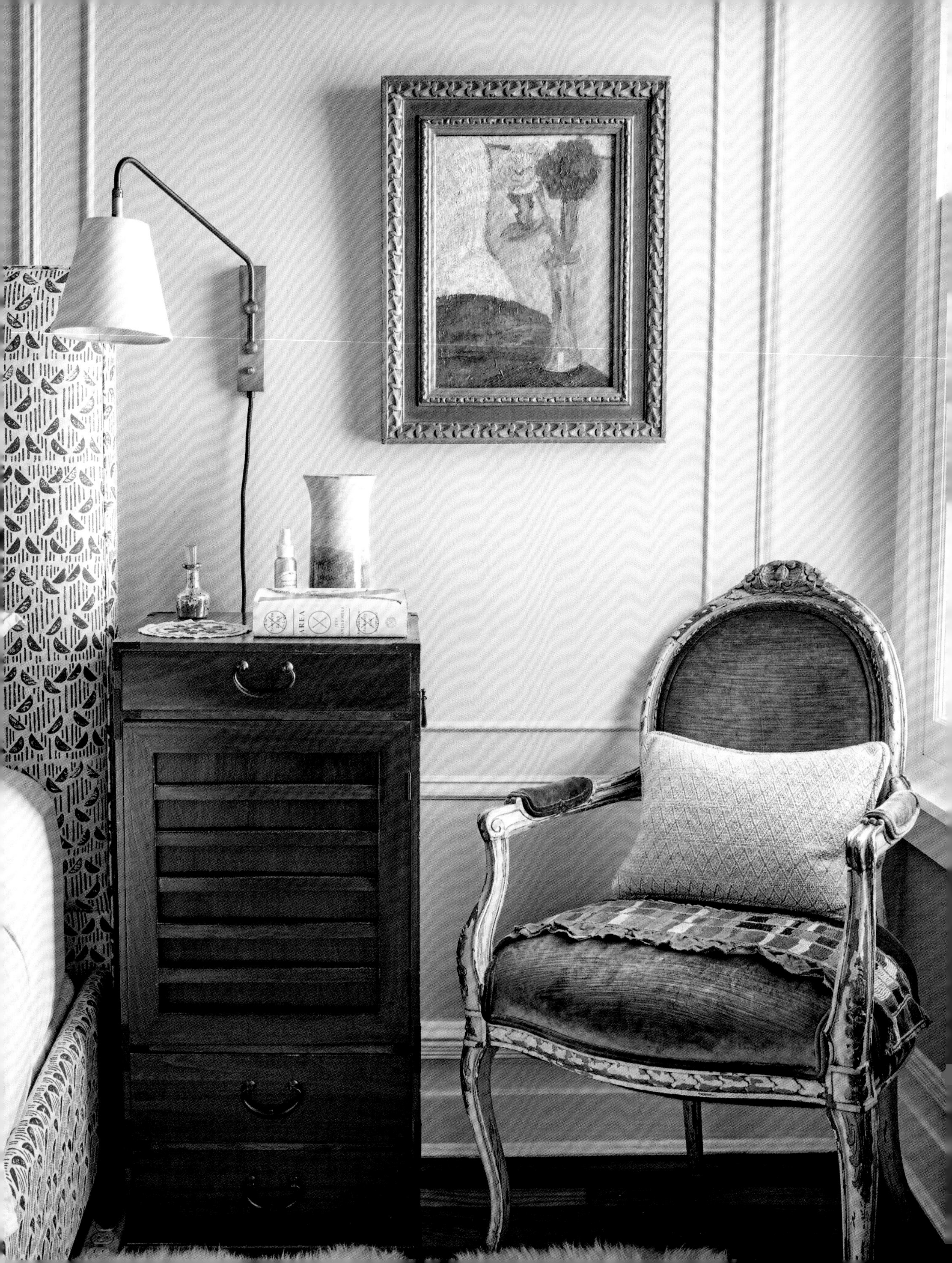
AREA

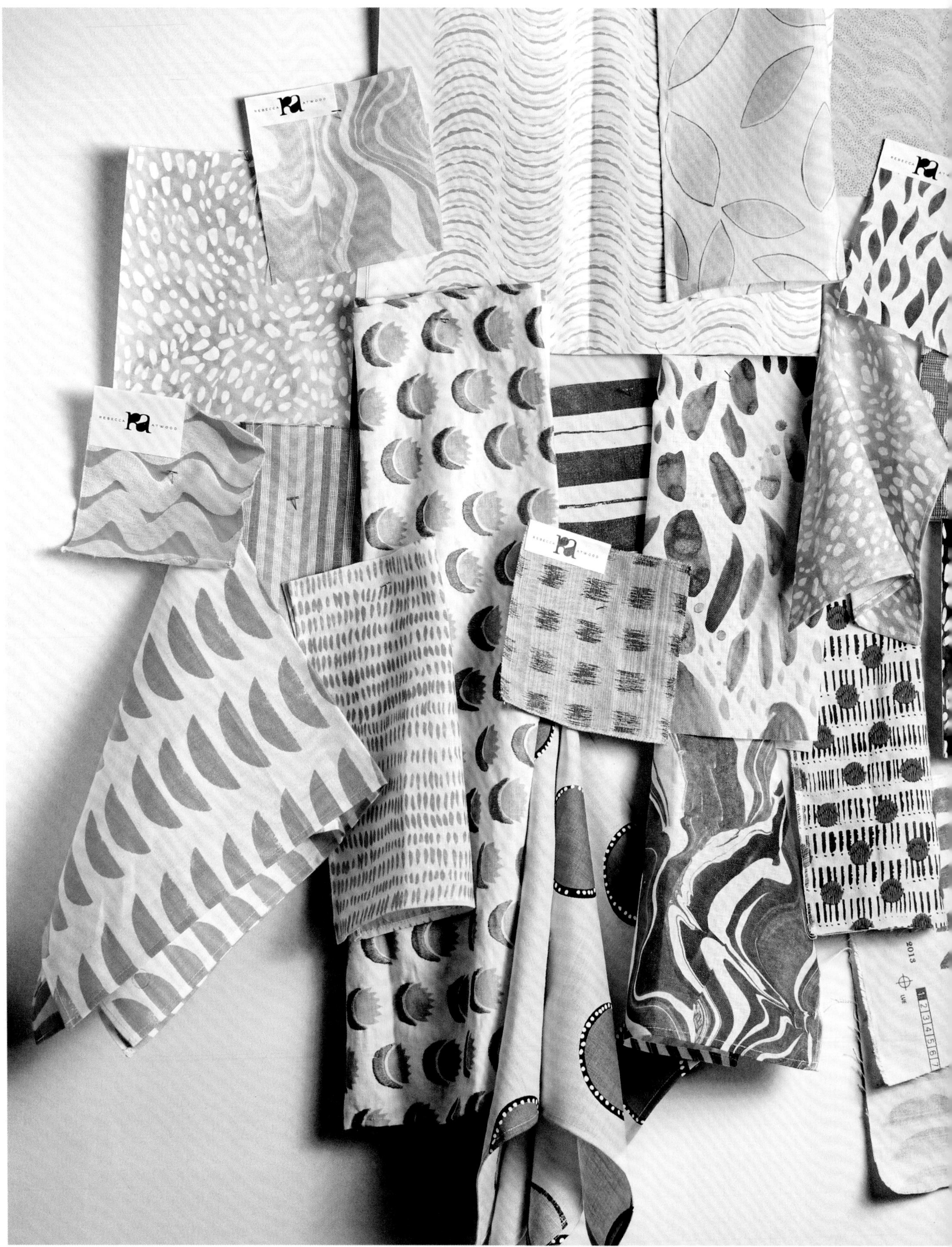
REBECCA ATWOOD
REBECCA ATWOOD
REBECCA ATWOOD
REBECCA ATWOOD
2013

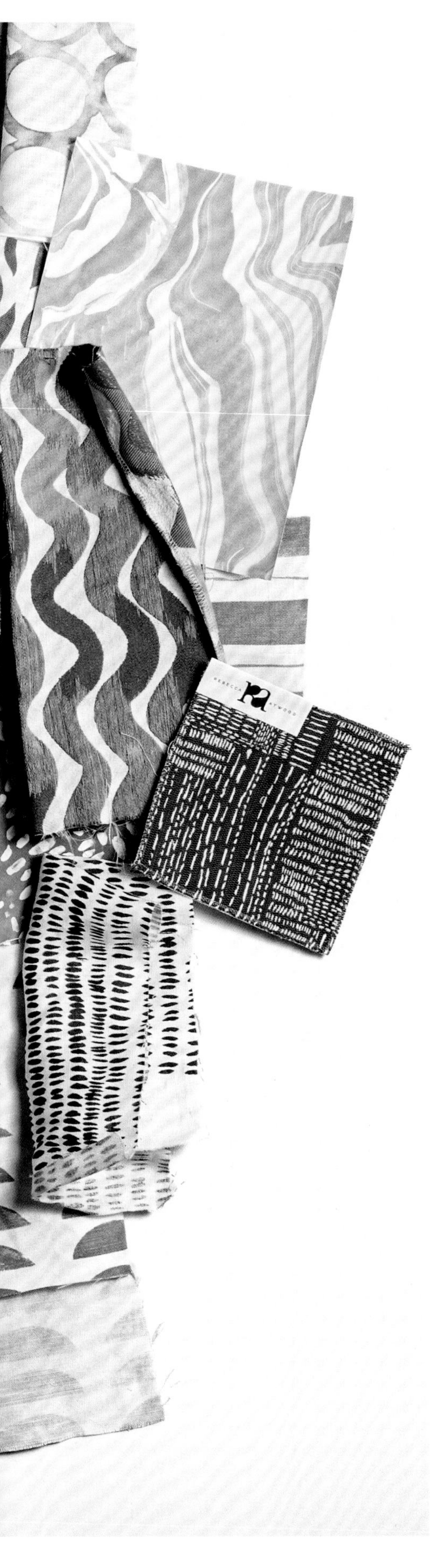

This is where you fall in love with color. Imagining it in all its beauty and wonder is the key to opening the door to a truly colorful life. You don't have to use every color in your home, or love multiple shades of every color, but embracing the color all around you can open up your palette in new and imaginative ways. As we discuss each color of the rainbow, open your heart and allow space for colors you might think you don't like—or even hate. I encourage you to explore your relationships with colors to determine the shades that speak to you. You'll learn that every color has had different meanings and cultural associations throughout history. Let this information empower you to assign your own meanings to these colors. Most of all, wash yourself in each color. Step into the pages and experience it.

NEUTRALS

SAND, BLUE-SLATE, CHARCOAL

Neutrals are your foundation. They are the base of your canvas. They often go unnoticed because of their subtlety, but they are inevitably found in every space or environment. Expand your notion of a neutral beyond the traditional definition of "colorless" because being completely devoid of color is almost impossible. In fact, you can create a whole color wheel out of only neutral shades, as we saw on page 21.

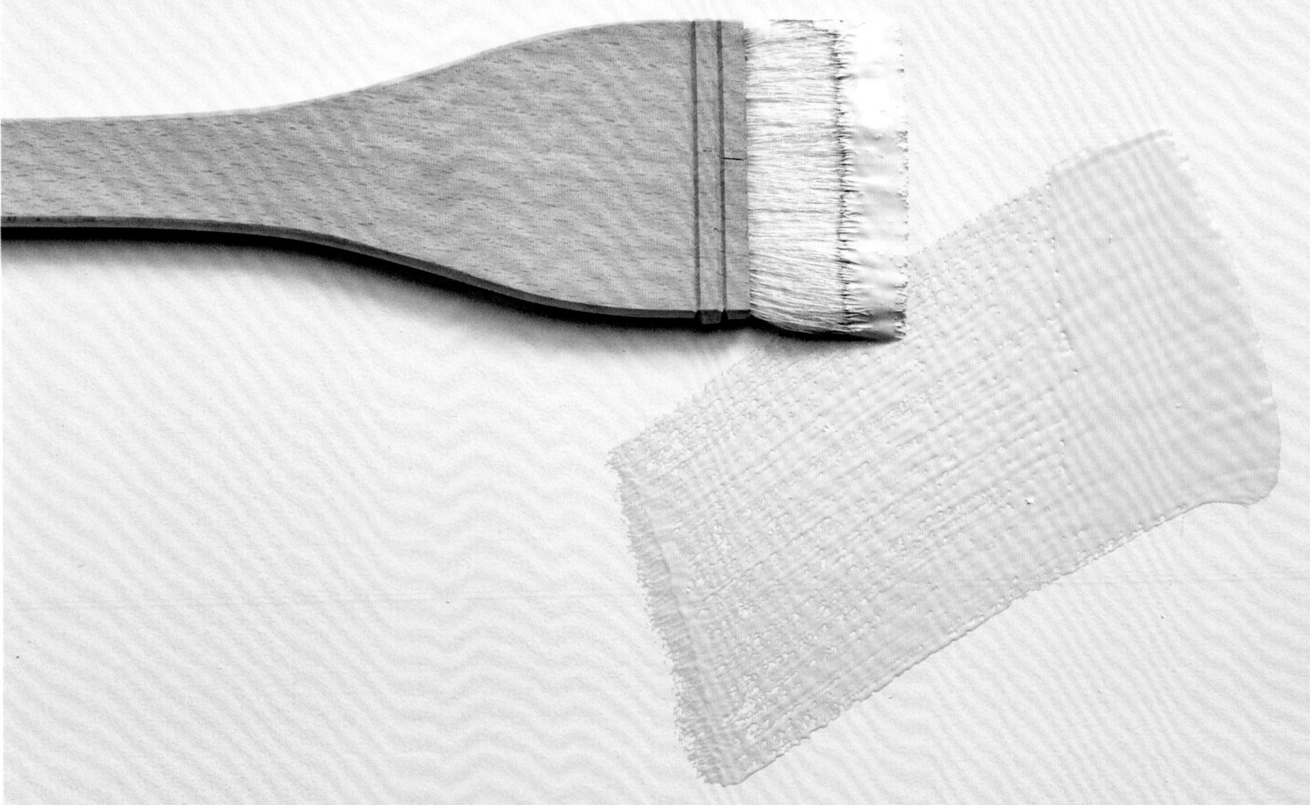

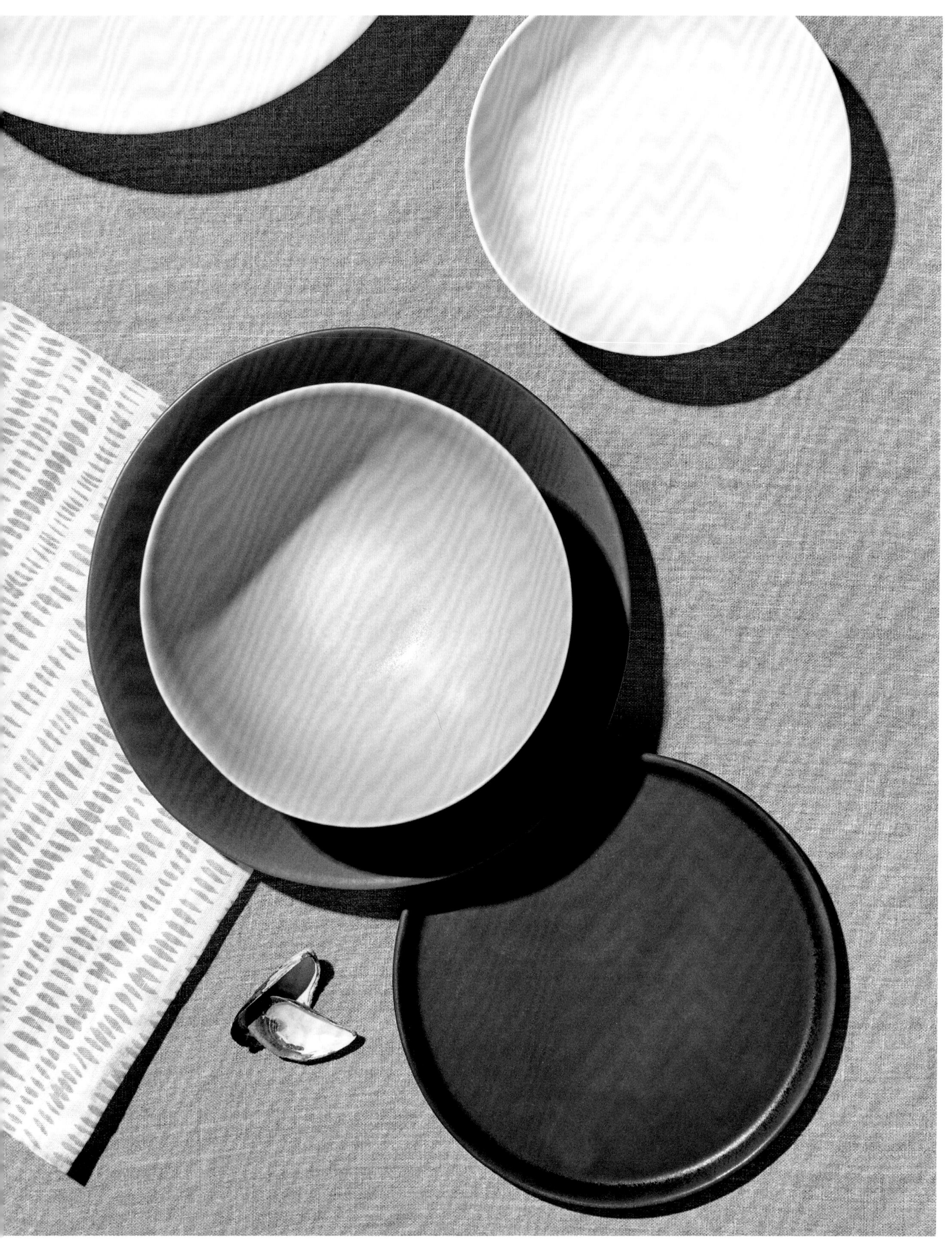

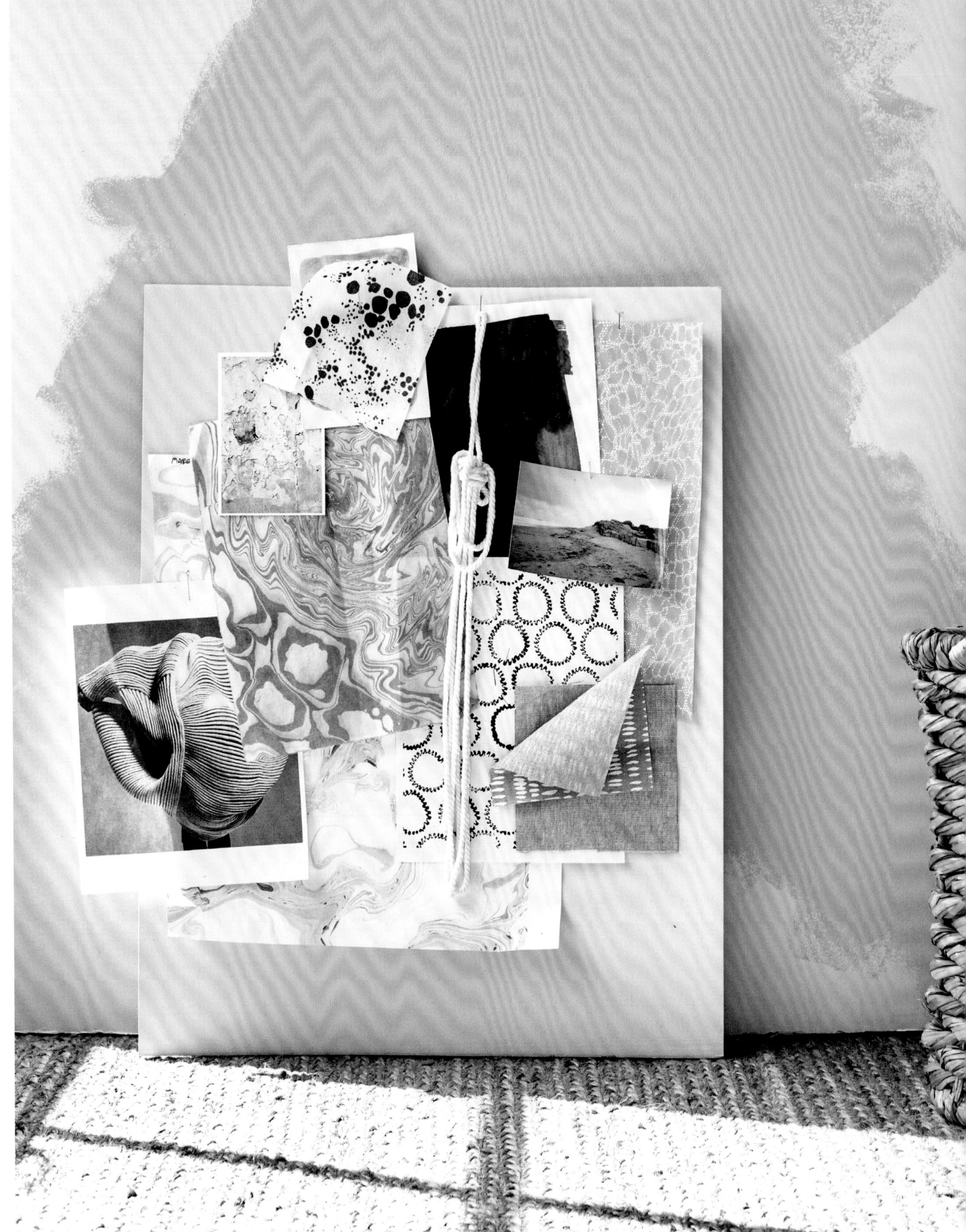

KNOWING WHERE TO LOOK . . .

My memories of neutrals

If you're looking for neutral inspiration out in the world, I would suggest taking a cue from natural materials. The first neutrals I fell in love with were at my childhood home—the cool gray-blue slate stones in my backyard and the warm mahogany wood of the curved banister that wrapped around the staircase. Ultimately, though, I am always most inspired by the beach. Sand was the neutral of my childhood because I spent countless days walking Cape Cod beaches. I loved the gradient created by darker, wetter, and colder sand closer to the water in contrast to the lighter, brighter sand closer to the dunes. I even loved the beach in the winter, with the dried grass by the shoreline being another inspiring neutral. Shifting light can be dramatic, and when it hit the dried grass, it glowed gold. Paying attention to the way light plays with neutrals is the key to finding the perfect ones for you.

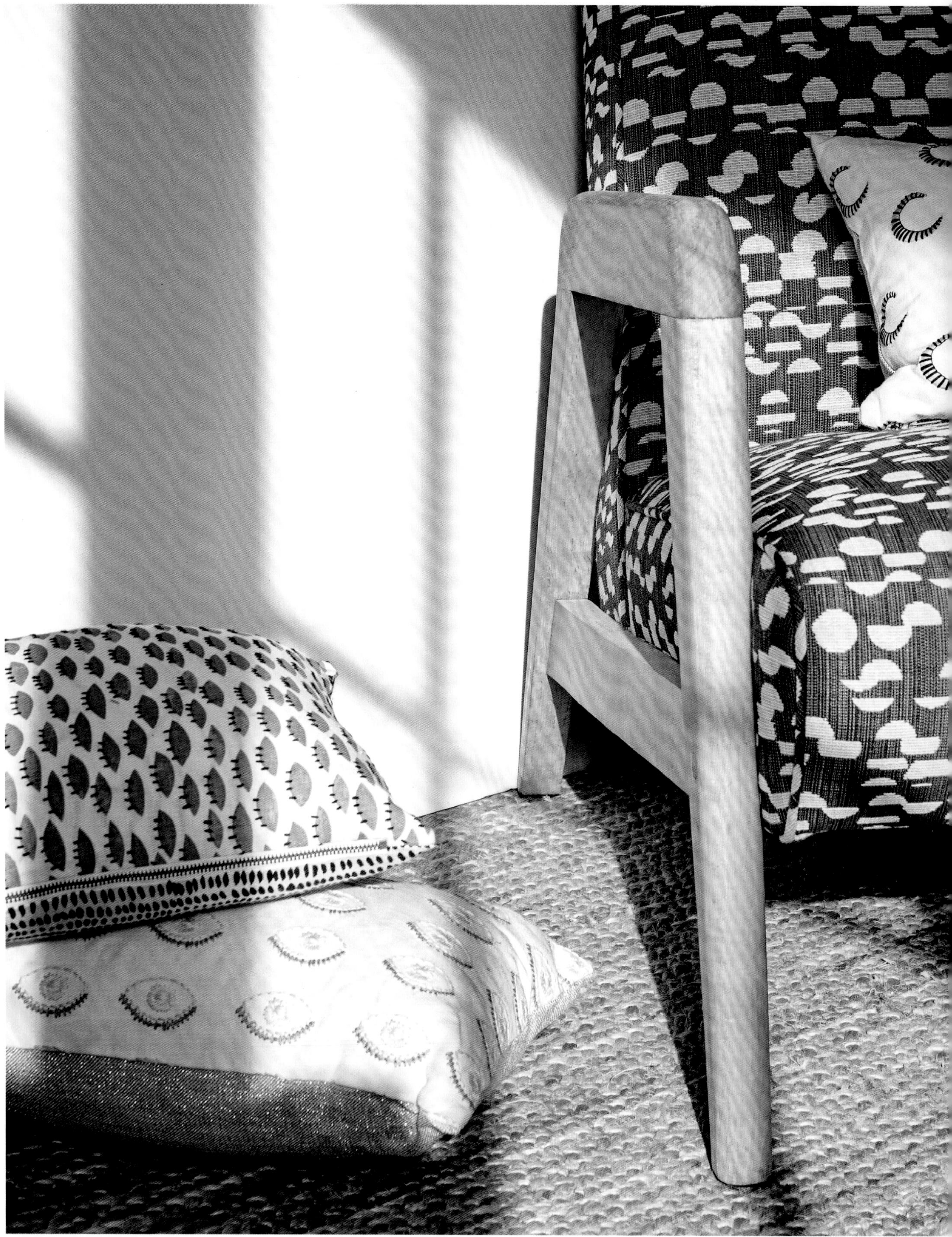

- What kind of neutrals do you remember from childhood?
- What neutrals can be found in your favorite painting?
- What natural materials do you instinctively gravitate toward? Why do you think that is?
- Imagine your happy place. What neutrals do you see there?

LIVING WITH NEUTRALS

The more you experiment with neutrals, the more interesting your home will be. Neutrals are the building blocks of a room, and every palette must have these quieter moments; however, quiet doesn't have to mean boring.

First, explore the full range of neutrals when decorating your home. Don't choose all warm or all cool (think all grays or all tans). If you're working with a very subdued color palette, widen your neutral options and play with texture. If you're using a narrow range of color, think about matte and shine, textured linen, velvet, pattern, and embroidery. These little details and materials become much more important in a minimal space.

The most important tip to remember is to push the boundaries of what you consider neutral. Think of pale versions of a hue (tints), desaturated versions of a hue (tones), or deep, rich dark versions of a hue (shades). Colors that appear in nature in vast amounts (like sky blues, grass greens, purple mountains, or golden hay in the winter) can be used the same way in your home and feel "neutral" because they're mimicking something we all know.

As you read further into this section about other colors, imagine what version of each feels like a neutral to you. Visualize how a soft pastel or a moody deep version of a bright color could be used as a neutral. Even a brighter, more saturated version of a color can feel neutral depending on how you use it.

There are some neutrals that can help bridge the gap between gray and tan. These colors are warm grays that have a little bit of tan to them, or cool tans that have a bit of gray in them. I love linen because it's almost in between a warm and cool color because of the fabric. The material naturally has both tan and gray, and it's a nice way to bridge an all-neutral palette.

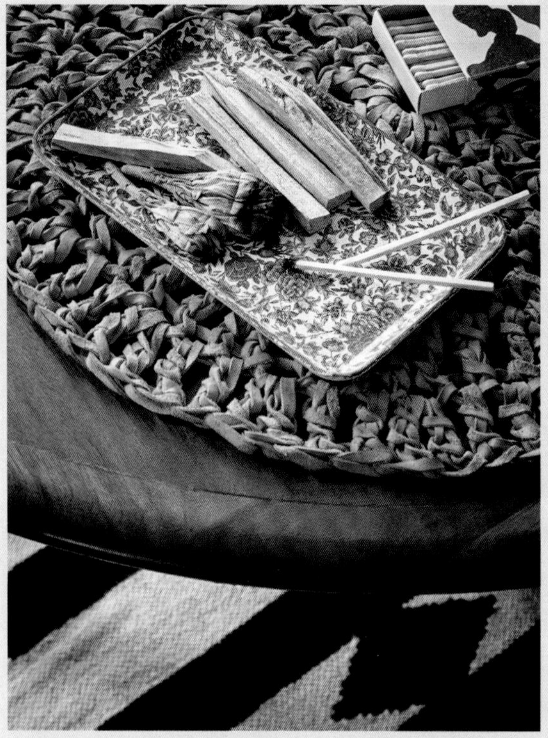

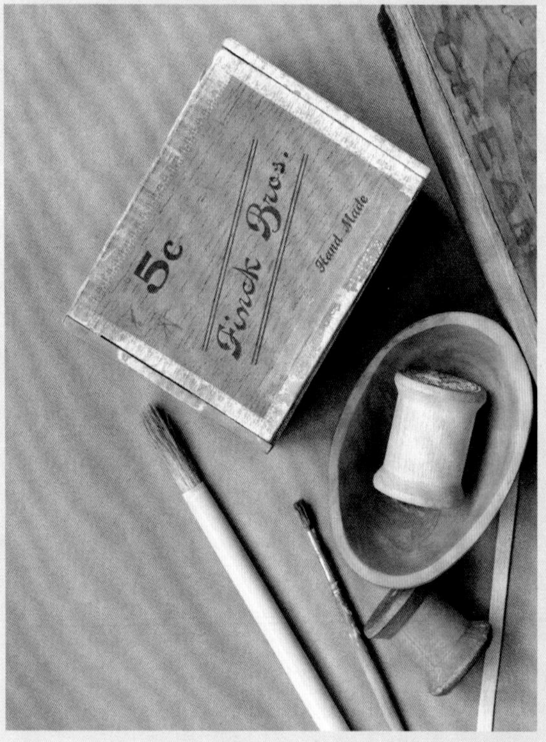

Making Neutral Colors Impactful

1 Consider finish. Think about dry textures against shiny, rustic textures mixed with elegantly polished ones. When your color is more muted, turn up the variety of textures, finishes, and materials in your space to create quiet drama.

2 Use a range of values. Contrast is an important tool for creating interest in a space. If you want to stick with a truly neutral palette, explore both light and dark. Deep charcoal gray, opalescent white, rich peat-moss brown, and linen hues can be beautiful together.

3 Explore the undertones. Take a close look at the neutral hues you choose. Notice if they have hints of pink, purple, or green. Noticing the variations of a neutral allows you to play off that with the other colors you layer on top. For example, if you choose a tan with a lot of green in it but plan to put it in a room with a lot of warm colors and reds, the sofa might look too green and appear out of place. The subtle undertones of a neutral can be the difference between a sad beige couch and a beautiful one.

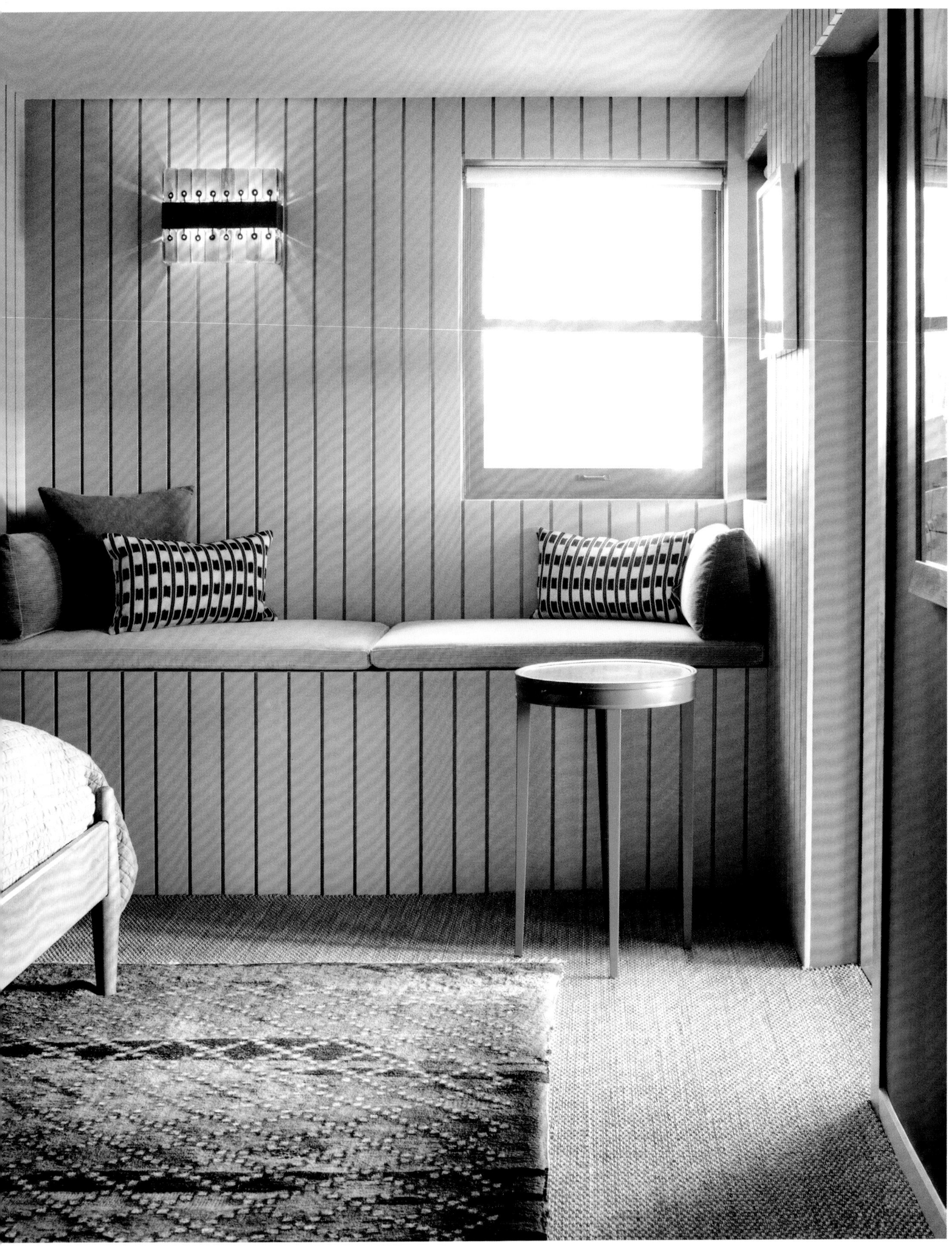

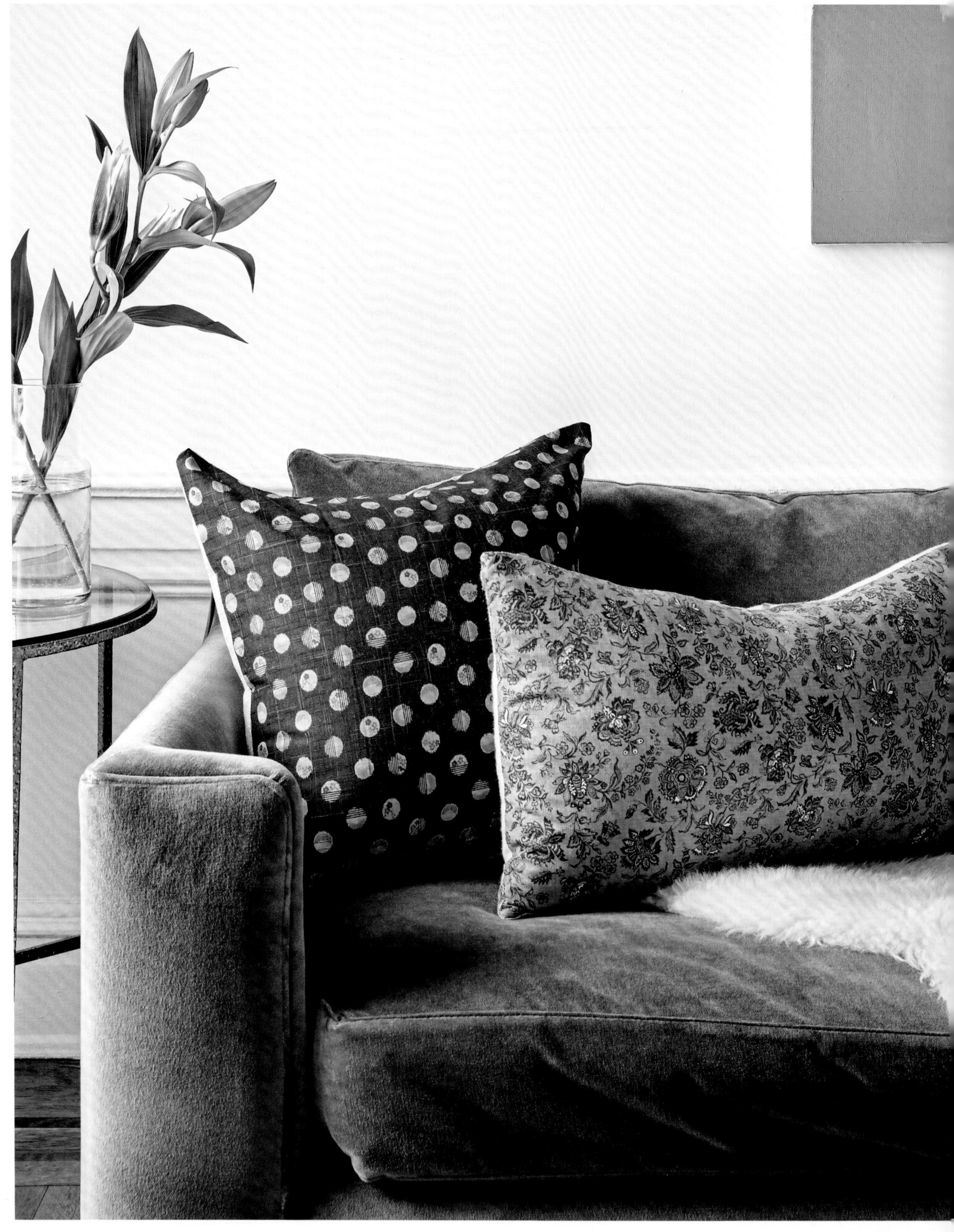

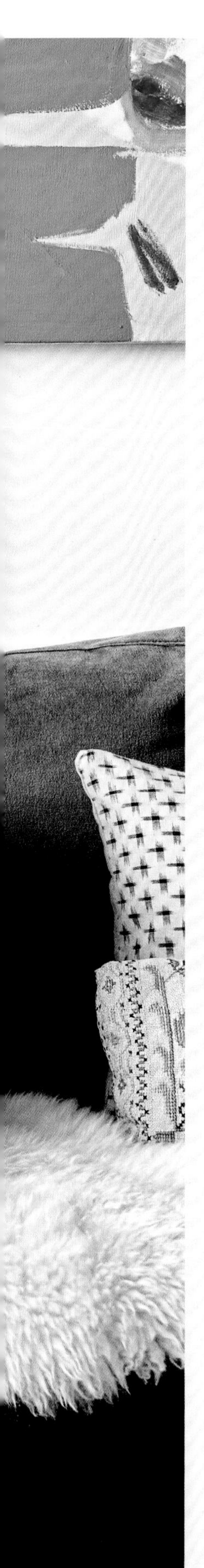

Make Any Color a "Neutral"

TEMPER IT WITH WHITE

When you use a brighter color in a pattern with a white ground, it feels less intense and more neutral. Proportion is the key. A small amount of a bolder color and more white, tan, beige, or gray can make a brighter color more subdued. Take this into account when choosing a patterned fabric—or when considering a space as a whole.

CONSIDER PLACEMENT

Bolder colors feel more rooted in the ground when you use them on the floor, so rugs are a place where more vibrant colors still feel neutral. Think about walking through a field of grass—it doesn't feel so green since it's underfoot, because it's not in your direct line of vision. Next time you're visiting a new place, look down. Notice the floors, sidewalks, and nature. The same can be said for what's above on the ceiling!

USE NATURAL MATERIALS

Whether it's green plants, exposed brick, or even a bowl of lemons, any color will feel less contrived (and more neutral) when it's used in a material that is organically that color. Natural materials feel neutral because we associate them as being that color. We don't think about a plant as adding color to a space in the same way that we do painting a green wall. It's a good way to bring in colorful neutrals.

REMEMBER THE COLOR BASICS

Tint, tone, shade, material, and even finish can all make a color feel more absorbable. Remember the basics in Part One. For example, the palest tint of red would act as a warm neutral, a barely pink-white. A tone of green could be army green or dark khaki, and a shade of blue is navy, which is a basic neutral you can't help but love.

RED

BLUSH, TOMATO, RUBY

Red is a stimulating and powerful color but it can also be tempered and rosy. From the pink sand beaches of Bermuda to The Pink City of Jaipur, India, I've always thought of pink as synonymous with magic and associated red with home and happiness. With such an arresting color, we often conjure the most saturated version of red like fire-engine red, stop-sign red, and Valentine's Day red, but shades of red also include apples, a changing maple leaf, and the inside of a redwood tree. For me, red has always been a comforting color. I grew up in a barn red house, where my family owned a restaurant called the Red Pheasant, and, because of that, I associate that color with tradition and warmth. The dining room in the restaurant had white walls with red trim and warm wood floors, which made red feel like a neutral, not a bright or bold color.

The brighter, bolder red I fell in love with was tomato, which is apparent in my designs. I remember growing my first tomatoes and watching them go from green to yellow to orange-red, which taught me that color is alive, because the change in colors signals to the world it's ripe, ready to become food and nourish. Looking at the entire spectrum of red from pink to barn to bright reminds us there are infinite ways to engage with seemingly intense colors.

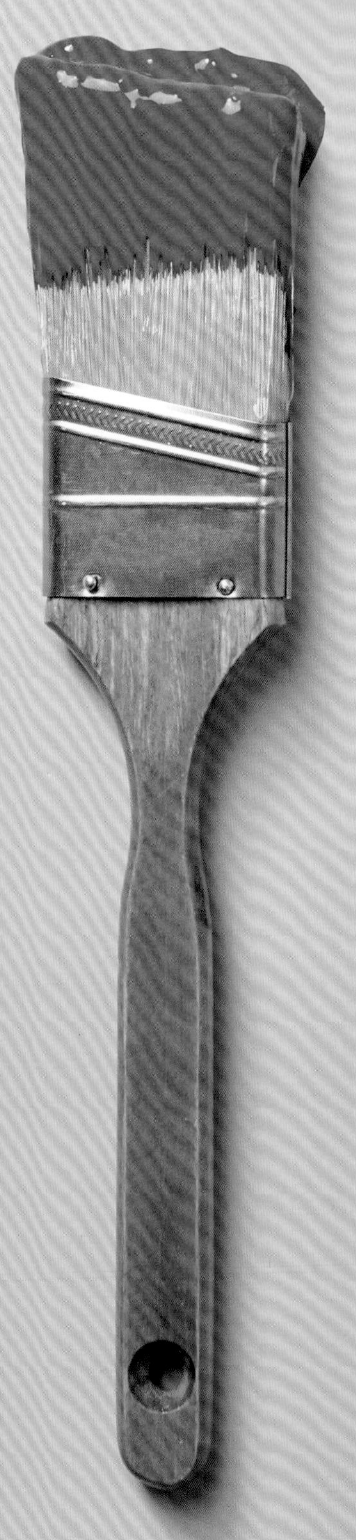

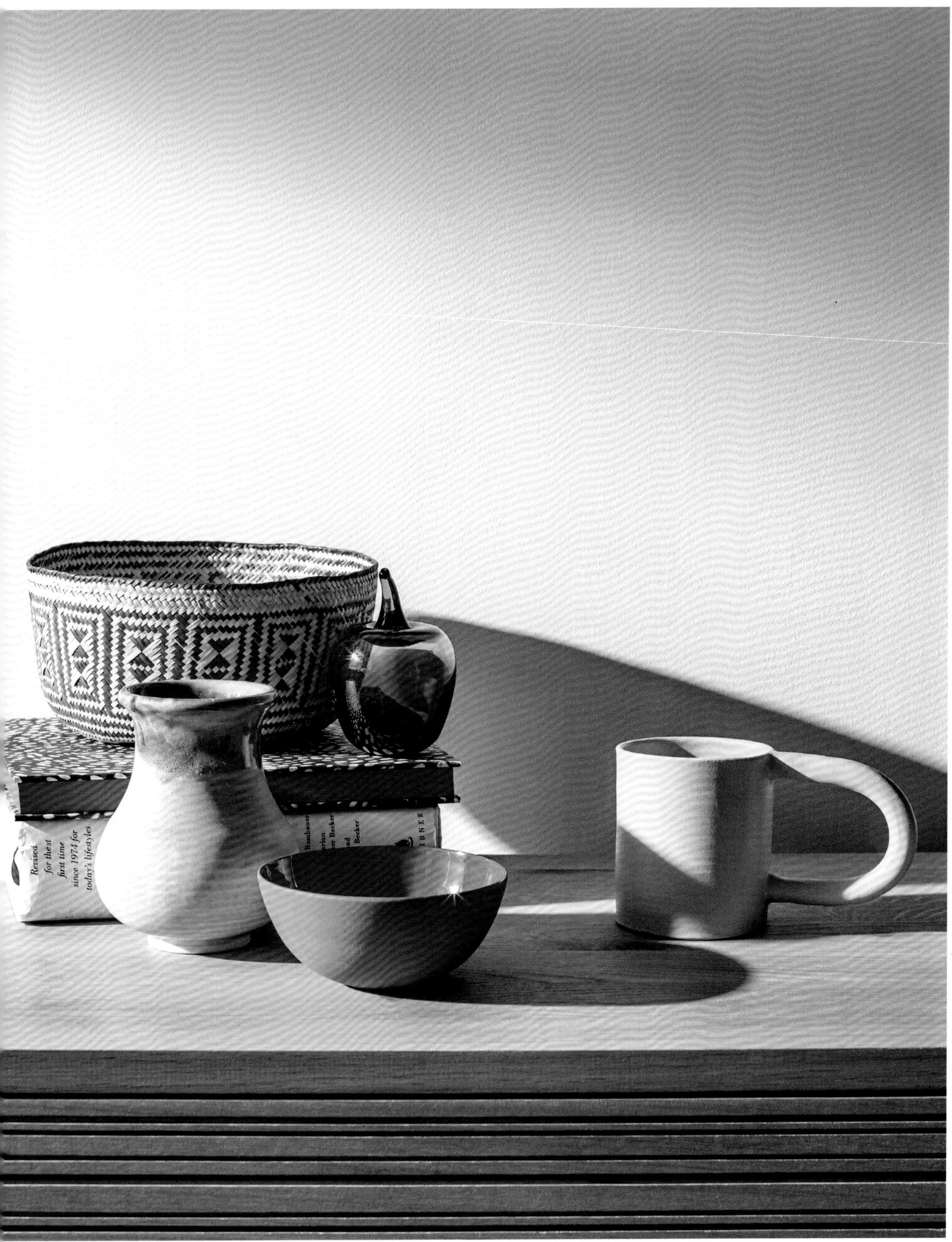
Revised
first time
since 1974 for
today's lifestyles

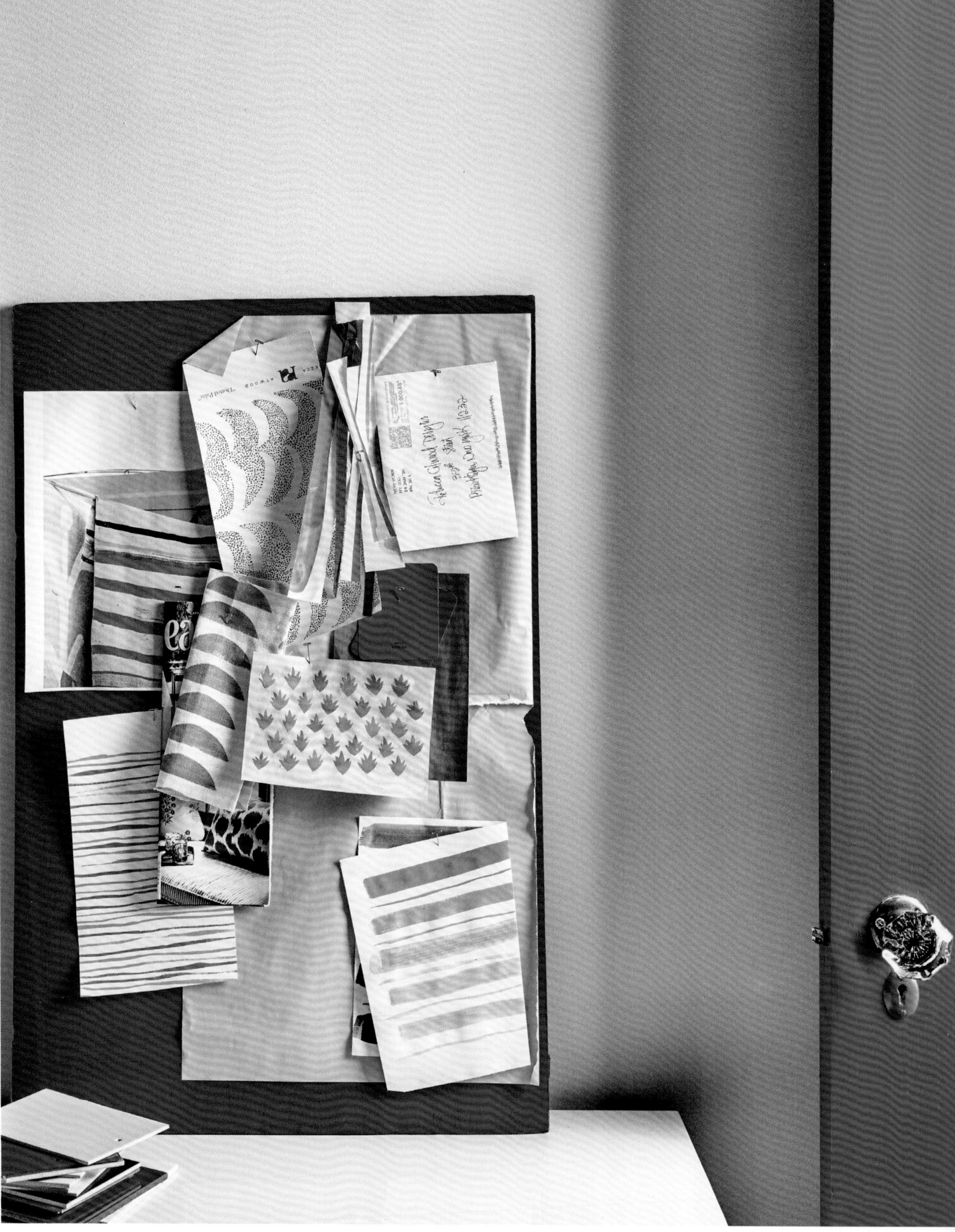

THE HISTORY OF RED

Written acknowledgment of the color red is so ancient that in early Rome, the word for *color* and the word for *red* were one in the same. Prior to the written word, the world was colorless with regard to language. With only black and white having names, a way to describe seeing color had not yet been invented. However, the first color human beings *were* able to describe was red. It is mentioned fifty-two times in the King James Bible, second only to white, most notably to describe the Red Sea.

Cultural associations with red abound. Red has long been connected to courage and sacrifice, because it is the color of blood. Around the world, red is aligned with political strength, which is why the majority of countries' flags feature the powerful color. Statistically speaking, Olympians who wear red are more likely to win, because the color inherently intimidates the competition—and the athlete wearing red feels powerful. In China, red represents death when mixed with black, but it also signifies good luck and good fortune. Hindu brides wear red saris in part to signal prosperity, fertility, and the rising sun.

Because red is alarming, it is also used to symbolize "stop," as in lights, stop signs, and tape. In fact, the term *red tape* comes from the red wax seals of yore used to seal the letters King Henry VIII sent to Pope Clement VII begging for an annulment of his marriage to Catherine of Aragon. To read these negotiations, you would have to "get past the red tape."

And the phrase "seeing red"? Well, it doesn't come from bullfighting. While it might seem like bulls in a fight charge at the red muleta waved by a matador because of its color, bulls are actually color-blind and just reacting to the motion.

In art, the paint colors red ochre and sienna were found in many of world's earliest works, and artists continue to use these colors to create drama and make statements.

The Aztecs were the first people to create red dye by harvesting cochineal, a tiny gray insect that, surprisingly, creates a bright red color when squashed. They dried and crushed the bugs into a fine powder and created a rich and lasting red. The Aztecs relished their red and adorned their rulers in it until the Spanish arrived, then conquered the people and quickly exported the dye to Europe. For the next two hundred years, the Spanish enjoyed a monopoly on the production of red dye and built an empire on the color.

Nevertheless, the original cochineal prevailed and is still used today in everything from lipstick to jams to maraschino cherries to M&Ms, disguised as the ingredient E120. So, the next time you eat something with red dye, be sure to thank the Aztecs, the Spanish, and the tiny gray bugs that made it all possible.

RED PALETTES

To create a palette with red as the focal point, choose your favorite version and get clear about how it makes you feel, which will help determine what other colors you mix with it, and the proportions you'll use as well. Like a painting, a beautiful palette should have depth along with dimension. The main color needs support to create that story. A few of my favorite shades of red are blush, tomato, and ruby, and you'll see inspiration in the book for using all of these colors.

Let's explore tomato in more depth. Tomato red is bold and vibrant, and verges on orange. For me, it's a happy color, so I want the palette it anchors to feel cheery and fresh. To keep it light, I chose a base of ivory, as well as peach and blush, to act as connector colors to bridge the gap between the soft and vibrant tones. I also picked a cornflower blue; because blue is a complementary color to orange, it brings out the orange in the tomato red, and using a lighter blue, in a smaller amount, reduces the red's intensity because the blue color is calm. Proportion also plays a role in the overall feel of a palette, so if you are making heavy use of ivory and using smaller amounts of the brightest colors, you'll create a very livable, airy palette with ribbons of color.

By pulling these fabric swatches, painted color chips, and objects together, we can start to create a mood. Imagine all these colors together in a room. Let's say it's a living room, with soft creamy walls, a blue armchair, patterned curtains in ivory and tomato, and peachy accents in pillows and throws. To fully incorporate the palette into a space, you'd need more neutrals, such as natural linen, as well as materials like mixed woods, but it already has the overarching feel for the layers of color.

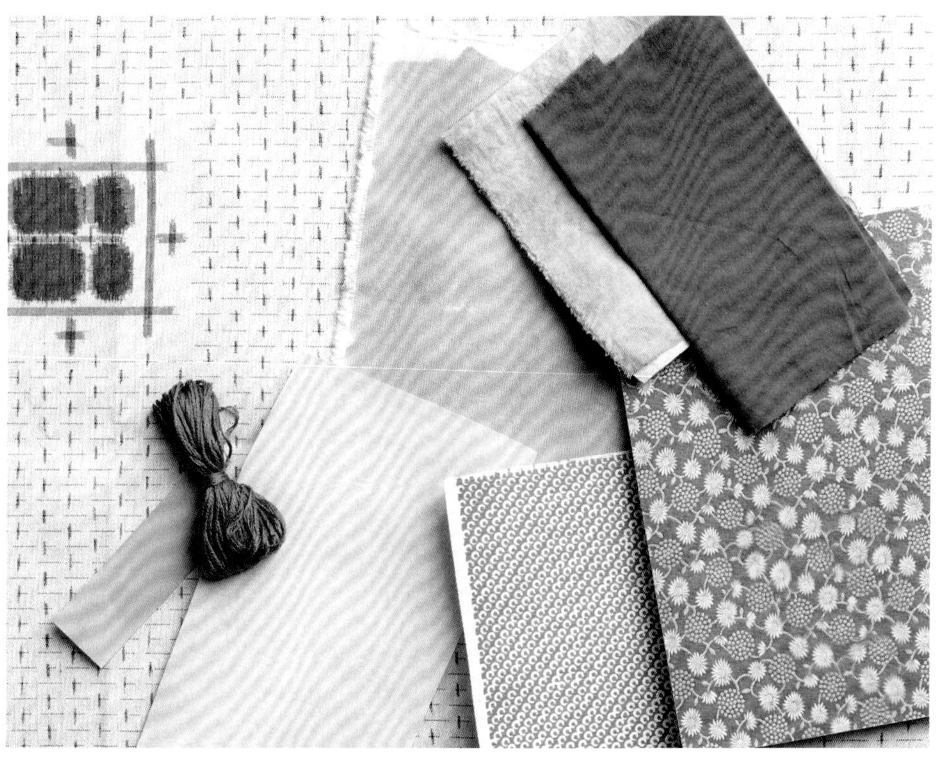

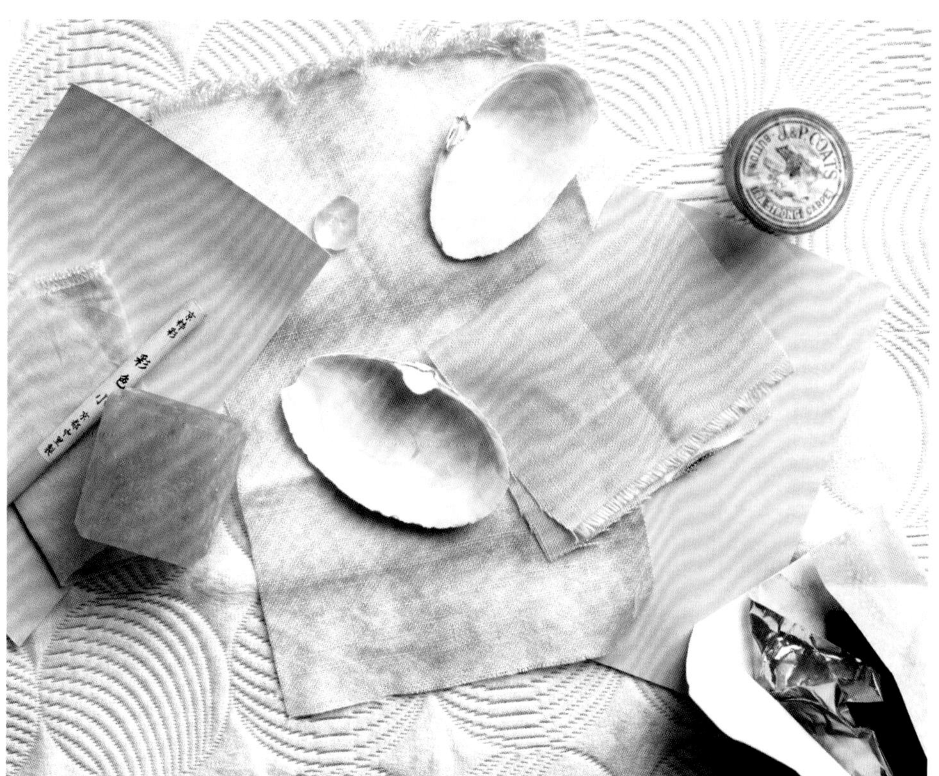
J&P COATS

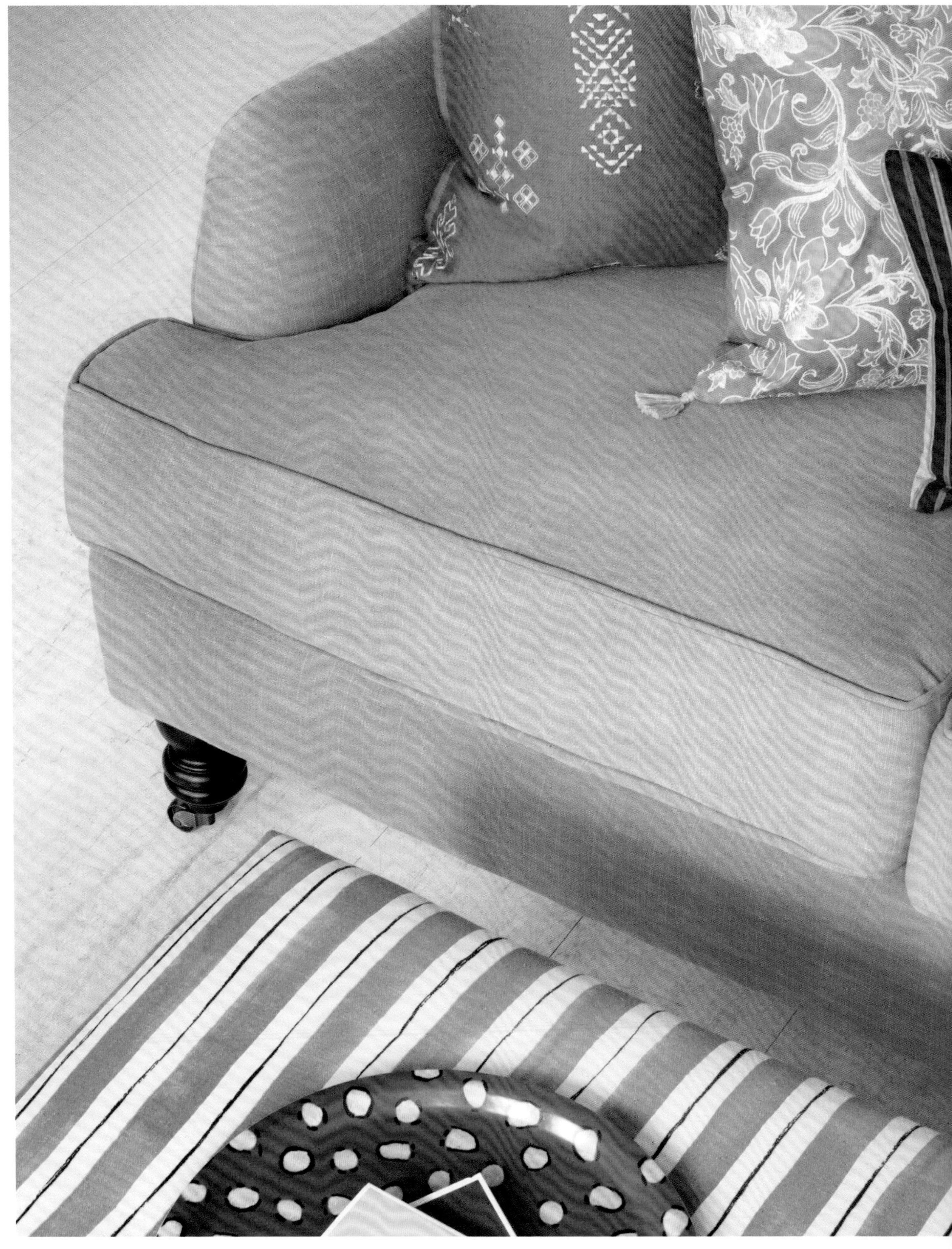

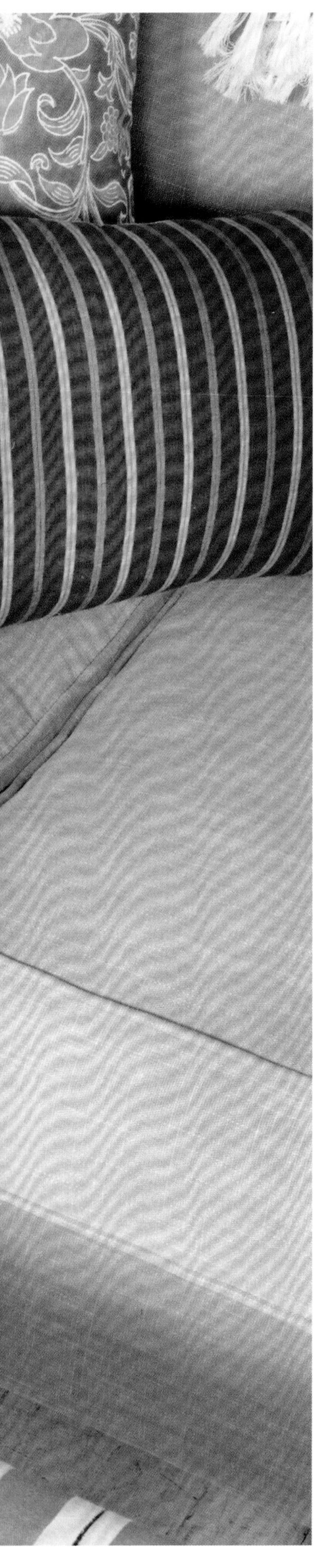

- What is one of your earliest memories of the color red?
- What version of red do you gravitate toward?
- With which rooms in the house would you associate this color?

LIVING WITH RED

Red is a robust color. When fully saturated, it can quickly overwhelm, so think about tints, tones, layers, finishes, and shades of red. If you're still wary, consider pinning up several different reds in your space to see how it reacts with the existing colors before you commit. A brighter, more saturated red can bring definition to an otherwise neutral space and keep things from feeling too dull, while a softer version can add warmth and energy. Vibrant red usually feels invigorating, cool shades feel romantic, and deep, bold shades feel powerful. The right shade comes from how you want the room to feel.

DECORATING WITH RED

Add a Pinch

Add a bright, happy version of red to your living room with a lampshade, vase, or pillows. Brighten a kitchen with a red bowl or teakettle. Using a vibrant red accent can pull a room together and bring the colors around it into sharper focus. It enhances other colors through contrast. Just remember, you may need to add in a different color to create balance—it could be a midtone connector color, or even a darker neutral.

Consider Softer Tints

If you want to warm up a space but keep it feeling calm, consider what pink can do. A blush hue that has orange in it (think more peach and less of a blue-pink) won't feel overly feminine.

Pair with White

Red works well in living rooms, kitchens, and areas of activity, since it a lively, energizing color. But white can soften it, making it appropriate for places like the bedroom. Think about a red-and-white tacking stitch, or red-and-white quilts. All that white dilutes the strength of the red but doesn't make it quite as soft as a blush.

Welcome with Red

A red doorway can also be energizing and symbolize good luck. It can feel welcoming, lively, and exciting.

Promote Movement

Hallways are areas of transition, and since red is an active color, they're a great place to use it. Hint: If you can see any red from another room, be sure the two colors work together. That means you may want to place a small red accent (or a warm hue that connects to that red) in the room from which you can see the red. For more inspiration on using red in a hallway setting, see how Emily Butler uses it in her home on page 128.

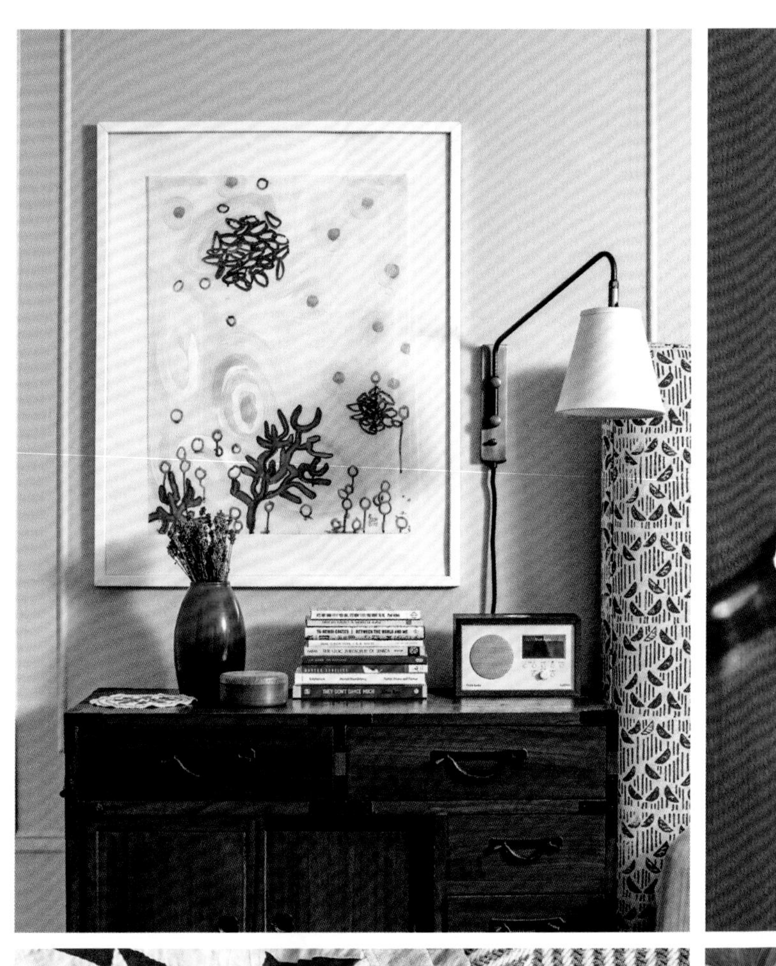
TA-NEHISI COATES | BETWEEN THE WORLD AND ME
THEY DON'T DANCE MUCH

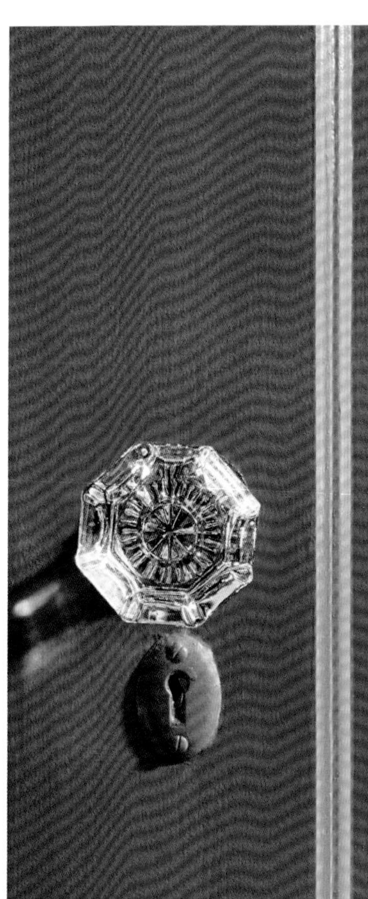

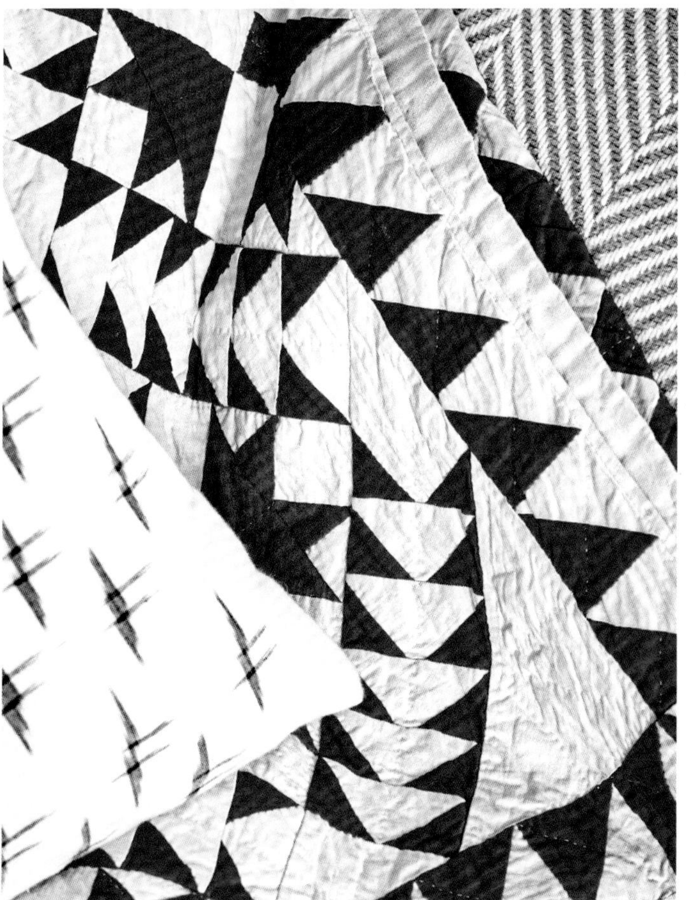

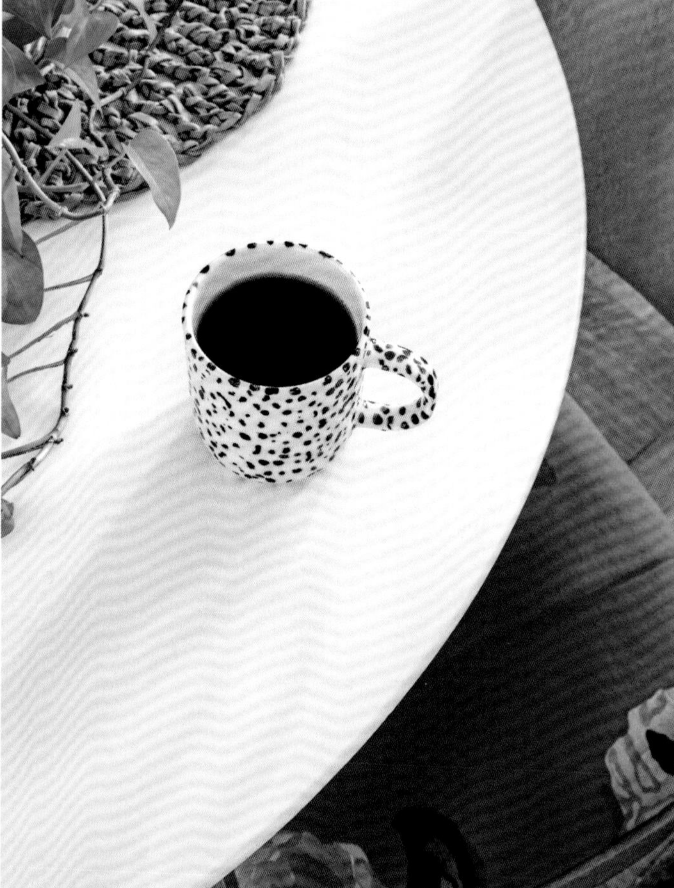

ORANGE

PEACH, TANGERINE, TERRA-COTTA

Orange has rich associations in the natural world. Imagine a desert landscape or gazing at the vastness of the Grand Canyon, surrounded entirely by orange. Orange is invigorating and happy; it's also warm and has a certain spirited energy. When dialed up, orange is modern and eye-opening, and when turned down it's rocklike and grounded. Think of orange fruit dangling from trees, the bright orbs dotted amid the lush greenery. It's hard not to associate orange with citrus. Personally, I think of the clementines we always had at the bottom of our Christmas stockings. It was a family tradition and I loved peeling them and uncovering that citrus scent.

Orange also reminds me of carving pumpkins with my sisters, cutting into the center and finding all that stringy flesh and the seeds. I liked how the thick skin of the pumpkin became a bit lighter toward the inside as you cut into it. We would save the pumpkin seeds and my mom would roast them with some salt for a snack. It was such a tactile experience, and it revealed a world of many shades of orange, from the calm yellow-nude of the seeds to the more saturated, hard outer shell. To me, orange is a color that shows us how we can take beautiful and varied color cues from food.

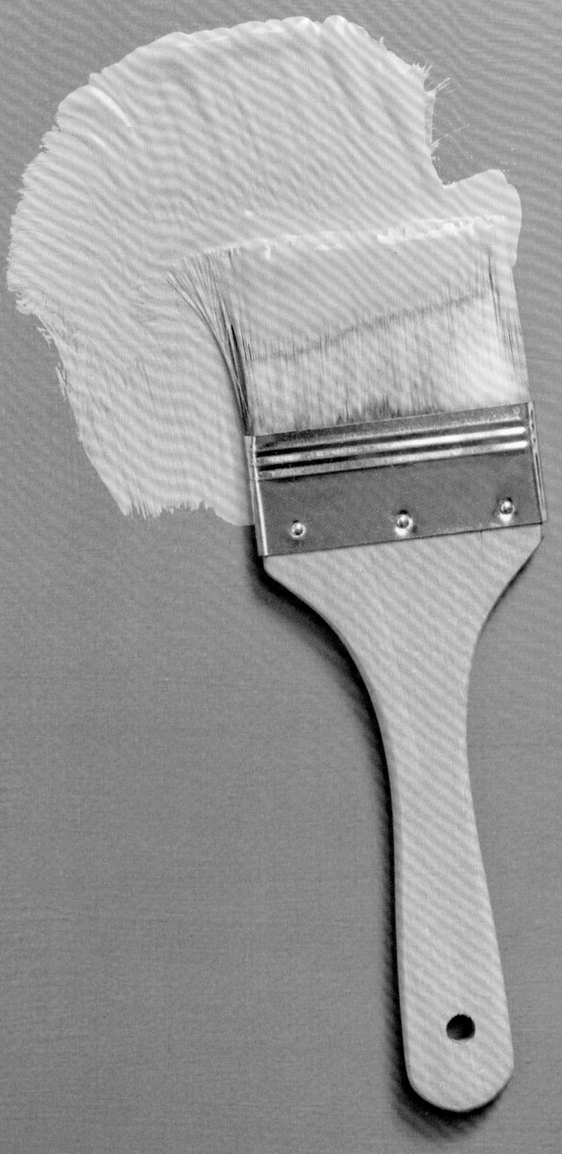

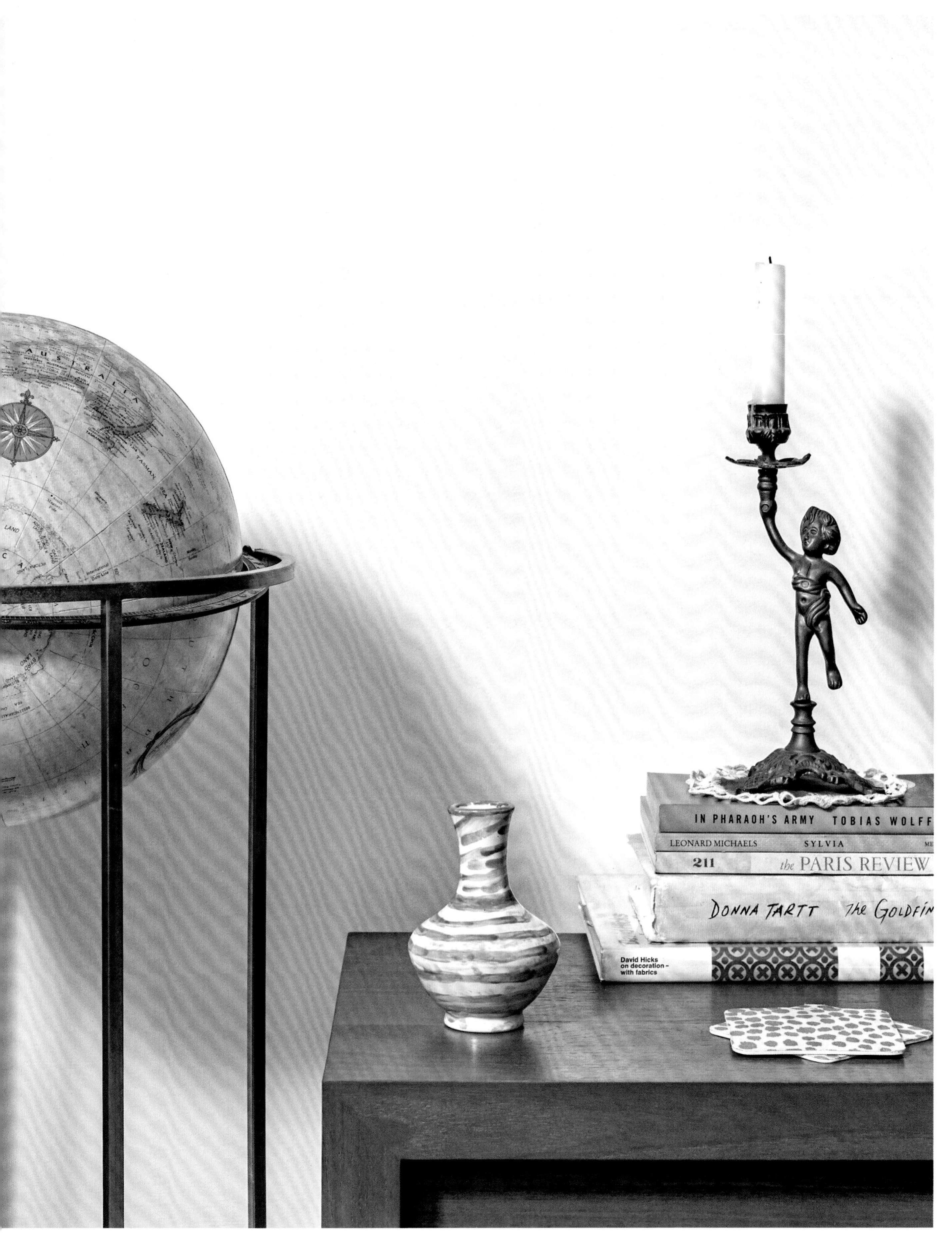
AUSTRALIA
IN PHARAOH'S ARMY
TOBIAS WOLFF
LEONARD MICHAELS
SYLVIA
211
the PARIS REVIEW
DONNA TARTT
David Hicks
on decoration –
with fabrics

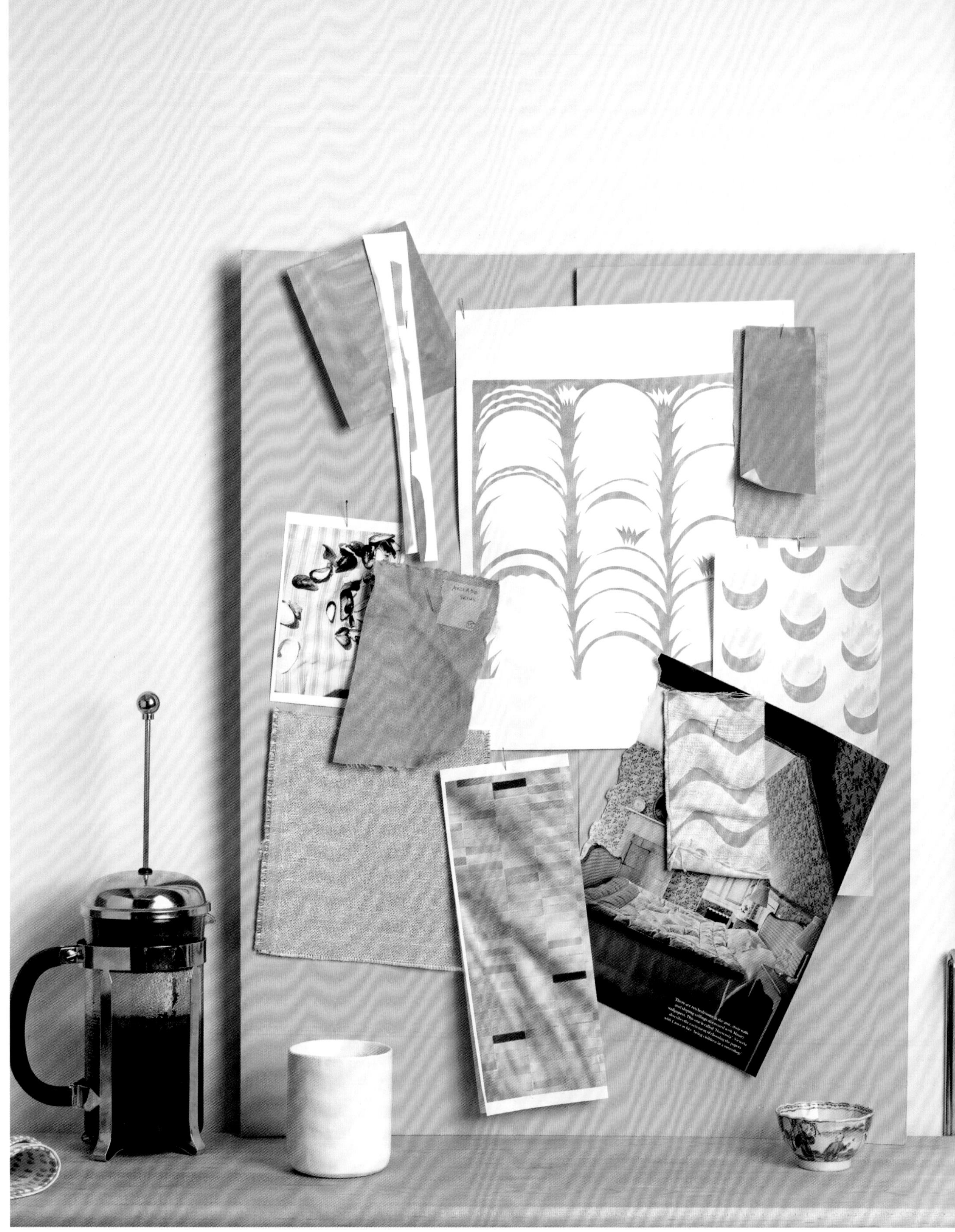

THE HISTORY OF ORANGE

Orange had to fight for an identity. Before the sixteenth century, it was simply referred to as yellow-red. However, all that changed upon the cultivation of a certain fruit, the color of which begged for its own description. The journey of the orange citrus fruit began, it is believed, in China and the first recorded use of the word *orange* as a color was in 1512.

While orange hardly boasts the regal or esteemed history of purple or red, it is the color of the world's most expensive spice. Trading between $2,000 and $10,000 a pound, saffron is one of the most expensive delicacies in the world. The reason for the hefty price tag stems (pun intended) from its fickle cultivation. Saffron threads come from the stamens of the *Crocus sativus,* a violet-colored flower that blooms for just one week each year. Each flower produces about three stamens, which must be picked delicately by hand and carefully dried. It takes thousands of flowers to produce a single pound of saffron. Whether or not it's worth it is debatable, but foodies describe the spice as heavenly, elevating entire dishes to new heights. Though much too expensive to be used as a dye, you might recognize saffron from the Buddhist robes that copy its color.

Arguably orange's most powerful association is with the Dutch. The great hero of religious freedom in the Netherlands, and eventual king of England, was William I, who hailed from the House of Orange. He and all his descendants are depicted in paintings draped in the bright color. In turn, the Dutch adopted orange as a symbol of freedom, calling themselves the Orangemen. In fact, they so embraced the color that when they captured the city of New York, they briefly named it New Orange—even today the Bronx flag still bears the traditional Dutch tricolor.

It wasn't until 1797, when the French scientist Louis Vauquelin discovered the mineral crocoite (which led to the 1809 invention of the synthetic pigment chrome orange) that orange became popular for artists. Though ancient Egyptian and medieval artists had previously produced orange with a variety of minerals, Impressionists in France were particularly enchanted with the way orange offered a complementary contrast to azure blue, and in 1872 Claude Monet painted *Impression, Sunrise,* which gave the artistic movement its name.

Though one of the most luxurious and enduring uses of orange is actually the result of an accident. Dye shortages among Parisian fashion houses during World War II resulted in labels and packages being printed with orange pigment instead. After the war, the color stuck; the luxury brand Hermes still retains their orange boxes and horse carriage logo, and orange remains an integral part of the brand's identity as a symbol of serenity, wisdom, and joie de vivre.

ORANGE PALETTES

My favorite orange hues are terra-cotta, tangerine, and peach. I also included soft versions of tan here, because while they are neutrals, at their core they are a dialed-down version of orange.

Let's look at the palette in two ways—first as a story in richness. Mix it with earthy neutrals and warm jewel tones—linen, soft brown, washes of pink, hints of cobalt, and even purple. This warm, robust palette is a great foundation if you plan to bring in more vibrant colors because it can handle colors like rich cobalt or punchy saturated orange. Your neutrals should have enough strength to complement the accent colors used (in this case, the warm jewel tones). This palette would work well in a kitchen or dining space.

Next, let's look at a softer palette. In this palette, I am still treating terra-cotta as a neutral, but I'm making it understated with blush hues as well as taupe. Those softer hues help absorb the orange color. Subdued orange goes well with both sage green and spicy yellow-green. This palette would be nice in a bedroom, because it's soft and dreamy but still unexpected.

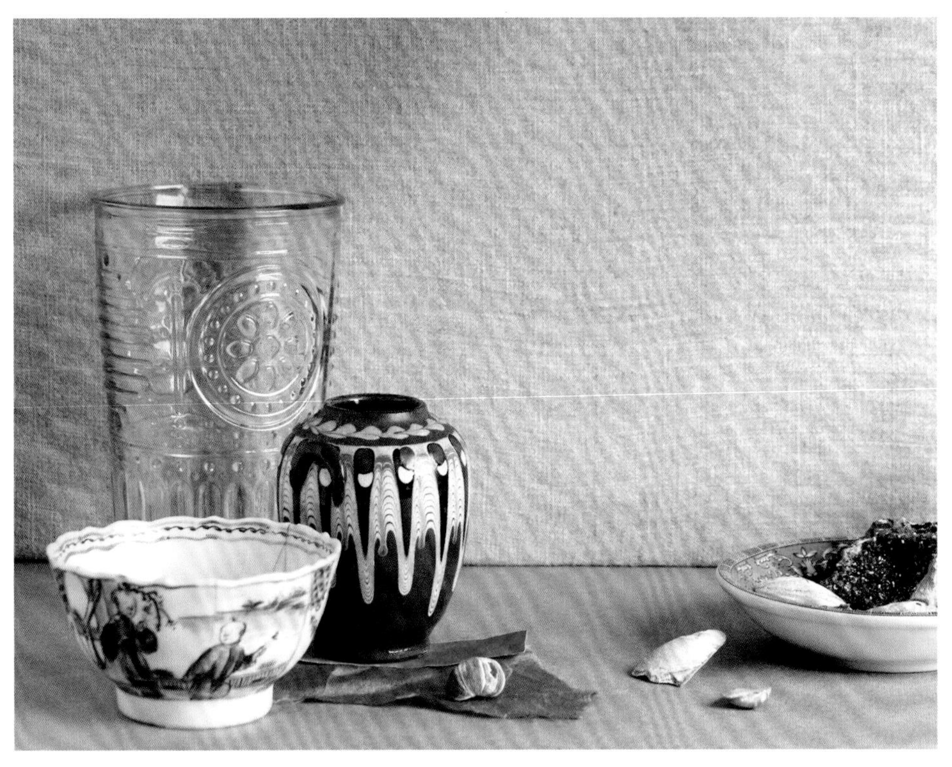

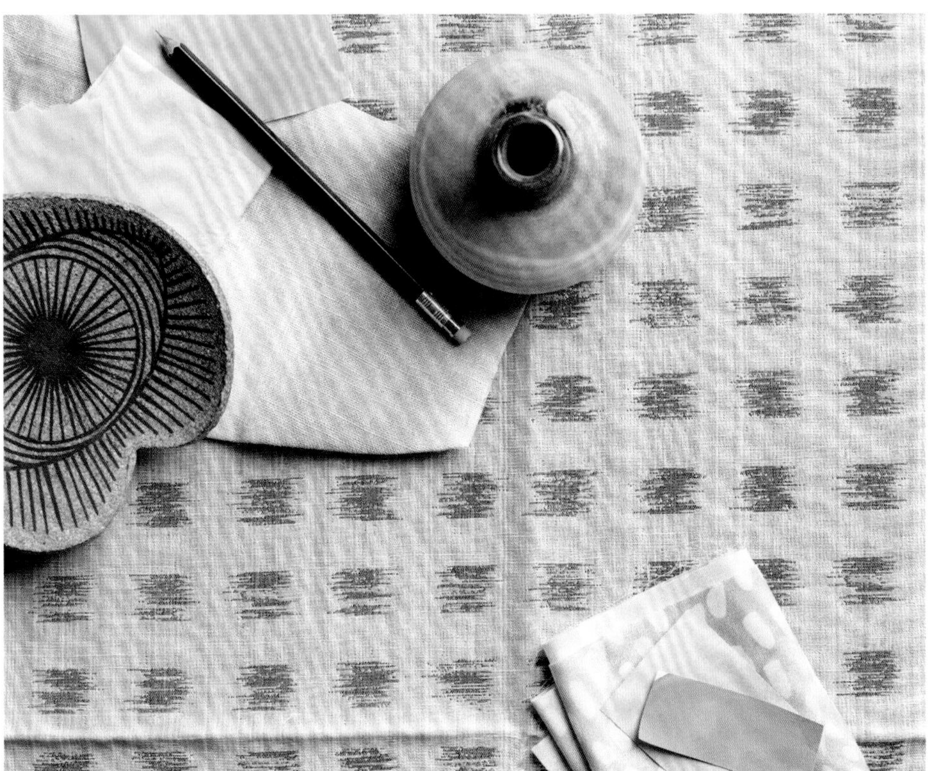

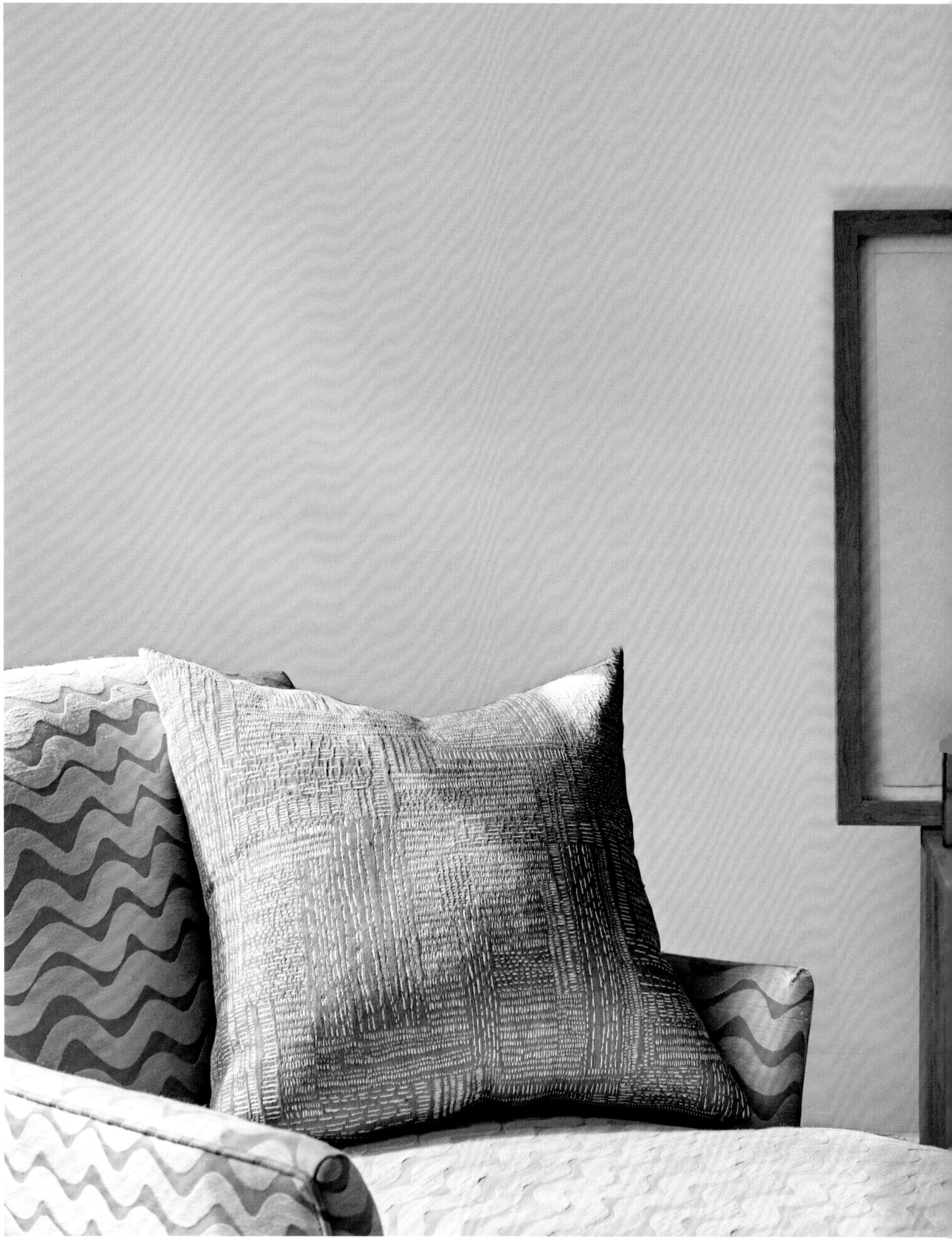

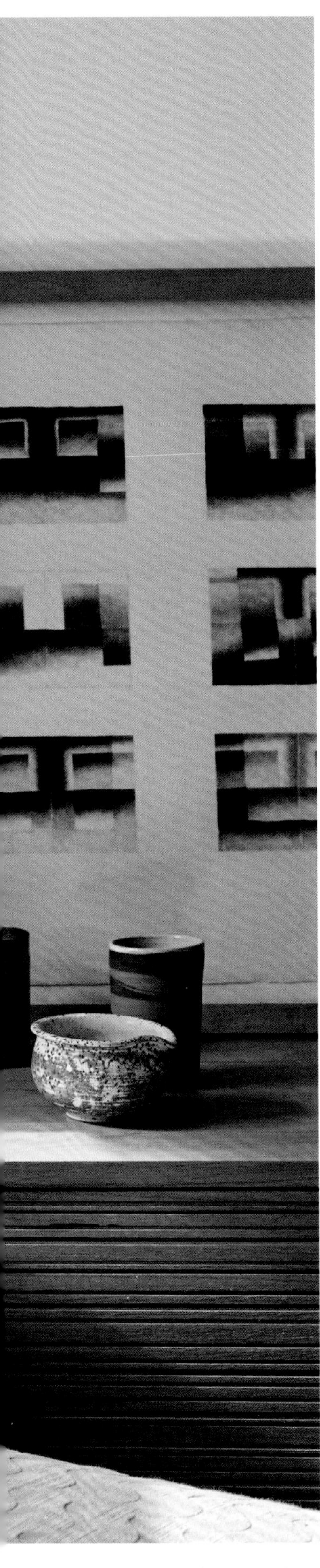

- When you think of the color orange in nature, what do you remember?
- What softer or deeper versions of orange can you imagine? How does this change how you feel about the color?
- What foods do you think of that are orange?

LIVING WITH ORANGE

When approaching a room, remember that orange can range from burnt, earthy neutrals to bright and vibrating or soft and peachy. It's the first color I think of when I imagine a sunset. Then I think of pink and yellow ribbons running through the setting sun, and I start to dream about how I can capture this feeling in my home and translate the calm, warm layers of color into rooms. Imagining orange in nature immediately reduces the intensity of picturing orange in your home and reminds you that it can lend a dreamy, peachy glow.

Orange can also create a cool, bohemian seventies look, or bring a fresh, modern, bright touch to a space. Orange is a great color to use at home because it layers so easily with neutrals and acts as a bridge to other colors. A desaturated orange feels organic and is more vibrant than a taupe, gray, or tan, so it adds warmth and interest.

DECORATING WITH ORANGE

Think Materially

One easy way to incorporate more orange into your space as a neutral is to think about materials. Add clay, terra-cotta, and midtone stained woods. Bring in a leather chair with an orangish hue to it. Natural, untreated leather tends to have orange undertones as it deepens. It can be gorgeous and subtle at the same time. Often a color can feel more natural (and thus neutral) if it's not a painted hue but rather the original color of a material.

Discover Finishes

Copper finishes are also a great way to bring in orange. Remember that finish can change how a color feels. Here copper provides a richness and elegance. It could be on cabinet hardware, a backsplash, or even a collection of copper pots on display. The warmth of this metal adds richness to any space.

Go for Peach

Peach is one of my favorite colors because it's a little unexpected but also very neutral. This creamy version of orange is like using a nude shade of nail polish; it's pretty and soft but subtle, too. It can be great painted on walls.

Just a Bit

If you're worried about adding orange to your environment, start by living with a bowl of oranges on your dining room table for a week, or pumpkins in your living room, and see how you feel. Collect a few books with orange spines and stack them on a table. Test the color out in a small way, and then you may feel comfortable using it elsewhere. (This tip works with all colors!)

Stay Grounded

Like red, orange imparts a grounded, earthy feeling, so it's great as an accent color in a rug pattern. I'm imagining a dab of orange in a diamond-patterned Berber rug for a seventies boho look, or the rich oranges in a traditional Heriz Serapi Persian rug. Since orange is used in small amounts on the ground, it won't be overwhelming but will provide warmth and earthiness.

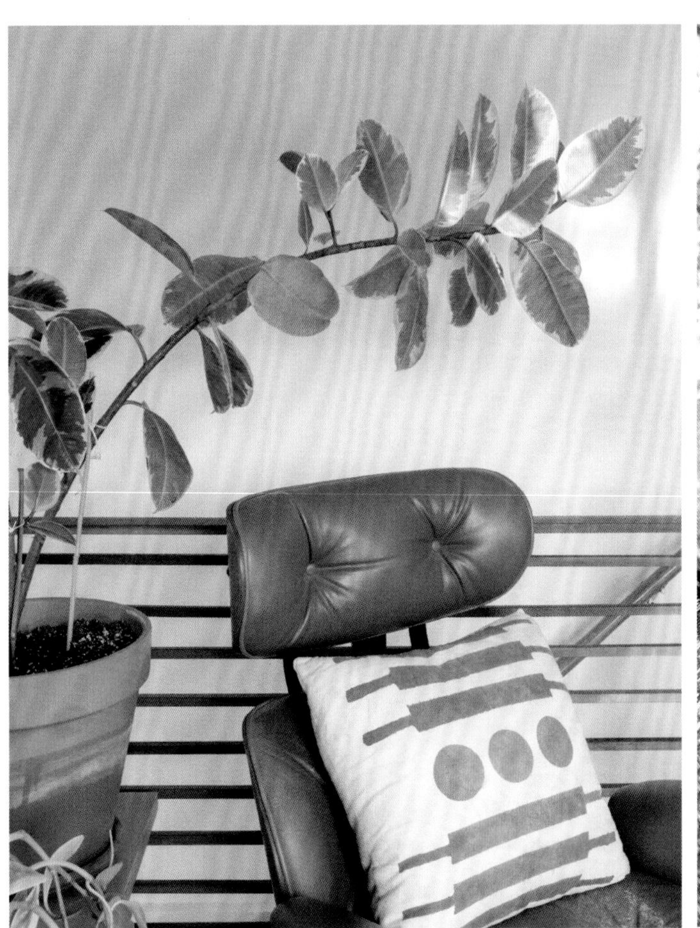

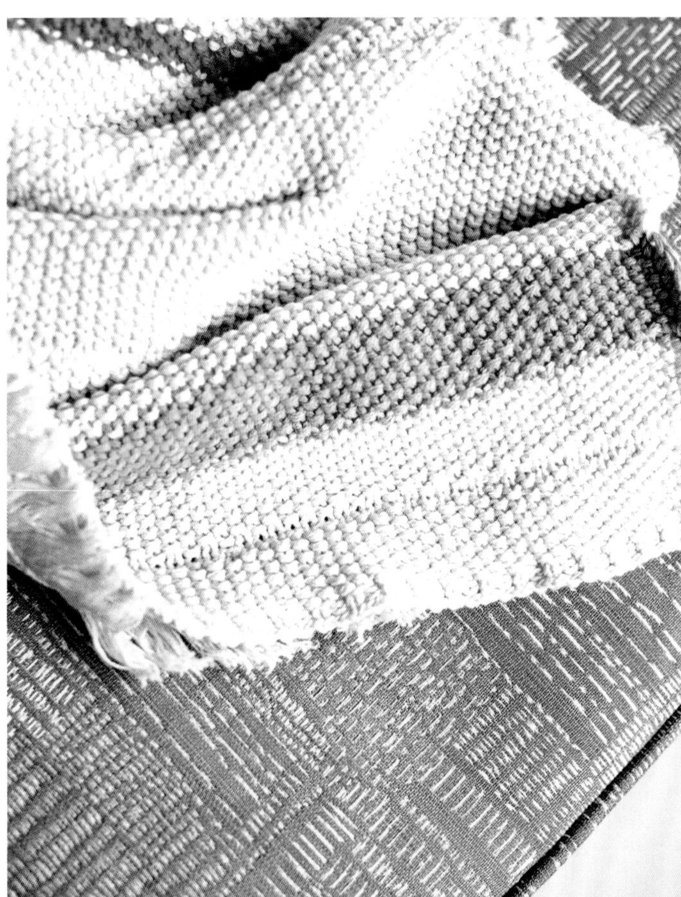

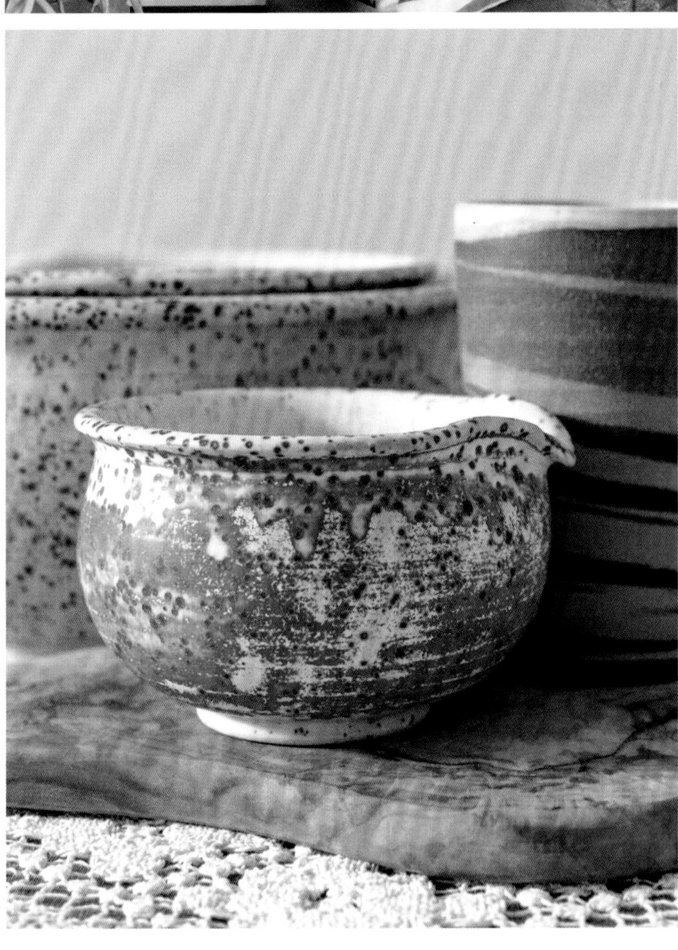

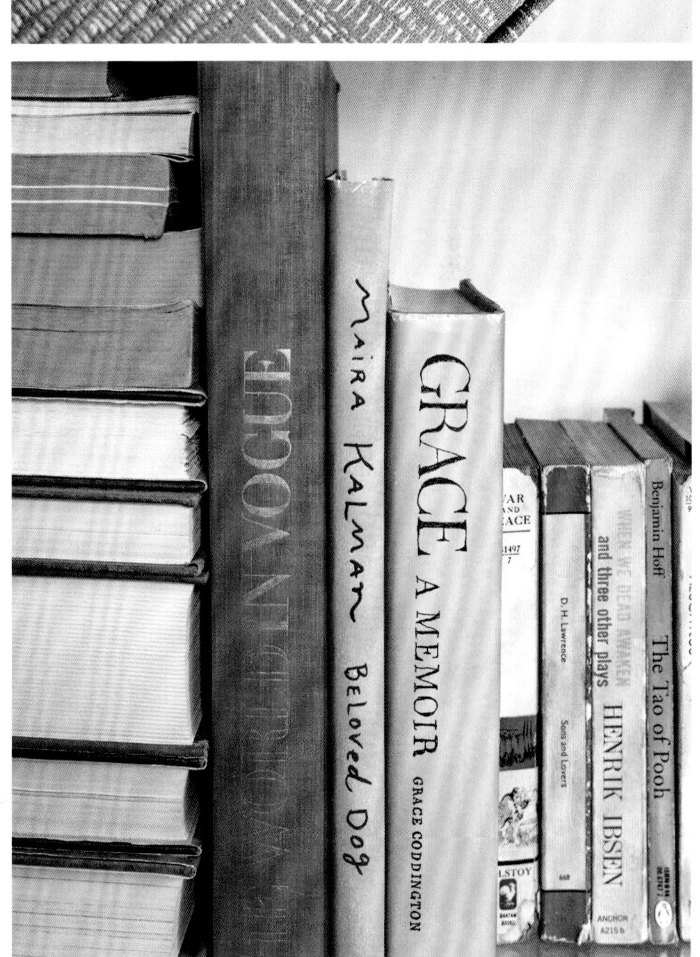
Maira Kalman Beloved Dog
GRACE A MEMOIR
GRACE CODDINGTON
D. H. Lawrence
Sons and Lovers
WHEN WE DEAD AWAKEN
and three other plays
HENRIK IBSEN
ANCHOR
Benjamin Hoff
The Tao of Pooh

YELLOW

LEMON-BUTTER, GOLDEN, OCHRE

I often think of yellow as sunshine. It brings me back to picking buttercups in the garden and plucking the petals off daisies, leaving the yellow center, or planting sunflowers in my mother's garden and watching the big flowers with bright yellow petals grow as if I were watching yellow sprout from the earth. Though I have other, less obvious associations with the color, like setting the table with beeswax candles and reveling in the varied color and soft waxy finish mingled with their gentle fragrance. I put them in brass candlesticks and light them to create dripping layers of yellow. I also like to think of unusual ways yellow shows up, like a campfire on the beach with the yellow flames piercing through the darkness in the surrounding woods or the faded butter yellow lines on a soft gray concrete street. Yellow can veer into the crisp yellow-green of a Golden Delicious apple to the muted color of honey and wheat to the brightness of a Meyer lemon. If you know how to look at a color like yellow, it can surprise and inspire you in the most interesting ways.

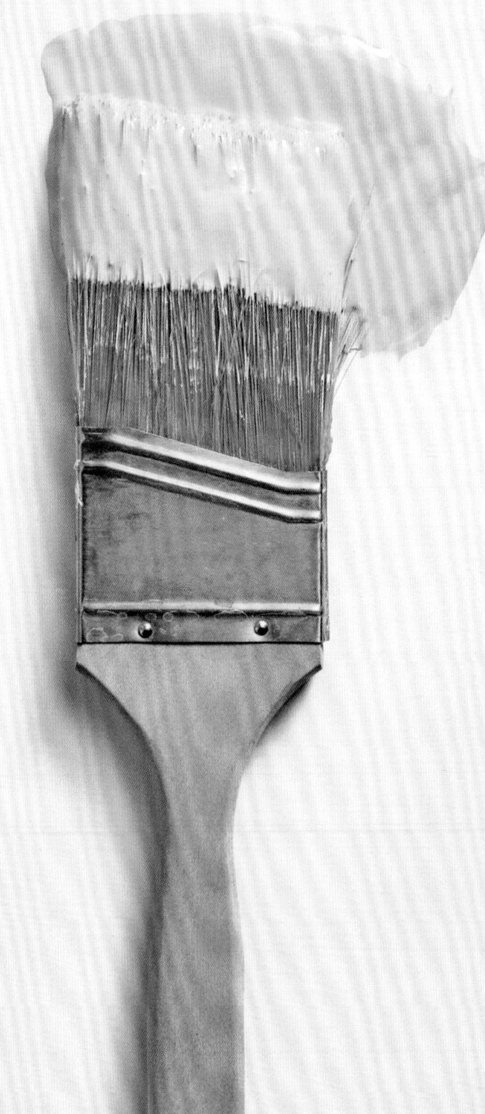

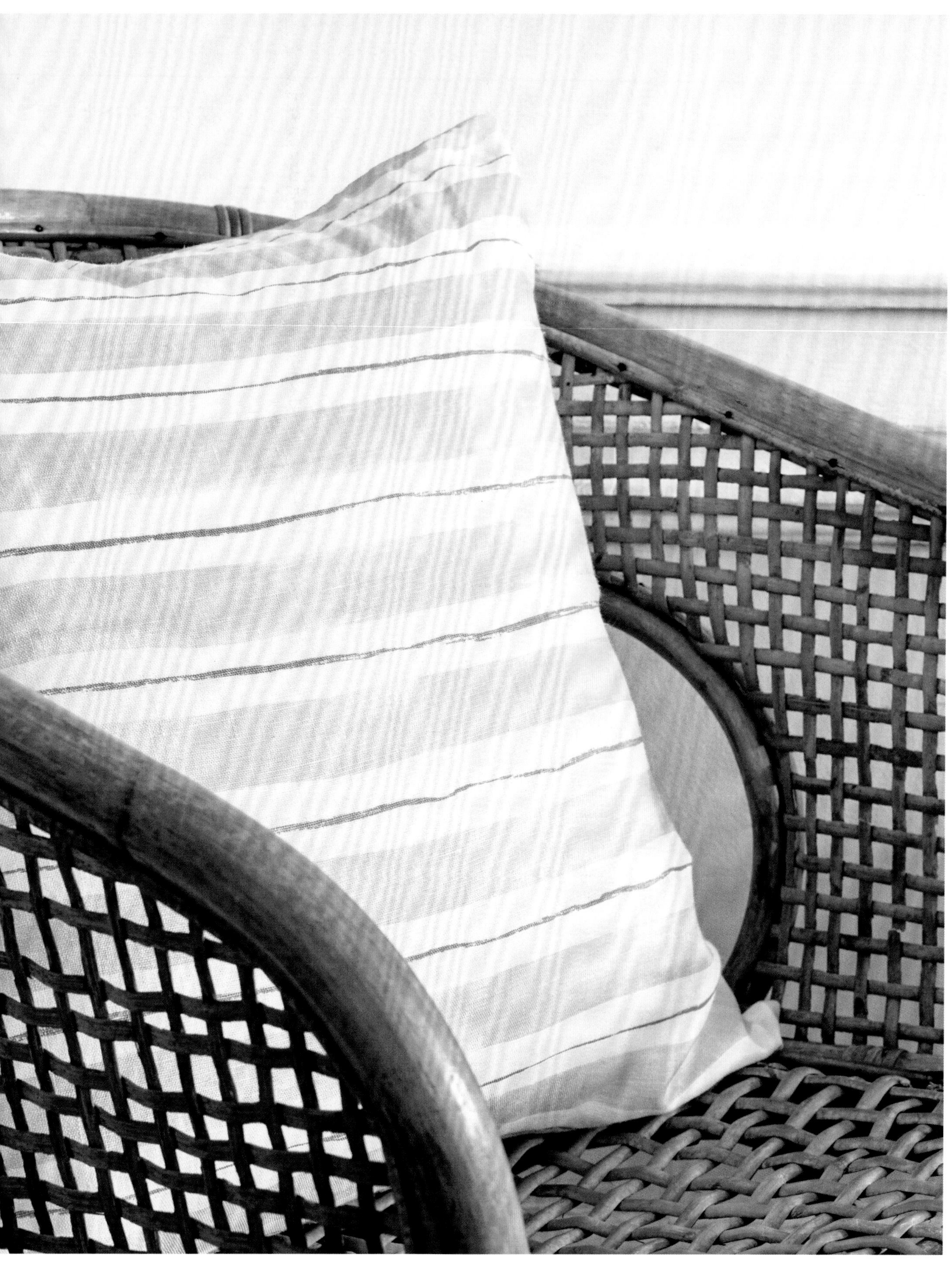

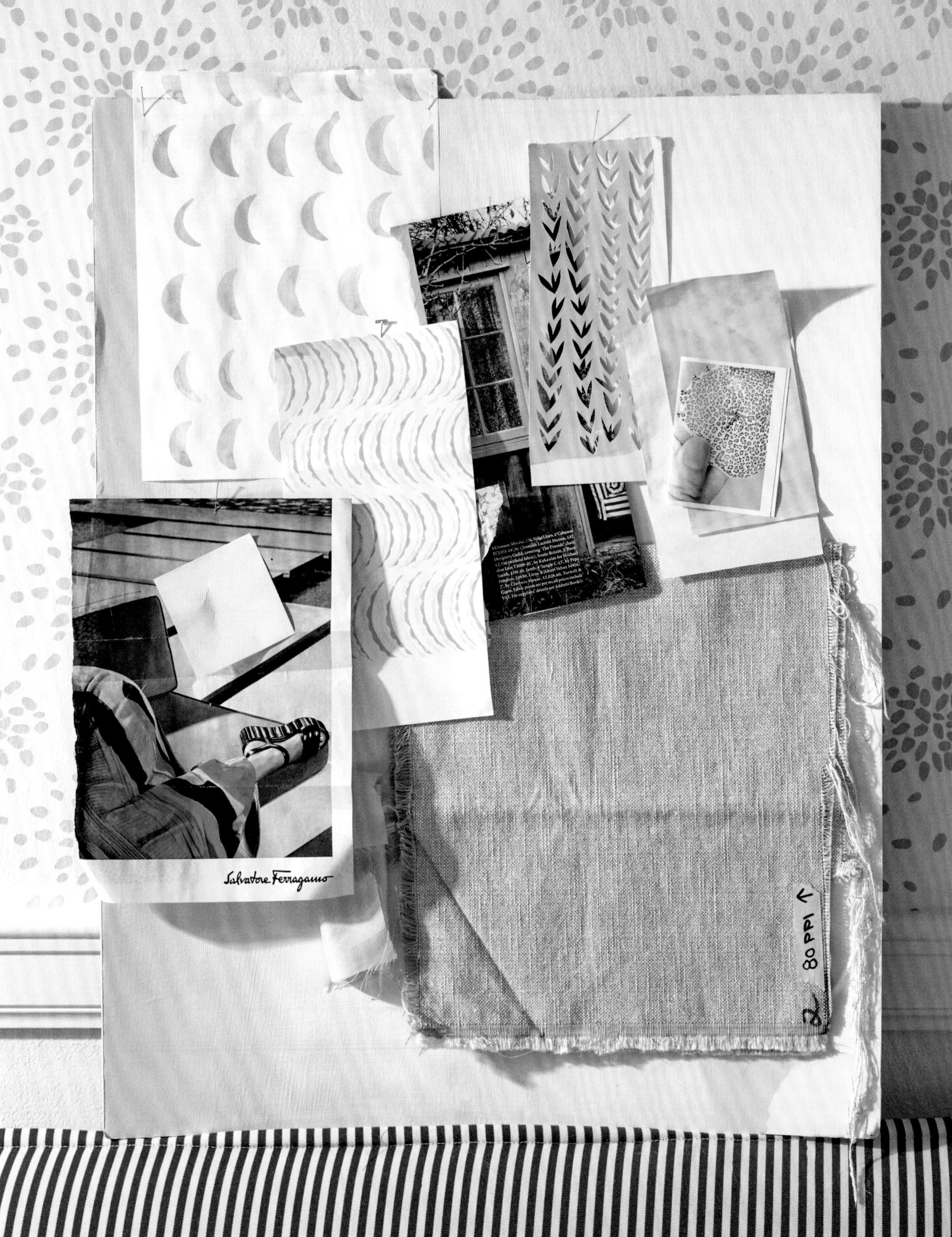
Salvatore Ferragamo
80 PPI

THE HISTORY OF YELLOW

Yellow's dichotomous meaning is in the eye of the beholder. On one hand, yellow is the stuff of smiley faces, rubber duckies, and buttercups, but it can also be associated with sickness and contamination. The reason for this dichotomy may have to do, quite literally, with both the eye and the beholder. The human eye is quite sensitive to yellow and can differentiate more variations of it than any other color. This explains why it is the color of choice for school buses, yield signs, road dividers, and countless other things we really *need* to see.

Plus, yellow's ability to stand out lends itself well to outlandish figures. Enter the mythical Yellow Emperor, Huangdi, in the twenty-sixth century BC. Whether man or myth, he nonetheless helped shape Chinese civilization—and its relationship to the color yellow. Because of the emperor's fondness for it, yellow became the color of rulers and one of the colors of the five-element theory in China. As the theory goes, yellow is the color that corresponds to the earth and is considered most beautiful and prestigious. Even though yellow lost its status with the fall of the Qing dynasty (1644–1912), it is still the chosen color of heroism and good luck. In China, it is sometimes paired with red in place of gold, and it graces the walls of many royal palaces and temples.

In Western culture, however, yellow was sometimes the opposite. Being called yellow or yellow-bellied is insulting. Its high visibility can also be used to label people as "others." It has been used to mark Jews throughout history, the most widely known example being the yellow Star of David from Nazi Germany.

Yellow also has close ties to sensational literature and journalism. The phrase "yellow journalism" originated with two feuding newspaper tycoons, William Randolph Hearst and Joseph Pulitzer, over a comic strip called *The Yellow Kid*. The comic strip was printed with a new type of yellow ink that didn't rub off on the readers' hands. When Hearst stole the popular cartoonist for his own paper, a rivalry ensued as the two strove to sell as many newspapers as possible, no matter how sensational those "yellow pages" needed to be.

Yellow pigment is also dualistic. Orpiment, a beautiful golden yellow used in ancient Egyptian tombs as well as the Taj Mahal, is laced with arsenic. The pigment Gamboge is fatal in large doses, though the color is beguilingly bright and sunny. This vibrancy made yellow a popular choice for artists, like Vincent Van Gogh. Eventually paintings like Jean Honoré Fragonard's *Young Girl Reading* in a lemon-yellow dress appeared on the art scene. Later, chrome yellow gave way to Vincent Van Gogh's iconic sunflowers. He proclaimed, "The sun, a light that for lack of a better word I can only call yellow, bright sulfur yellow, pale lemon gold. How beautiful yellow is!"

YELLOW PALETTES

Yellow, in all its forms, adds cheerfulness to a space. My favorite yellows are lemon-butter, golden, and ochre. These versions of yellow are easily digestible within a space. They give it warmth and sunniness without feeling excessively bright or colorful.

When creating a palette with yellow, starting with soft buttery shades is the easiest way to incorporate it. We want to create a color story for a room that can either be enough on its own or the foundation to add more color. Pair these buttery shades with slightly brighter shades of yellow. This blend will help the brighter shades feel softer, as if you're creating your own gradient of a hue. I like yellow mixed with linen, warm grays (think reddish gray versus bluish gray), peach, blue, and neutrals reminiscent of stones on the beach. This soft mix is a perfect base for a room—whether a living room, bedroom, or kitchen. Although it's not what you would traditionally think of as neutral, this palette is a great base to build upon, depending on the mood you're looking to achieve. It can handle some darker, moodier shades or bright, more vibrant hues. Having color in your foundation makes it easier to keep layering. If you want to take it a step further, consider adding ochre, burnt orange, and even a soft gray-lilac.

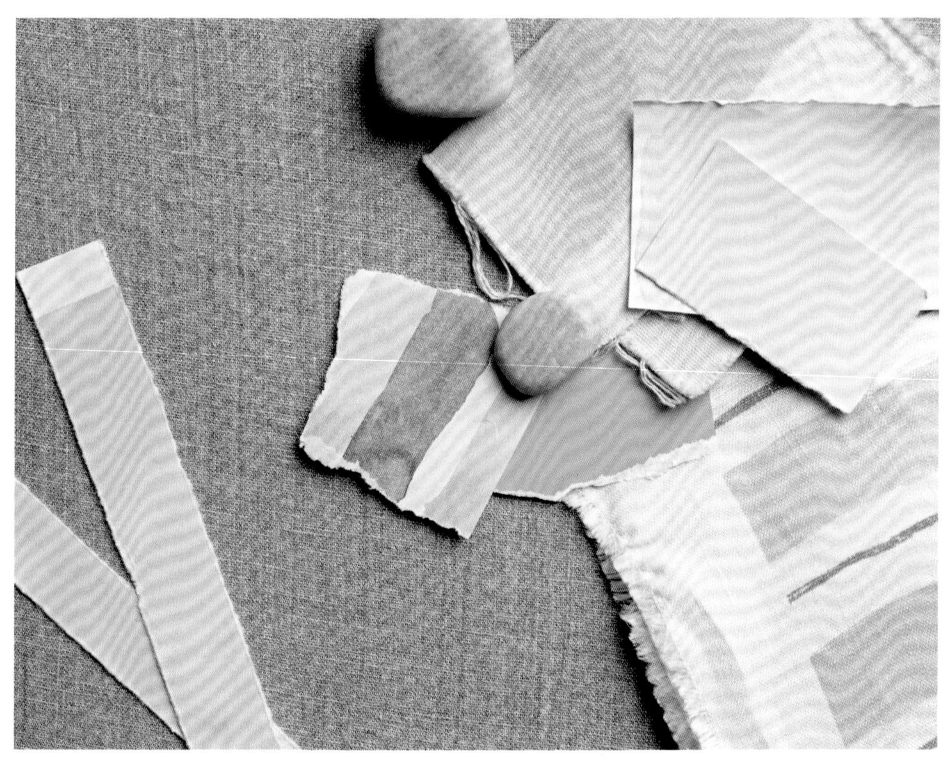

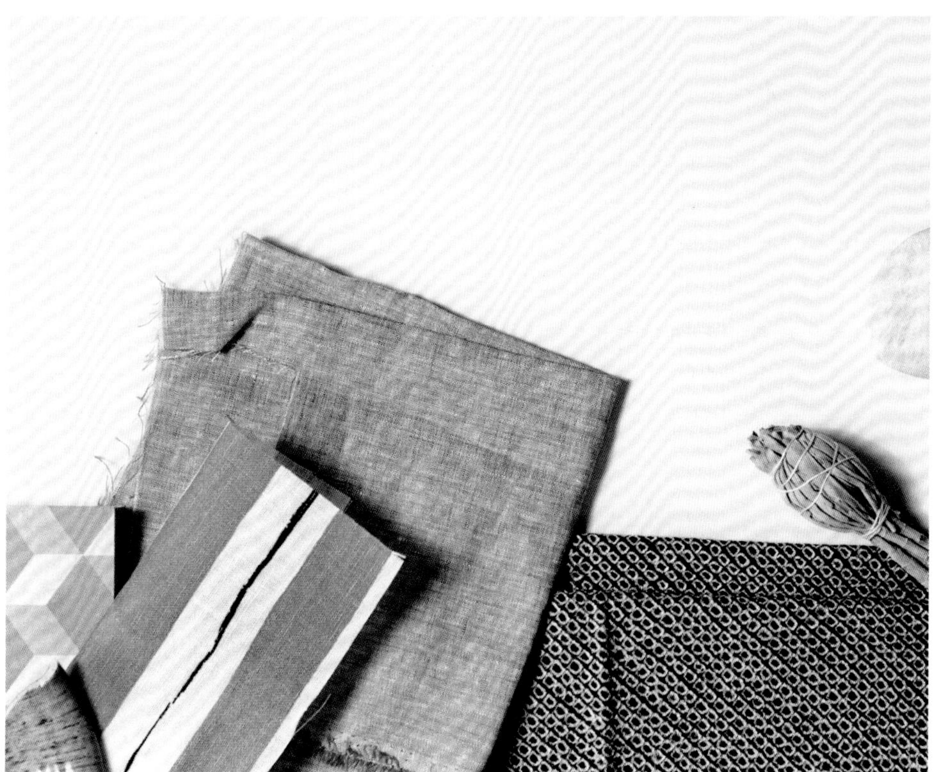

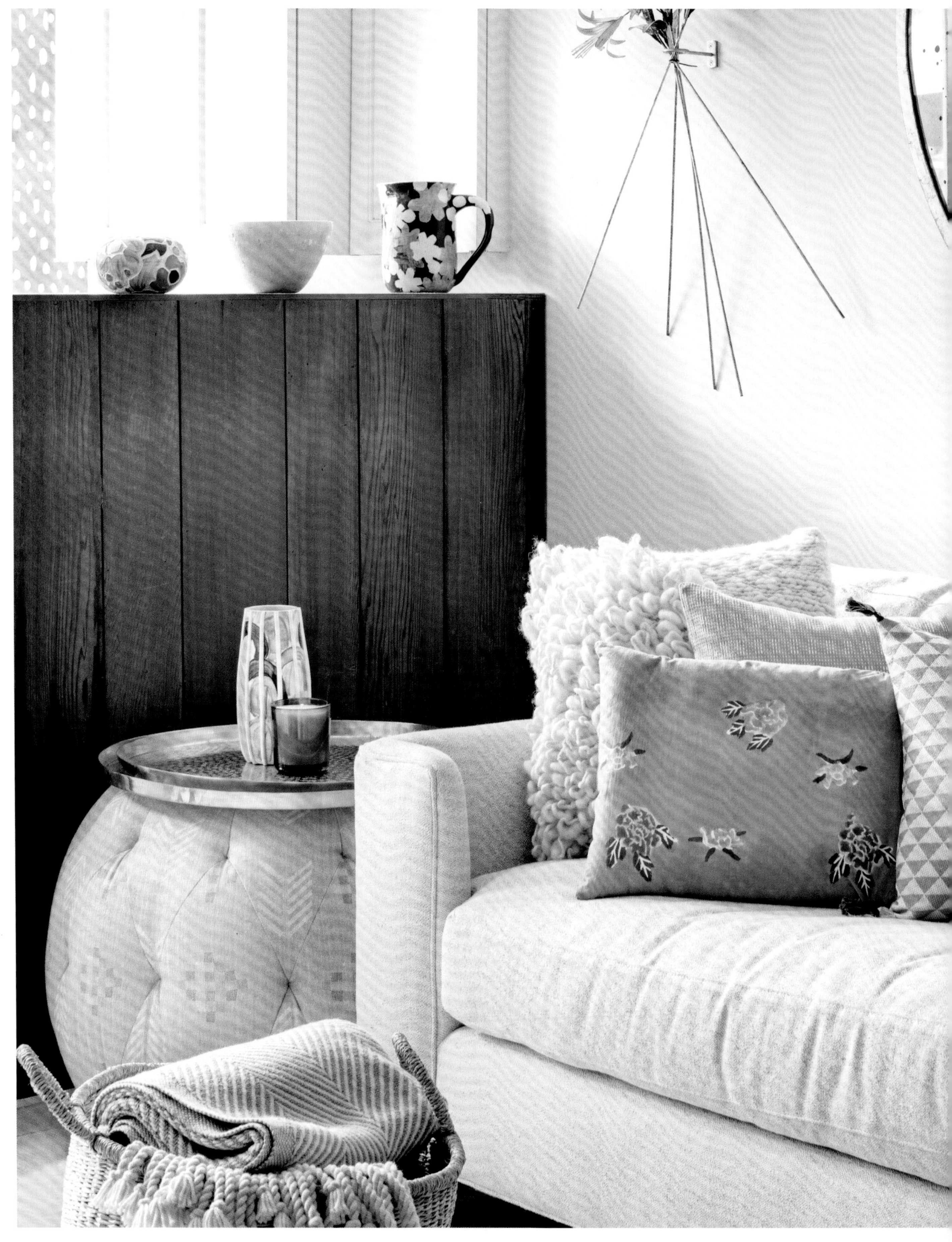

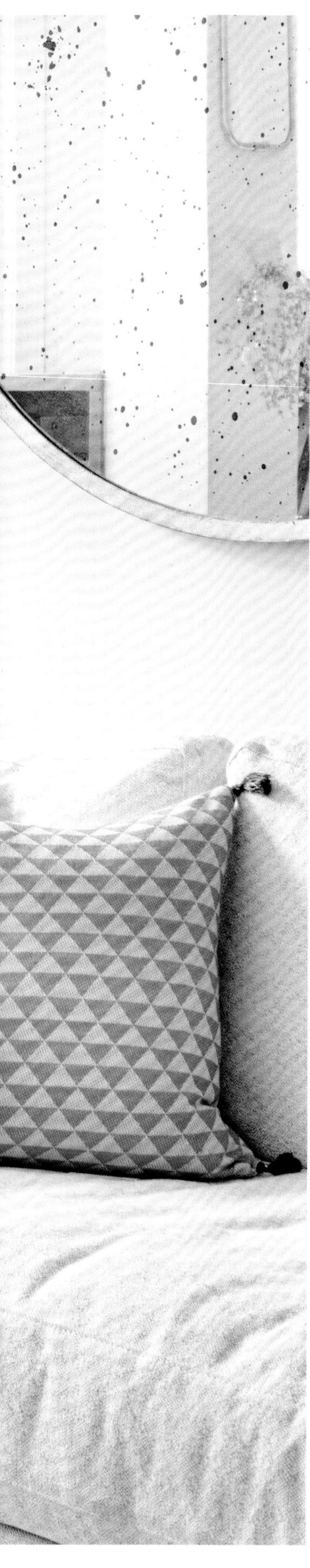

- What fragrances do you associate with yellow?
- Is there an unexpected version of yellow that you love?
- Do you remember any articles of clothing you wore that were yellow or had yellow patterns or buttons?

LIVING WITH YELLOW

Yellow is sunshine, and who doesn't want more of that in their home? Widening your view of yellow is the first step to using it when you decorate. While it's not as common as blue or green, it is likely that you already use versions of this hue more than you realize. For instance, many of the light-colored woods have yellow undertones, which you can use as the foundation of a color palette. Or consider metallics—brass and gold accents are yellow, too.

Think about the way yellow feels like a neutral in nature when you want to warm up your space to make it feel sunny but still blended. Imagine a field of grass in the winter when the light hits it. That soft golden glow is a nice alternative to beige, but it can still work as a neutral.

If you choose to use a brighter version, remember that a little can go a long way. Outdoors, true yellow arrives in small bursts in the form of spring daffodils in a field. In the fall, yellow leaves suddenly blanket everything while the rest of the world has become dustier, deeper, and muted but rich enough to balance it. Mirror this effect in your home, using yellow either sparingly and blended into a palette or widely using versatile materials, which is the most livable way to incorporate it.

DECORATING WITH YELLOW

Collect It

Repetition of simple everyday objects is a great way to bring in a color inexpensively. For example, a stack of old *National Geographic* magazines on your shelf can add a welcome brightness. My mom displayed a collection of old pale-yellow butter molds on a shelf.

Glisten

Yellow is joyful and bright, but it can also be sophisticated and even reserved. Gold accents are a great way to add the feeling of yellow to your space in a sophisticated way. Think about incorporating brass hardware, candlesticks with beeswax candles, and gold frames. These accents can act as jewelry for your home. When the light hits them, it adds a subtle glimmer and creates warmth. Look to these metallic versions of the hue to inspire yellow color choices in different materials like fabric, ceramics, and paint.

Come Home to Yellow

A yellow entryway can be a great way to welcome people into your home. The softest, palest yellow can be used to bathe your space in sunshine. Use it generously here. These soft, pale versions of yellow are easy to use in large amounts because they're so absorbable. They look great on walls and are a neutral use of the color.

A Kitchen Accent

Because yellow is so cheerful, it's a natural fit for the kitchen. Try a bowl of lemons, glass jars of honey, bright yellow tulips in a pale-yellow vase, or a clear bottle of olive oil on your counter. It's also easy to add yellow, without commitment, to table linens. If you love how that looks, consider yellow cushions for your kitchen chairs or collect ceramics that feature the hue.

Offset the Seasons

In winter, you need something happy, so bring in some bright yellow. Add a yellow lampshade or a painting in a spot you pass each morning to make you smile. Think about how good it feels to see that first daffodil in the spring—you can bring that into your home anytime you need an extra bit of happiness.

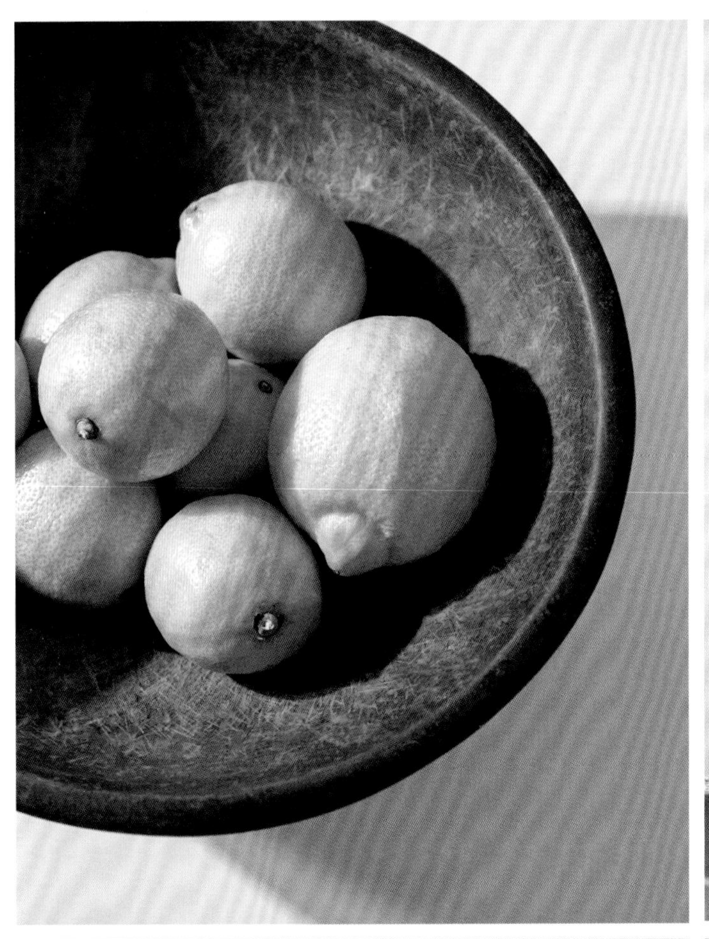

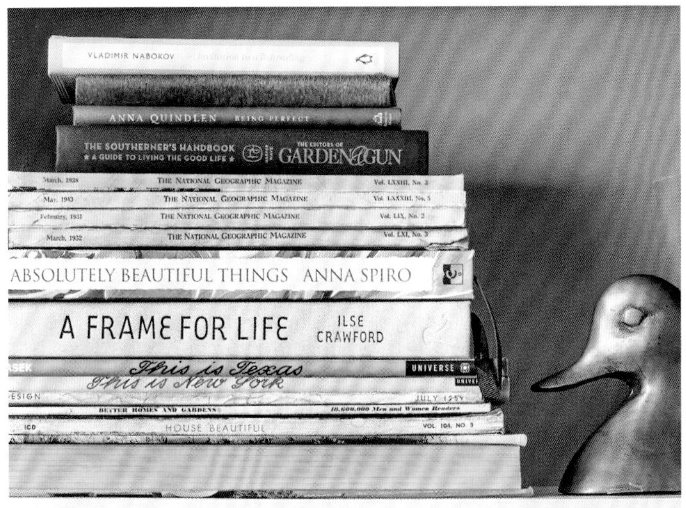

VLADIMIR NABOKOV
ANNA QUINDLEN
THE SOUTHERNER'S HANDBOOK
★ A GUIDE TO LIVING THE GOOD LIFE ★
THE EDITORS OF GARDEN&GUN
THE NATIONAL GEOGRAPHIC MAGAZINE
THE NATIONAL GEOGRAPHIC MAGAZINE
THE NATIONAL GEOGRAPHIC MAGAZINE
THE NATIONAL GEOGRAPHIC MAGAZINE
ABSOLUTELY BEAUTIFUL THINGS ANNA SPIRO
A FRAME FOR LIFE ILSE CRAWFORD
This is Texas
UNIVERSE
This is New York
HOUSE BEAUTIFUL

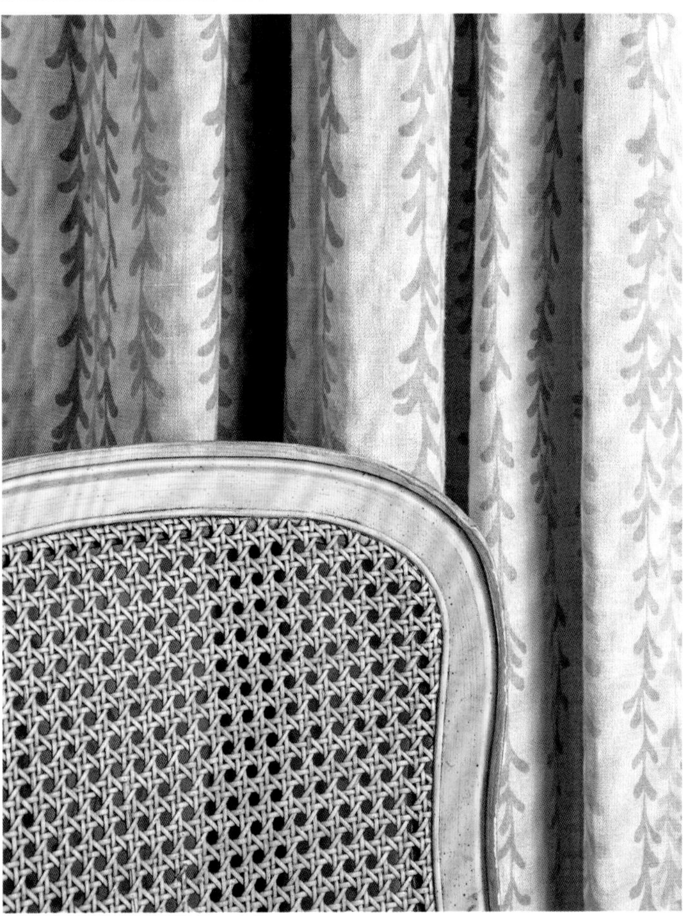

GREEN

MINT, DUNE GRASS, MARINE

Green is the basis of plant life, so it's a color that is often all around us in nature. The green spectrum can be calm and restorative, vibrant and energizing. Consider how many shades of green are in a single forest. When I visited Japan, I experienced the concept of forest bathing. I stayed in a room that overlooked a forest and spent time lying in a hammock, soaking in all the green. The ground was covered with moss, plants, and ferns. Looking up, the Japanese maple leaves appeared like green lace. I remember the muted hues verging on gray, yellow, and even blue.

Some of the greens reminded me of the mint that used to grow in our yard when I was young. It was so refreshing we would put it in our water glasses on hot summer days. We tried freezing the mint in ice cubes and letting them melt in our mouths and it was like eating the color green.

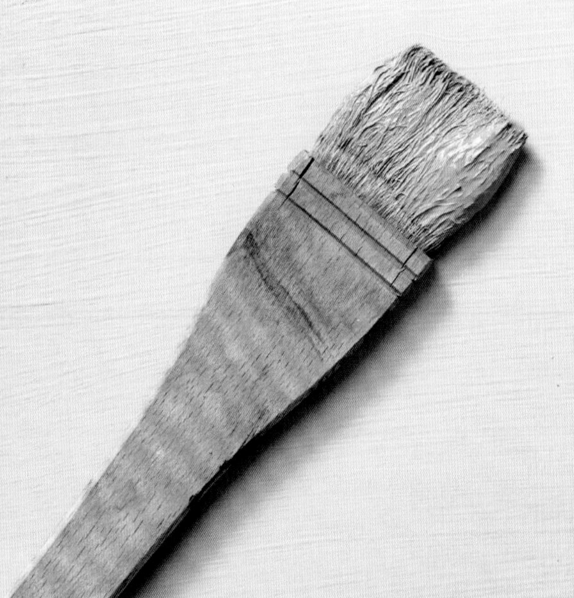

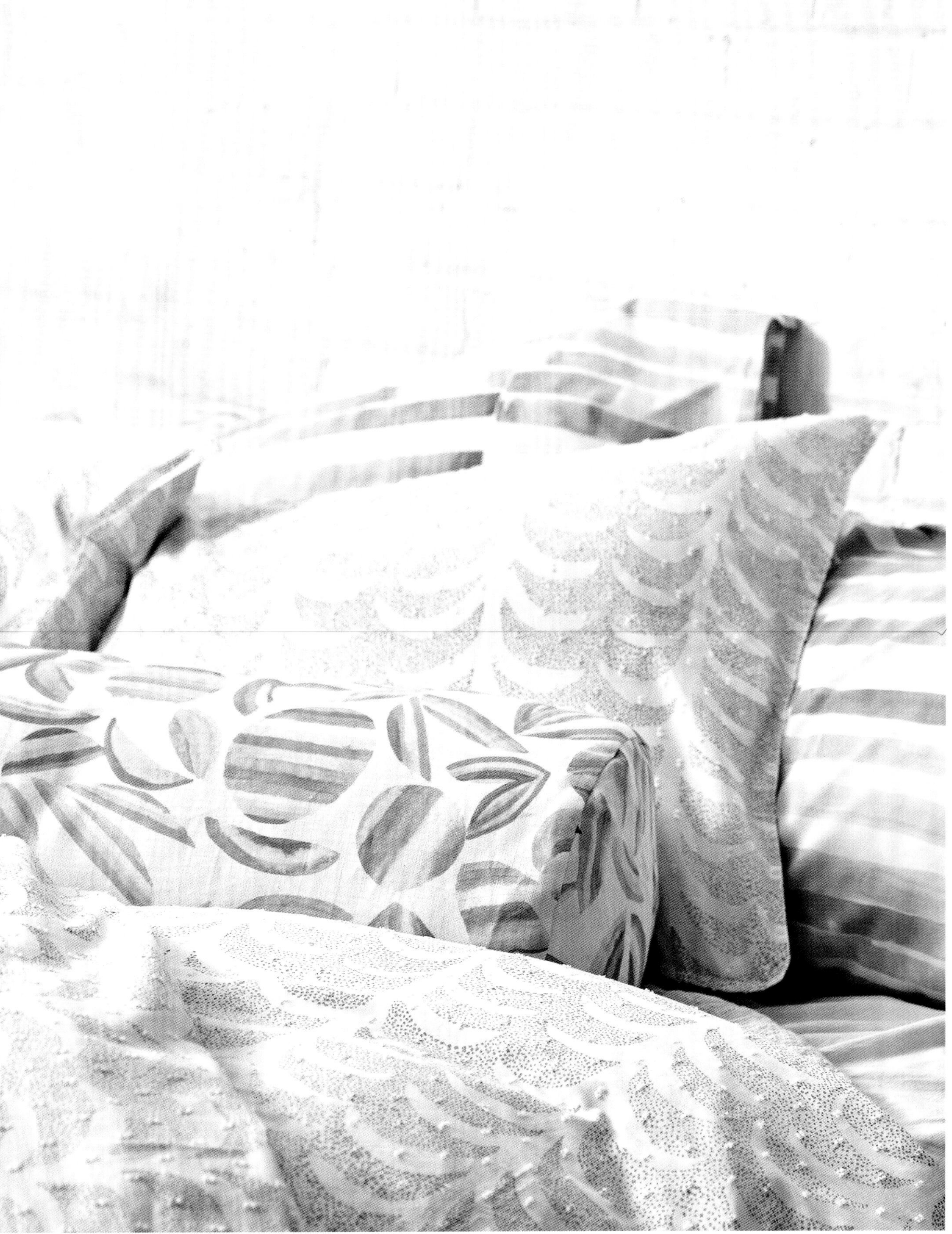

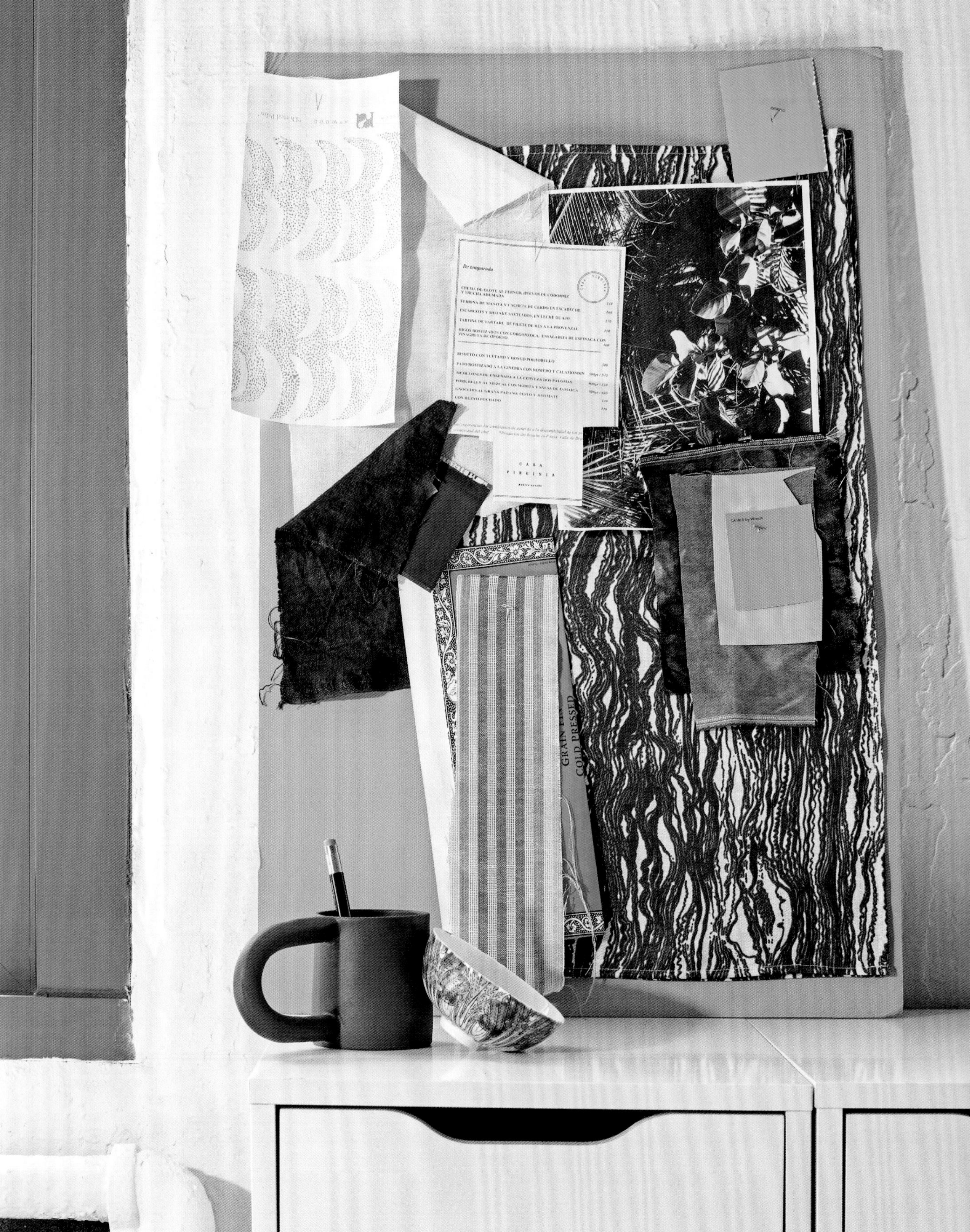

De temporada
CREMA DE ELOTE AL PERNOD, HUEVOS DE CODORNIZ Y TRUCHA AHUMADA
TERRINA DE MANITA Y CACHETE DE CERDO EN ESCABECHE
ESCARGOTS Y SHITAKE SALTEADOS, EN LECHE DE AJO
TARTINE DE TARTARE DE FILETE DE RES A LA PROVENZAL
HIGOS ROSTIZADOS CON GORGONZOLA, ENSALADITA DE ESPINACA CON VINAGRETA DE OPORTO
RISOTTO CON TUÉTANO Y HONGO PORTOBELLO
PATO ROSTIZADO A LA GINEBRA CON ROMERO Y CALAMONDIN
MEJILLONES DE ENSENADA A LA CERVEZA DOS PALOMAS
PORK BELLY AL MEZCAL CON MORITA Y SALSA DE JAMAICA
GNOCCHIS AL GRANA PADANO, PESTO Y JITOMATE CON HUEVO POCHADO
CASA
VIRGINIA
COLD PRESSED

THE HISTORY OF GREEN

Since the dawn of civilization, green has been synonymous with the very essence of life, vitality, and rebirth. Prolific gardeners are known as having a "green thumb," and the phrase "going green" is used for earth-friendly practices. The Latin word *vita* means life, closely related to *virita,* which means green. Green was later rooted in the word *grow* from the Old English *gro,* so it was often thought to mean "raw" and "immature," whether in plant life or young humans. As far back as the Middle Ages, the term *green* was used to describe novices or young people who had not ripened yet.

In terms of painting, green was a tricky hue to achieve. During the Renaissance, most painters had to work with verdigris, a color produced by a chemical reaction that resulted in copper carbonate, which became a greenish-blue color when scraped off. It's this same process that gives old pennies and the Statue of Liberty a green patina.

Perhaps the most famous use of this pigment is the green dress in Jan Van Eyck's 1434 painting *The Arnolfini Portrait,* a curious painting that was no doubt commissioned by a wealthy couple who could afford green paintings and clothes. The color became even more unpredictable with the rise of oil paintings, because, when mixed with oil, verdigris turns an unfortunate shade of brown over time; hence, the sludge color in many garden paintings we see today from that period.

Though artists were particularly frustrated with green as a pigment, they embraced it as a muse in the form of a green drink called absinthe. A variety of writers and artists, including the likes of Edgar Allan Poe, Oscar Wilde, Mark Twain, Vincent Van Gogh, Henri de Toulouse-Lautrec, Pablo Picasso, and Ernest Hemingway, paid homage to absinthe. Fashioned from medicinal roots of anise, fennel, and wormwood, it was used as an antiseptic by ancient Egyptians and Romans. But when French soldiers started drinking it to ward off malaria in the 1860s, they fell under its spell, and by the 1870s the cafés of Paris were teeming with absinthe drinkers. It became so pervasive that five o' clock became known as "the green hour."

To the Irish the color means hope and faith. Ever since Saint Patrick used the shamrock to explain the Holy Trinity to would-be Irish Catholics, green became the anti-orange (the symbol of Protestantism). Along with the four-leaf clover, the color green has come to represent "the luck of the Irish."

It is simply coincidental that money in the United States is green. During the Civil War, the greenback, a green currency, was introduced as an anti-counterfeiting measure. When the war ended, the U.S. Bureau of Printing and Engraving continued to print in green because they claimed "the ink was plentiful and durable and the color green was associated with stability."

GREEN PALETTES

Creating a palette with green should begin with imagining your favorite places in nature and envisioning where you would like to have that same feeling in your home. Green is a versatile hue, and a few of my favorite shades are mint, dune grass, and marine. These shades can take you from soft and airy to deep and moody, and you'll see inspiration here for how you can layer them. If you're unsure about how to add green, start with softer shades and then build upon them and deepen them.

Let's look at a few ways of using a soft green as a base. Mint green makes for a great backdrop. Whether it's truly minty or verges more on sage, these tips apply. Pick soft cream and sand hues to keep the palette feeling natural and grounded. If you want it to stay calm and beachy, play on the soft variations within this world. Most of the time, you'll want to bring in a deeper color to contrast. Here I used a deep marine hue that verges on black. These images give examples of how proportion can change the overall vibe of this palette. When deeper marine is used, the vibe feels more like fall; it's moodier and cozier. When the softer shades are the focus, it's beachy and breezy. Make it feel more playful by introducing a peach and a citrine color. This base is a great starting point for adding a natural vibe to your space. These palettes are versatile and would work well in any space in your home.

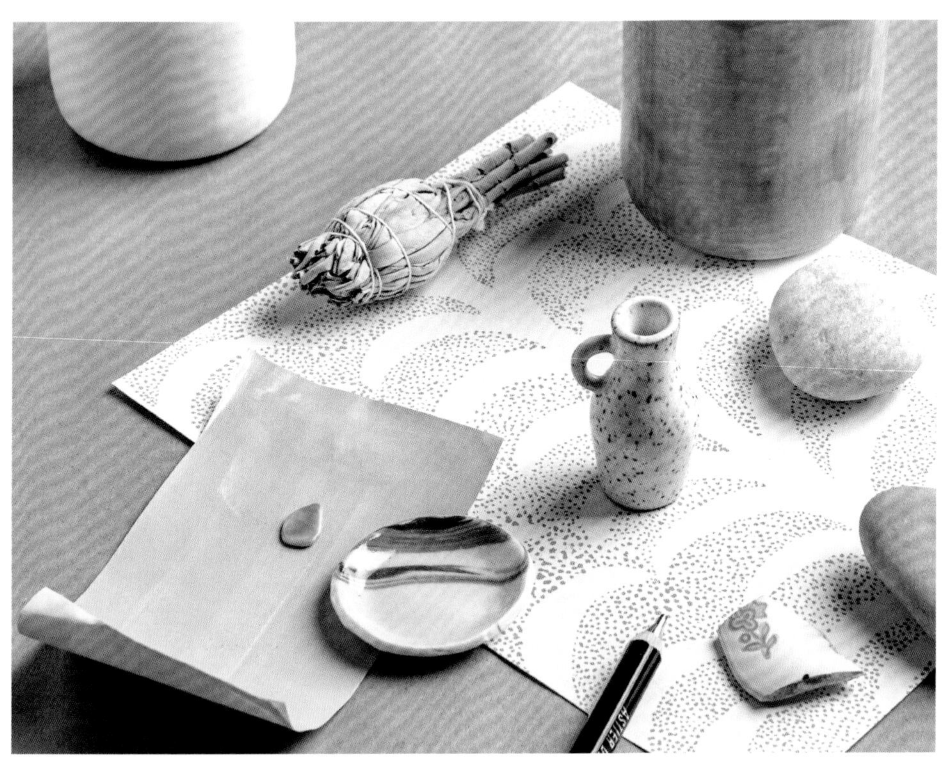

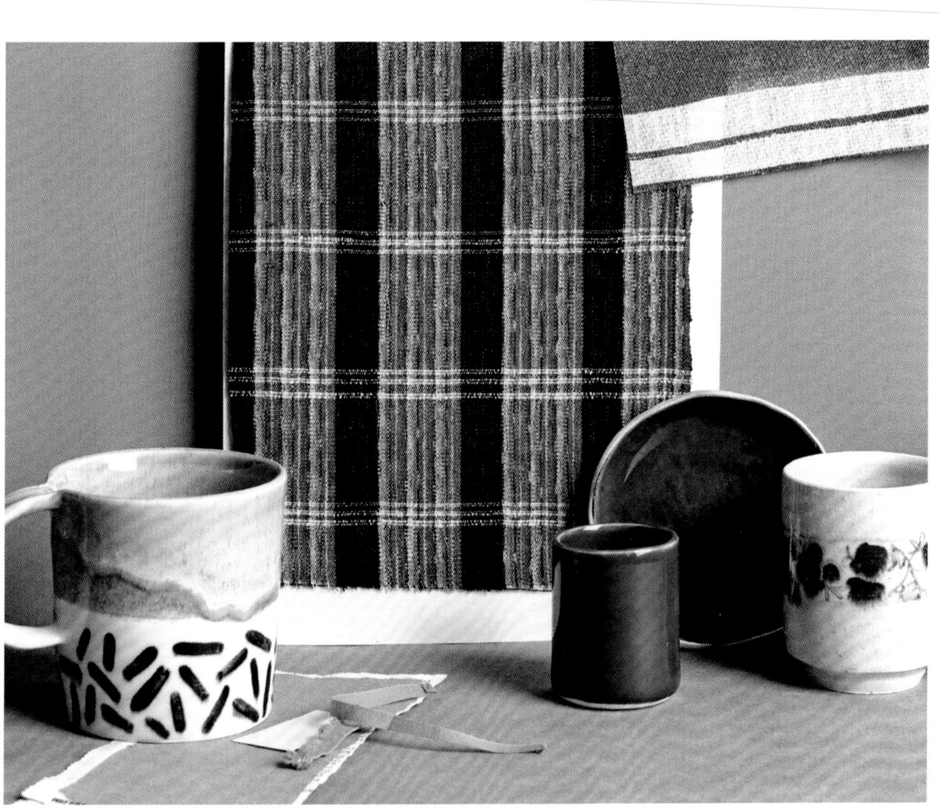

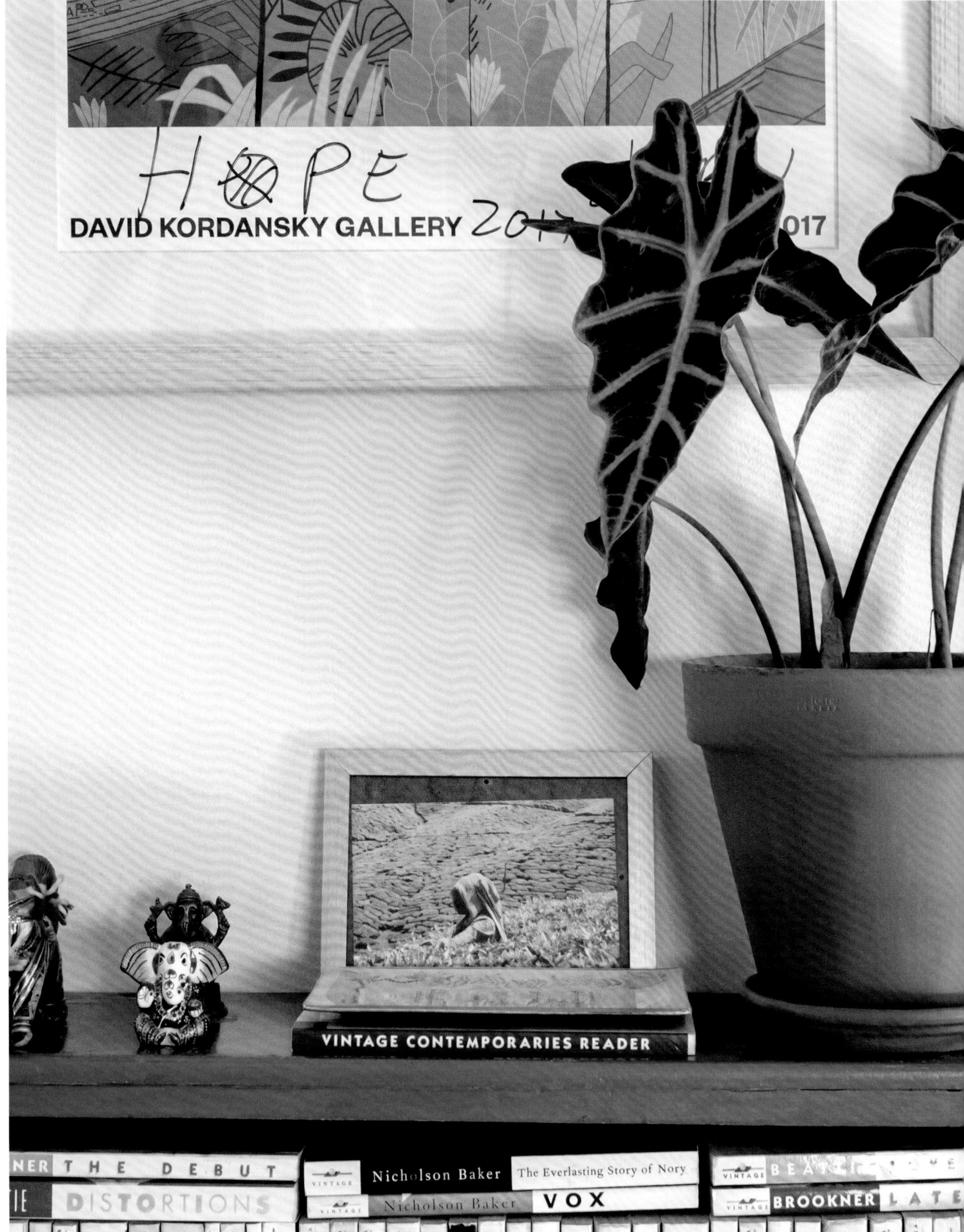
HOPE
DAVID KORDANSKY GALLERY
2017
VINTAGE CONTEMPORARIES READER
THE DEBUT
DISTORTIONS
Nicholson Baker
The Everlasting Story of Nory
Nicholson Baker
VOX
BROOKNER

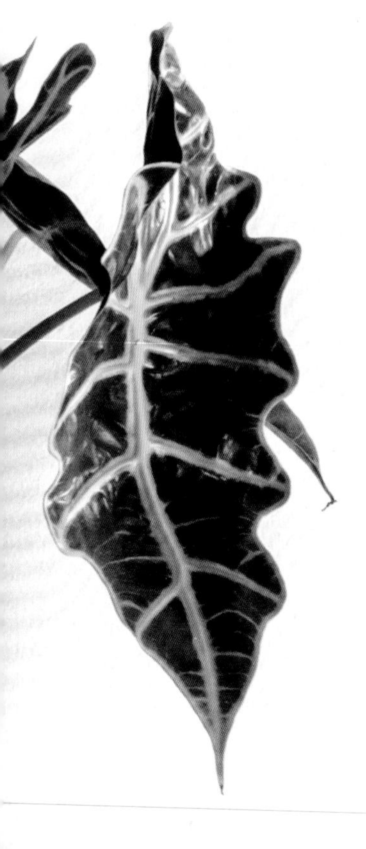

- Can you think of unexpected memories of green? Can you push yourself beyond the obvious?
- Do you have travel memories of green?
- Do you associate it with a particular place from your past?

LIVING WITH GREEN

Green is rejuvenating and restorative. While green is a cool color, it still feels very alive. One of the easiest and most natural ways to bring green into your home is with plants. I love the many different textures of plants: fuzzy, glossy, waxy, dry. It's hard to mimic nature's complexity of a color, so bringing in the real thing is best.

If you're looking for a more vibrant but livable way to bring in green, consider layering it in a monochromatic way. This will make you feel like you're soaking in the greenery of a forest. If you choose a shade of green for the wall, break it up with shelves of books or artwork. If you're looking for a richer but more muted version, think about that particular shade army green. It's a great neutral that works just as well in an outfit as it does in a room. Verging on olive with hints of brown, it's more muted and blends in with nature. Use it in place of gray or tan.

DECORATING WITH GREEN

A Refreshing Place

Because green is associated with rejuvenation, using it in the bathroom is a natural place to start. Try something simple and small, like a bundle of eucalyptus in a vase. The fragrance alone will conjure the color. Tile is another beautiful way to bring this color into the bathroom. Consider a matte geometric pattern or a glossy jewel tone in simple handmade shapes.

An Indoor Garden

Channel the feeling of a greenhouse. Bring in plants and flaunt their color. If you don't have a green thumb, start with something easy to maintain, like the snake plant. Or consider wallpaper or fabric inspired by vines or a lush painting of a landscape. Think sage velvet, vibrant jade ceramics, subdued wool, or matte pine paint. The possibilities are endless (but remember, finish is important; see page 25).

Soft and Minty

If you're looking for a neutral green, mint is a great choice. Just like a pale shade of yellow seems to bathe a room in sunshine, mint, too, lends a subtle vibe to a space. This pale shade isn't as obvious—it almost feels like the light is giving the room that hue.

An Unexpected Alternative

We often think of blue for bedrooms, but green is also a natural choice. Think about places where you'd use blue (see page 104), and try green as a refreshing alternative. It's more unexpected than blue but feels equally calm. You can also choose shades of green with more blue in them if blue is one of your favorite colors.

Go Bright

A vibrant green can be just the thing to make a room feel alive. When you go with a bright version, be sure it feels luxe. If it's paint, choose one with the most pigment and use it sparingly but with impact—for example, on the trim around a window. Look for saturated hues that have depth versus ones that feel too flat. Another route to create impact is to display multiples of an object (like my great-aunt's beautiful jadeite pieces). Consider green glass cups or vases on open shelving.

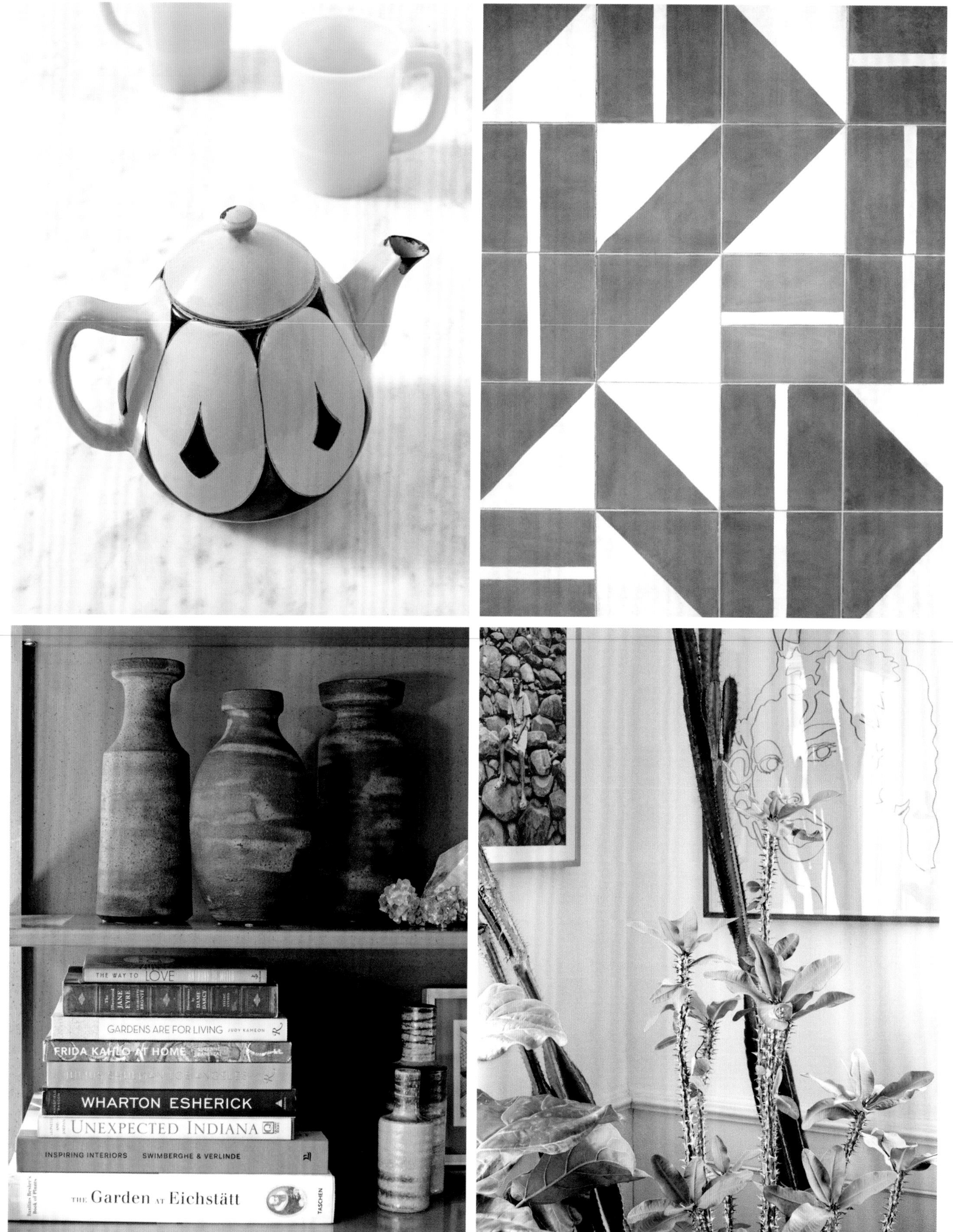
THE WAY TO LOVE
GARDENS ARE FOR LIVING JUDY KAMEON
FRIDA KAHLO AT HOME
WHARTON ESHERICK
UNEXPECTED INDIANA
INSPIRING INTERIORS SWIMBERGHE & VERLINDE
THE Garden AT Eichstätt
TASCHEN

BLUE

ICE, OCEAN, DEEP NAVY

Blue feels expansive, cool, and full of possibility. It reminds us of everything from “clean” to “peace” to “freedom,” and it’s always changing, like the blue of the ocean. Some days it’s calm and reflective with soft bubbly surf, other days it’s dark, rough, and filled with whitecaps. Growing up, our house was a fifteen-minute walk from the beach so I spent many hours just taking in the lapping waves. Depending on where in the world you are, the ocean can range from brilliant turquoise to deep and moody. This may be where my love for tonal hues originates. I love looking for the stripes of color and the changing light. Layering blue in a home can be a gorgeous homage to the ocean. These layers can range from the classic cobalt of china patterns to the happy blue of a hydrangea to the sky blue used on ceilings throughout history to inspire people to look up and dream.

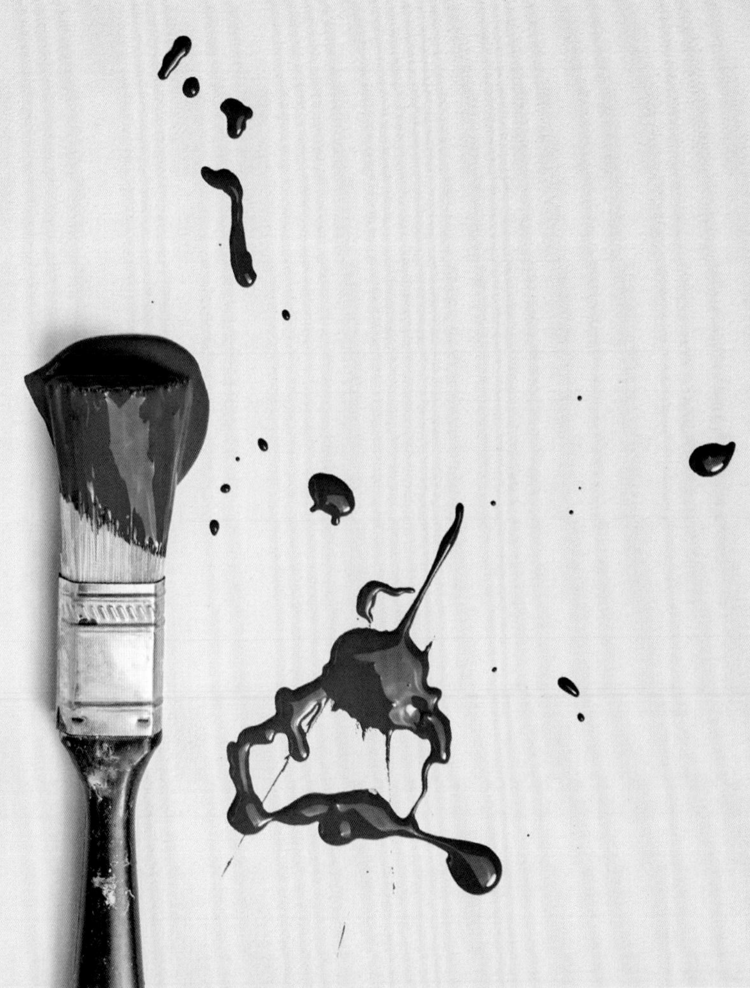

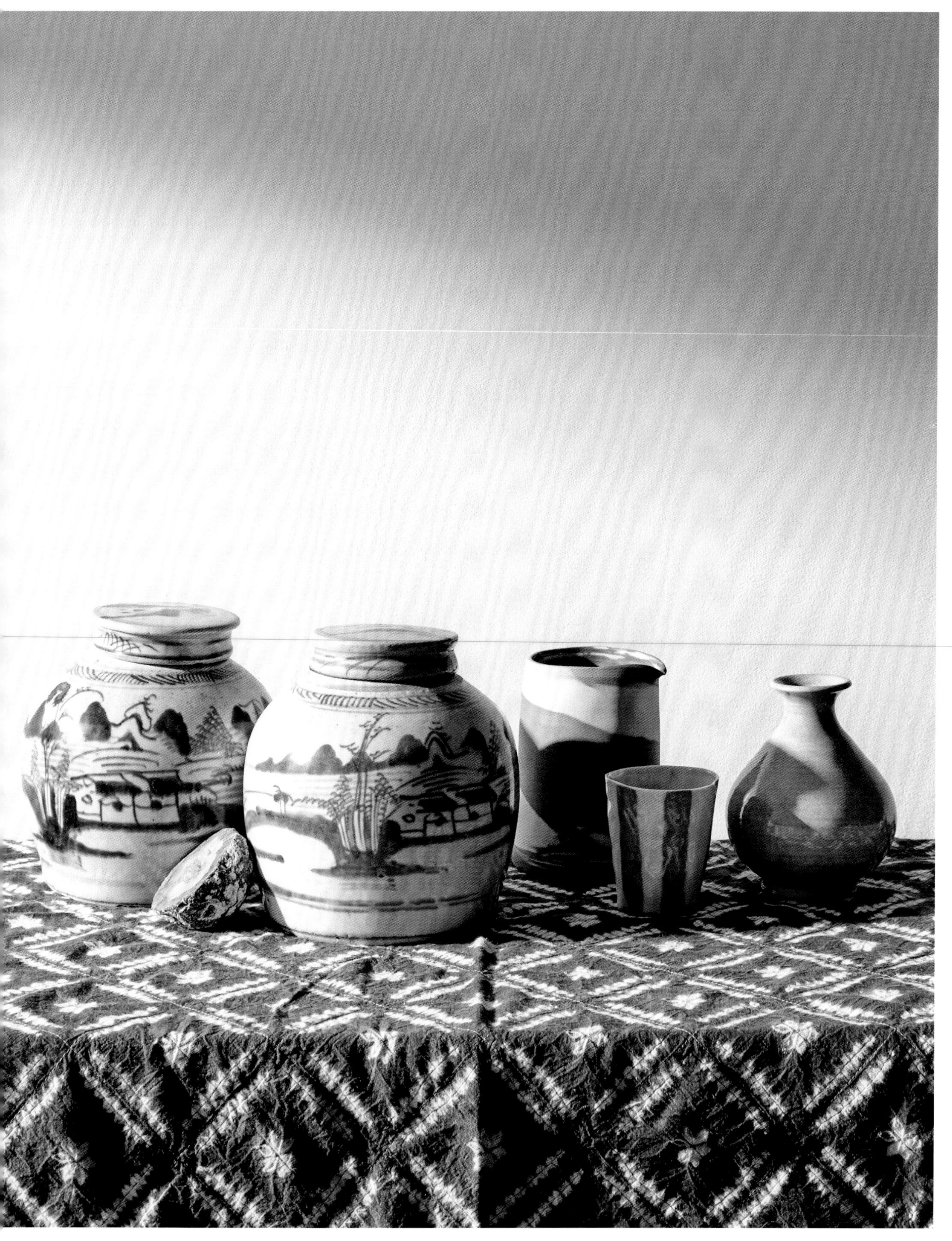

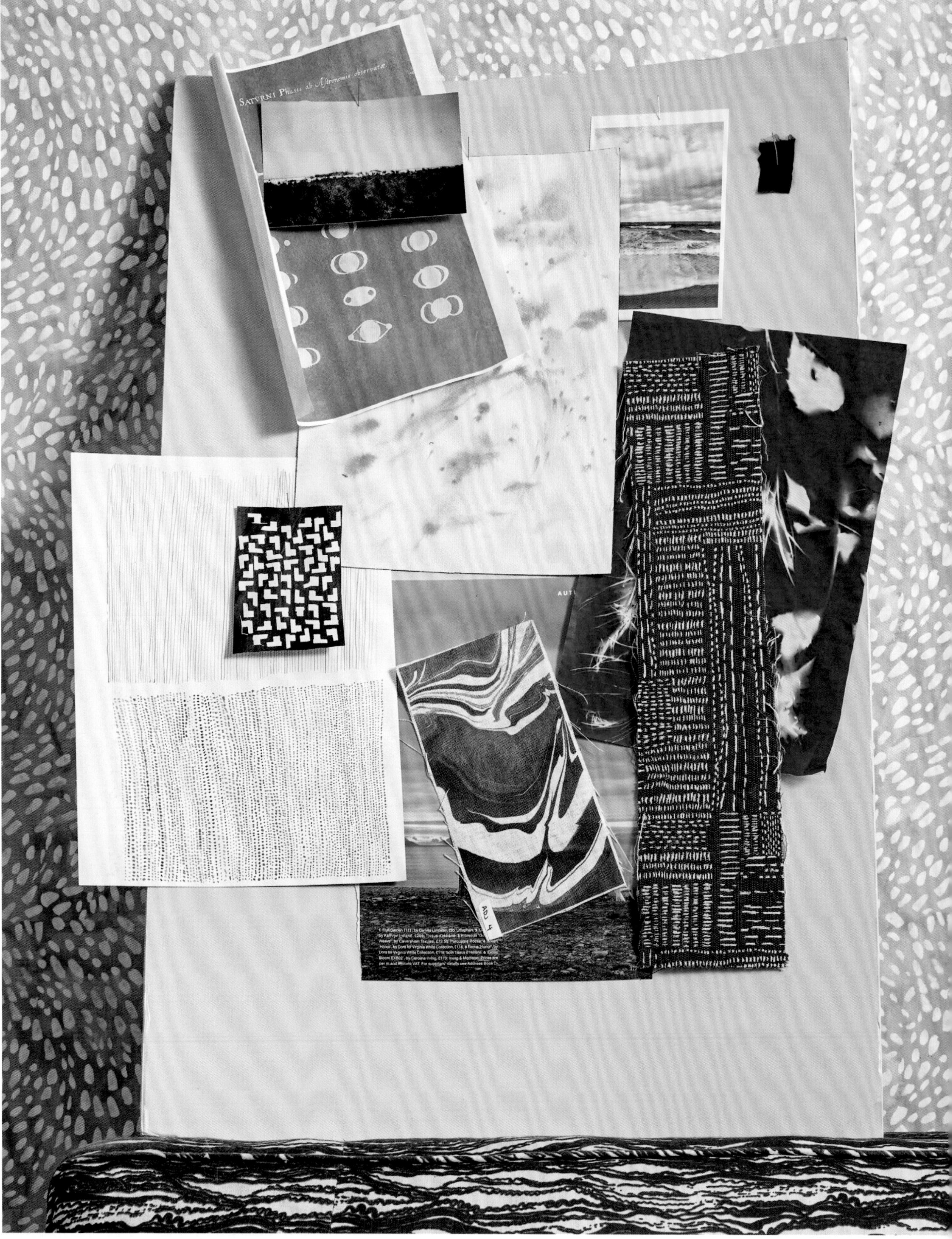
SATVRNI Phases ab Astronomis observatæ
ADJ 4

THE HISTORY OF BLUE

For most of early human history, blue was ignored. This is particularly surprising given that studies show blue has been the perennial favorite color worldwide since World War I. But not once is it mentioned in the *Illiad* or the *Odyssey,* and hardly at all in any early Christian writings. Though the sky and ocean are often considered blue, they are ever-changing. Thus, blue as a solid concept took quite some time for humans to adopt. In later works of art, however, the Virgin Mary is often depicted in blue robes, representing tranquility, holiness, and humility.

While ancient Egyptians valued the brilliance of the blue gemstone lapis lazuli, it wasn't until synthetic ultramarine (original ultramarine was made from the royally expensive lapis lazuli) was created in 1826 that painters began to use the beautiful color as the foundation for a pigment. Yet even then only wealthy patrons could afford the steep price tag. Many merchants and artists were on the lookout for a less prohibitively expensive option, but ironically an affordable blue pigment was discovered by accident in 1706 by an alchemist in Berlin named Diesbach, who was sold bad potash laced with contaminants. The result was Prussian blue.

Thus, blue became widely available to artists across Europe. One artist in particular, Pablo Picasso, favored Prussian blue during his famous blue period, along with other shades like cerulean. While Picasso's somber paint choice was said to be the result of his depression over the death of a friend, we still do not know the origins of the phrase "feeling blue." We do, however, know the origin of many other associations. "Royal blue," for instance, was the result of a contest to design a dress for Queen Charlotte of England. Most theories behind the origin of "true blue" have to do with consistency, whether it's the constant blue sky or blue dye that doesn't run or fade, and "blue chip stock" stems from the most valuable chip in a simple set of red, white, and blue poker chips.

The story behind "blue blood" reaches all the way back to 1492. During the Spanish Inquisition, Catholic rulers King Ferdinand and Queen Isabella of Spain forced Jews and Muslims to either convert to Catholicism or flee the region; since they were often of North African descent, they were darker skinned than their European counterparts, whose blue veins, or "blue blood," could be seen through their fair skin. The first usage of the term, though, was in 1809, and it eventually became synonymous with the aristocracy.

Blue jeans, however, are quite the opposite: a stiff fabric designed for hardworking miners and cowboys. Traditionally, jeans were dyed a blue color using natural indigo dye, made from a variety of pretty but temperamental plants, but today most denim is made using synthetic indigo. The arduous process of making real indigo is still carried out by a handful of skilled artisans across the globe.

BLUE PALETTES

In many instances, blue acts like a neutral; shades like deep navy look good with everything. Personally, I've always preferred navy to black, because there's a little more energy to it. Two of my other favorite shades are ice and ocean.

Let's explore creating a soft neutral base. Icy blues keep a space feeling cool and collected. Bring in soft buttery yellow, deep navy, and rusty brown to keep them from feeling too monochromatic. These toned-down hues, mixed with a few darker shades, create a neutral base for a room that goes beyond desaturated color. You can even consider a deep but subdued blue-black stain for wood floors, or bring in the shade with rugs. Soft ice-colored walls act like a cool white.

Next, let's look at how blue can be a great partner for a bolder color. While blue is a nice neutral, it still has a lot of strength, so it can balance a bolder hue like tomato red. You may think red, white, and blue would feel very traditional and patriotic, but it doesn't need to, if you pick shades that are less expected. Think a dash of maroon and a hint of tangerine. Then, play with proportion. Sky blue can act as a pop—try pairing it with a soft orange, a dusty green, and a deep navy.

These ideas for blue translate easily into a room and are a great base for layering on additional color. A soft, paler palette is a good choice for calm places like the bedroom and bathroom. A bolder, punchier palette is perfect for an entryway, powder room, or living room. If you want to add another color, consider picking up some paint swatches and even placing them next to this page to see how they work.

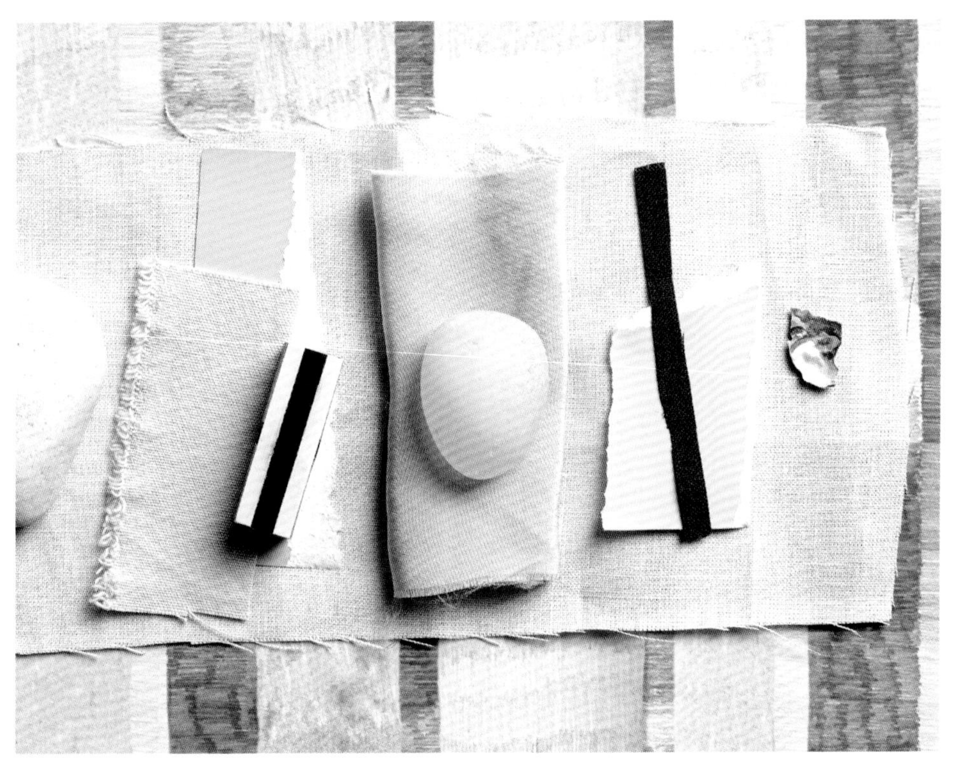

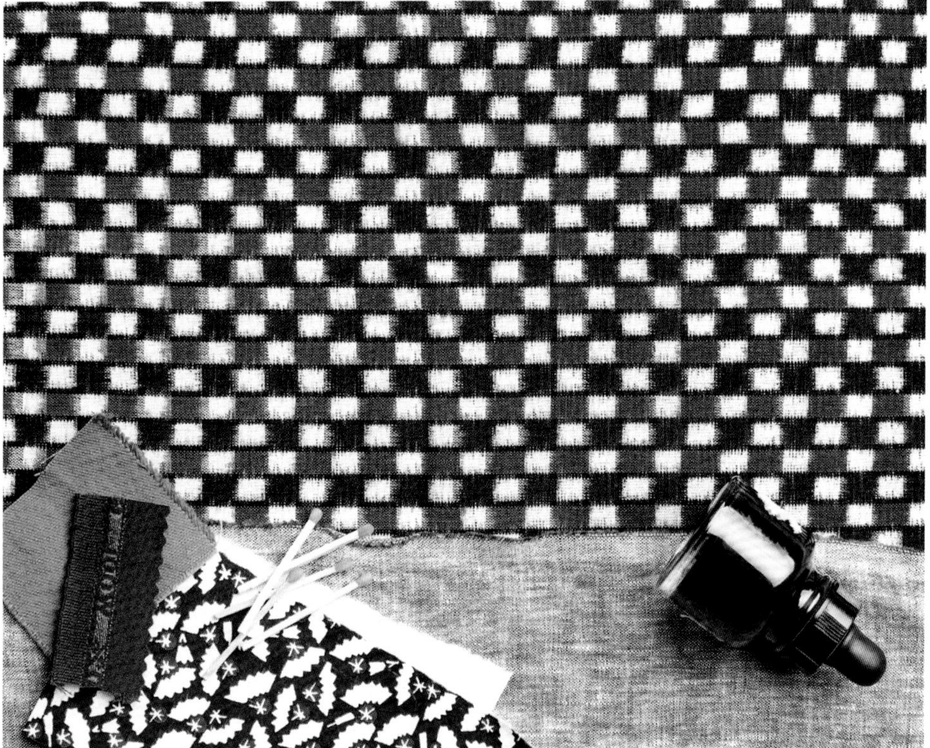

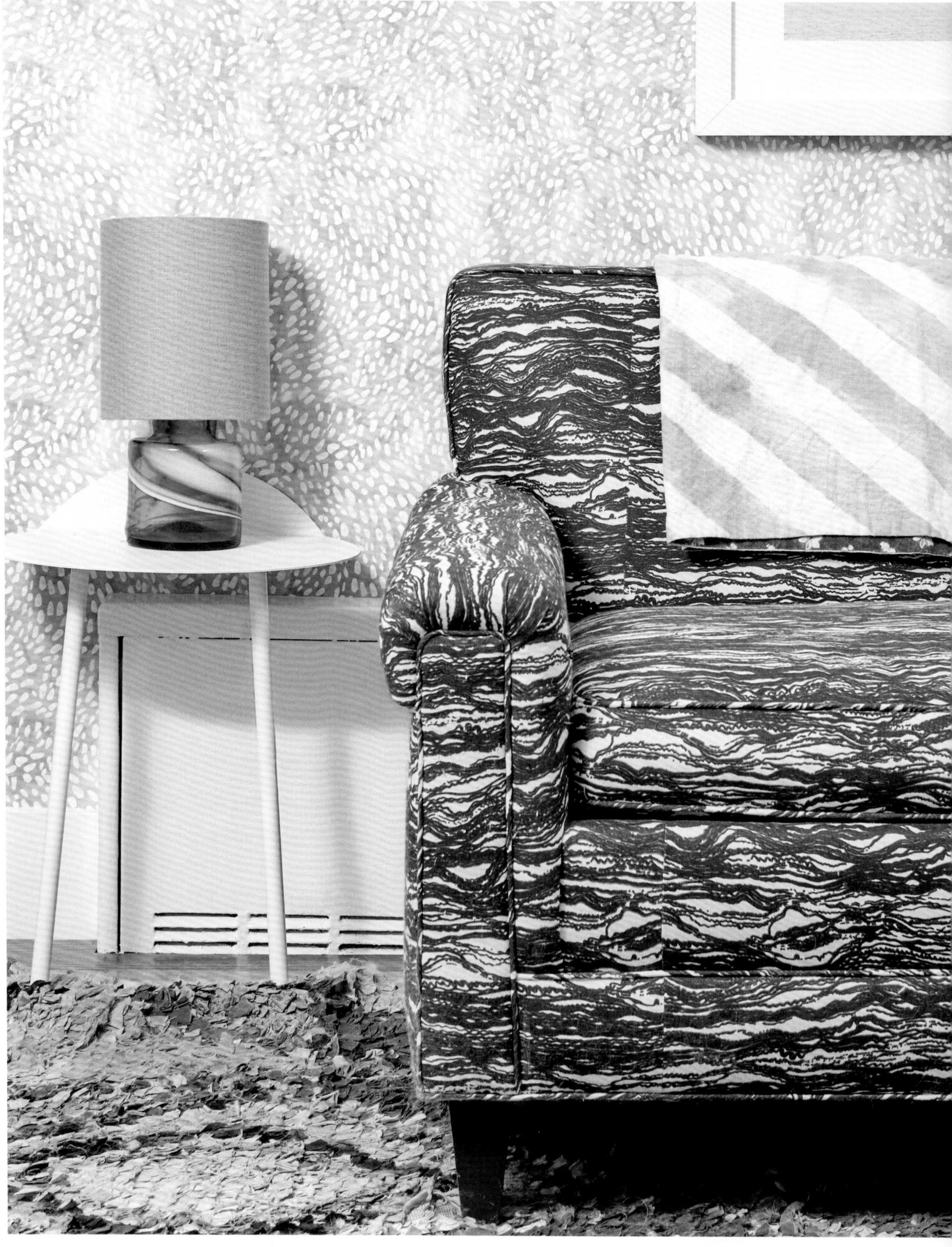

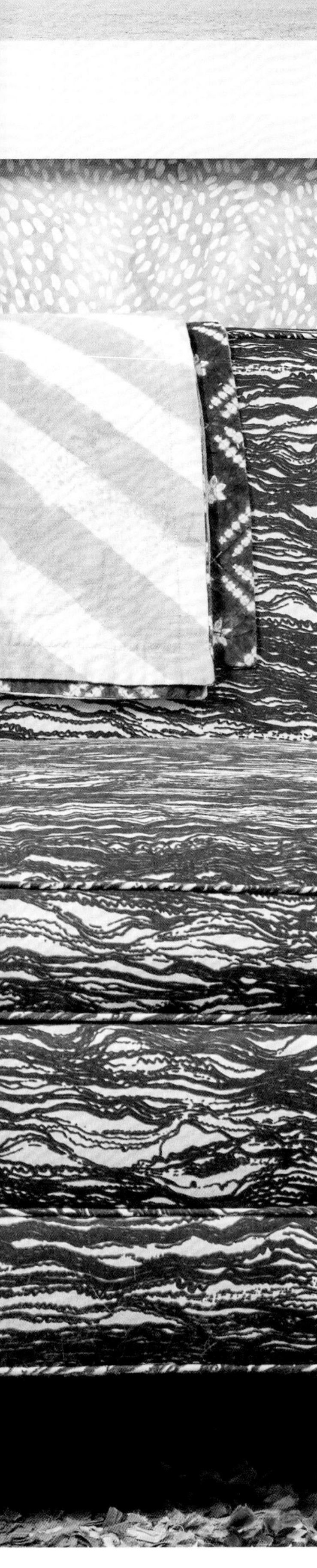

- What are your happiest memories of blue?
- Are there people in your life whom you associate with blue?
- What does blue signify to you? What are your immediate associations?

LIVING WITH BLUE

Blue is a common favorite, and it's used frequently at home. Most people feel comfortable using blue, so that's why this is a great color with which to experiment. Explore all of its moods. Push this familiar color to the edge of its boundaries. Nature uses this color in large amounts, and you can do the same in your home—remember, the sky and ocean are never just one color. Use an inky midnight blue where you might otherwise use black, or substitute blue-gray in place of gray. Layer blue on top of blue, or paint the edges of a door or a bookshelf with this color. Try something unusual, like electric blue on the inside of a lampshade, so you see it only when the light is on. Play with other colors that are the same value as blue; put them next to one another and watch the gradient you create. Push the edges toward green and purple. Give the feeling of blue but use many colors. Blur the edges. Rethink blue and explore it.

DECORATING WITH BLUE

Look Up

Mimic the sky and paint the ceiling blue. Consider a glossy finish—I love this trick. In the Deep South, especially in the historic homes around Savannah, Georgia, and Charleston, South Carolina, many people painted their porch ceilings a specific shade known as haint blue, a soft blue-green, to ward off evil spirits called "haints," which is a variation of haunts. It can work on inside ceilings, too, conveying the sense of being outside.

Go Dark and Moody

Use rich, deep blues to impart the calm of a midnight-blue sky. Feel how it can be expansive yet comforting, such as swimming in the ocean at night or stargazing. This color works well for a small space. You might think it would make it feel smaller, but dark blue can play up the coziness and make the room feel purposeful.

Build a Peaceful Retreat

Use soft, varying blues to create a bedroom oasis. Think washed, worn, and faded versions of this hue, as if you were sleeping on a cloud within the blue sky. Stain your floors a dark, almost-navy color on the verge of gray—it's a great neutral and extremely livable.

Be Bold

If you really love blue, go for a vibrant cobalt in the form of a stack of books or piping. If you push the saturation level, it can be an exciting surprise. However, if you do this with paint, make sure you go for high quality, especially if you're using it in a larger area.

Revisit Tradition

Blue-and-white china is a classic to which I constantly return. I love collecting old and new pieces, because together they create something new. Here it's about the mix and finding a way to make a traditional palette feel fresh. Cream grounds and white grounds, handmade ceramics and fine bone china can all play together.

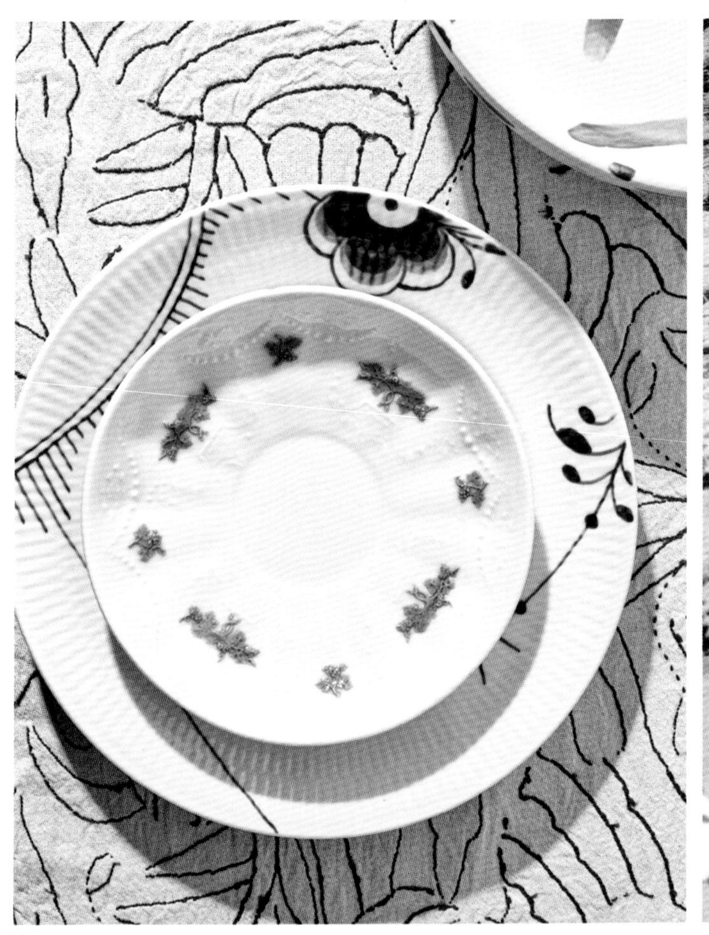
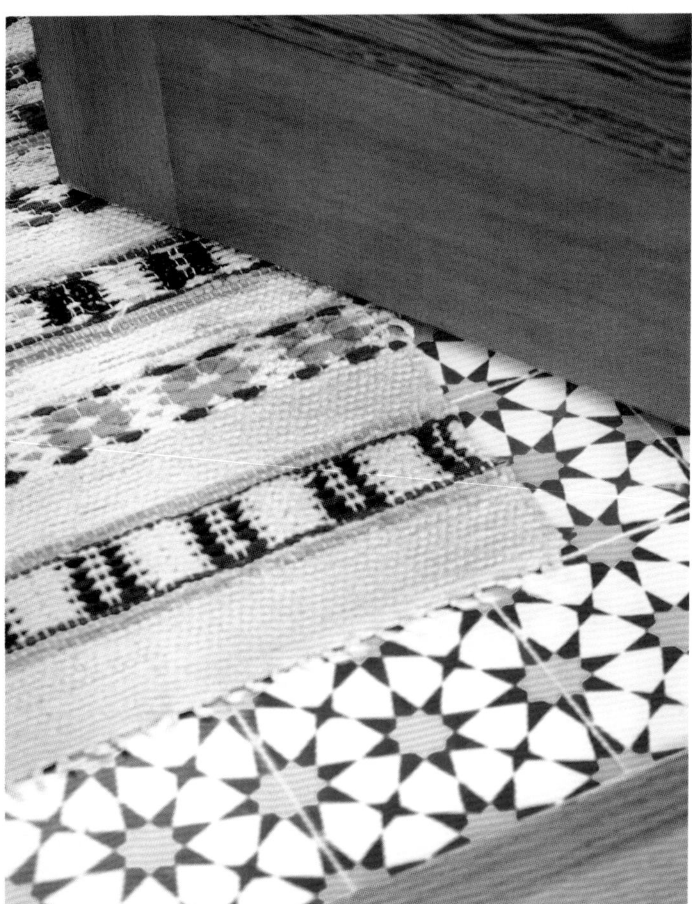
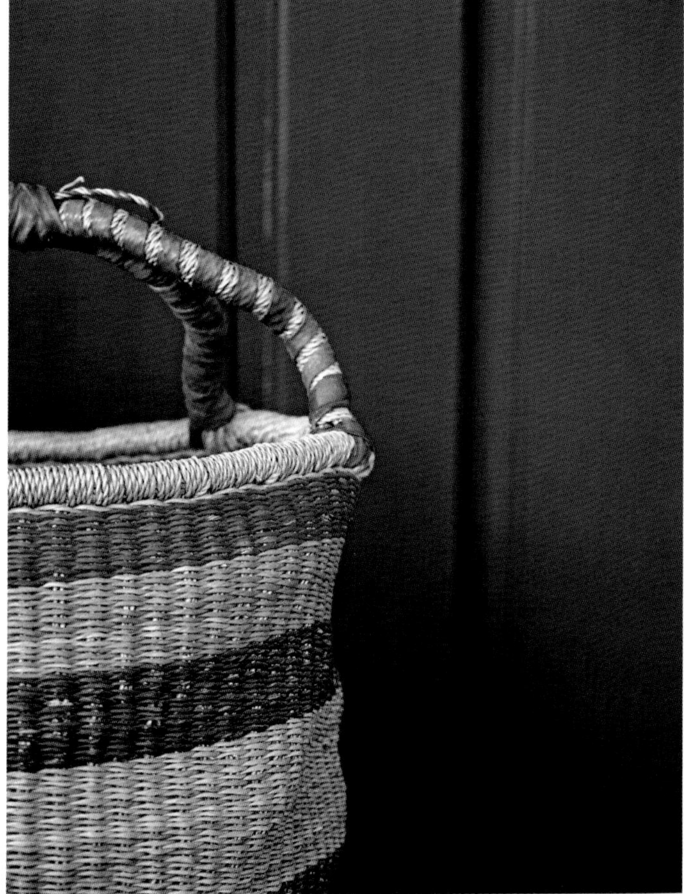
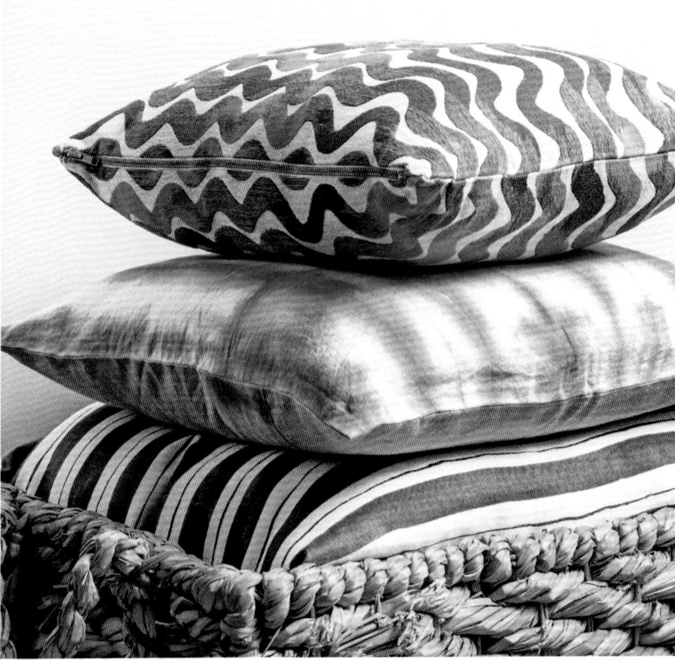

PURPLE

GRAY-LILAC, DUSK, MIDNIGHT

Purple is a moody and complicated color. When the sun has gone down but there's still some light, the darks of a landscape feel purple to me, and I always think of the shadows in a room as purple. Monet said it was the color of the atmosphere. Purple feels rich like lustrous amethyst stones, which makes sense because it is traditionally known as the color of royalty. It's also associated with the magic and mystery of the unknown.

I never thought of myself as someone who loved purple. Growing up, it was my mother who loved purple. She also loves lavender, as a color and fragrance, and I have so many little memories of purple that now I associate this color with her: a purple top or violets in small pots on the windowsill and lilacs in the garden.

However, when I first started working with dyes for fabrics, I found many of the colors I was drawn to verged on purple—from a gray that had hints of lilac to deep blues with purple undertones, and I realized how much I'd been unwittingly pulled toward purple. It's easy to miss the soft sheen of dreamy, smoke purple, or the rich depth of an eggplant or a mussel shell, but purple is present in more of our world than we realize.

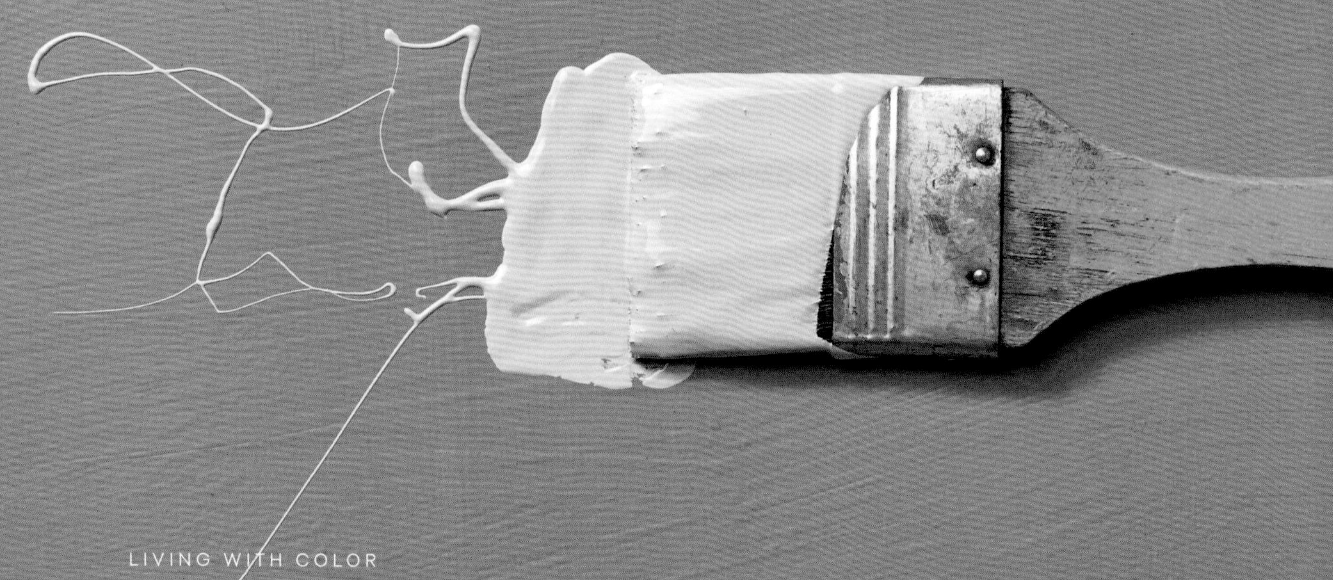

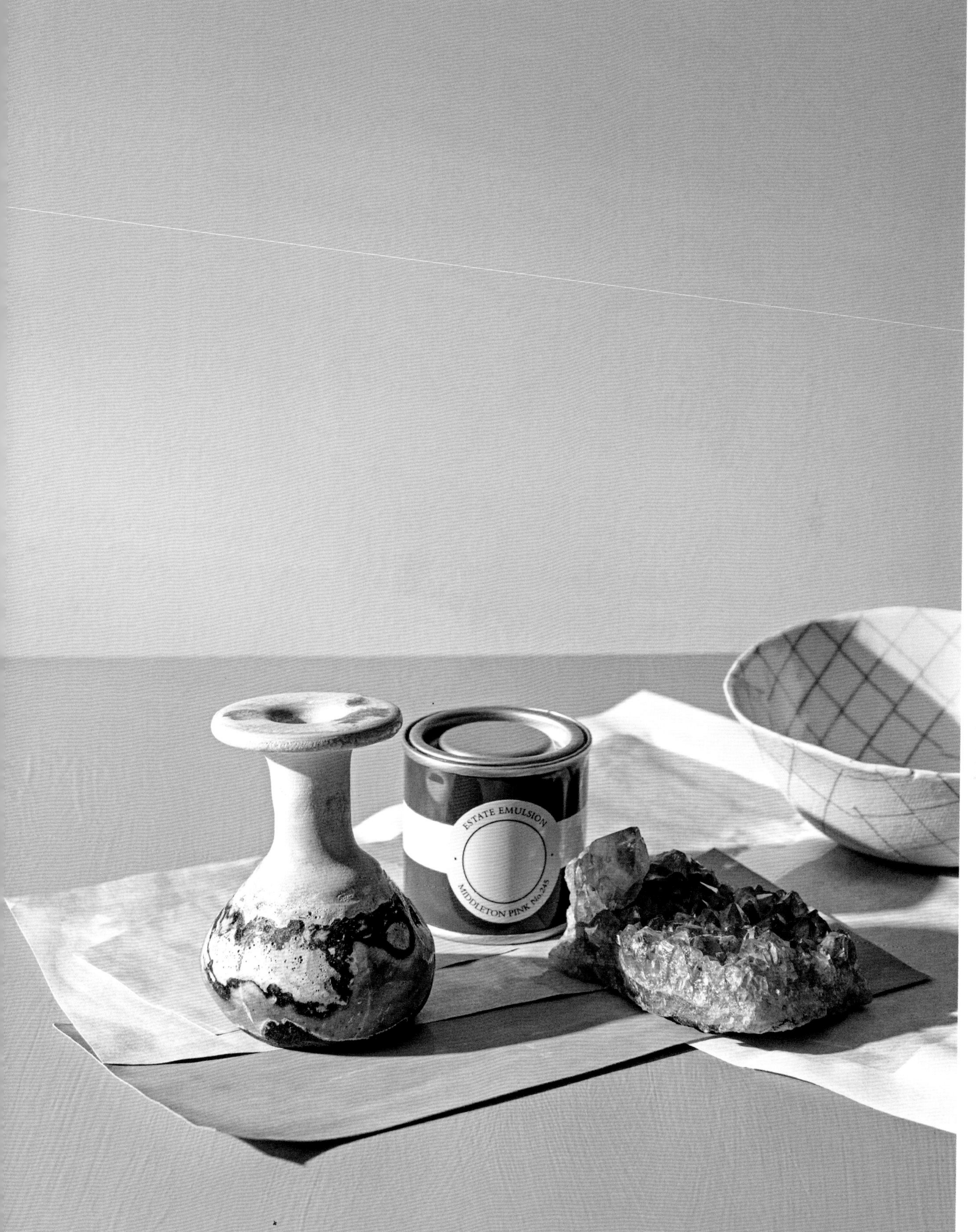
ESTATE EMULSION
MIDDLETON PINK No.245

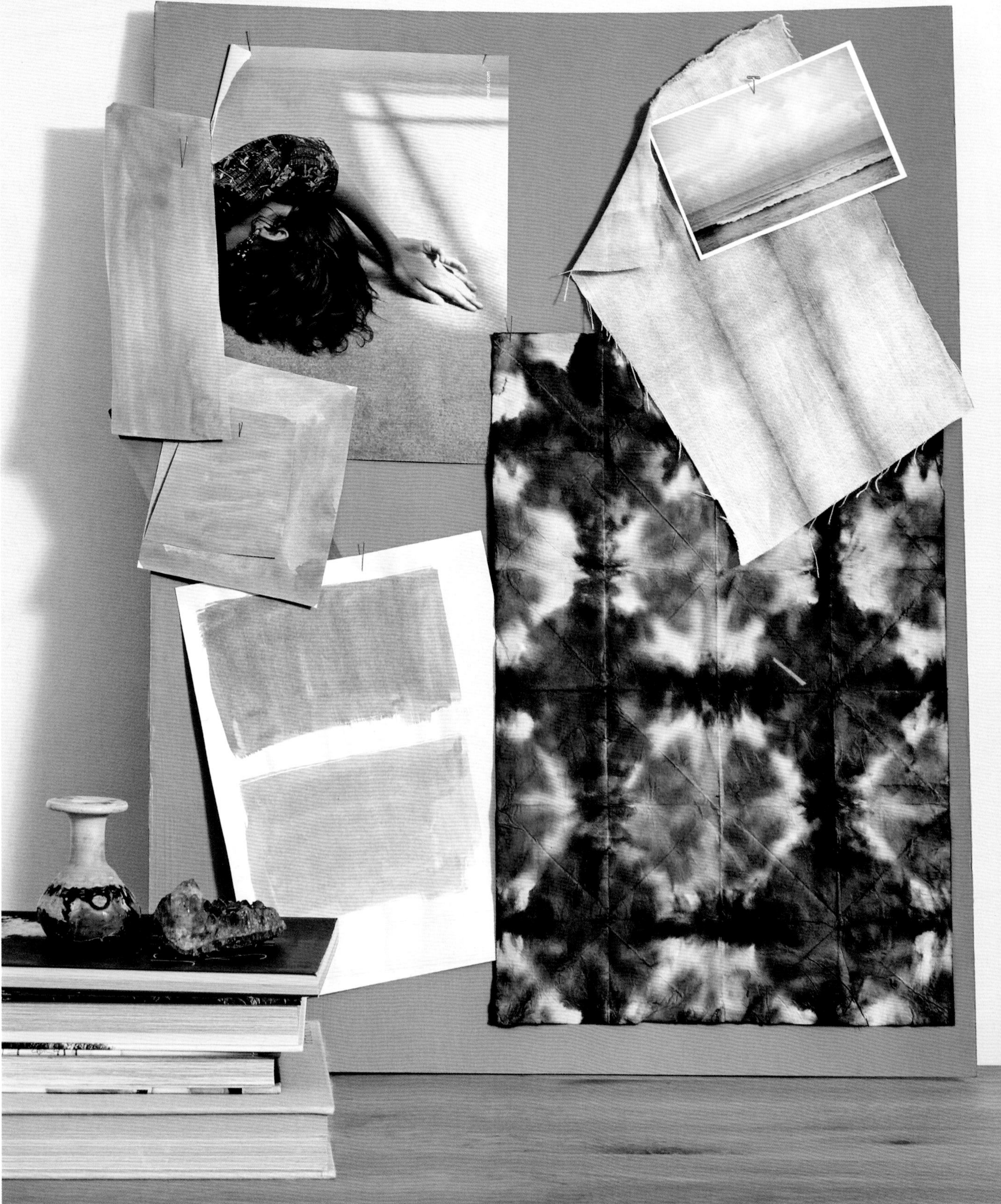

THE HISTORY OF PURPLE

Purple is a mythical and ethereal color. According to the ancient Greeks, the myth of Tyrian purple is said to have been discovered by the Phoenician god Melqart. Purple was first created from a snail called spiny dye-murex found in the Mediterranean Sea. Creating the dye was an expensive and laborious process; to turn just a single garment purple, many thousands of snails had to be separated from their shells, their glands extracted, and the liquid drained from said glands and put out in sunlight. The liquid needed to be removed from the sunlit basin at the exact moment it turned purple, lest it turn red. It's no wonder, then, that purple became associated exclusively with royalty, nobility, and luxury. In fact, Tyrian purple became as prohibitively expensive as silver, and in the first century AD, only the Roman emperor Nero was allowed to wear it. In ancient Rome, generals were decorated in purple and gold robes, and later archbishops, knights, senators, and other noblemen wore purple as badges of honor and status symbols.

Luckily for the snails, the recipe for Tyrian purple was buried for centuries after the fall of the Roman Empire and didn't resurface again until 1856, when a young chemist by the name of William Perkin accidently discovered the synthetic version of the color at the Royal College of Chemistry during a failed experiment. He called the color mauveine, from the French word, *mauve*, for mallow flower, and from then on it was produced inexpensively and worn widely. Purple continues to be associated with opulence and high honor. The Purple Heart created by George Washington in 1782 to honor military heroes still adorns veterans. In "America the Beautiful," schoolchildren across the United States sing of "purple mountain majesty." In language, the term "purple prose" still refers to lavish and over-the-top writing.

PURPLE PALETTES

Creating a livable palette based around purple is all about the right tint, tone, shade, and finish for the space. Remember, purple doesn't need to be highly saturated; it can be more muted and atmospheric. Or, you may find that a saturated ultraviolet hue looks amazing when used in a smaller proportion, or in a space where you want extra vibrancy. A few of my favorite shades of purple are gray-lilac, dusk, and midnight. They resonate strongly because of their versatility and association with nature.

Because purple can be intense, I want to specifically look at how neutrals can influence its feeling, which will help you control the vibe and create a base that you can layer other colors onto over time. Purple is a cool color, so your first inclination may be to mix it with cool neutrals for a softer feeling. If you go this route with grays, whites, and even linen (remember, linen is so versatile because it's almost in between a warm and cool color depending on the fabric), you can create a cloud-like feeling with softer, paler purples. Stone, marble, and even pale purple glass work well as materials. This palette will feel cool and airy. The soft gray tones will slightly diffuse the soft purples.

You can also balance purple's richness with the earthiness of warm neutrals in sand, clay, coffee, taupe, and linen hues. Purple and yellow are complementary colors, so purple will accentuate the yellow in some of these warmer neutral hues. You can also add more neutral tones, such as a warm brown with purple and red undertones. The richness will help balance the purple. While the first take on a purple palette felt soft and the cool neutrals diffused the color, this second palette works because of the balance and strength of those warmer neutrals.

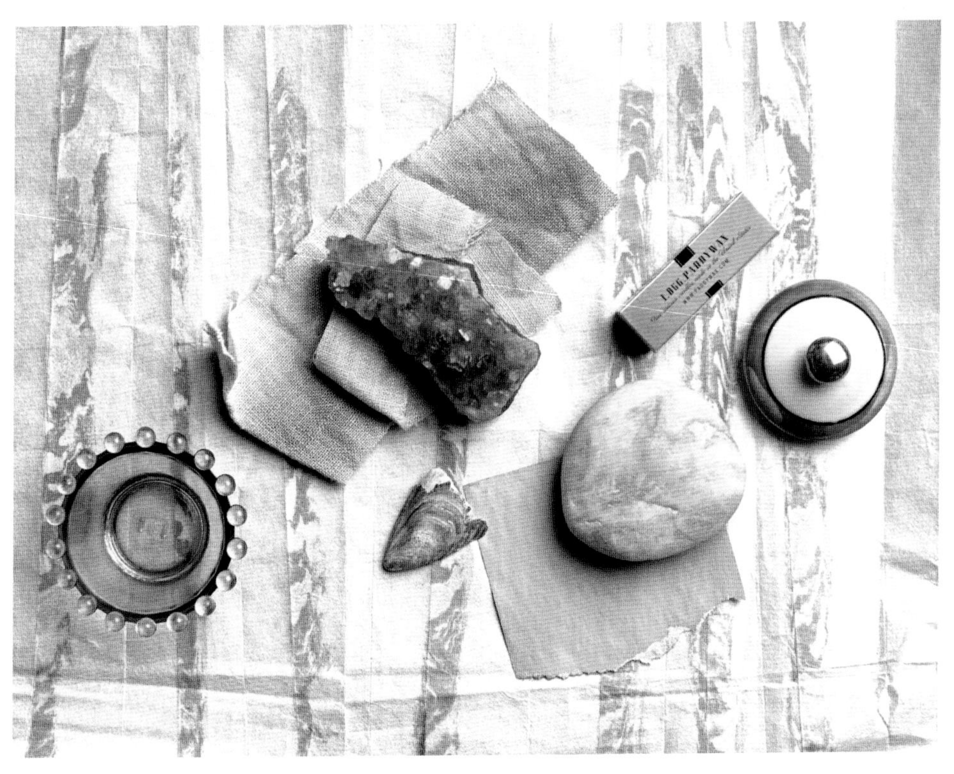

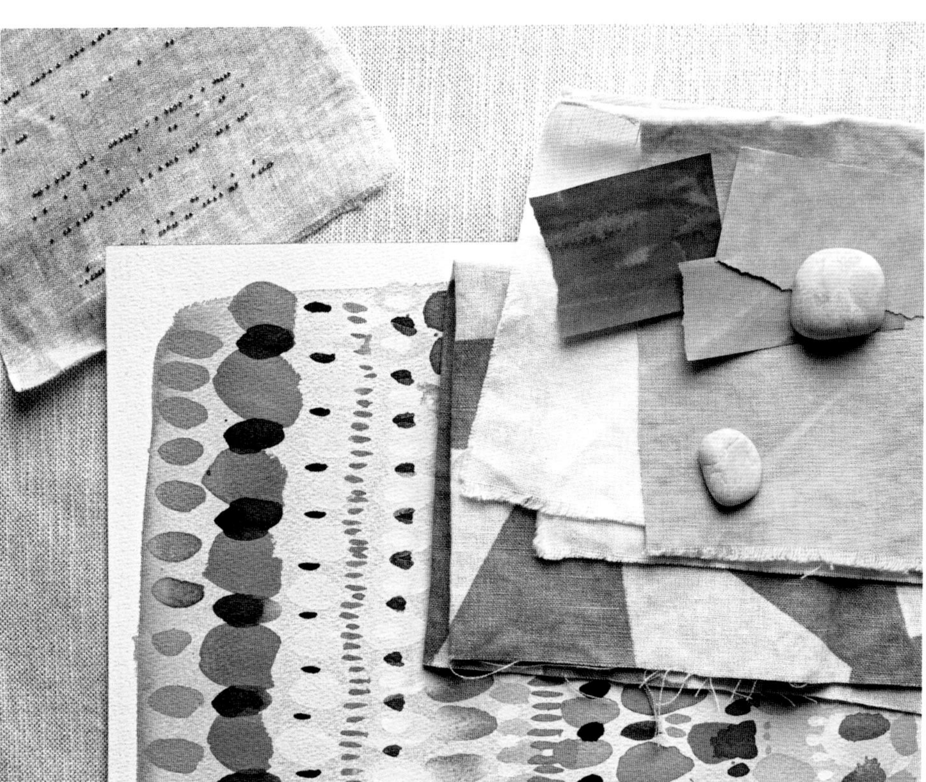

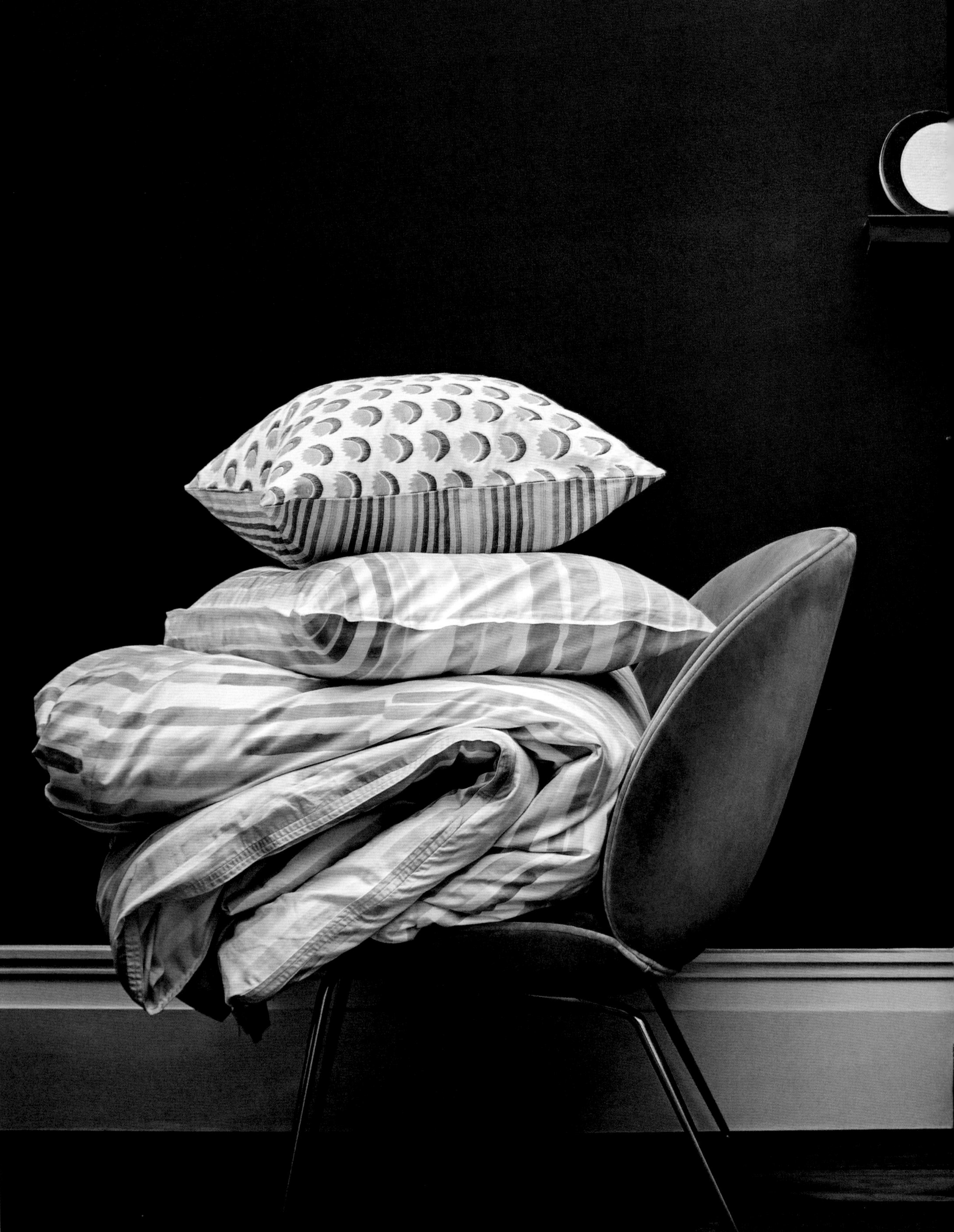

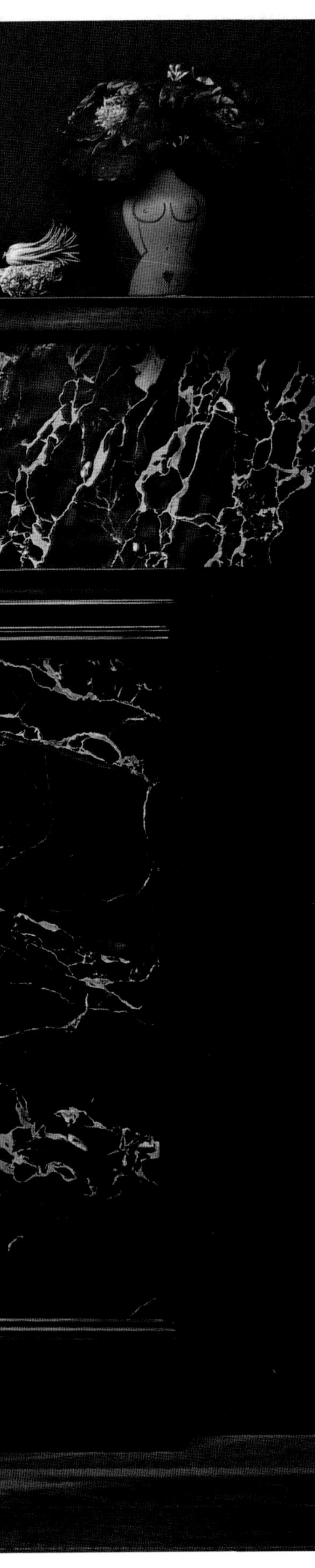

- What scents do you associate with the color purple?
- During which seasons do you see more purple in nature?
- How can you envision purple being used as a neutral color?

LIVING WITH PURPLE

Purple may seem potent, but it's a great color to use at home. It's a way to add passion to a room, or to create a dreamy, calm vibe. To avoid using purple in a way that feels overly feminine or rich (unless that's your intention), try mixing it with earth tones. Engage with brighter versions of purple and counterbalance them with warm wood tones, terra-cotta, ochre, and taupe. These natural hues balance out the opulence of the color and help keep it grounded. They bring to mind the rolling hills of a landscape. I think about a golden field of natural hues against purple mountains in the fall, and it feels natural and cozy.

You can also explore the edges of purple by using a gray-lilac when you would normally just use gray. Sometimes when you're unsure how to use a color, think about the analogous colors on the color wheel—in this case, blue and red. If you love blue, you might consider using purple tones that have more blue in them, or, on the other hand, purples with more red. Exploring the edges of a color is a good way to expand your mind about new ways of using it. Blue-purples can lend depth to a monochromatic blue room and add surprise. Red-purples can add depth to a warm space—even if it's mostly light blush hues. Contrast is important in creating an interesting room.

Soft, subdued versions of purple feel beautiful and atmospheric. They could include a shade that's just a step up from white, and one with enough gray in it that it's not overpowering. I'm drawn to these shades time and again, and I use them often—although I don't typically think of them as "purple" hues. They're great for the bedroom, as they are soothing and relaxing but less expected than blue. Adding a soft purple-and-white pattern can be a great place to start.

DECORATING WITH PURPLE

Start Slow

If you want to slowly introduce this color into your space but you're overwhelmed by the idea, start with something small like a flower with purple petals, such as an orchid. You can even paint your bathroom this color once you get used to it; it can be beautiful in a small space. Or, take a cue from the color of dried lavender and go soft and more muted when introducing it in larger amounts. Pale lilac sheer curtains or blinds can cast a dreamy light on a room.

Deep, Dark, Mysterious

Think about the shade of an eggplant and go dramatic. This darker shade is a great way to enrich a room, without the purple seeming overpowering. Deep, midnight-purple hues like this work well in a bedroom, closet, or library.

Weave It In

Weaving purple fibers into a fabric can help make this color feel more natural, because it's dimensional, textured, and blended with other colors. Take this literally and look for textural upholstery fabrics that have a purple yarn mixed with neutrals and other colors.

Be Intentional

Purple inspires thoughtfulness, so consider using it in places you spend time introspectively—an office or a spot where you practice yoga or meditate. This could be as simple as placing an amethyst stone on your desk. It is thought of as a healing and protective stone, known for purifying the mind and clearing it of negative thoughts.

Reinterpret Traditional

A little purple can go a long way, but it can also add just the finishing touch you need to a room. When using a bolder color such as purple, introduce it into a scene that's more traditional. Consider, for example, classic bedding that has a frame of color around the edge. This classic concept can feel fresh when the purple is vibrant. Use purple in places in which a more neutral color might feel boring.

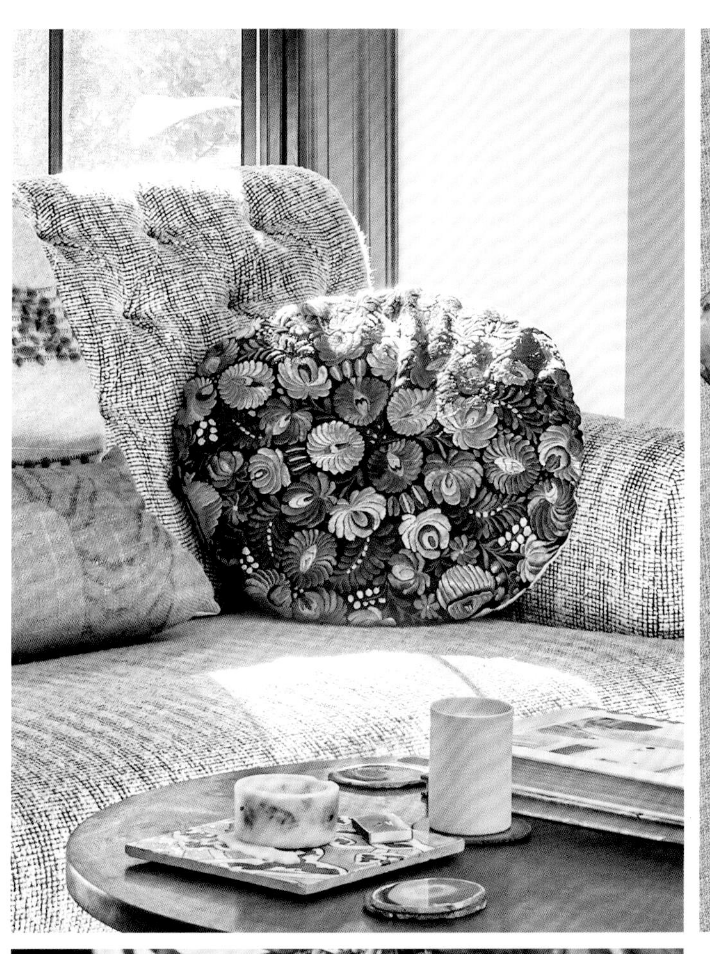

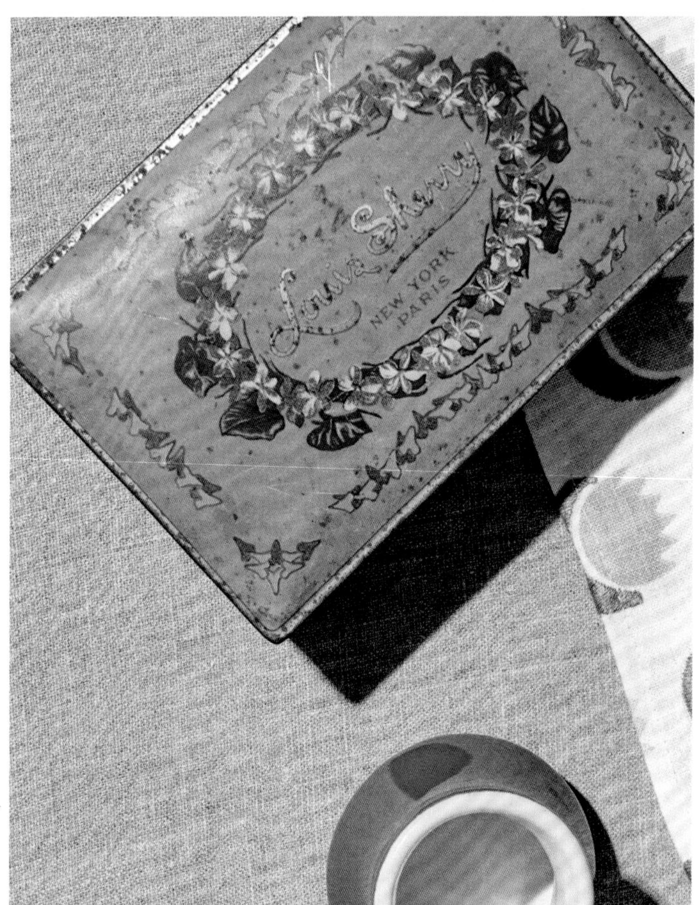
Louis Sherry
NEW YORK
PARIS

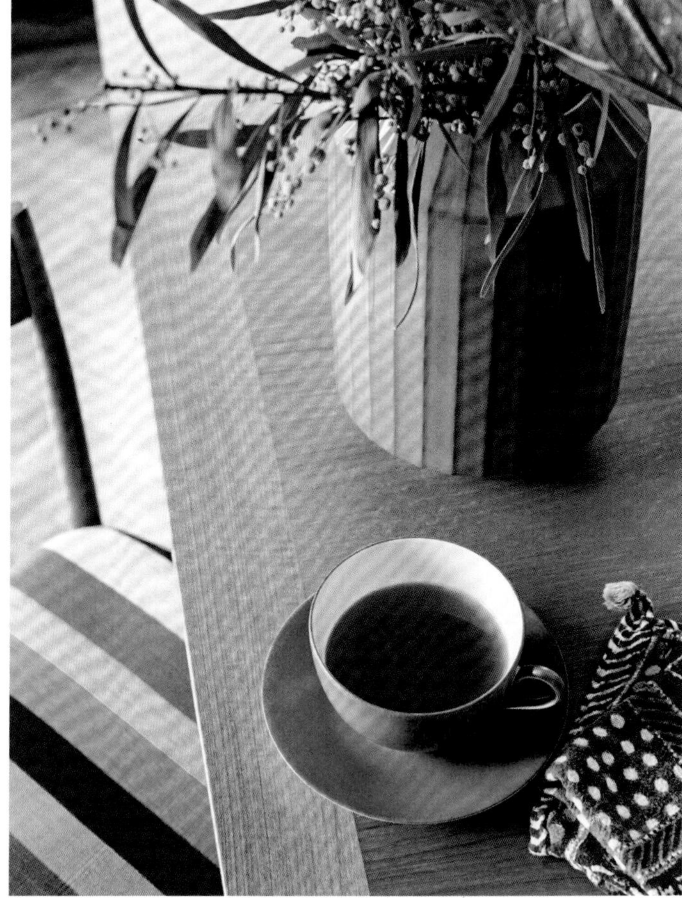

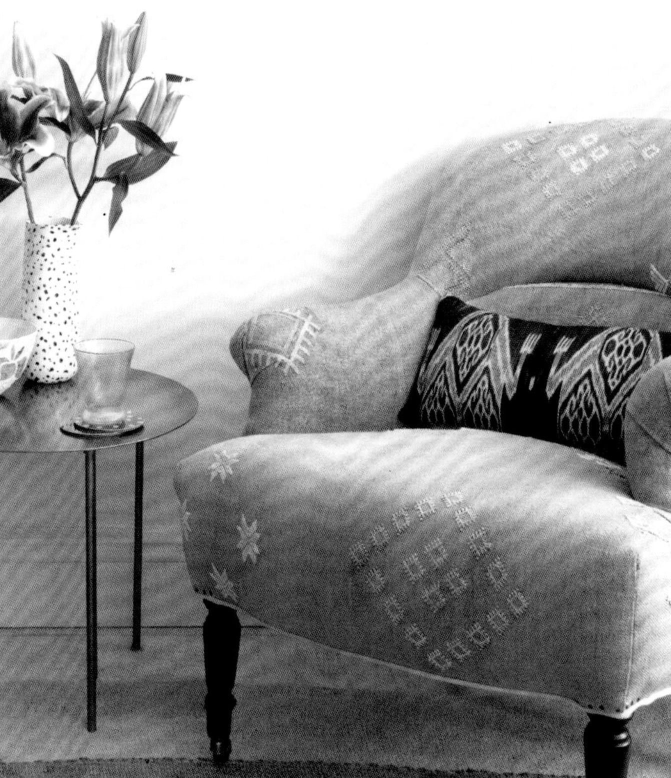

Getting Close to Color

STEP 1

Look to your memories. Spend a few minutes jotting down ideas for each color and the times and places where you remember seeing that color.

STEP 2

Write down words that describe how a color makes you feel. Explore your own personal associations with a color—what makes color magical is how you feel about it.

STEP 3

Place an object with a color you love, but don't currently use, somewhere in your home. Notice how it looks with the other colors you already have, and how it makes you feel. Move it around, try it in different places, and let it spark your imagination.

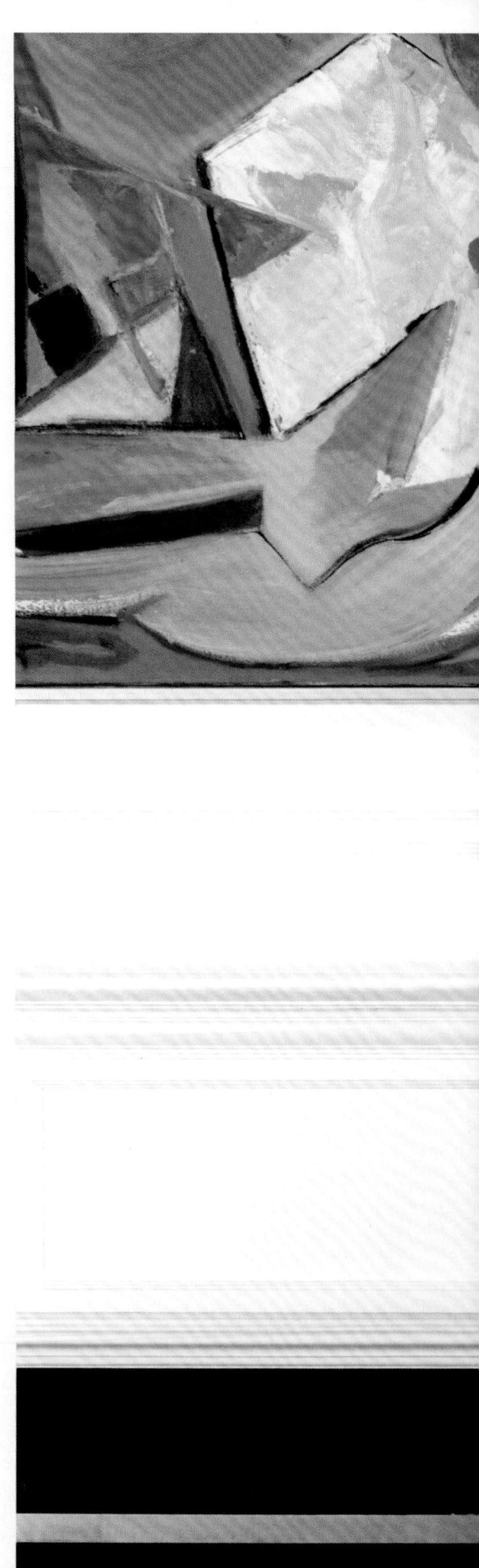

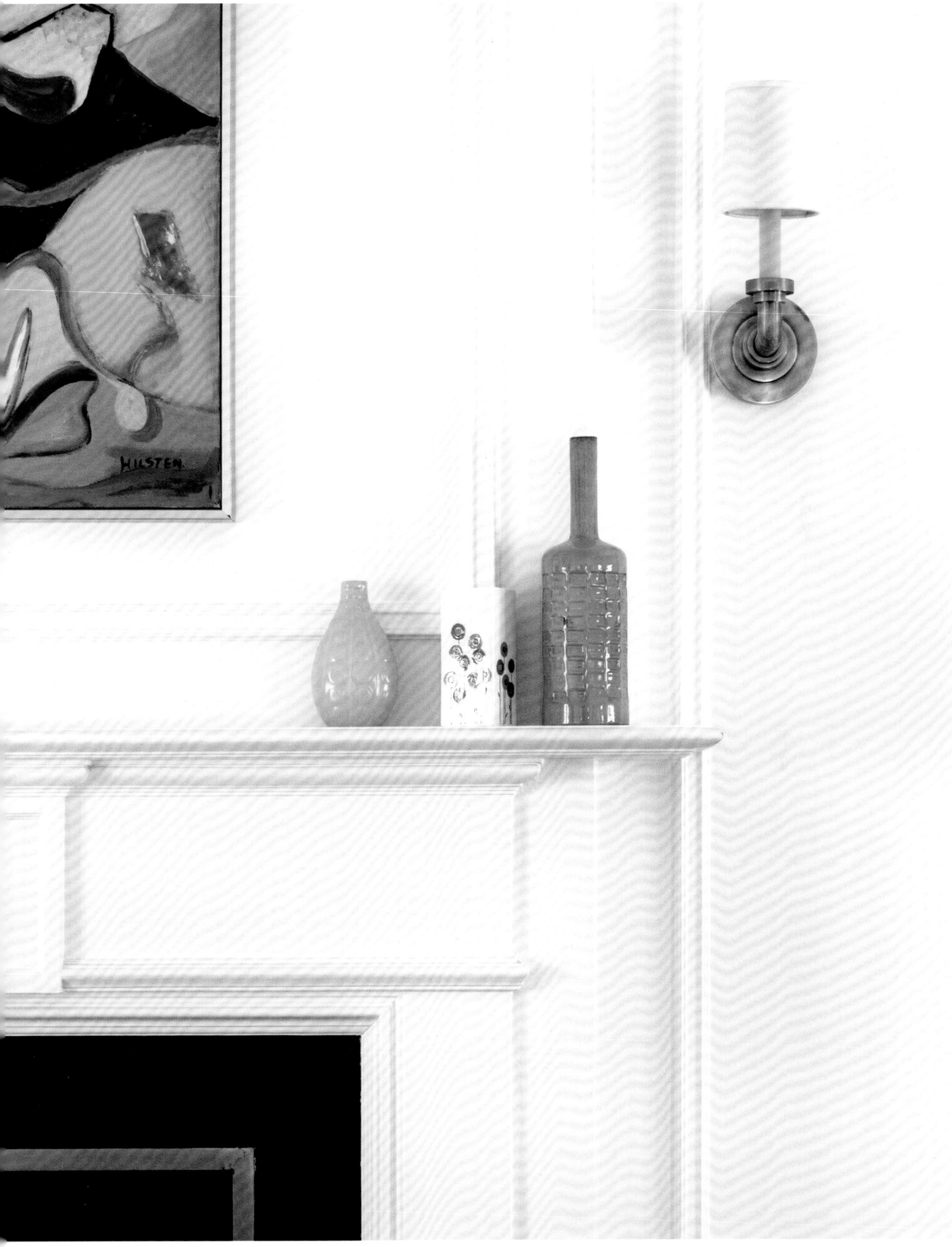
HILSTEN.

PART FOUR

living COLOR

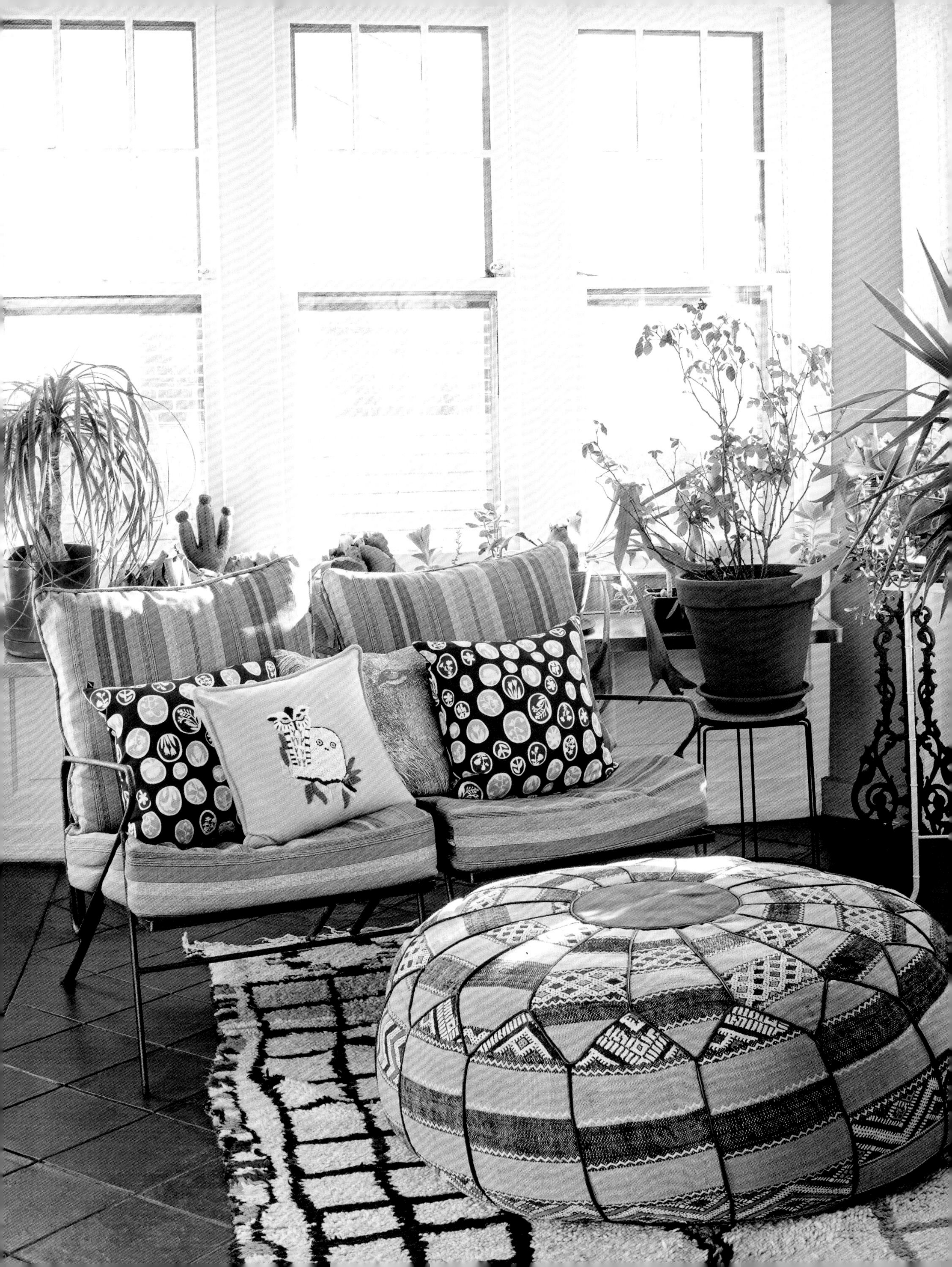

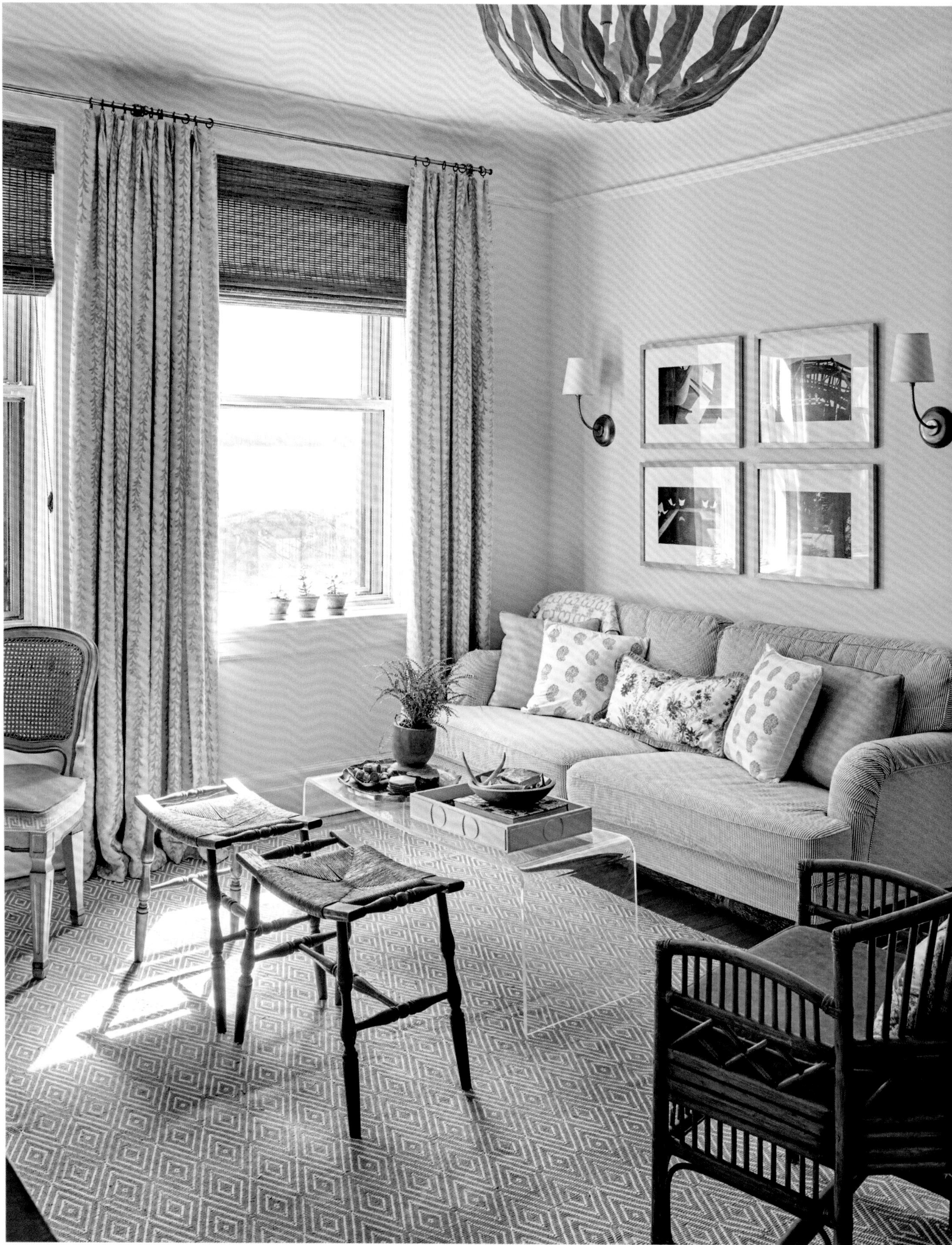

FIXER-UPPER CHARM

EMILY C. BUTLER
Interior Designer
& Decorator

As a Texas native who spent her childhood in rural Kentucky, Emily got her love of projects and fixer-upper grit from her parents and the pride they took in their home. "They strongly valued having a comfortable place to live," says Emily, "which I appreciate now more than ever."

She summoned these skills when, just in time for Thanksgiving 2016, she and her husband, Jonathan Kemp, moved into their prewar apartment in Jackson Heights, Queens, after a six-week renovation. Their landmark building is now celebrating its one hundredth birthday, and they couldn't be happier with the beautiful, historic neighborhood in which they've settled. "All the [prewar building] fuss isn't for everyone," Emily cautions, "but we can't get enough [of the] charm." The apartment was in estate condition and poorly maintained when they bought it, so it took a bit of imagination to shift her focus away from the grime to its beautiful bones, but luckily most of the original details were still intact.

Emily decided to go with her gut and paint all the original interior doors tomato red, then build a palette from there. "I never considered myself a 'red person,'" says Emily, "but for some reason, it just felt right for this apartment." She knew she wanted to paint the living room walls blue and the bedroom walls a minty green, so the red helped warm up those cooler tones. She also loved that the red complemented her existing drapery panels (Clay McLaurin's Weeping Willow in yellow), which she adores. "Plus," she adds, "I decided that if we change our minds—or our palette—down the road, it's just paint." She finds it satisfying to commit to a bold selection, "even if all that really means is you have some crazy red doors." Emily loves color so much and feels each strong color choice is so personal that she finds it hard to use desaturated neutrals. Instead, she leans on darker colors in smaller spaces to accentuate the coziness and lighter hues in larger spaces to allow them air to breathe. When approaching a new space, she tries to be practical and utilize what she already has, but she still allows herself to dream and pull wish-list fabrics and furniture pieces. "There is a happy medium where you aren't buying all new things but you are freshening up what you already have—and love," she says.

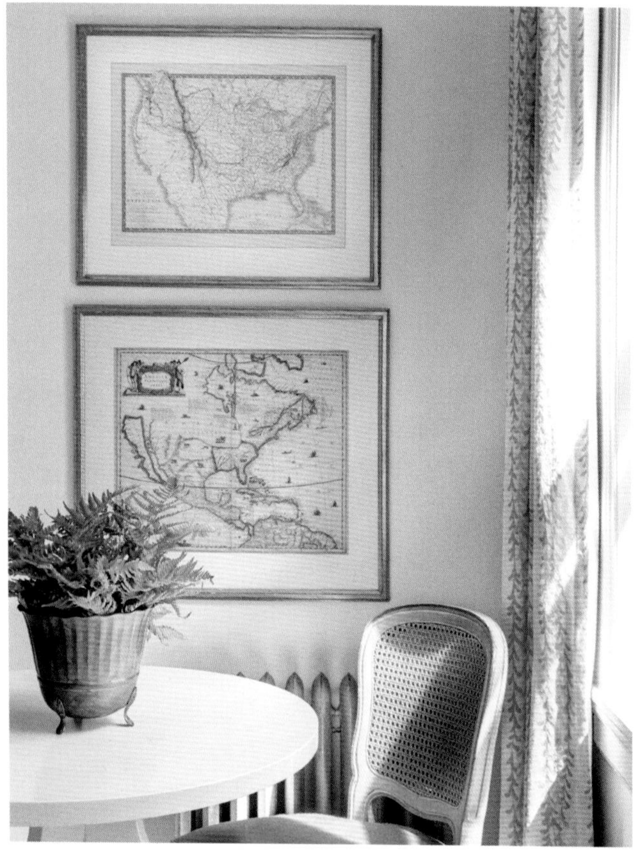

COLOR CONNECTION

Emily's style is more traditional, but it feels fresh because of the intentional use of color. Her home is a great example of an unexpected primary colors (red, yellow, blue) palette. Instead of being overwhelming, the colors feel calm. Soft blue walls are a natural backdrop, like the sky, and the yellow is more of a weathered golden hue, which connects with the warm neutrals in the space, like cream, rattan, wood, and gold accents. The reds, varying from faded Nantucket red to red mixed with white, are accented by bolder red doors. The red on the doors is vibrant but also feels livable and not too extreme. Not only is it a great shade, but it also encourages transition within the spaces of the home. Layering a hue with varying shades within a space makes it feel more natural, and a bolder version seems less of a shock. The doors feel connected with the living room because of the softer red hues and the color choices in the hallway and the other rooms surrounding it.

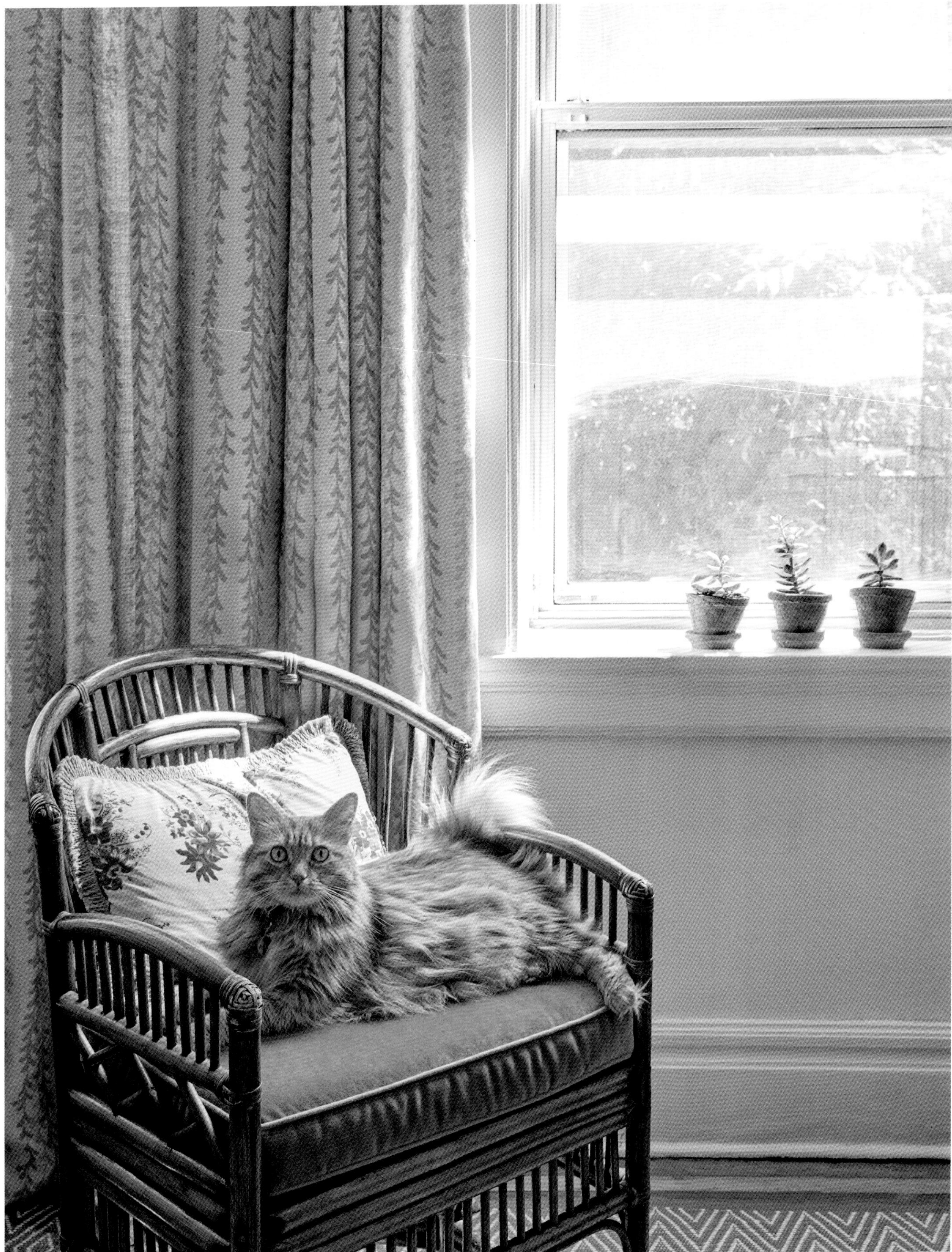

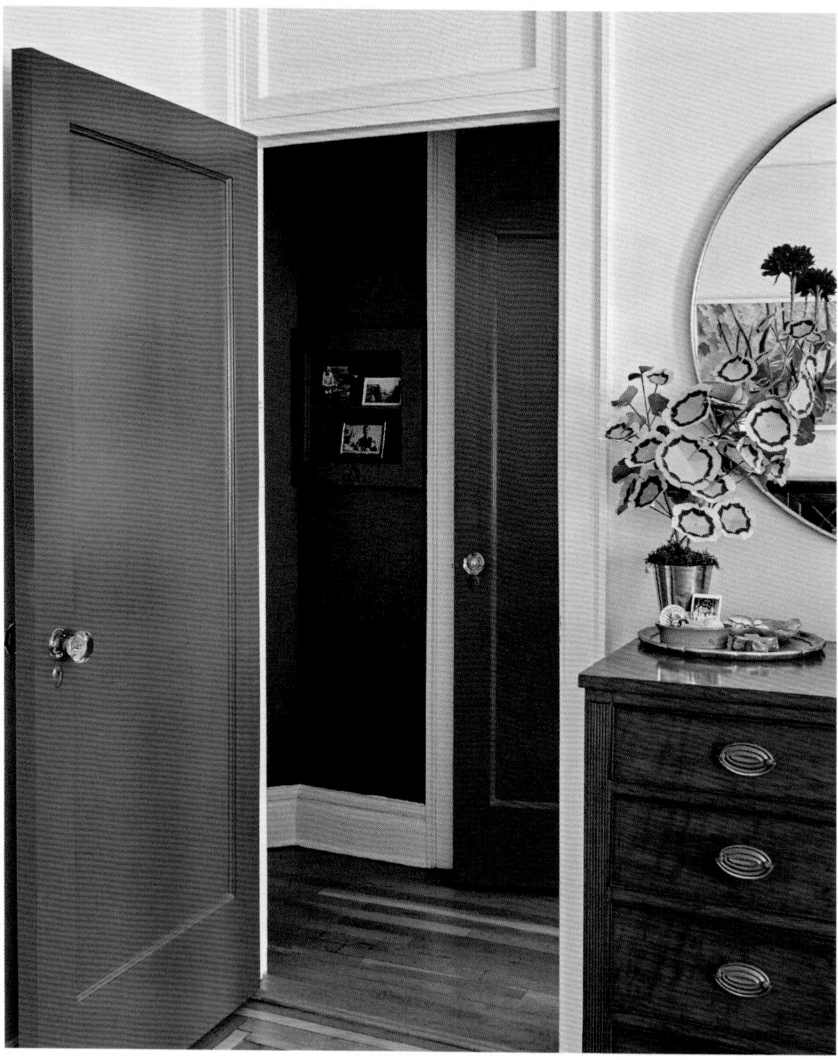

ELEGANT HALLWAY

A New York apartment can easily seem small, and often is, but the layout and clever design decisions make this home feel quite spacious. The hallway, which could appear like a tight space, instead feels thoughtful and elegant with its dark walls in deep marine green, which is a complementary color to the red. This hue is a neutral version of green, but it pops because of the red doors. The color also pulls out a bit of green in the living room's blue walls to connect everything.

SUNNY KITCHEN

Emily loves to host (she even baked homemade banana bread for our visit), and her kitchen reflects this. The area is more neutral but feels very sunny and yellow—even though the wallpaper is taupe. The yellow accents on the chair and the bowl of lemons make it appear sunny and warm. Those golden-yellow vibes also play off the color in the living room. Little touches of yellow can make taupes, gold, and warm neutrals feel golden and sunny, and this kitchen proves you don't have to use bright shades all over a small space to achieve that feeling.

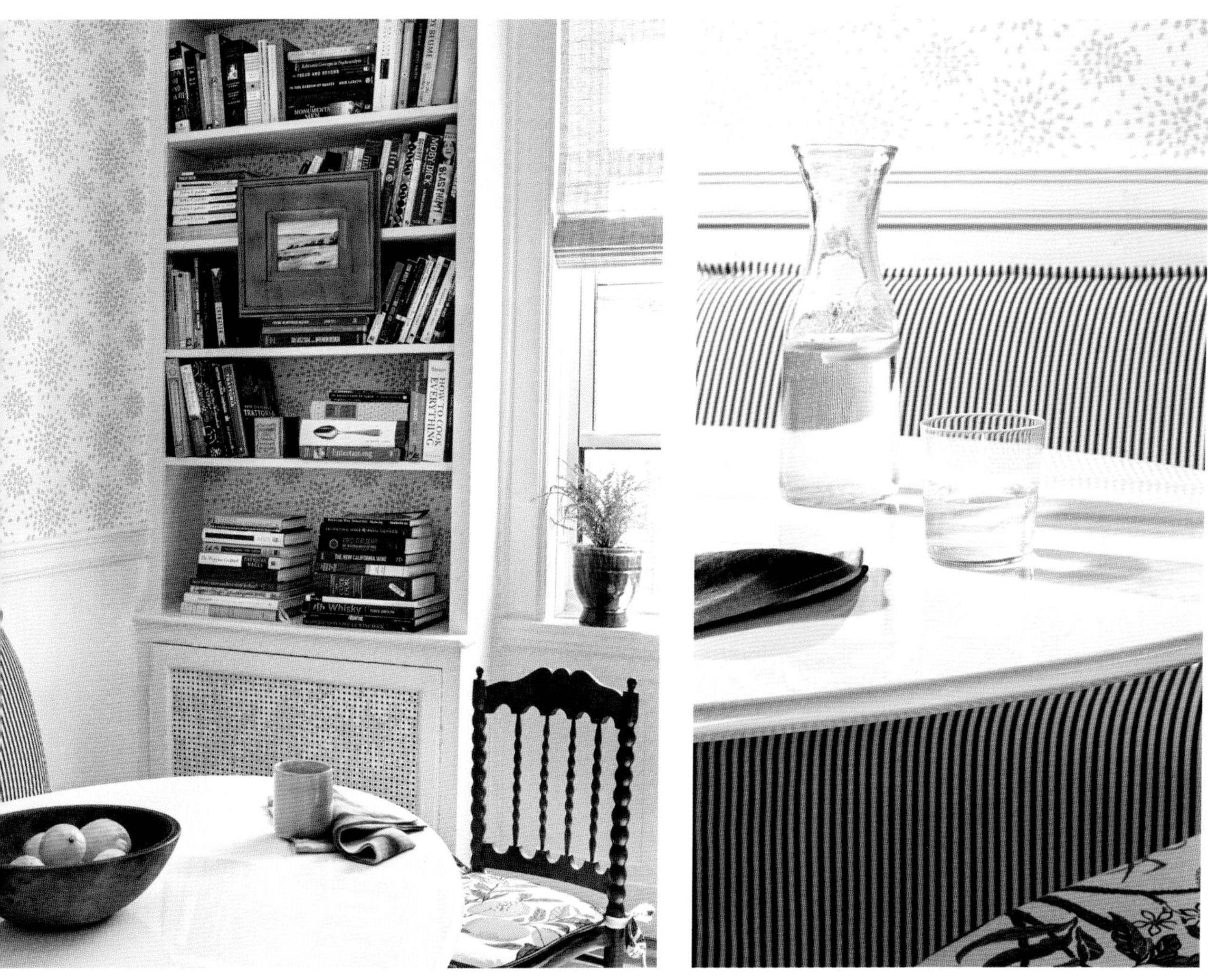

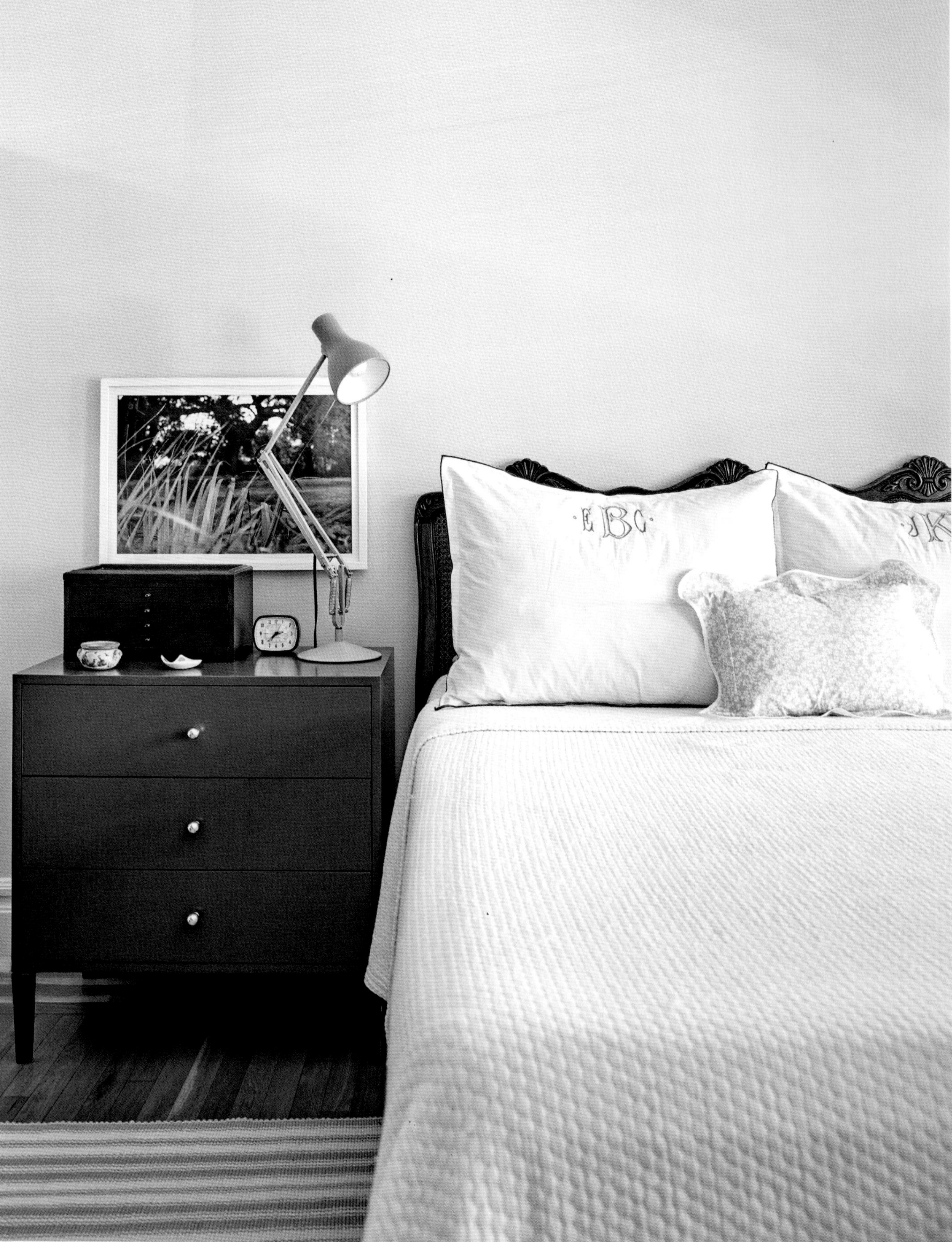
EBC

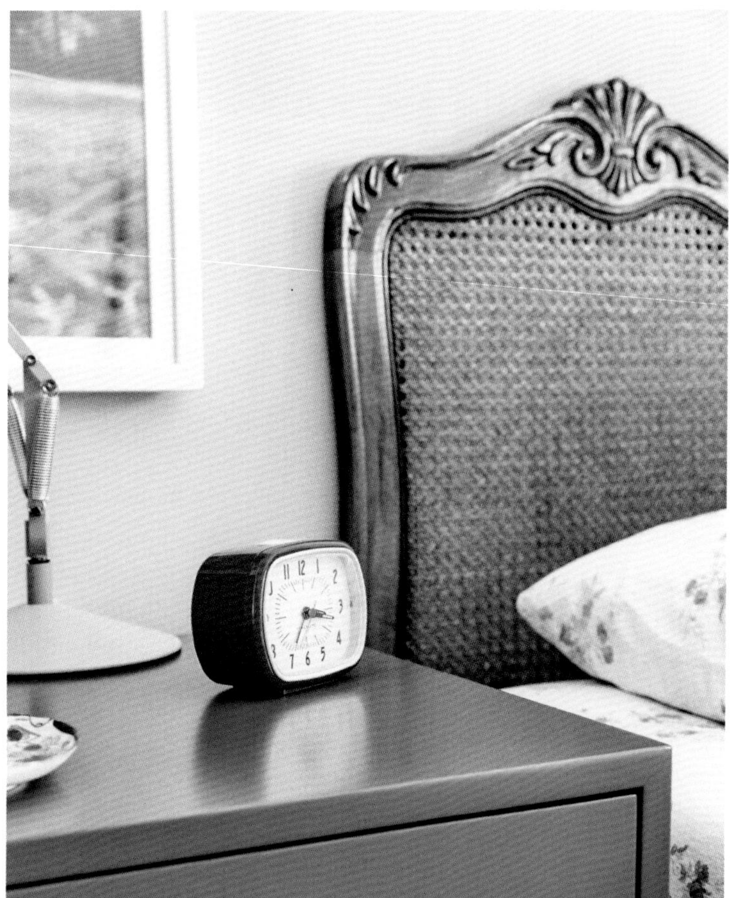

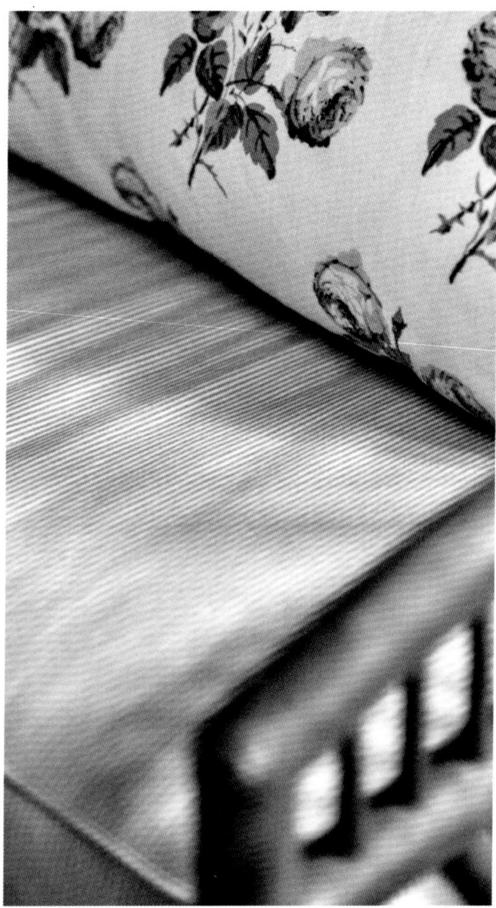

CALM BEDROOM

In the bedroom, the colors from the living room continue to be an influence, but they shift toward more restorative hues. The red accents are small—just an alarm clock and a softer version in a print on the sheets—but the natural dark wood tones also connect the reds. Instead of yellow, green is used here, lending the space a calmer vibe with the mint lamp and the greens in the photography. It's natural to want the bedroom to feel quiet and rejuvenating, and these color choices are appropriate for a bedroom but still relate to the rest of the home.

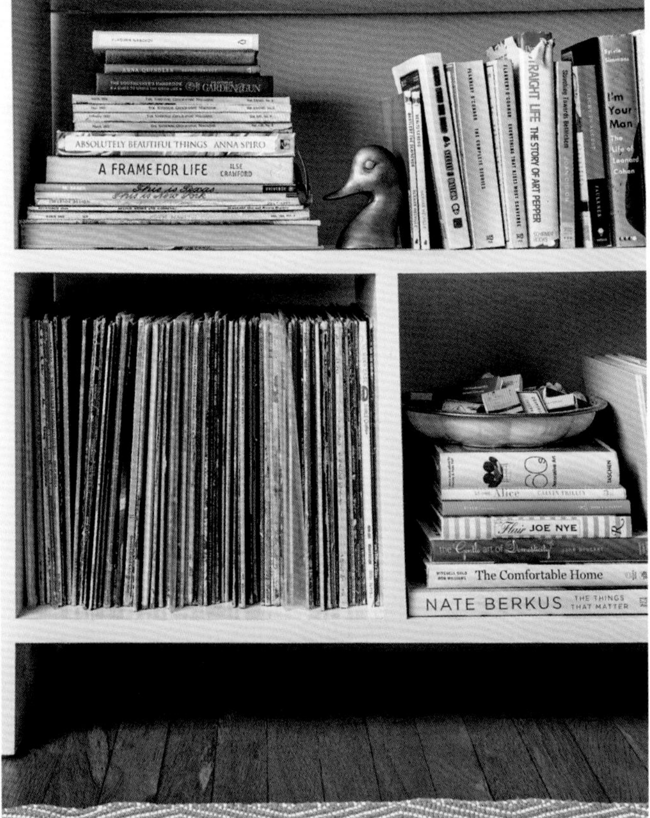

AREAS FOR INSPIRATION

To spur creativity, Emily pores over the work of her design peers and idols. "I will never tire of print publications," she assures, but she finds the Internet to be an incredible connector for ideas, friendships, and sharing resources. Over her desk, she has a mood board, which acts as a spot to gather inspiration, and her books are stacked on the shelves, which makes this another place to play with color. She believes in allowing yourself time to browse, grow, and evolve throughout the design process. She implores anyone approaching a new home project to "always try to remember that decorating has a long arc, and it takes time to create something really meaningful."

MAKE IT YOUR OWN

- Reimagine a primary color palette by playing with tints, tones, and shades of this palette.
- Promote movement, and make a small space feel larger by paying attention to the transitions.
- Paint your doors red!
- Reinvent an existing color palette you love by making subtle changes for different rooms. By emphasizing one color more than another, you can change the entire mood.
- Subtle taupe and neutral hues paired with a few yellow accents feel warm and sunny.

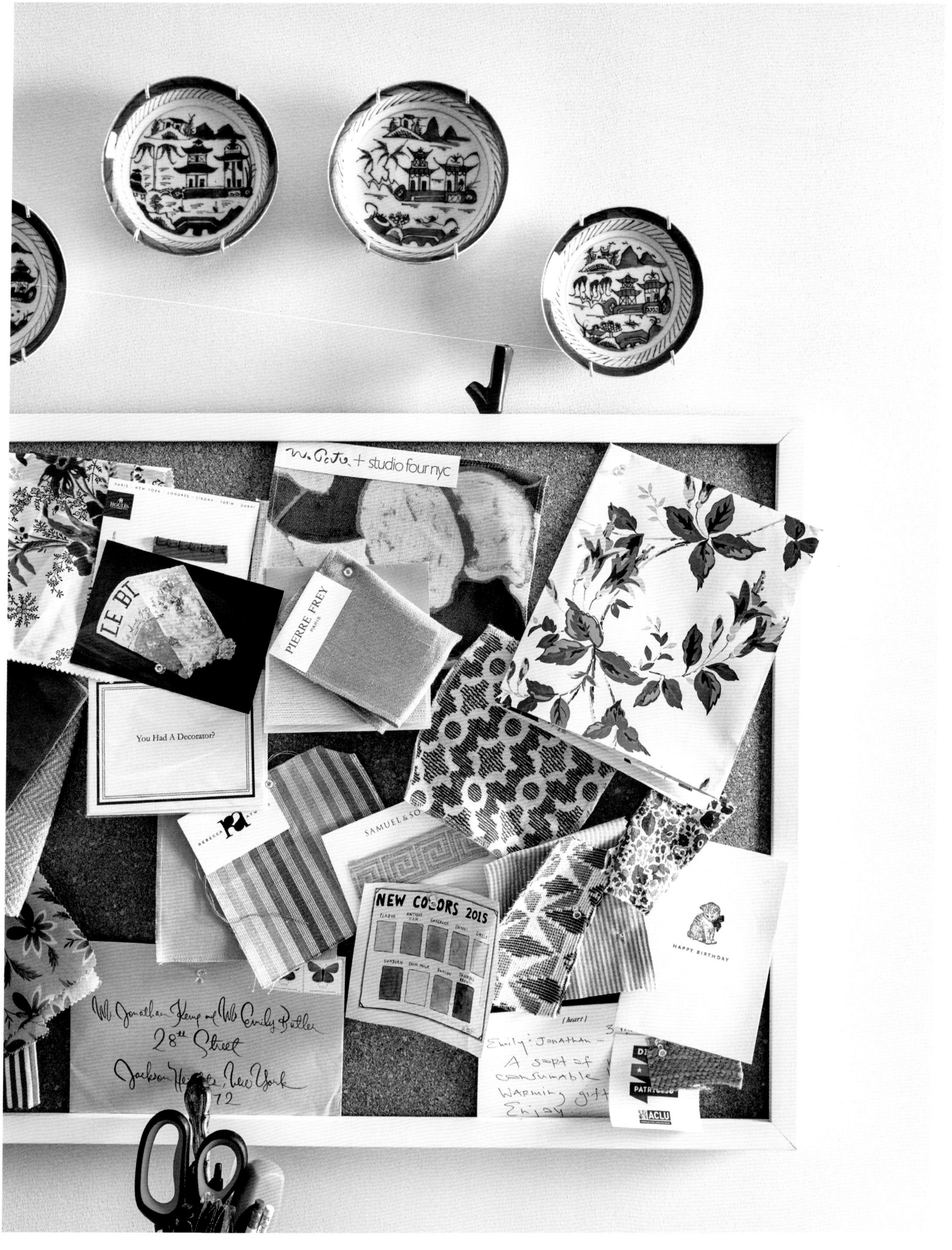

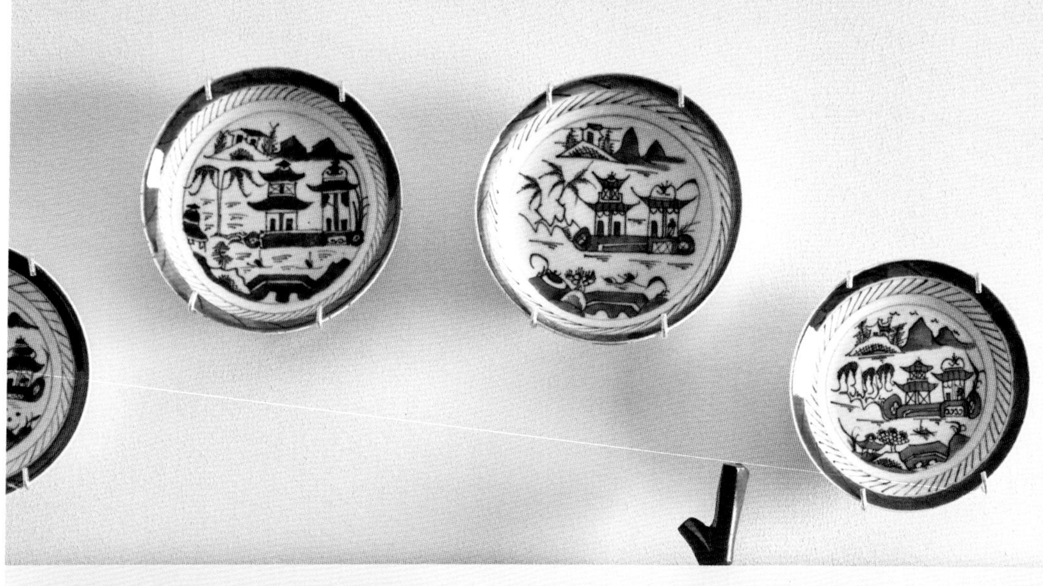

+ studio four nyc
PIERRE FREY
PARIS
You Had A Decorator?
NEW COLORS 2015
HAPPY BIRTHDAY
28th Street
ACLU

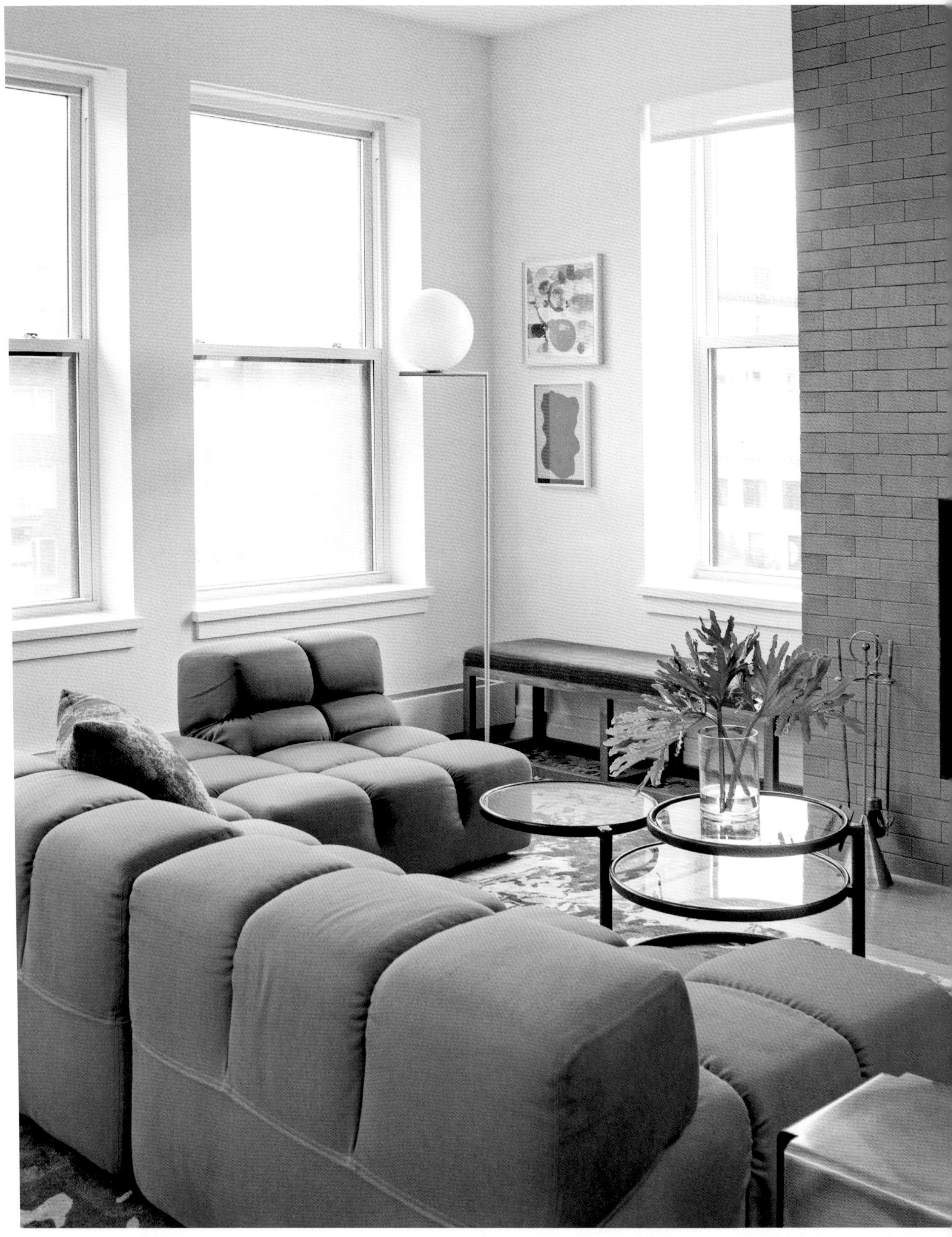

FLORAL ART

LUCY HARRIS
Interior Designer

For designer Lucy Harris, her grandmother's flower arrangements were an art form. "My grandmother had a way of mixing unusual heights, textures, and colors from her garden," says Lucy. "I think of her tiger lilies in July, sprigs of evergreens in winter, and flowering branches in spring." Looking at the assemblage, Lucy understood that the bouquets were not just about color but also about texture, shape, and seasonality, impacting the whole. "She [her grandmother] was an artist and furniture designer, and totally fearless and bold," says Lucy.

To this day, the memory of her grandmother's arts-and-crafts summer home evokes positive associations with color: the blue sky, the dark creek water, the green of the trees, and the brick red of the exterior. The very memory still conjures the smell of boxwood.

PAINTERLY PALETTE

For color inspiration, Lucy turns to art and shies away from standard color palettes. "In art, there is more freedom for unusual color combinations; I look to Josef Albers, David Hockney for his blues, and Georgia O'Keeffe for mixing warm and cool tones," says Lucy. "I find Farrow and Ball's paint colors an absolutely indispensable resource." She suggests those decorating a new space think beyond white walls and use color in a thoughtful way. While she cautions against going too dark or choosing overly saturated colors for walls, she notes you can always use a pigmented color that feels like a neutral, such as Farrow and Ball's Cromarty No. 285 or Light Blue No. 22. "I used these both in my last home and adored them for years," she offers. "Art and your furniture will pop beautifully against them."

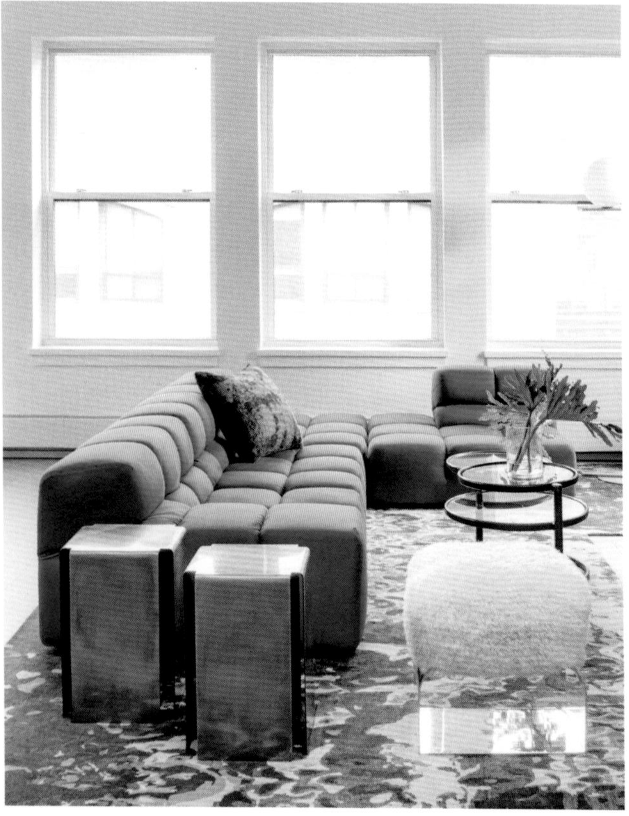

UNEXPECTED CHOICES

This home demonstrates what happens when you open your mind to unexpected colors and palettes. It features soft pastels mixed with brighter hues, and it's a beautiful example of how layering softer tones of a hue makes those brighter versions feel connected. Pastels might be a turnoff, making you think of Easter or the dated looks of the 1980s, but they can be fresh and modern when paired thoughtfully. With Lucy's styling layered into it, this home has a contemporary and urban vibe. This is partly because Lucy makes sure to factor in a home's location and time period when she's designing, and she began by using this Chelsea apartment's industrial roots as a jumping-off point. Then she used color as a wonderful punctuator in a way that is both soothing and energizing.

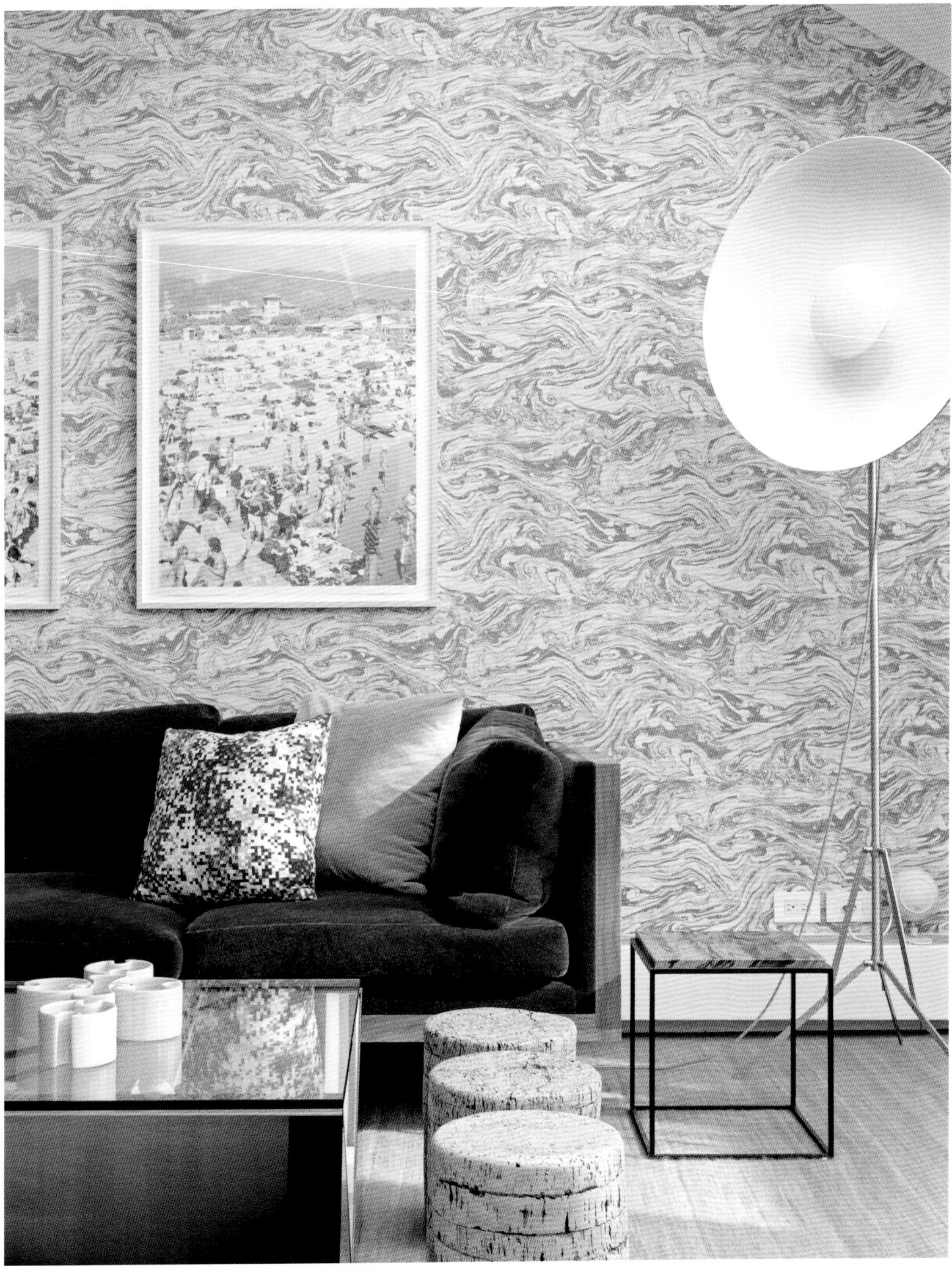

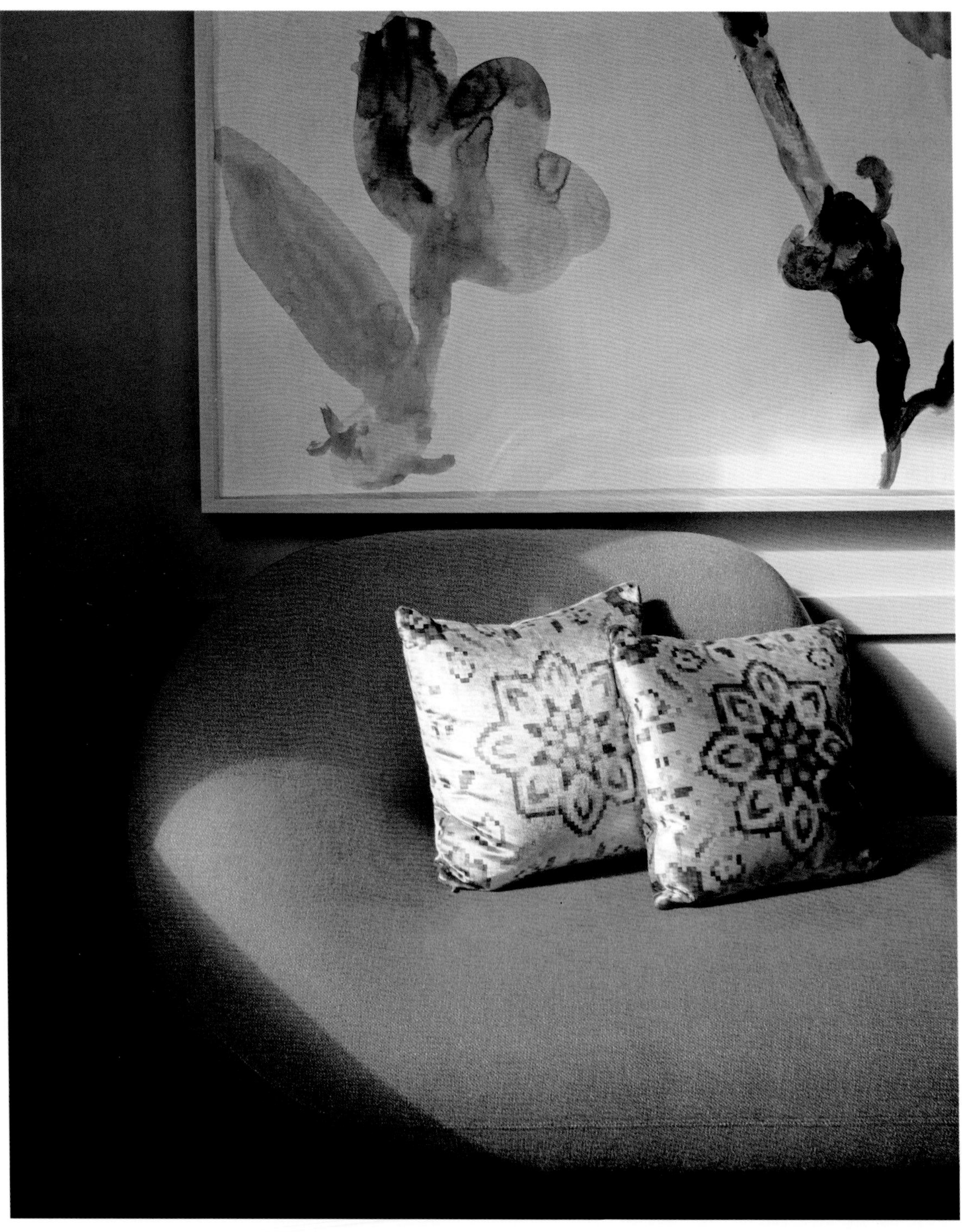

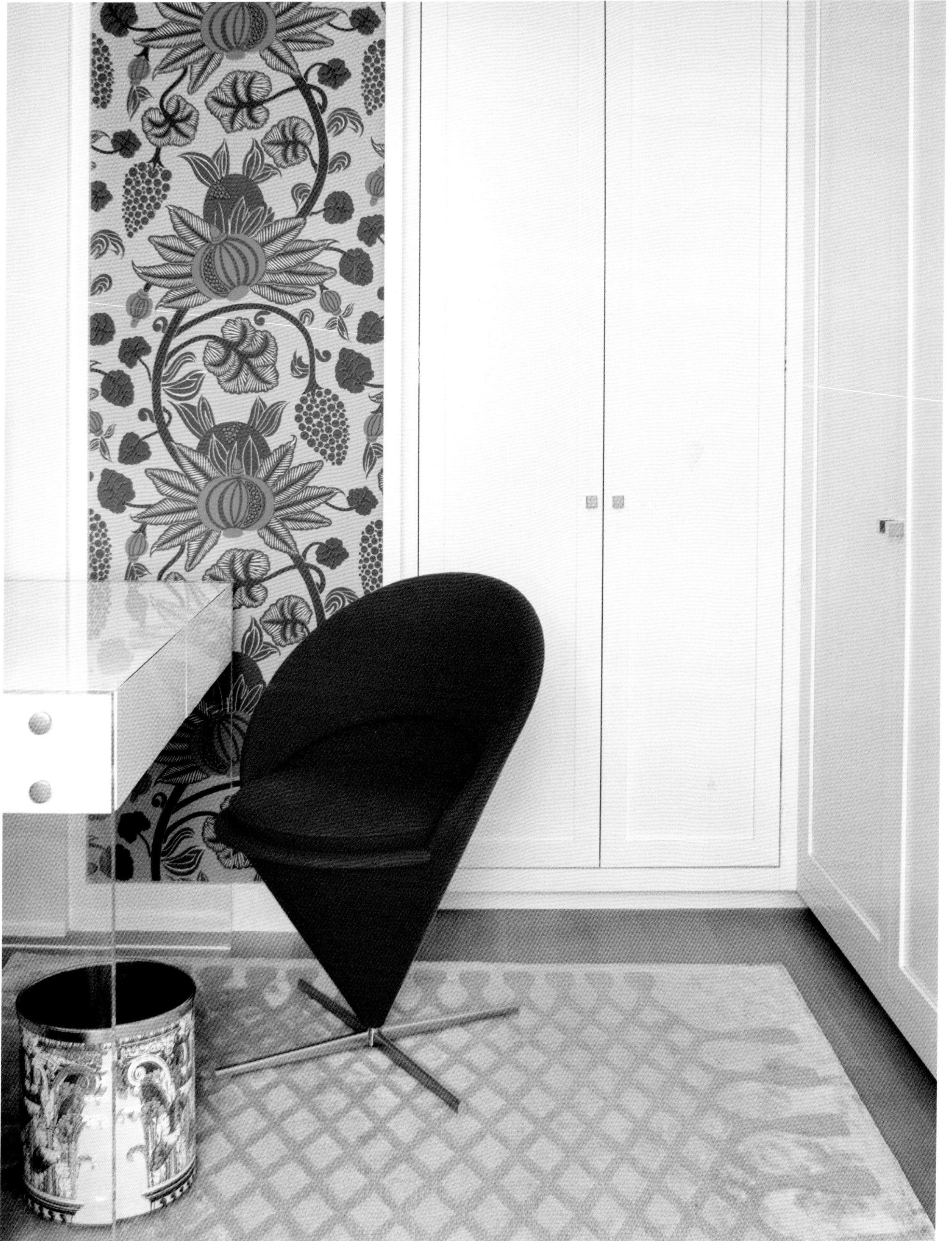

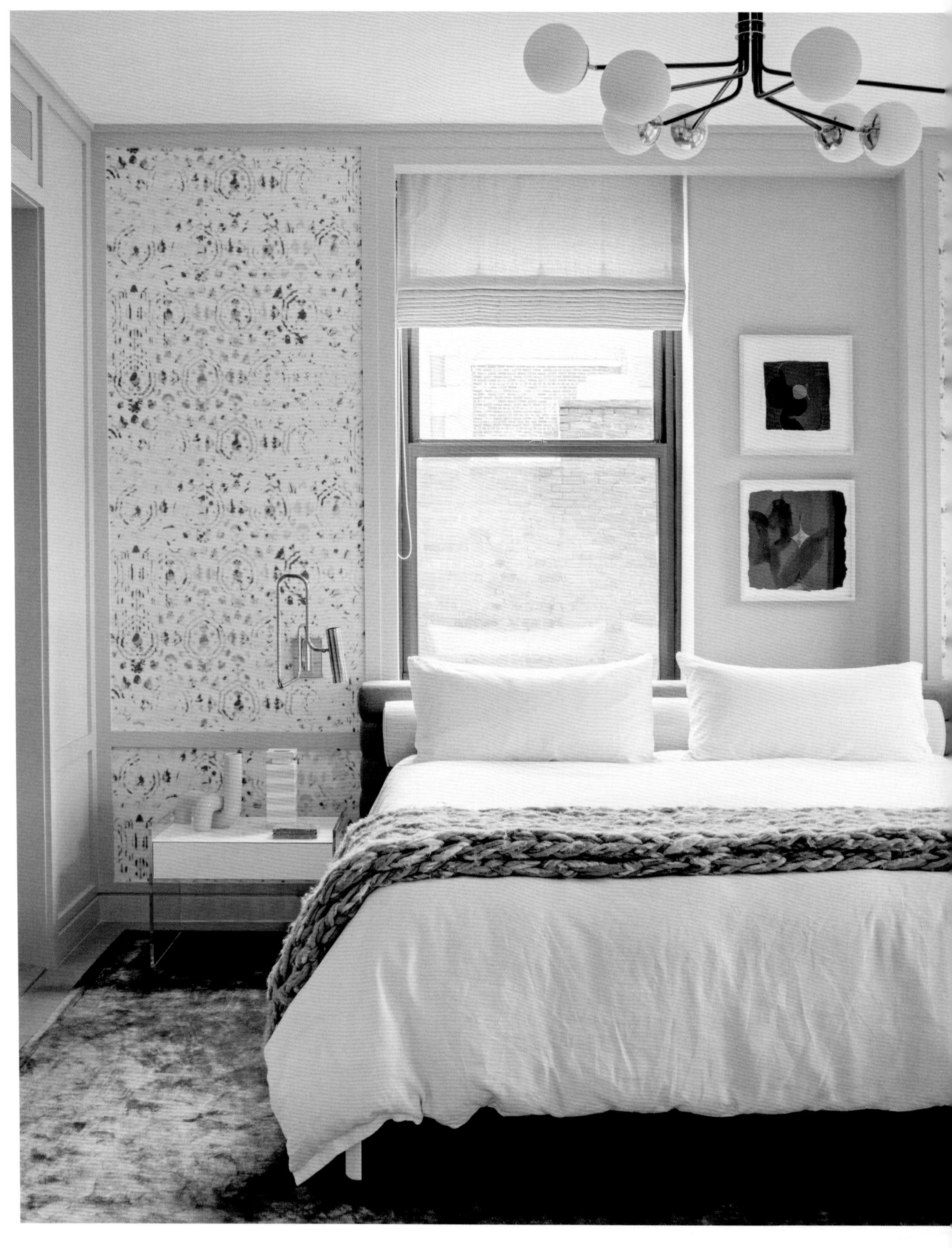

WHIMSICAL BEDROOMS

The bedrooms are whimsical and filled with colorful wallpaper that gives each room personality. The use of yellows and purples in the master bedroom play off one another perfectly. Although yellow and purple can be difficult colors to use together, Lucy pairs them expertly, and you can tell she considers composition when she places objects in the room. She also chooses objects and materials that move your eye around the space and keep it light and lively.

The guest bedroom's floral wallpaper lets company feel like they are sleeping under a jungle canopy of mystical blooming plants. Lucy's choice of color in this room is gorgeous and exciting, because it feels very painterly, like thick strokes of color. The yellow lamp floating on the wall also adds to the fantastical vibe of the room. The glow of the lamp fills the space with warmth. In each room, Lucy adds surprising objects in the space. The painted nightstand is not the obvious choice, which makes it a point of interest, and she plays up that choice with the items she places next to the bed. These bedrooms transport you to another place with the use of whimsy and color.

MAKE IT YOUR OWN

- Mix brighter, saturated shades with pastels.
- Add materials like Lucite, brass, and cork.
- Use bright yellow accents to make a bedroom feel sunny.
- Wallpaper within molding. It's less intense than a full wall but still adds impact.

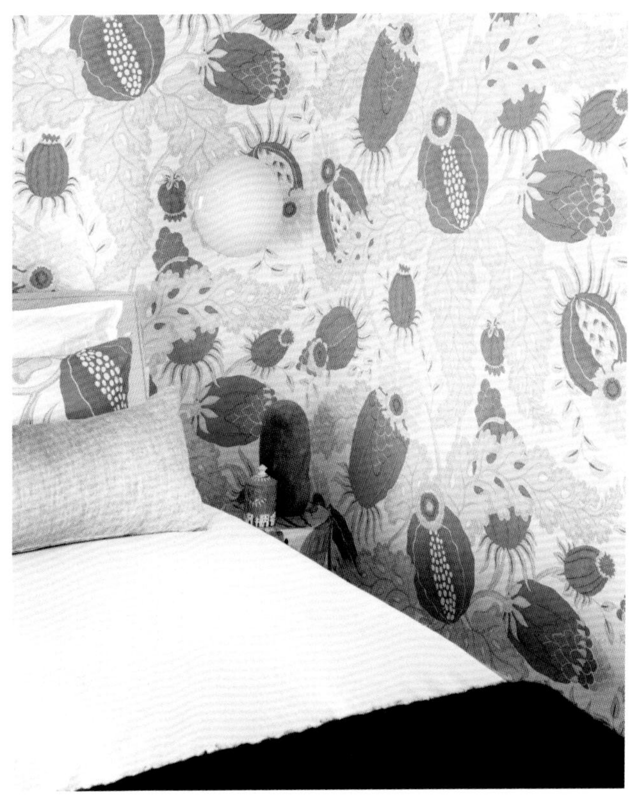

ARTFUL OBJECTS IN THE KITCHEN AND DINING AREA

The kitchen is simple and minimal. Lucy uses soft pastel purples and greens to bring a subtle pop to the space. Even the red and black lines in the painting minimally push the color as well.

Lucy has a great eye for choosing artwork and photographs. She draws the eye in with these interesting sculptural objects, combining them with the space in a natural way. Her attention to detail shows in her interior compositions, and they, too, make it feel as if you are walking into a work of art.

She highlights the architecture of the objects as well. She finds unique pieces and knows how to pair them together. You can see this in the way the dining room chairs mimic the shapes in the painting. Lucy shows off their unique qualities and illustrates how to bring unusual works of art into your home. Everywhere you look is a piece like nothing you've ever seen before that catches your eye. Her choice of materials is also clearly important; cork stools, puzzle-piece ceramic elements, and lamp fixtures are chosen with the utmost intention and style.

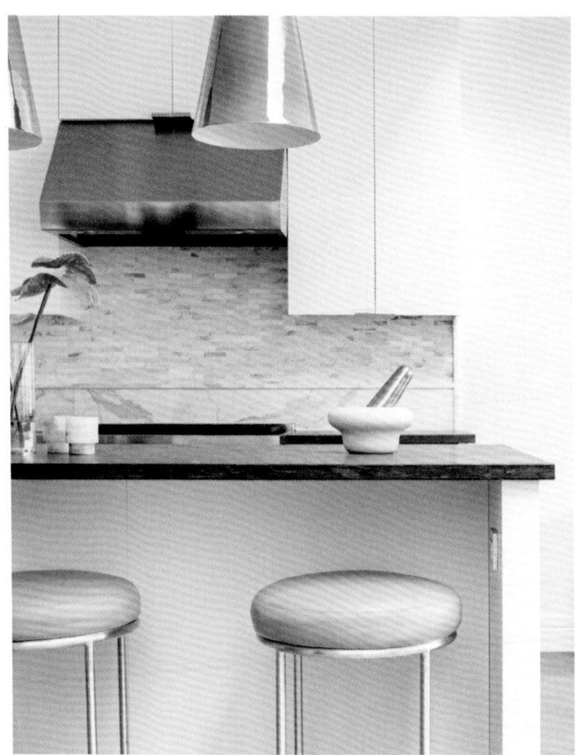

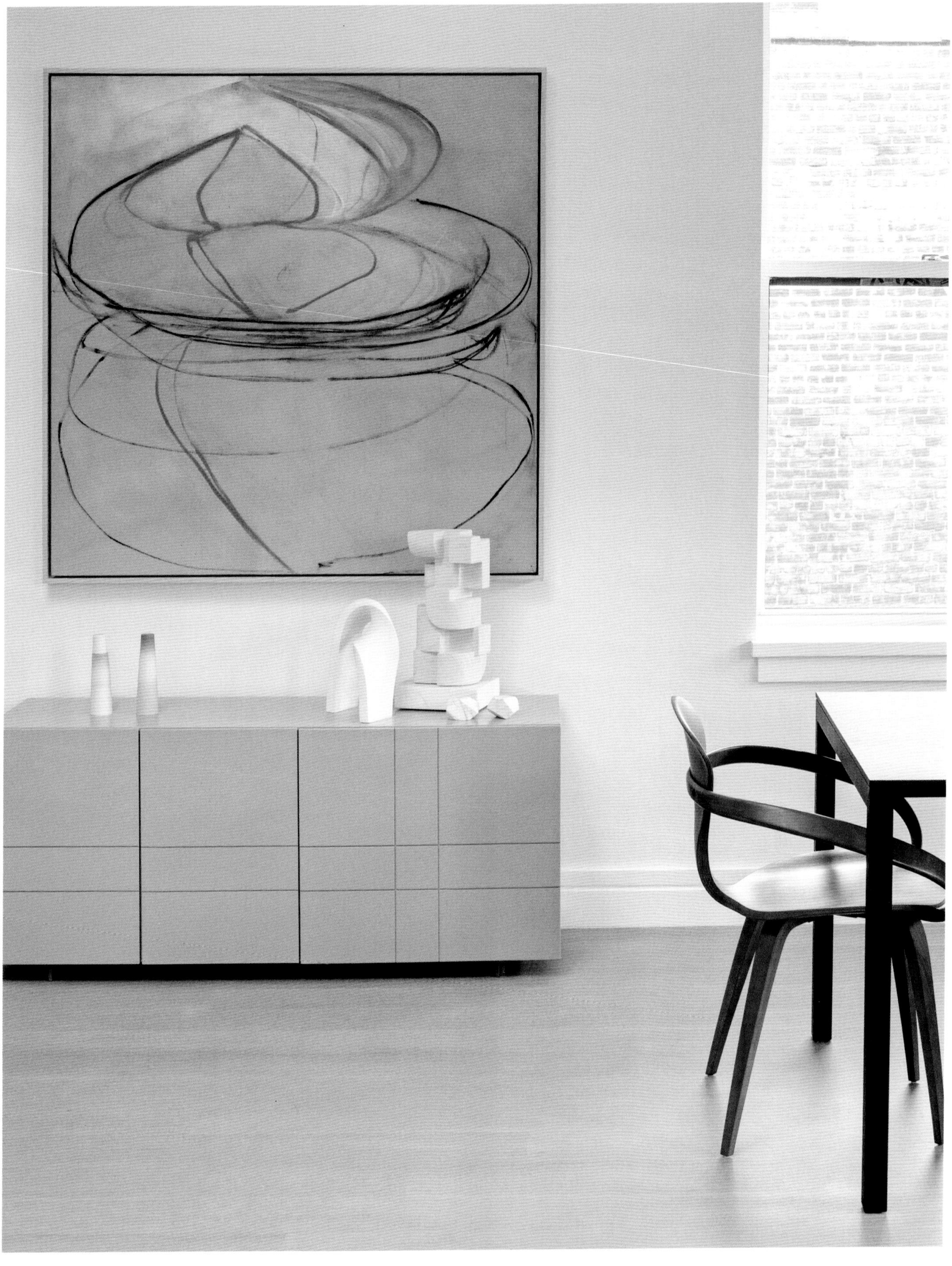

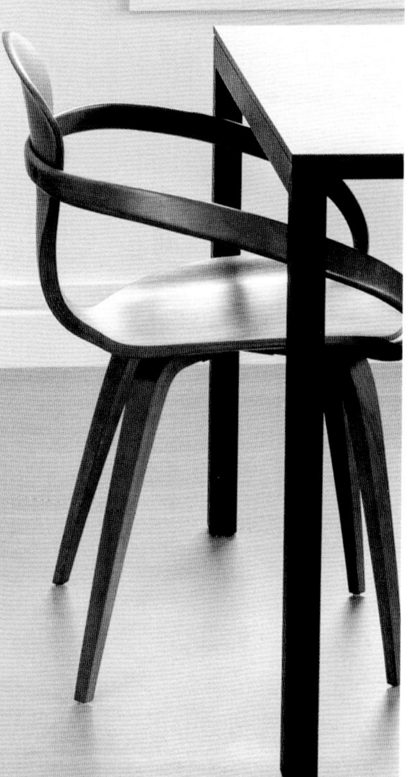

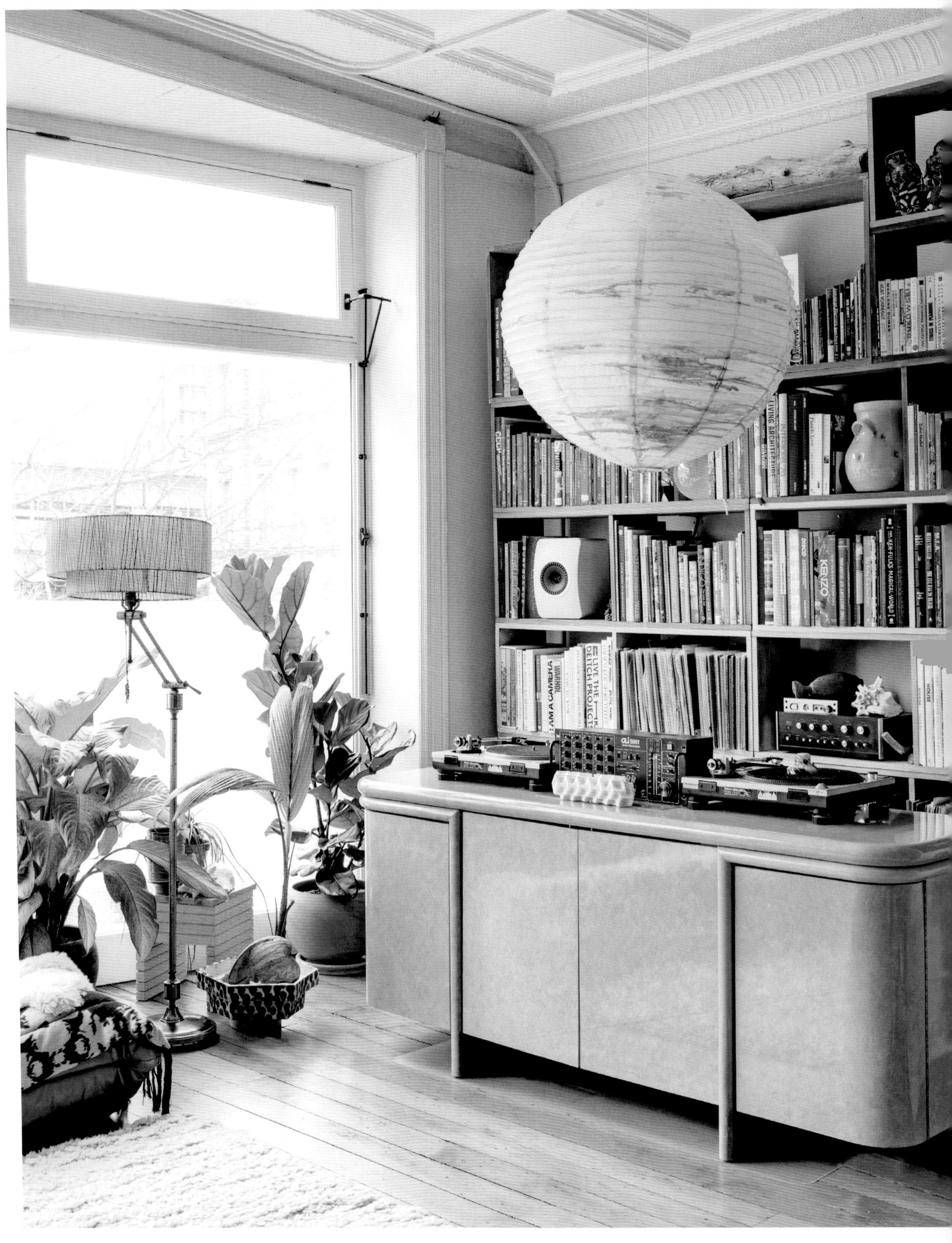
LIVING ARCHITECTURE
KENZO
I AM A CAMERA
WARHOL
DEITCH PROJECTS
BUKOWSKI
HOUSE

OCEAN LAYERS

SHANAN CAMPANARO
NICK CHOCANA
Eskayel Wallpaper,
Fabric & Rugs

For Shanan Campanaro, founder of the Brooklyn-based textile and design firm Eskayel, color is life. Not only does she work with color daily to develop patterns drawn from her original artwork, but she also values it as a key element in the Williamsburg, Brooklyn, home she shares with her husband, Nick Chocana. Originally hailing from San Diego, California, Shanan wanted a home that reflected her seaside-living aesthetic. That meant turning a 1905 live/work space initially built as a New York architect's office into a cohesive interconnected home that felt like being on a permanent summer beach vacation.

To ensure the space felt comfortable, clean, and airy, she chose rich textured fabrics, white walls, and an intentional layering that felt like soft ocean waves lapping over one another. Then she set her sights on greenery, and luckily the generous bay windows flooding the space with light allowed her to engage lots of plant life. Finally, she chose colors and natural materials that reminded her of the ocean. The result is nothing short of breathtaking; rooms awash in oceanic layers of indigo, marine blue, turquoise, green, sage, peachy pink, warm whites, and contrasting blacks that all add up to a sophisticated "under the sea" feeling.

ANCHORED SPACE

Shanan urges anyone decorating a new space not to worry about things "matching," because if you have a strong palette of colors you love that work together (which you're learning to do!) they will all look good and fall into place. She admits that as a textiles and wallpaper designer, she found it hard to pick which favorites among her own work to use at home. The rug, on the other hand, she designed specifically for the space and was set on it from the beginning (though at the time of this photo, it had not yet arrived). For those who have a hard time making design decisions, Shanan suggests starting from the ground up and anchoring a room like this with a rug because it lays a solid foundation upon which you can build.

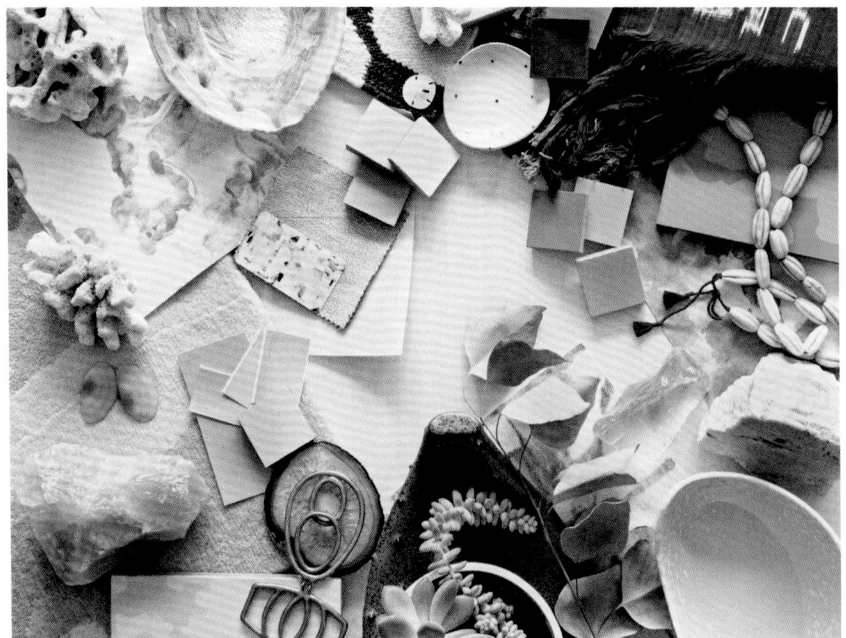

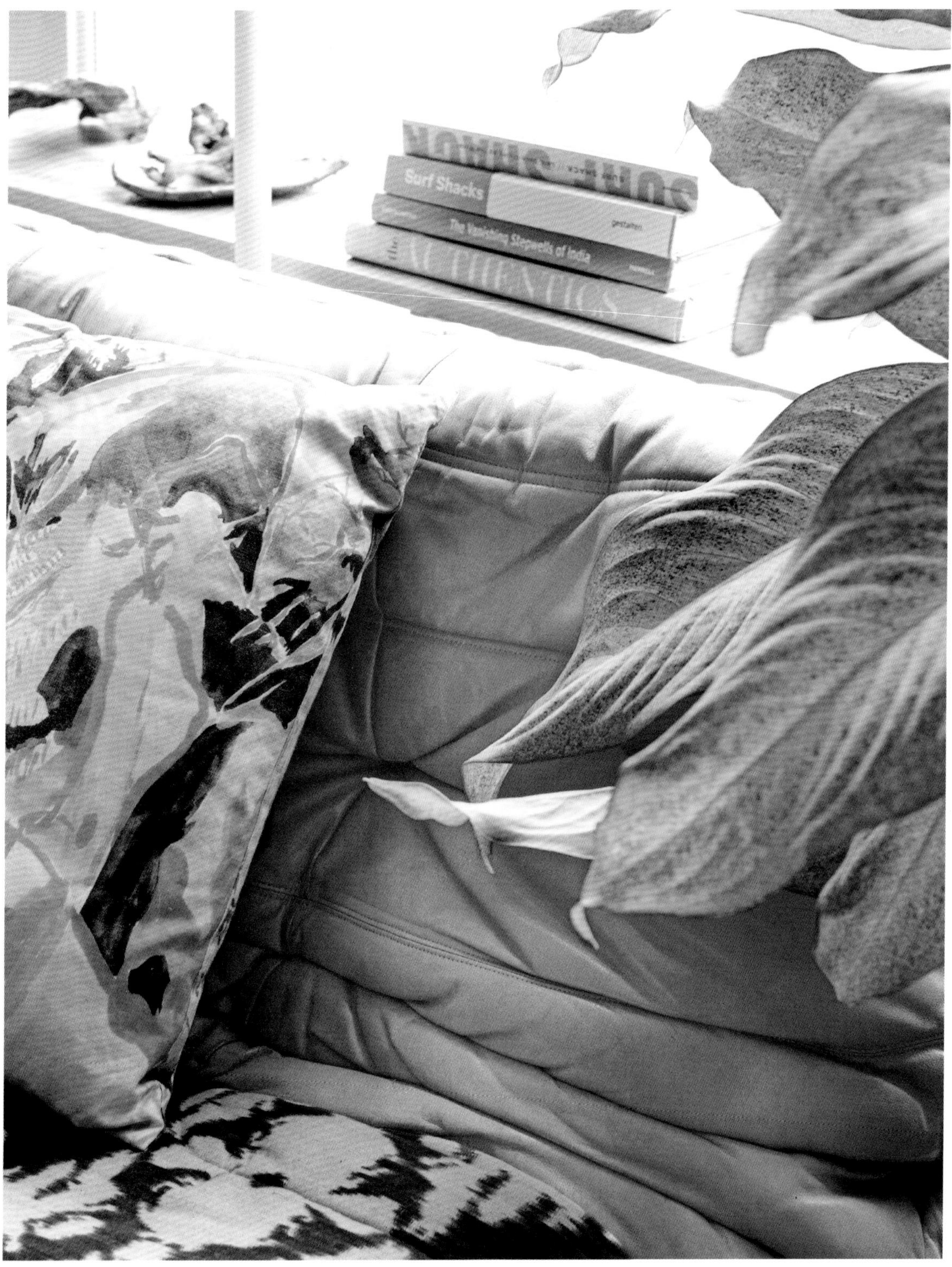
Surf Shacks
The Vanishing Stepwells of India

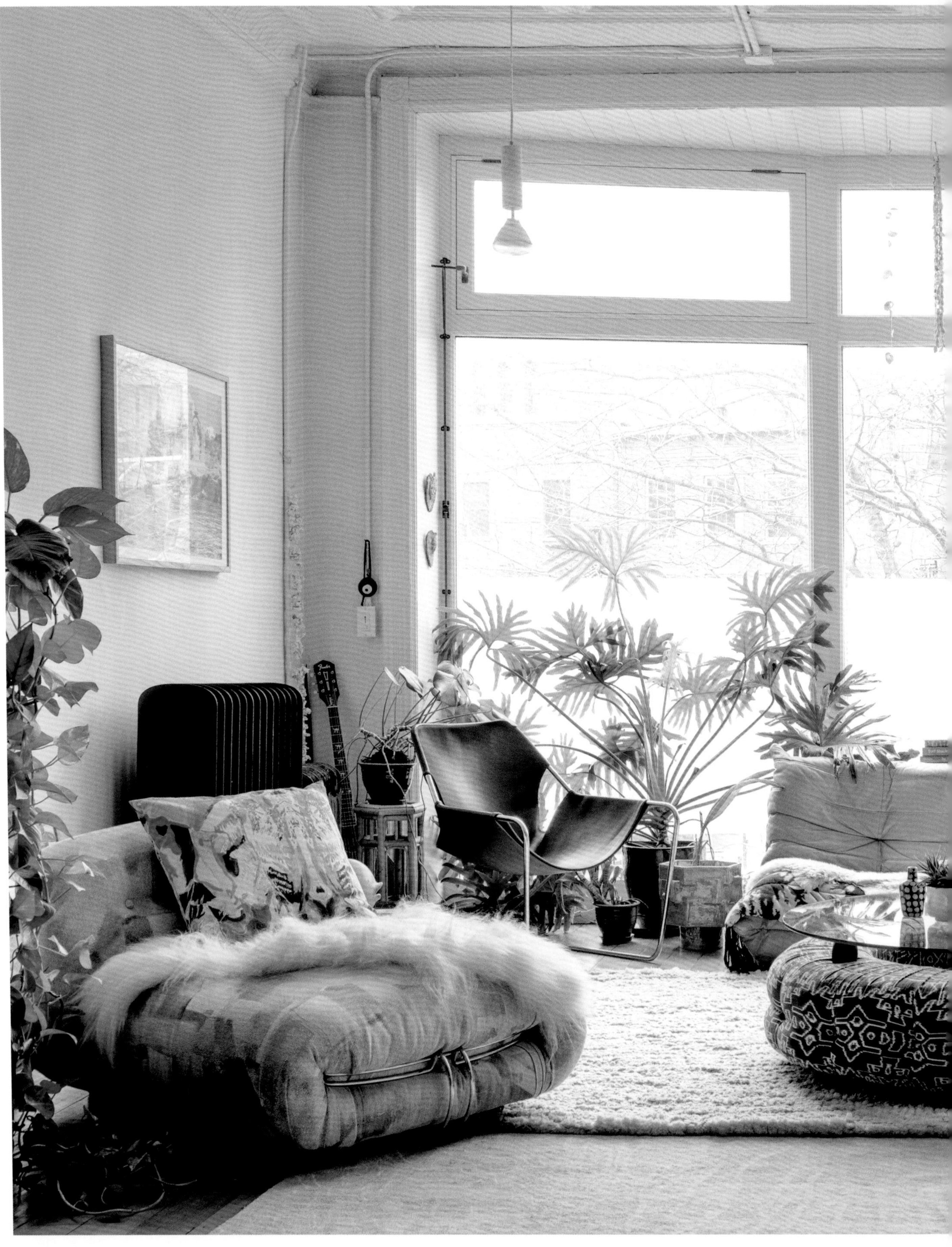

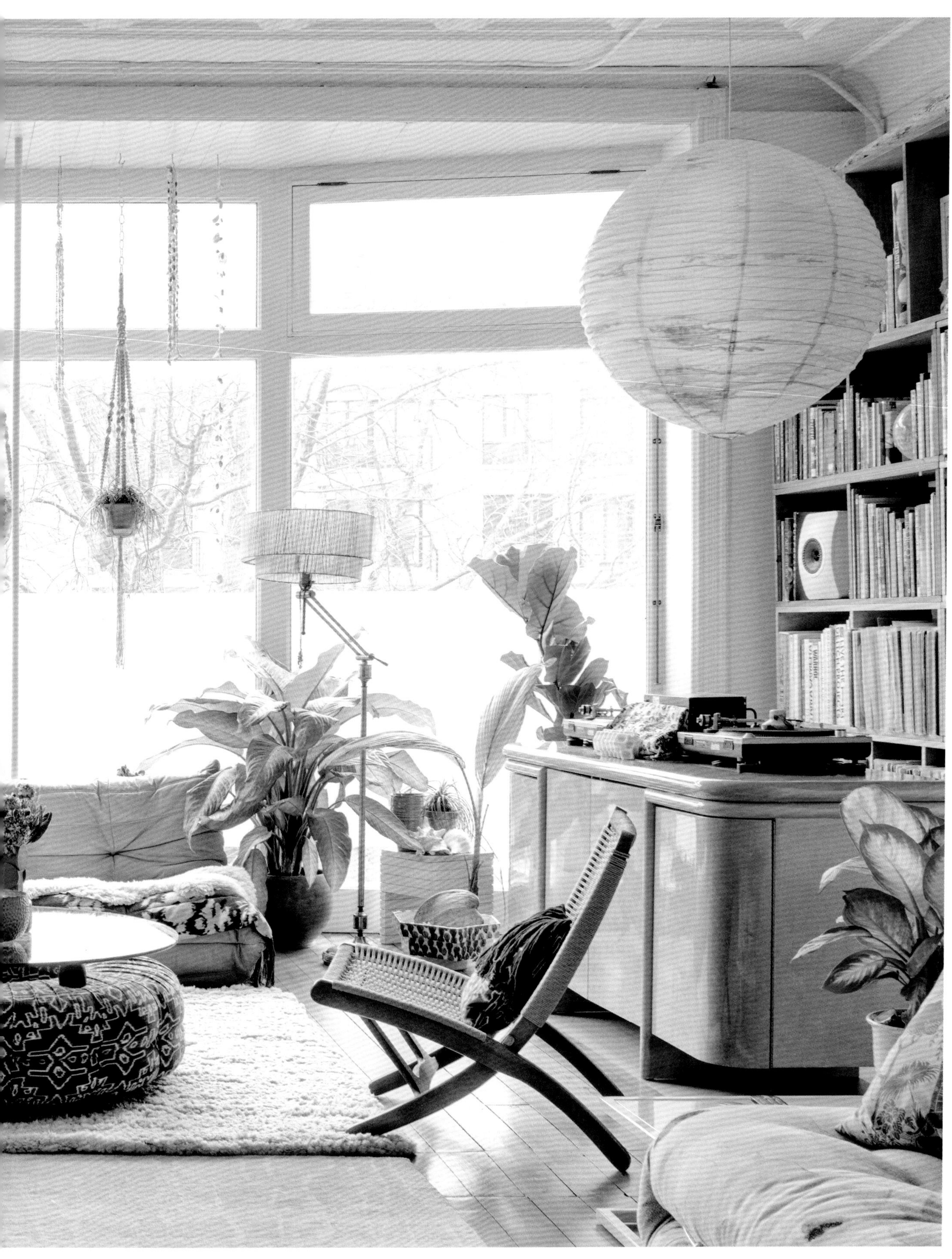

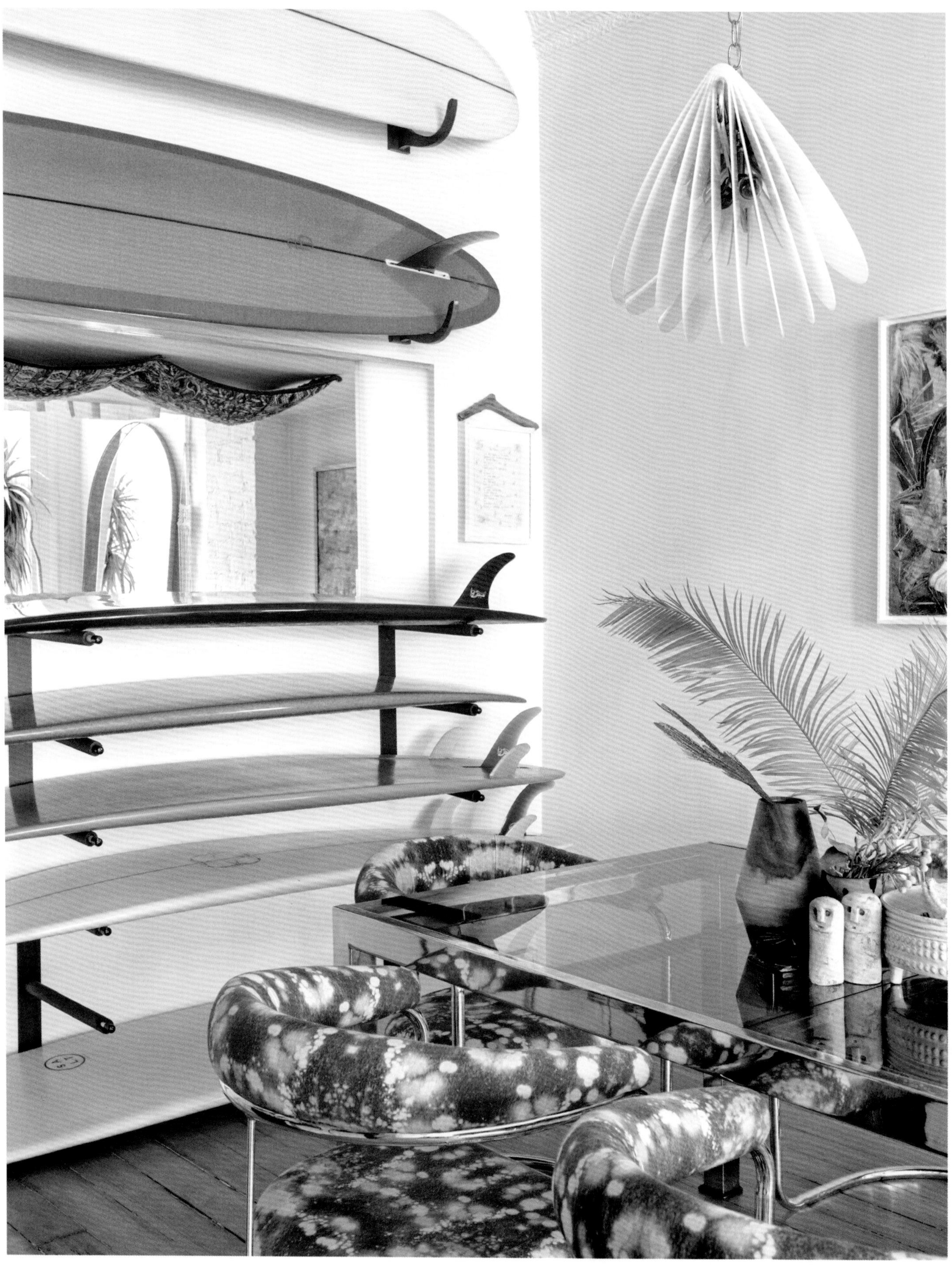

TONS OF COLOR

Shanan fell in love with color at an early age in a painting class and has been drawn to it ever since. She feels that color "just appears" in their home, and Nick doesn't shy away from it either. Her approach to decorating is to use piles of tints, tones, and shades, and then sprinkle in neutrals to balance things out. For instance, they recently acquired a large green credenza, but numerous plants act as neutrals to tone down the mint color of their new piece. She also tried to edit her colors to gradients of green and blue for a calm atmosphere rather than using reds and orange to bring out the blues. She also chose ultra-subtle neutral complements, like the soft, desaturated orange of book spines on the shelf to gently "pop" in the room.

DINING ROOM

Shanan and Nick love taking vintage furniture and reupholstering it in their fabrics for a personal touch. Their dining chairs are a perfect example, and they lend a unique yet cohesive look to their eating area, complete with surfboard décor that carries the ocean vibe throughout the breezy space. The chair pattern also lends movement and life to the area, which allows it to feel open and welcoming for home-cooked meals and casual gatherings with friends and family. Yet, she still maintains a cohesive color story with soft, neutral complements on the underside of the surfboard, which tie into the orange book spines from the living room. Overall, the transformation of this home from office space to flowing, organic home is natural and inspiring, just like the homeowners themselves.

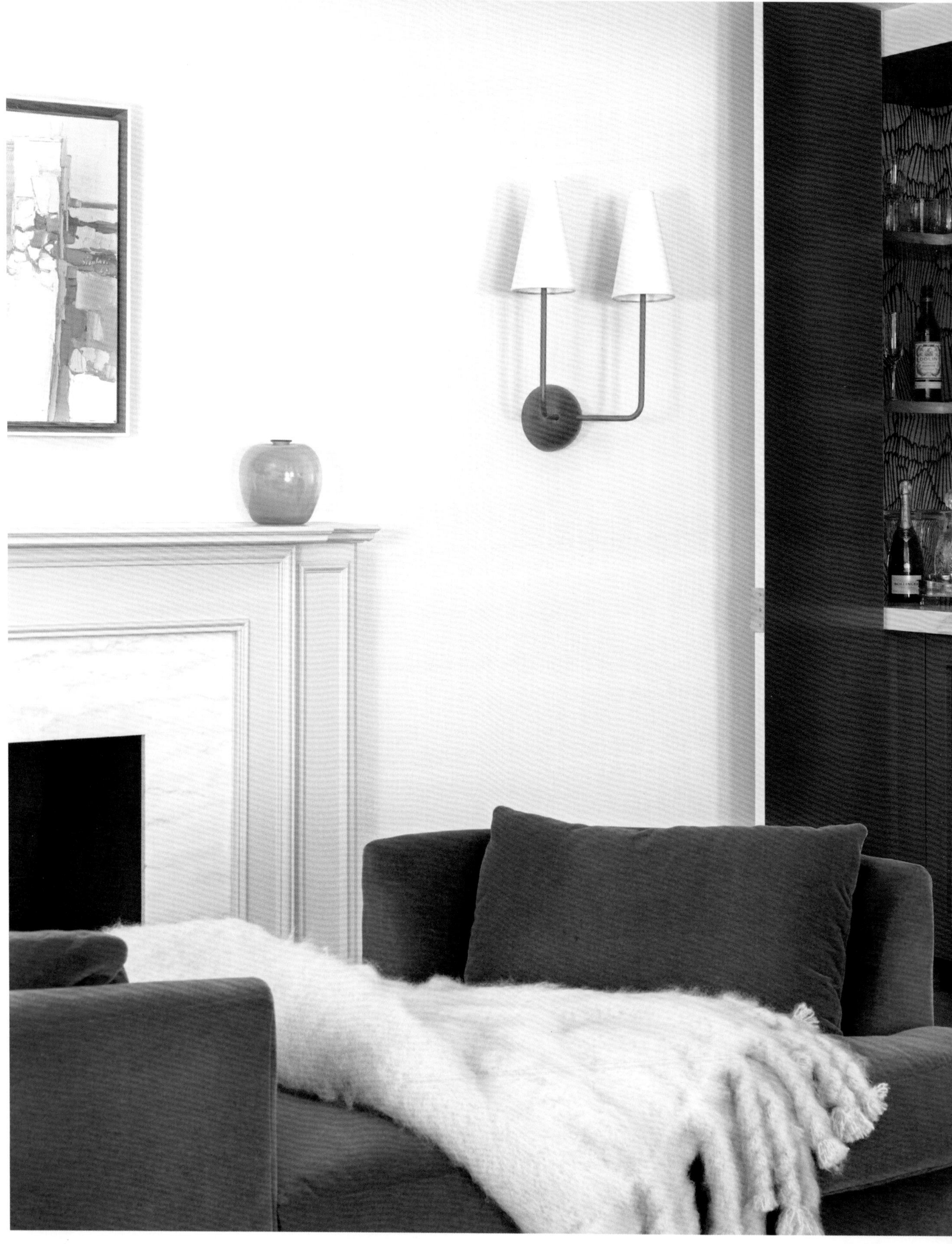
DOLIN

CONNECT WITH COLOR

BRITT ZUNINO
Interior Designer
with Studio DB

Britt Zunino and her husband, Damian, founded their interior design firm, Studio DB, on the principle that the most interesting homes are the ones that show the true character of the occupant, not the designer or the architect. While Britt and Damian impart their own vision to a space, each project speaks foremost to the clients' individuality. They believe their job is to create a cohesive vision for a space and to enhance the positive while editing the choices. The most important question they ask clients when beginning to design a space is "What's your favorite color?" Then they inquire as to how the client envisions using the room. For instance, should it be invigorating and playful? Or calm and soothing? When the program includes all the above, they must find a common thread to connect the home, and in that endeavor, color often plays the starring role.

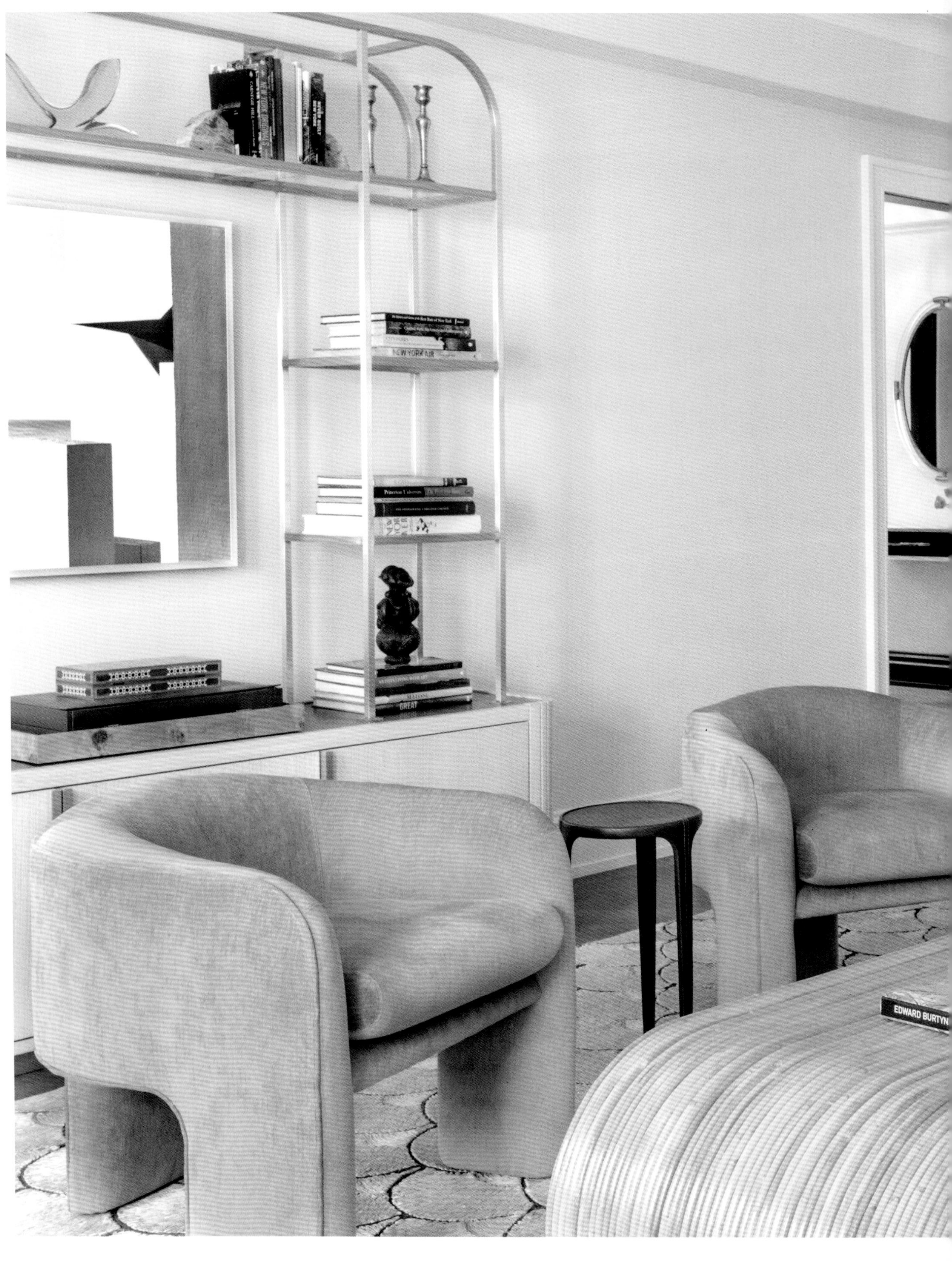
NEW YORK AIR
EDWARD BURTYN

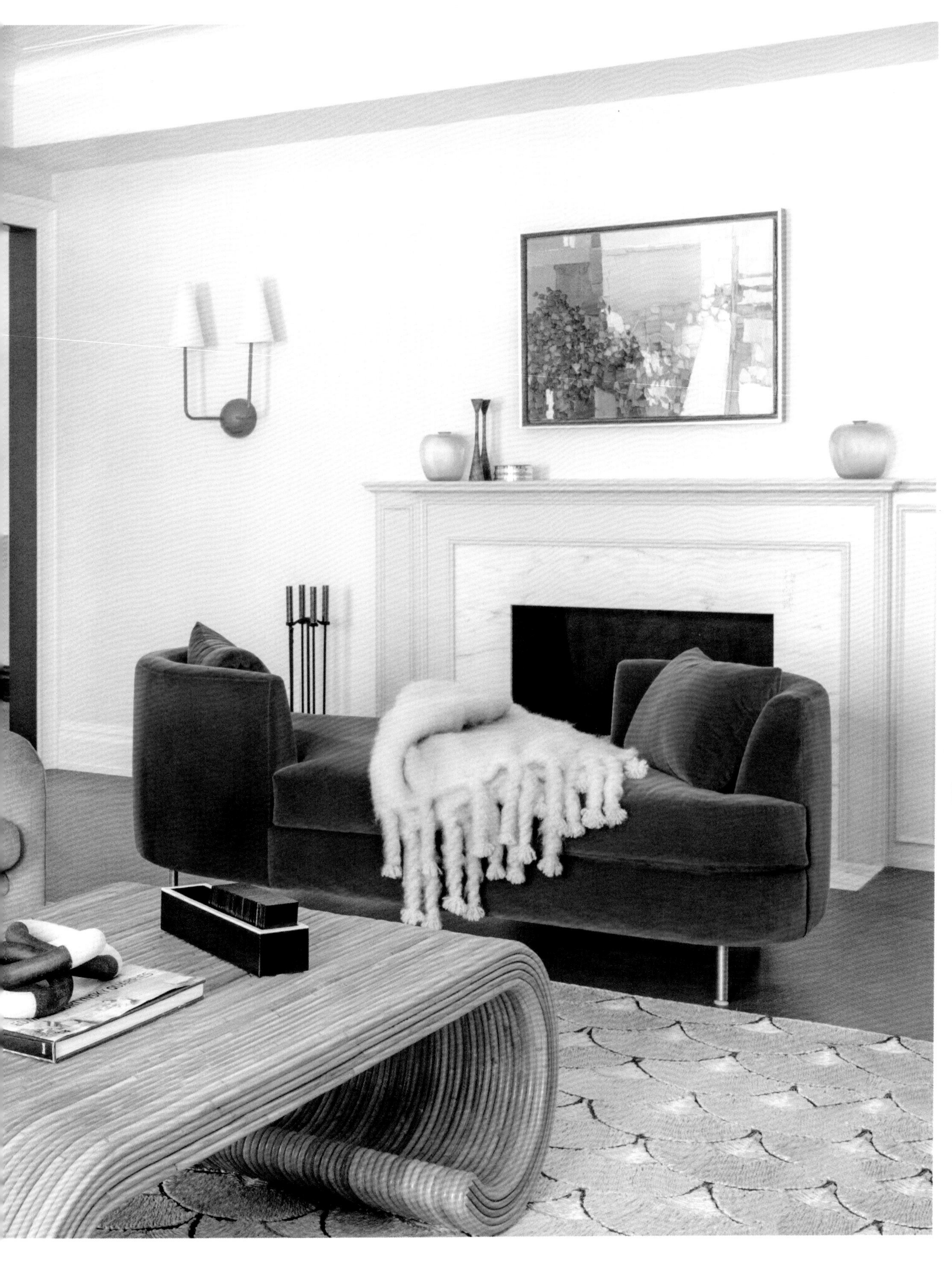

PALETTE ANCHOR

When they first met the clients for this project—a lovely Southern couple tasking them with renovating and furnishing a New York City apartment that would be functional for themselves, their two children, and a dog—color was at the center of the discussion. "Color sets the mood for every space," says Britt. "With a coat of paint or a new upholstery fabric, you can transform your entire experience of a room." The clients wanted a lighter, brighter space without the addition of recessed lighting, as well as a more cohesive flow from room to room. For Britt, that meant editing down the pieces already in the space, while keeping each room unique. "We started by paring back the colors in the old apartment and introducing lighter and brighter neutrals, but really it all went back to the amazing de Gournay mural," says Britt. The mural had been an early find for the dining room, and they used it as a palette anchor. "It was an incredible place to start," Britt adds. "You need a springboard."

For anyone undertaking a renovation project, Britt suggests using art to drive a palette, as well as taking in the architecture and outdoors. "I like to mix cooler colors with warmer woods," she says, "and since our home upstate is essentially a glass box, we must consider the role that our outside environment plays." She takes her inspiration from nature and fashion, and is forever walking the line between a space that feels fresh and new but not trendy. That is why she emphasizes the importance of a room that reflects personal taste, thoughtfulness, and a general sense of the colors and surroundings that make the homeowner happy. "Own it if you love it," she advises, "despite a shift in cultural taste."

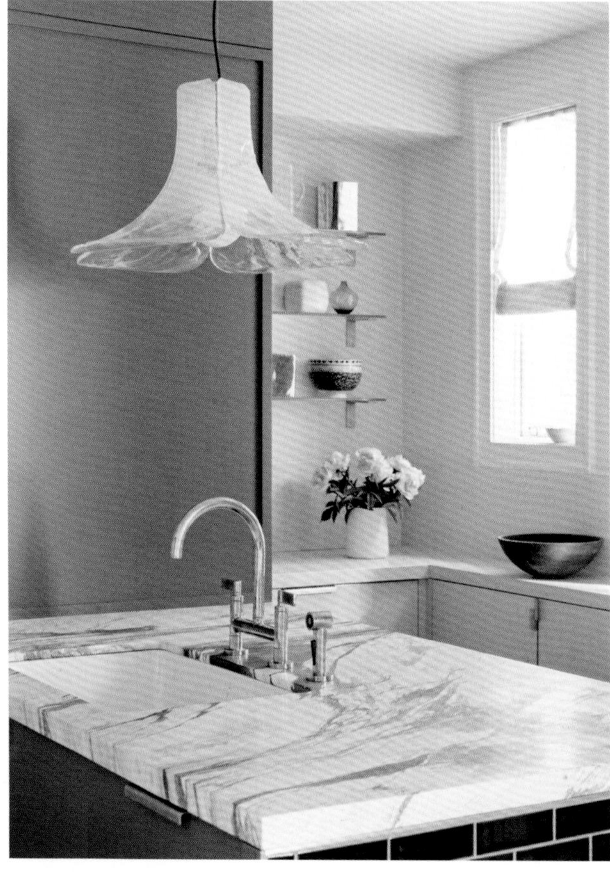

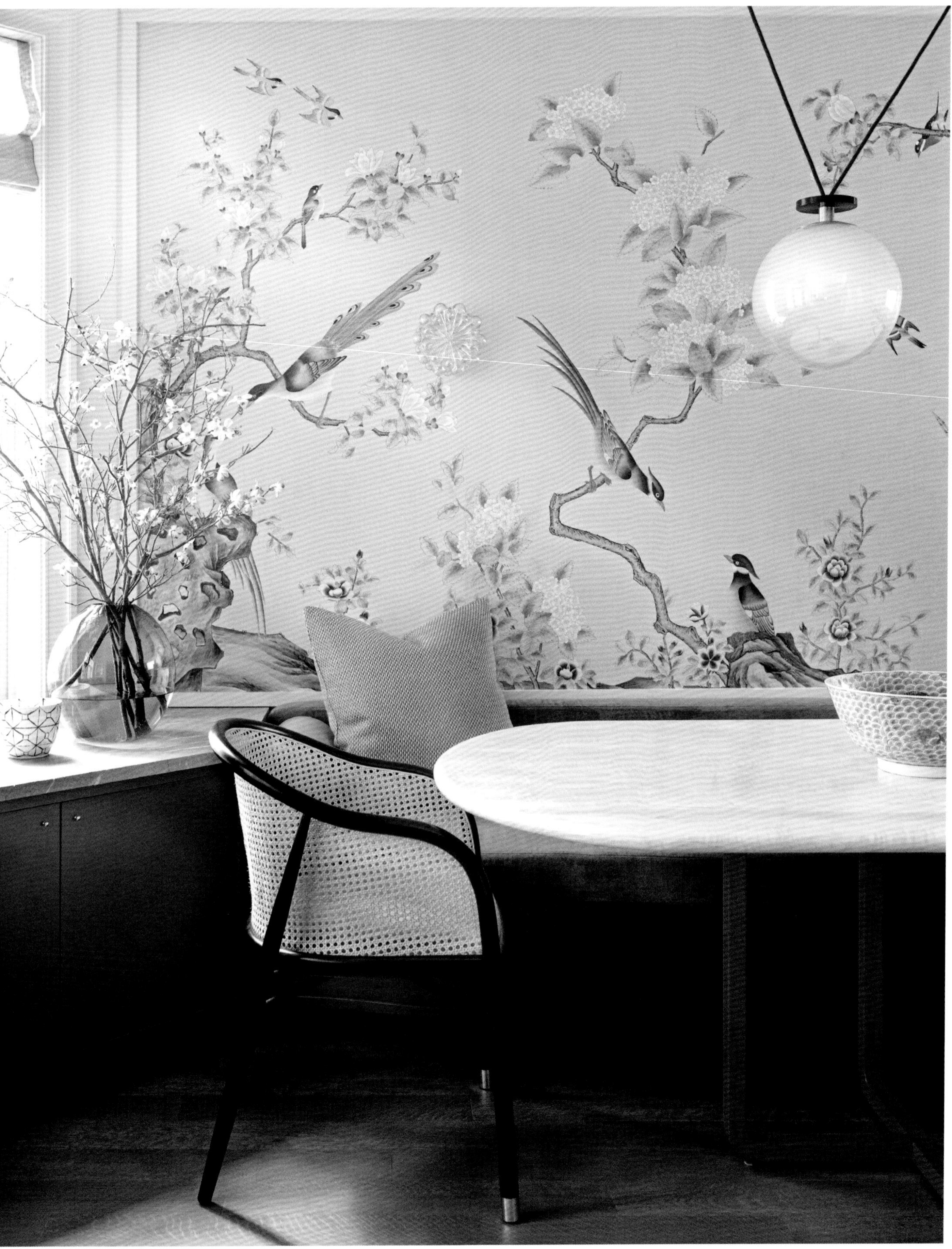

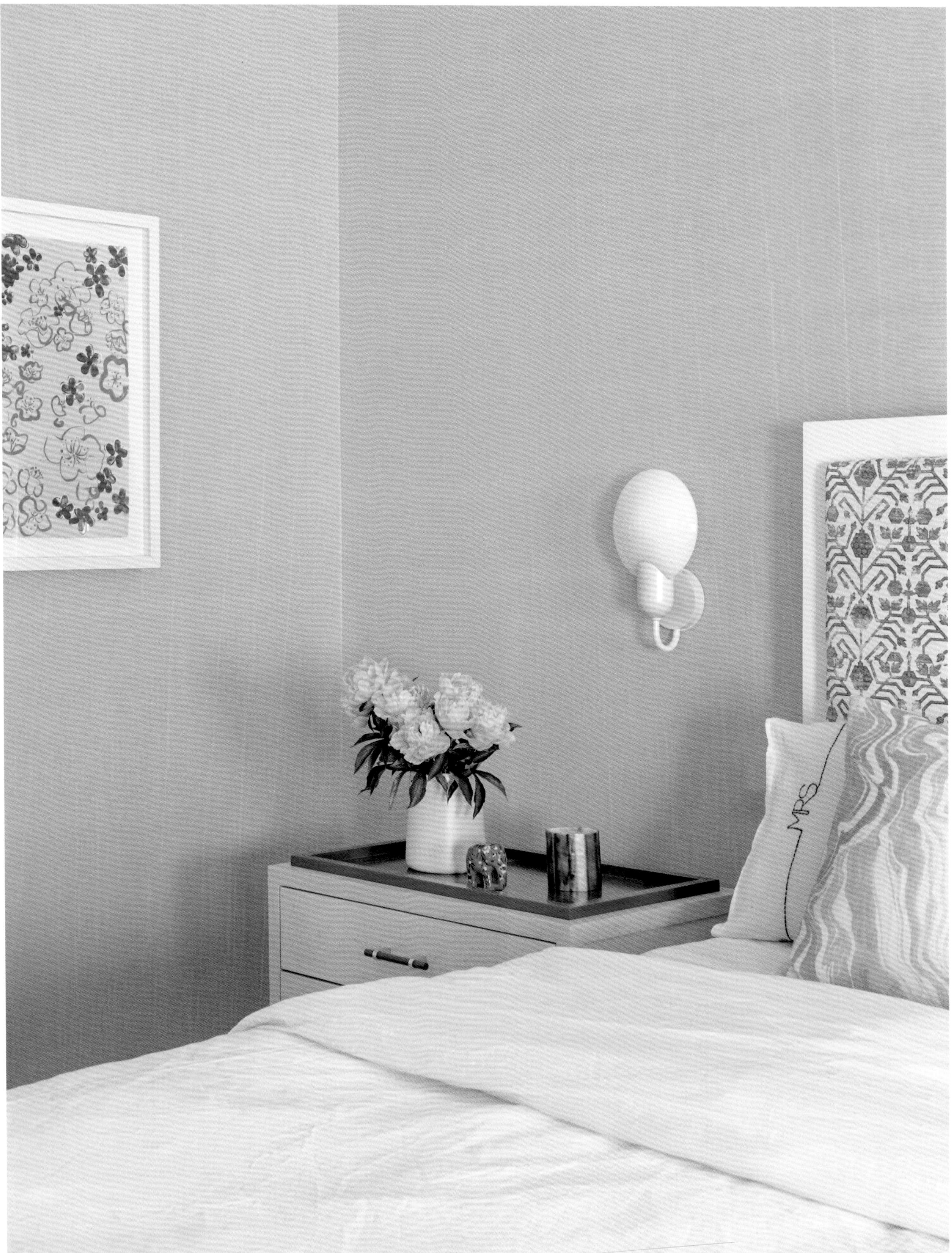
MRS

COLOR COMPLEXITY

From the perspective of a designer who chooses colors for her clients, Britt is particularly interested in the study of humans' biological versus cultural response to color. "It is very complex, and I'd love to learn more about it," she says. While she knows to use calming colors like blues when her clients request a room that makes them feel peaceful, she is also aware that color is personal and she must uncover her clients' individual color associations to understand how those will affect their feelings toward a room she designs. She is fascinated by the psychology of how our exposure to certain experiences influences our desire to live in specific environments. "Color can create a very emotional reaction to a space," she adds, "which I find so interesting."

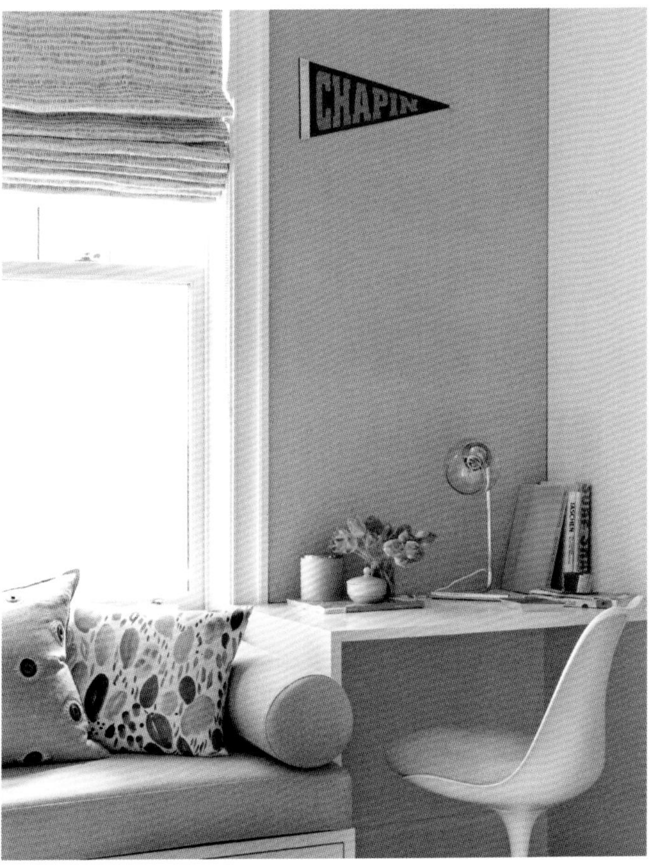

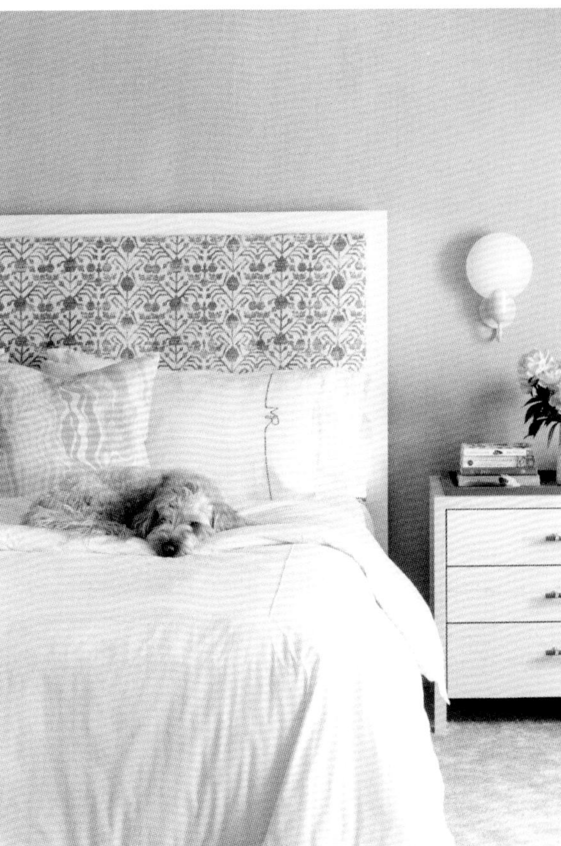

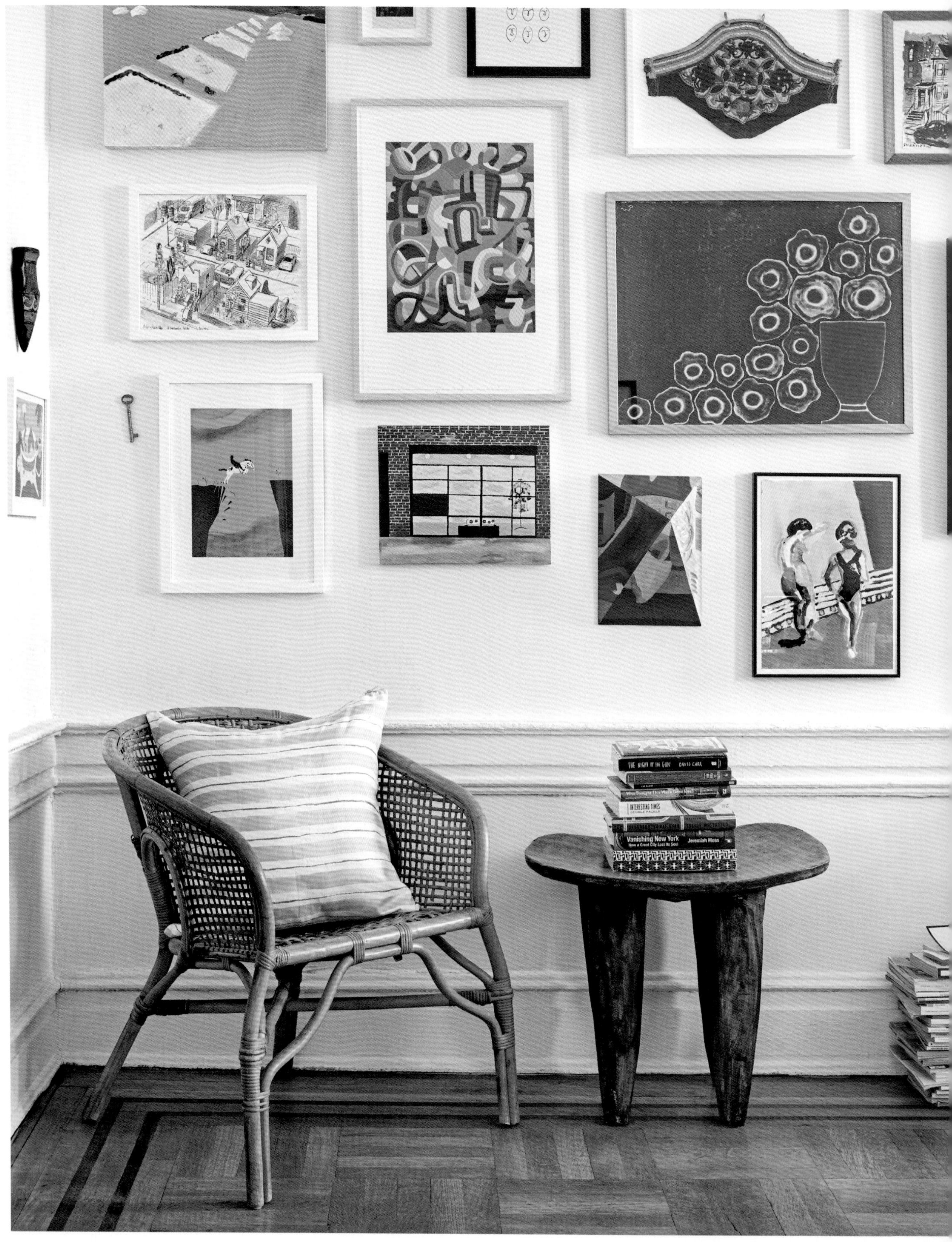
THE NIGHT OF THE GUN DAVID CARR
Who Thought This Was a Good Idea?
INTERESTING TIMES
GEORGE PACKER
Vanishing New York
How a Great City Lost Its Soul
Jeremiah Moss

TEXTILE LOVE

MAURI WEAKLEY
Owner, Collyer's Mansion

From vintage-clothing stores to flea markets to estate sale finds, Mauri Weakley is inspired by everything old made new again. This is clear in her choices as shop owner of the store Collyer's Mansion on Atlantic Avenue in Brooklyn and in her home. Both spaces are filled with lovely, colorful furniture and prints for the home, and both come from a unique point of view. Mauri grew up in Tennessee; her mother was a seamstress, often sewing costumes for Mauri and custom pieces for others' homes. She also hails from a long line of quilters on one side, and women who created custom window treatments, cushions, and bedding on the other, so you could say patchwork is in the blood. For this reason, textiles are her favorite aspect of home décor.

Naturally, she also finds the most interesting part of a vintage-clothing collection to be the prints and the fabric designs. "The color palettes in vintage clothing are often unusual and playful," she says. Her creativity is similarly ignited when she tours historic homes with lots of wallpaper and printed upholstery. "The way they decorated and really created a room, oftentimes with very bold color and upholstery, is really inspiring," she says. "I always think of how I can use this as inspiration to make [my own home] feel current and timeless." Mauri is clearly a collector, as is evident in her wall of art. She's always adding new pieces and finding a different spot for a piece she's had for a long time. Simply moving things around can give them new life.

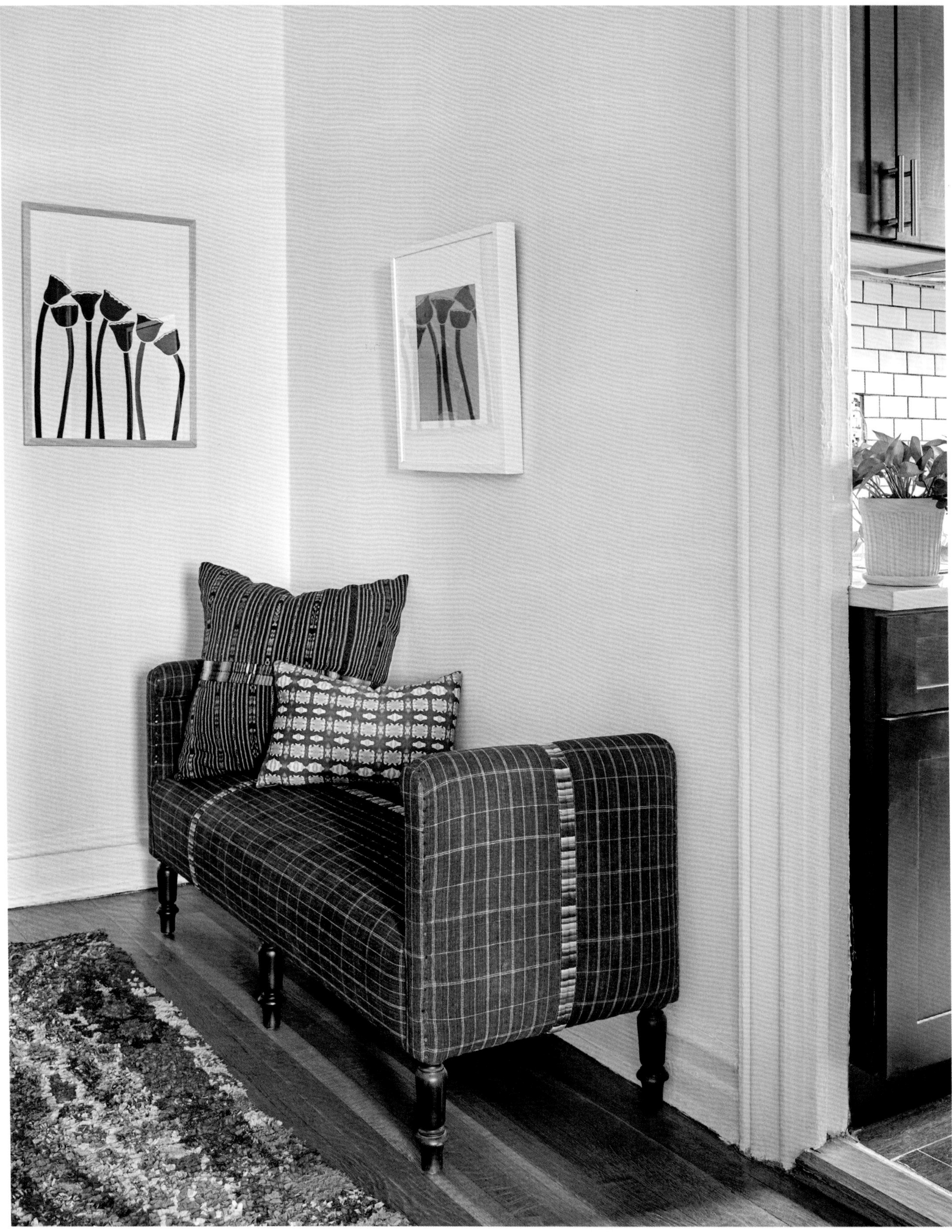

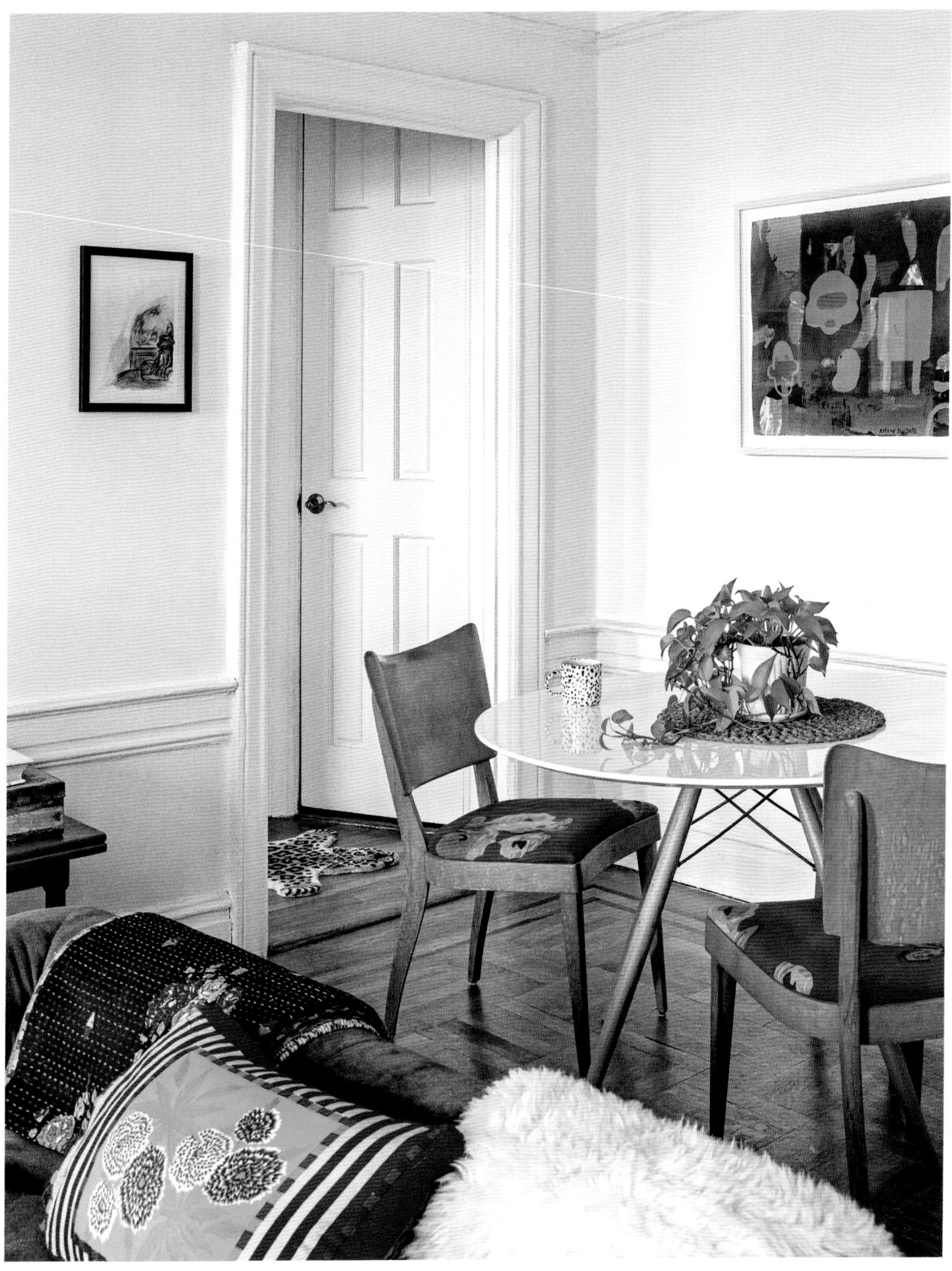

ORGANIC LAYERS

Mauri's apartment is in a big, old building in Ditmas Park, Brooklyn, so it certainly has vintage charm, but it is also on a corner, so it has lots of windows and great natural light, which is a luxury in New York. For that reason, she often photographs objects for her shop in her home, which means it's constantly in flux. "The top layer of objects in my home, like pillows, artwork, throws, and accessories, is always getting moved around or rearranged," she says.

To ensure that her space feels organic even as she inserts new items, she starts with the bones of a room and lets them guide her in adding furniture and accents. Then she thinks in terms of layers. "I create a furniture arrangement I like best that feels the most functional and aesthetically pleasing for that room, and then I begin layering in things like throw blankets, lamps and decorative pillows," she explains. Then she simply moves small objects from room to room to make the space feel new and fresh, or works in new objects, but the bottom layers remain a solid base.

This home is a great example of an apartment where there's a neutral foundation—white walls—and the artwork, pillows, textiles, and accessories provide color and keep things fresh. Though this is a common practice, Maura's home illustrates it perfectly and shows you how to stay within your comfort zone but still have a home with a very distinctive, colorful, and personal perspective.

For instance, the pillows in her home have been collected over time, and they work together because she likes them, and because she's so sure of her own taste and style. She simply embraced what she loved and then brought in the multicolored painting in her living room to pull all of the colors together. You'll notice that green is the most prominent color in the painting, but she pulls out the less prominent colors for the rest of the room. The colors don't have to perfectly match, just relate. It's more about looking at an entire room when designing or adding something and making it a balanced composition, as in Mauri's rooms.

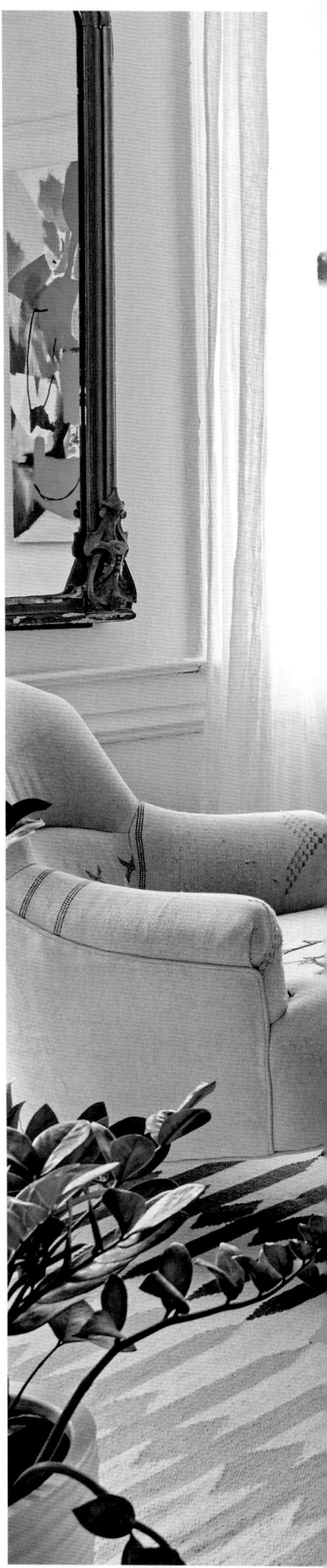

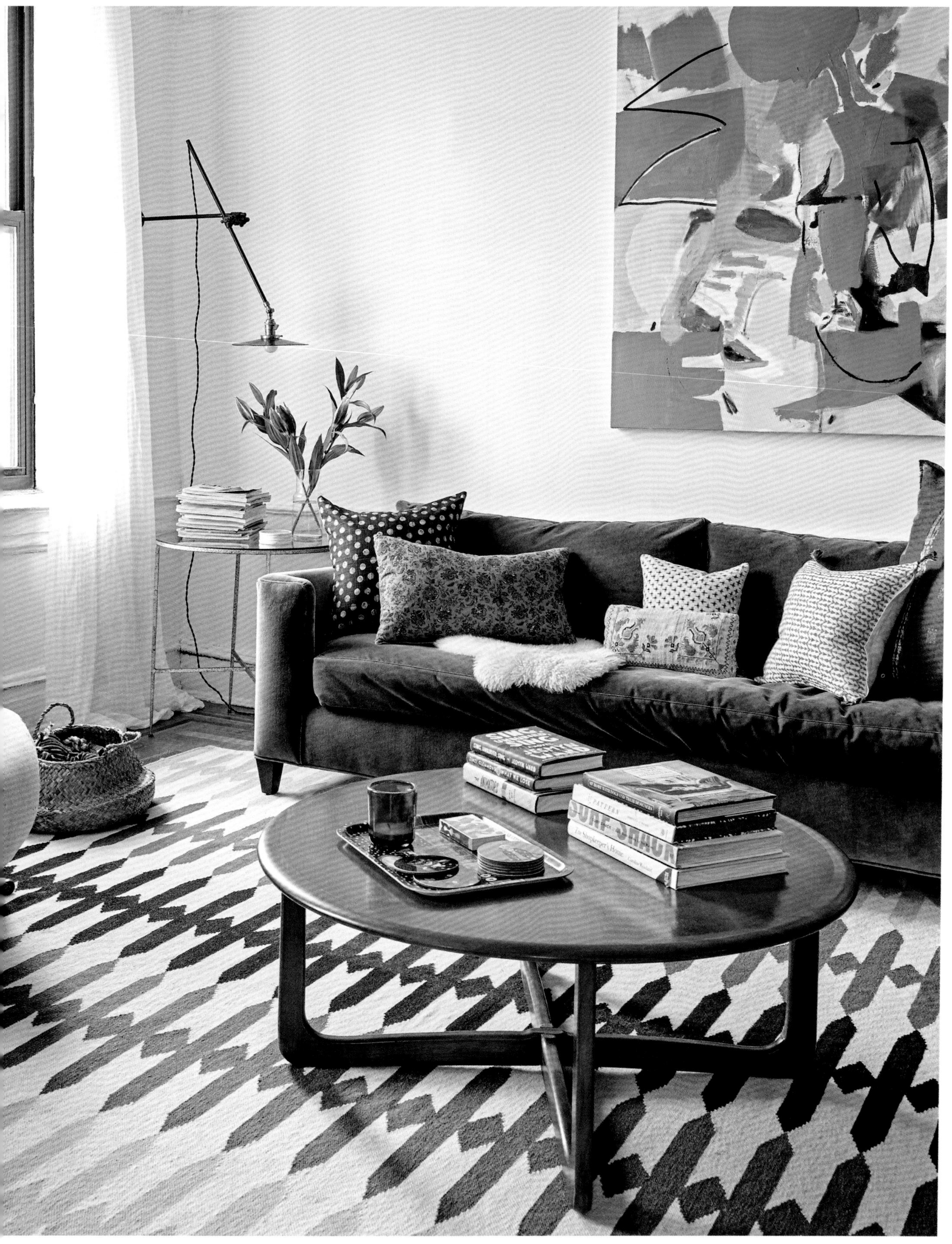
SING, UNBURIED, SING
JESMYN WARD
WHAT WE LOSE
PATTERN
SURF SHACK
The Shopkeeper's House

MAKE IT YOUR OWN

- Let a multicolored piece of art be the starting point for your color palette. Picking up on less prominent colors in the painting can make the space feel more unified.
- Don't be afraid to mix patterns. Look for interesting textiles you love and make them into pillow covers or upholster a chair with them.

CONNECTING COLOR

Her bedroom is just as layered but a little more subdued, using mostly blues and greens. The decorative pillow brings in a pop of pink that freshens the room. It doesn't seem disconnected because of the artwork on the walls, which have some earthy, warm tones, and also the color she uses in the adjacent living room. Consider color flow throughout the home. Color choices are most cohesive when they have some connection to one another but are used in interchanging ways in different spaces.

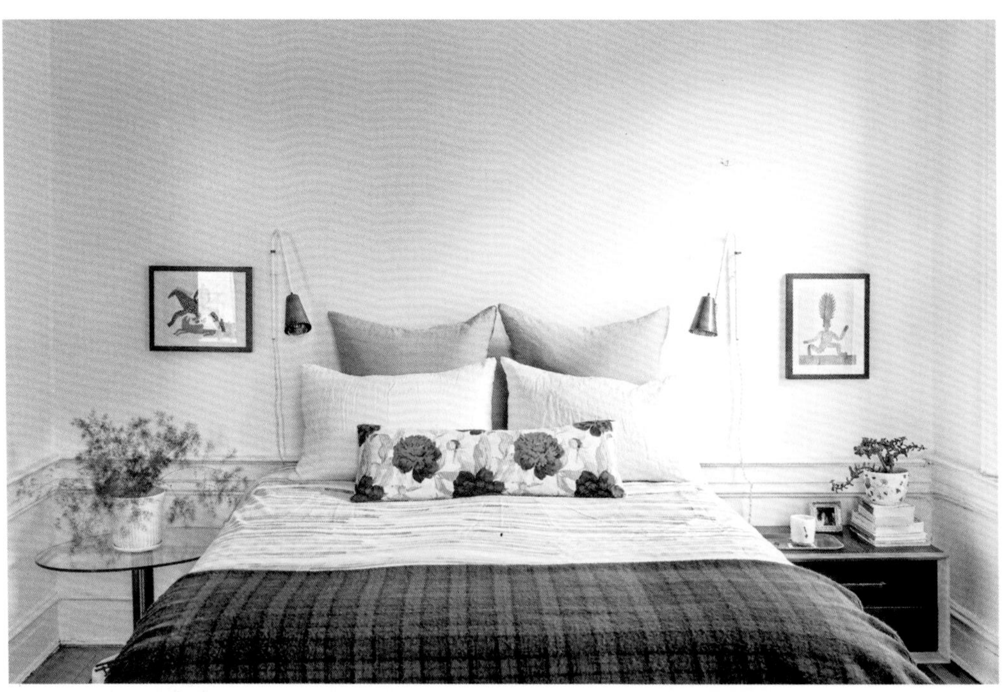

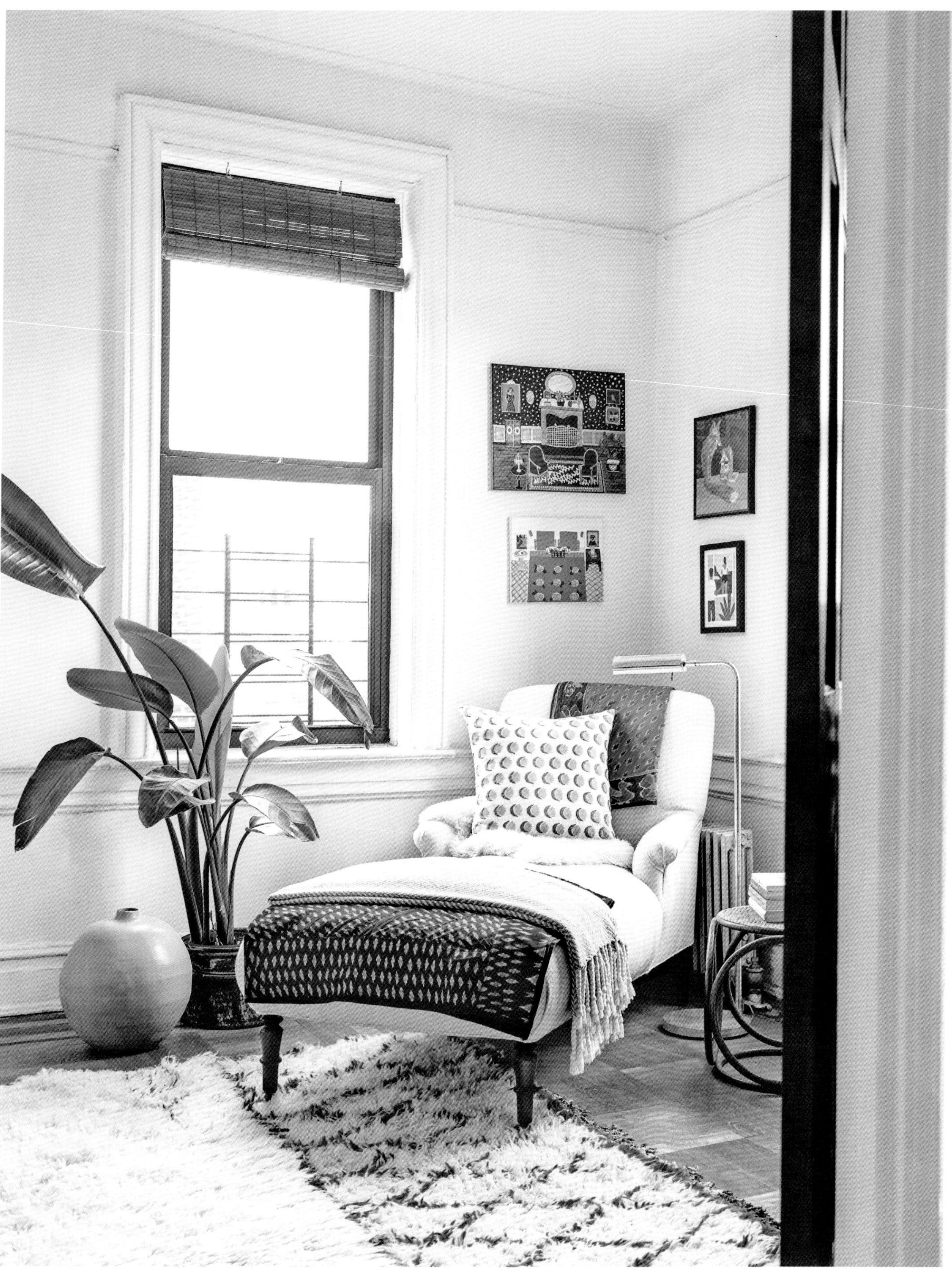

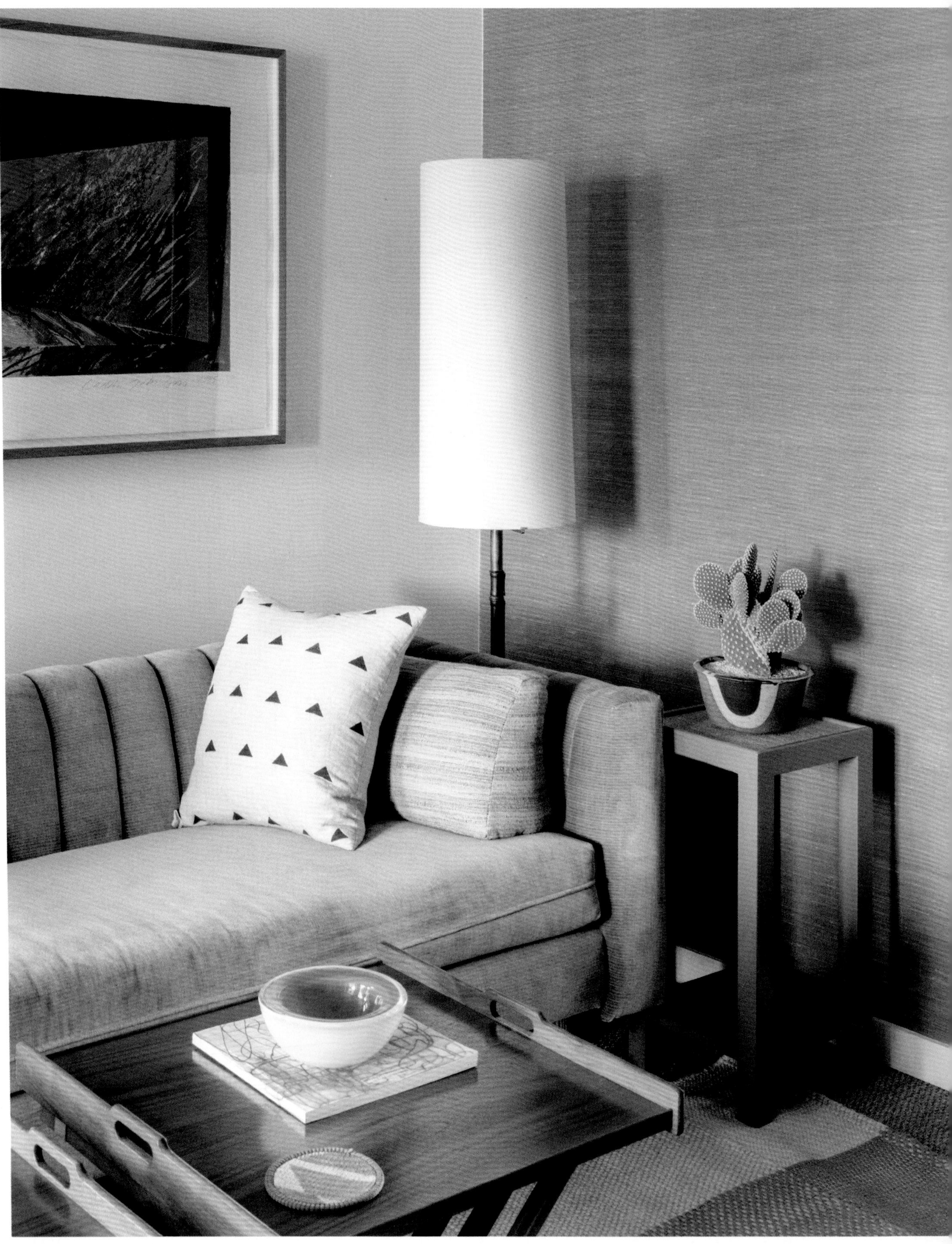

CALIFORNIA COOL

GRANT WILLIAM FENNING
Furniture Designer/ Shop Owner, Lawson-Fenning

Grant Fenning is the co-founder of Lawson-Fenning, one of the most inspiring home shops in Los Angeles, and when he's asked to describe what home means to him, "privacy, peace, and comfort" are the words he uses. They clearly capture the vibe of the laid-back California home he shares with his partner, Nicolas. Built in the 1940s, their Los Feliz house was an early prefab concept design called the California Cabin. They purchased the property in 2010 and spent over a year renovating it, but they kept the original compact pitched roof and beams. Positioned atop a steep hillside, the distinct dwelling features unique structural Y-shaped upright posts that are left exposed in most of the open floor plan. "It lives a bit like a tree house," says Grant, in a nod to the entire back of the house, which comprises windows that look out onto their densely forested yard.

This cue from nature informs many of Grant's design decisions, and he often draws on a color scheme from the natural world. Greens, blues, grays, and medium-brown wood tones with highlights of muted red and yellow ochre feature prominently in the upstairs, while downstairs it's a bit warmer and cozier with lighter wood tones. Grant describes all of his color decisions a as "emotional and instinctual, because this is my home."

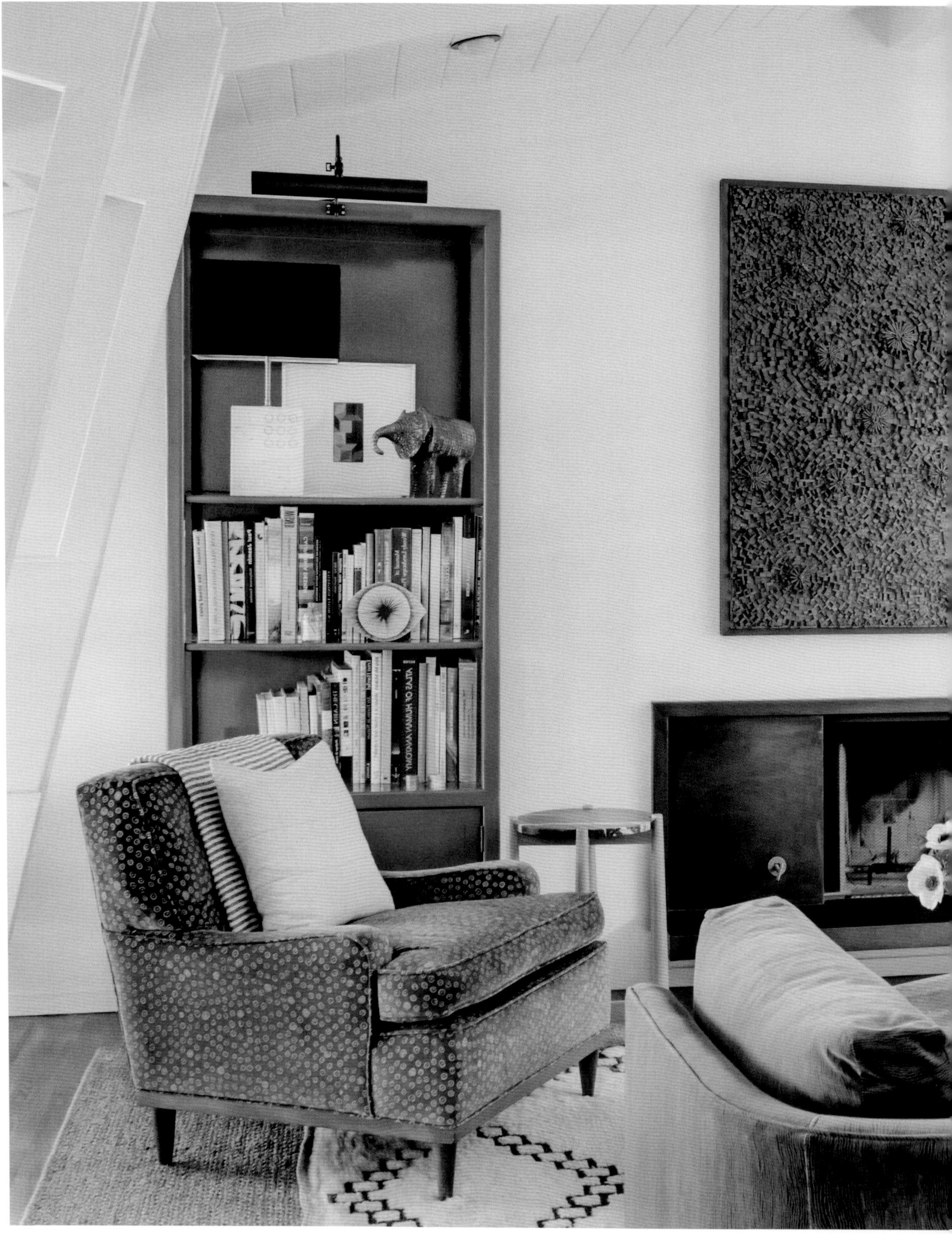
THE CABIN
ATLAS OF HUMAN ANATOMY

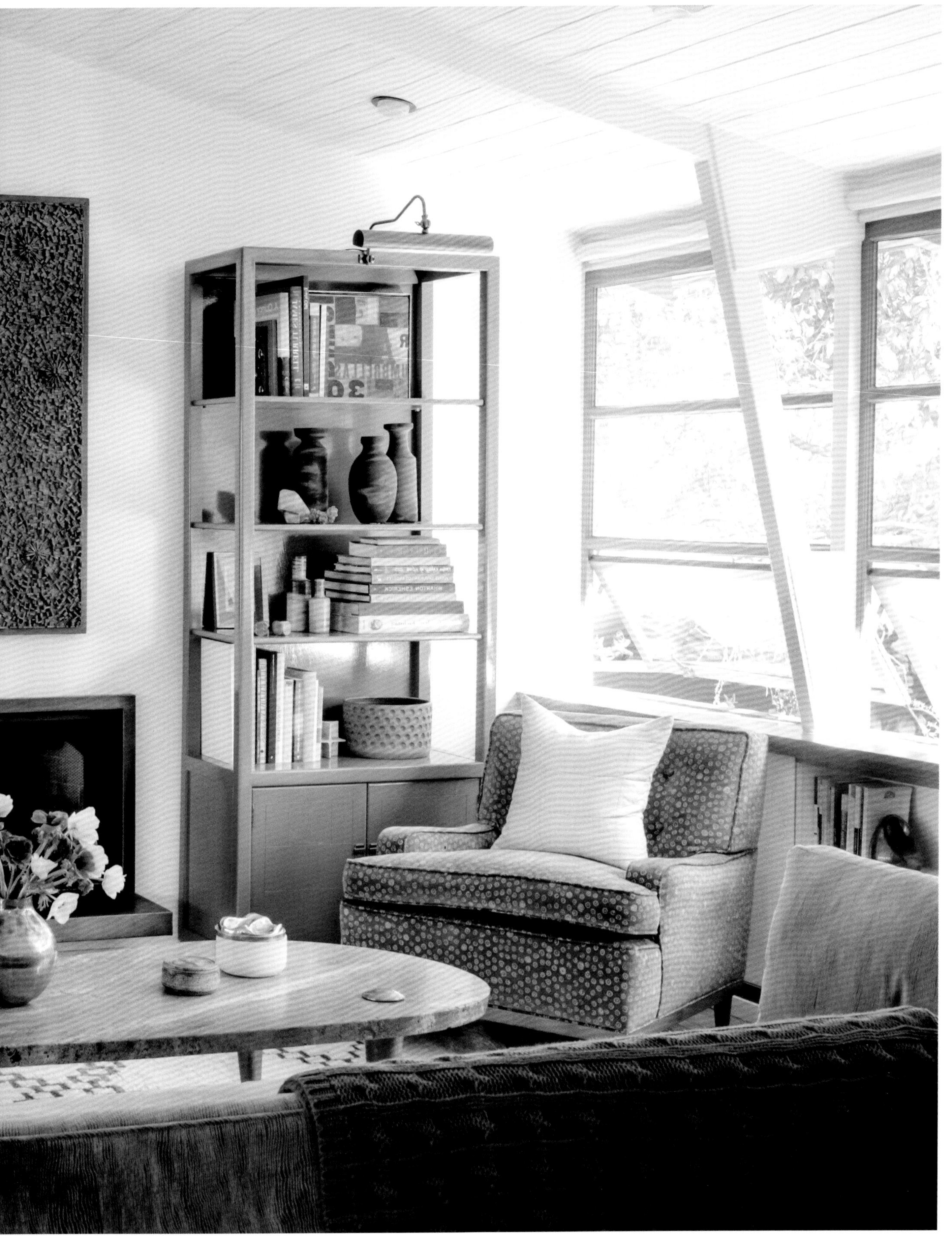

COLOR STRATEGY

Grant's living room reads primarily as neutral, but two vibrant emerald-green bookshelves give it energy. The upholstery fabrics on the sofa and chairs pick up on this hue with a subtle green tint. Throughout Grant's home, you'll see a strategic use of color. It's thoughtful and intentional. A rich hue, in a beautiful finish, can effortlessly add impact.

The pop of red you see here on the dining chairs is just enough to add vibrancy to a mostly neutral space. The warm wood acts as a connector color so that the red works in the space and doesn't feel out of place. Consider smaller touches like this for bringing in unexpected color.

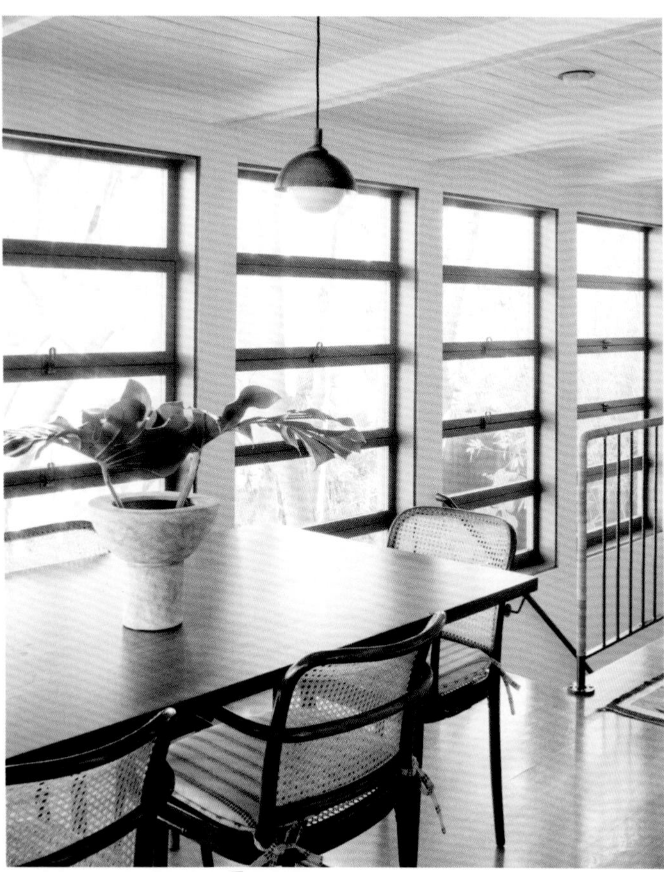

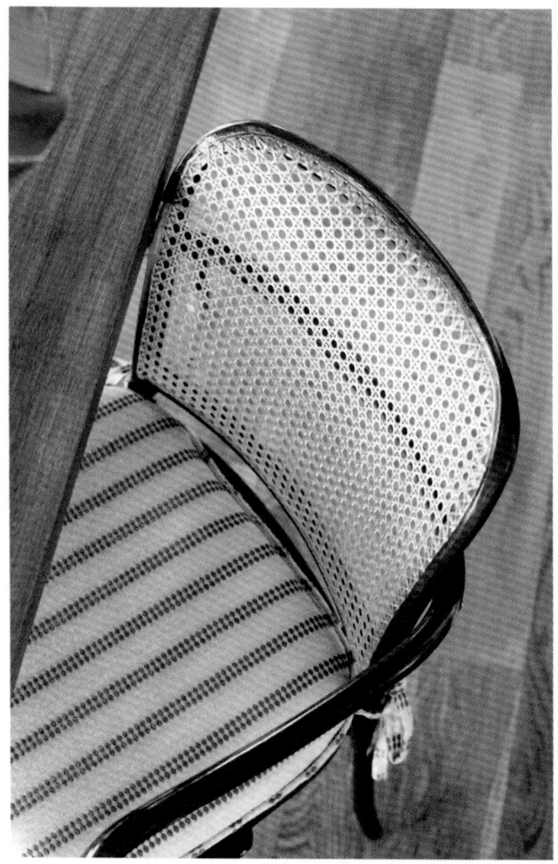

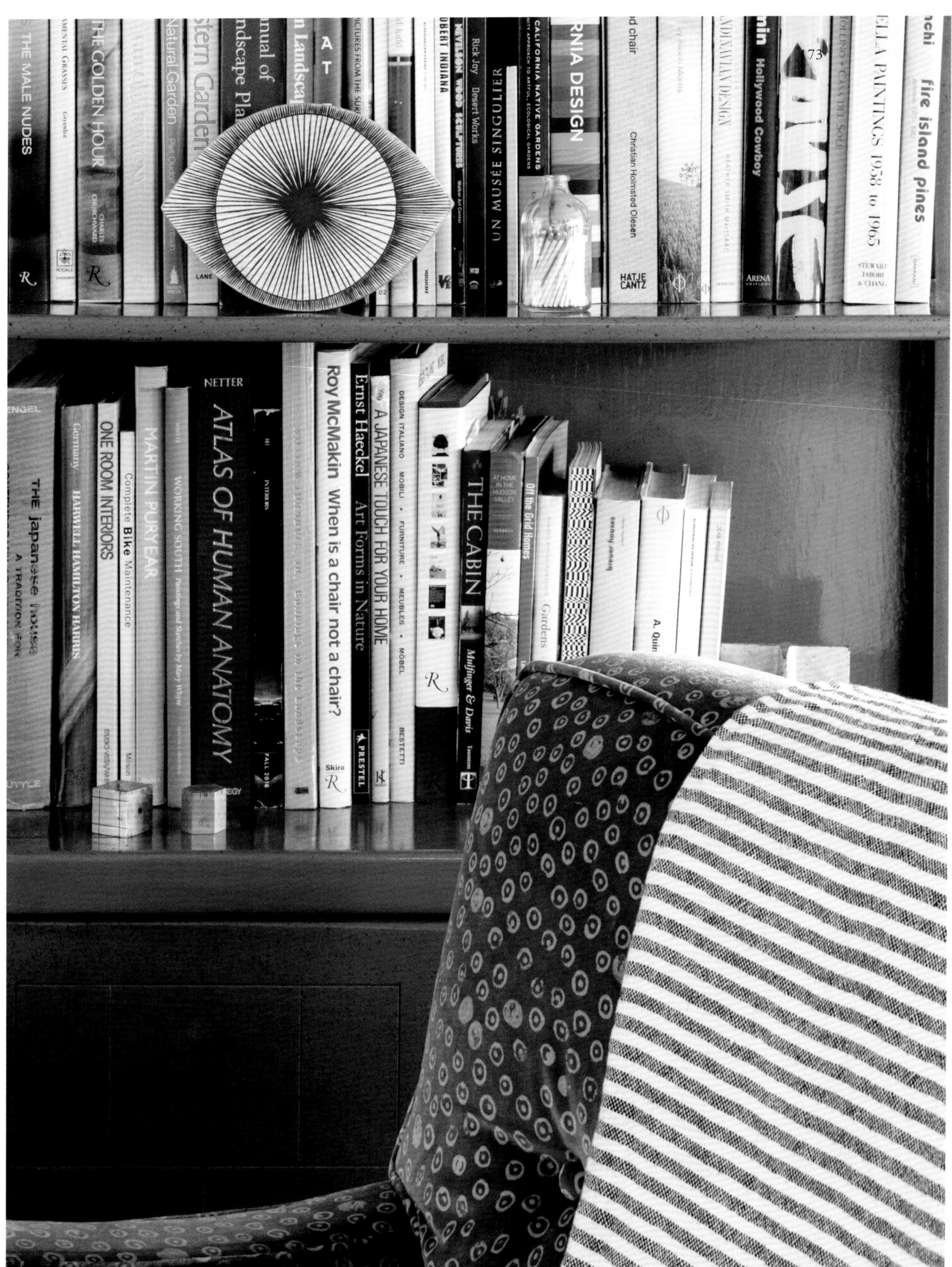

THE MALE NUDES
THE GOLDEN HOUR
NEVELSON WOOD SCULPTURES
Walker Art Center
Rick Joy Desert Works
UN MUSÉE SINGULIER
CALIFORNIA NATIVE GARDENS
Christian Holmsted Olesen
HATJE CANTZ
HEATHER SMITH MacISAAC
Hollywood Cowboy
ARENA
PAINTINGS 1958 to 1965
STEWART TABORI & CHANG
fire island pines
ENGEL
THE japanese house
A TRADITION FOR
Germany
HARWELL HAMILTON HARRIS
ONE ROOM INTERIORS
Complete Bike Maintenance
MARTIN PURYEAR
WORKING SOUTH Paintings and Sketches by Mary Whyte
NETTER
ATLAS OF HUMAN ANATOMY
INTERIORS
FALL 2016
Roy McMakin When is a chair not a chair?
Skira
Ernst Haeckel Art Forms in Nature
PRESTEL
A JAPANESE TOUCH FOR YOUR HOME
DESIGN ITALIANO MOBILI • FURNITURE • MEUBLES • MÖBEL
BESTETTI
THE CABIN
Mulfinger & Davis
Taunton
AT HOME IN THE HUDSON VALLEY
Off the Grid Homes
Gardens

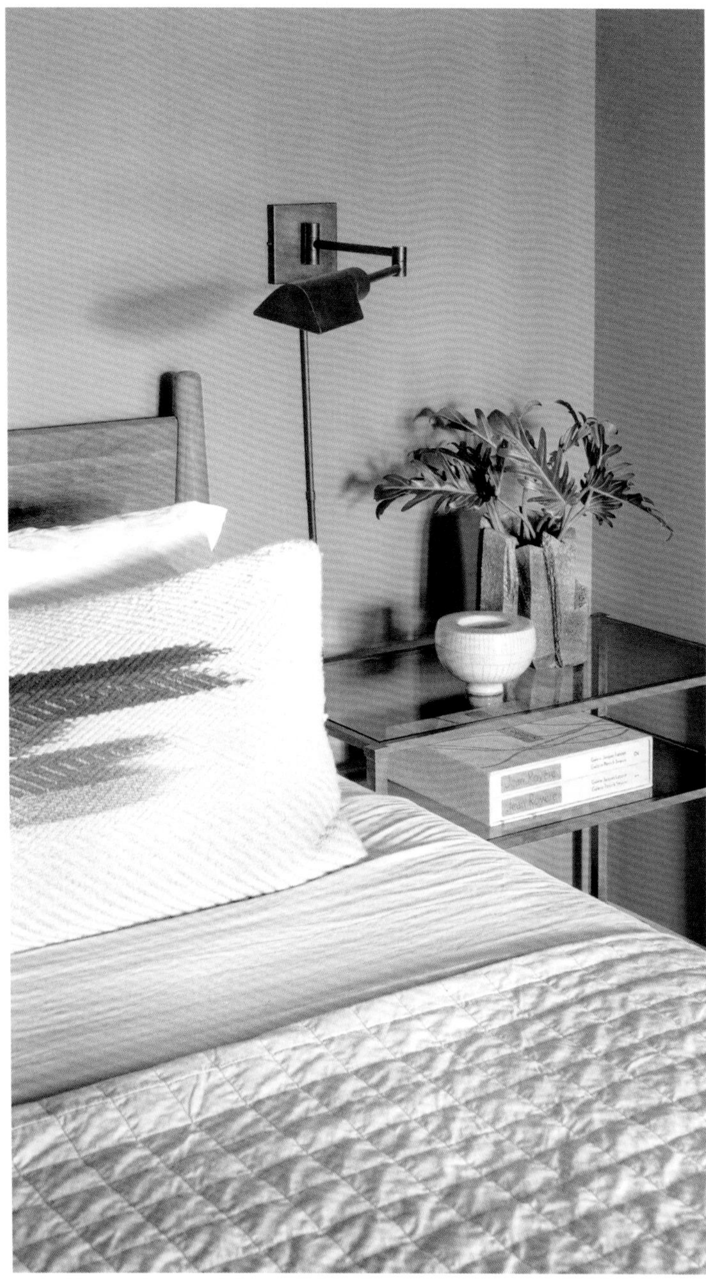

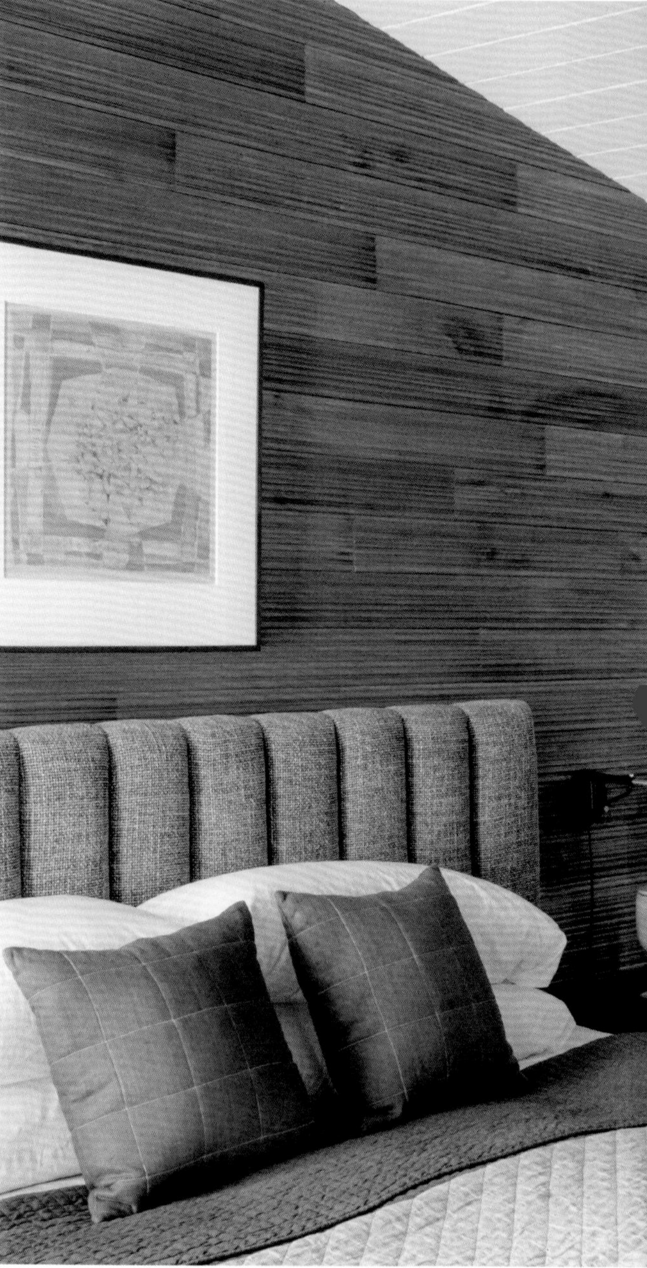

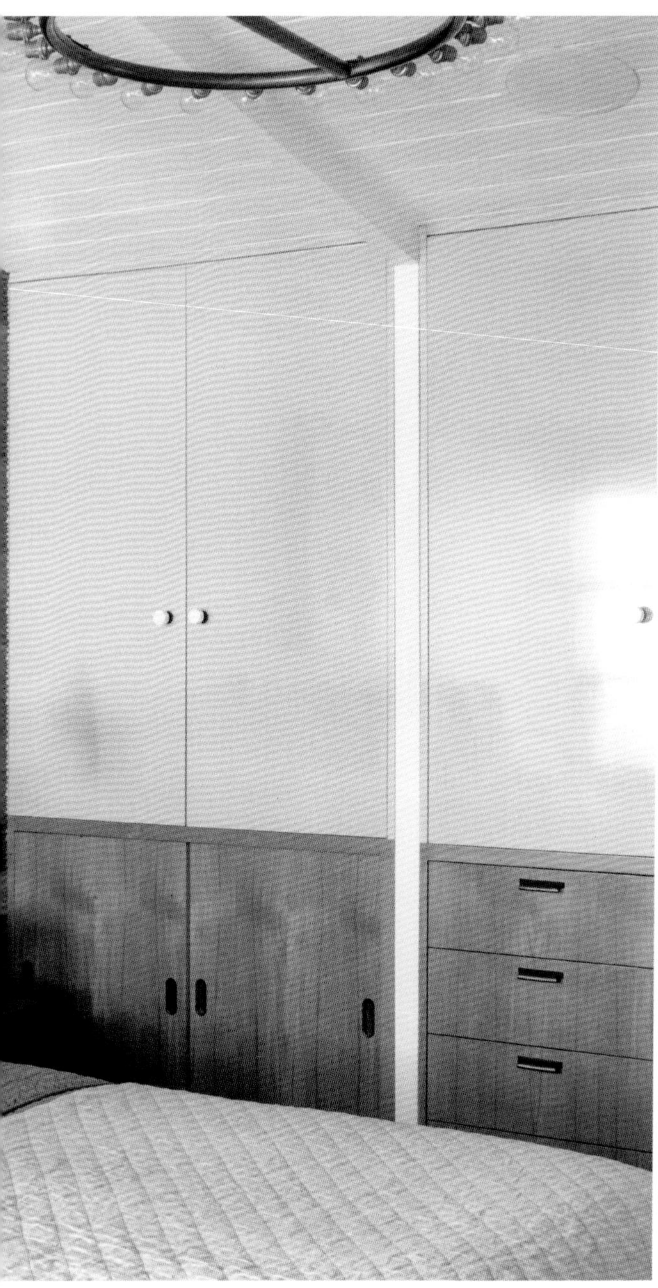

SUNNY BEDROOM

In the master bedroom, Grant chose calming colors—warm gray and dark wood—but also included yellow ochre polished lacquer closet doors because the color makes him feel happy and reminds him of one of his first design memories—his childhood bedroom. When he was young, he was permitted to decorate his own room; he chose an overscaled white-and-yellow checkerboard-pattern wallpaper for three walls, and on the fourth wall, he added orange cartoon cats and yellow birds. "I loved it until I didn't," he jokes. "When I was a teen, I convinced my mother to change it to a medium-gray leatherette paper." However, he still has an affinity for yellow, hence the closet doors in his current home, a friendly nod to his first foray into designing with color.

The guest bedroom plays with cool grays and a wash of bright sky-like blue. Both bedrooms are good examples of using color in a space intended for rest; the mix of neutrals is key to keeping the brighter colors grounded.

INFLUENCES AT HOME AND ABROAD

Though Grant grew up in a traditional redbrick colonial home in North Carolina, his mother and her decorator were very influenced by English designer David Hicks. "We lived with lots of color and pattern in a traditional home," says Grant. At some point, his parents also built a modern cedar-clad beach house on the coast of North Carolina; it had an origami roofline, and to this day, that remains his favorite house.

His own design influences stem from his travels and are the result of staying at properties that shift his worldview. "Last year after Milan Design Week, I took an inspirational trip to Lake Como, where I stayed at Patricia Urquiola's project, Il Sereno Hotel," says Grant. "I was very inspired by her use of color and materials. She took references from one of the most beautiful locations on the planet and created a palette that, to me, was as perfect as the place itself."

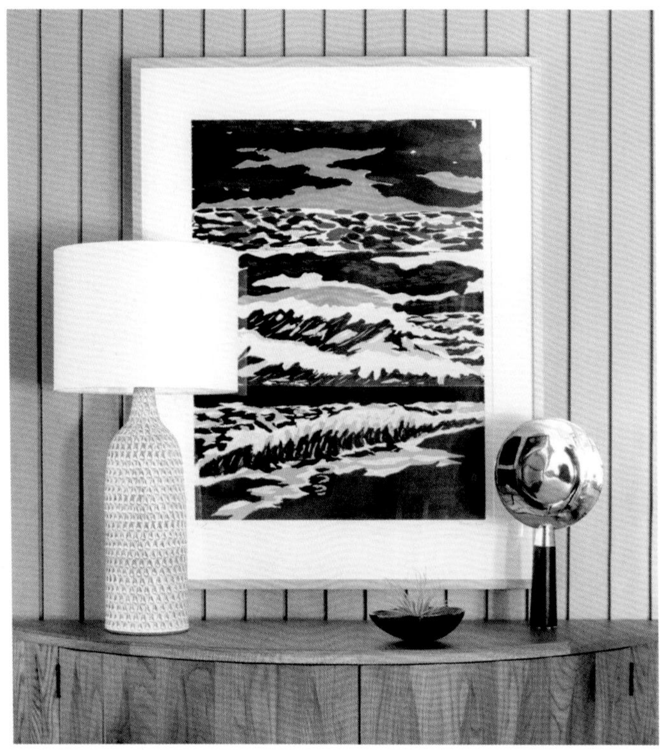

MAKE IT YOUR OWN

- Ground your space in interesting neutrals that are subtle colors: soft mossy green-gray fabrics, terra-cotta, grass cloth, lots of natural materials like sisal, and gray paint. Pay attention to your neutrals to help ground bolder pops of color.
- Choose a focal point in a room and use a rich hue for it. Pay attention to finish.
- Mix your wood finishes.

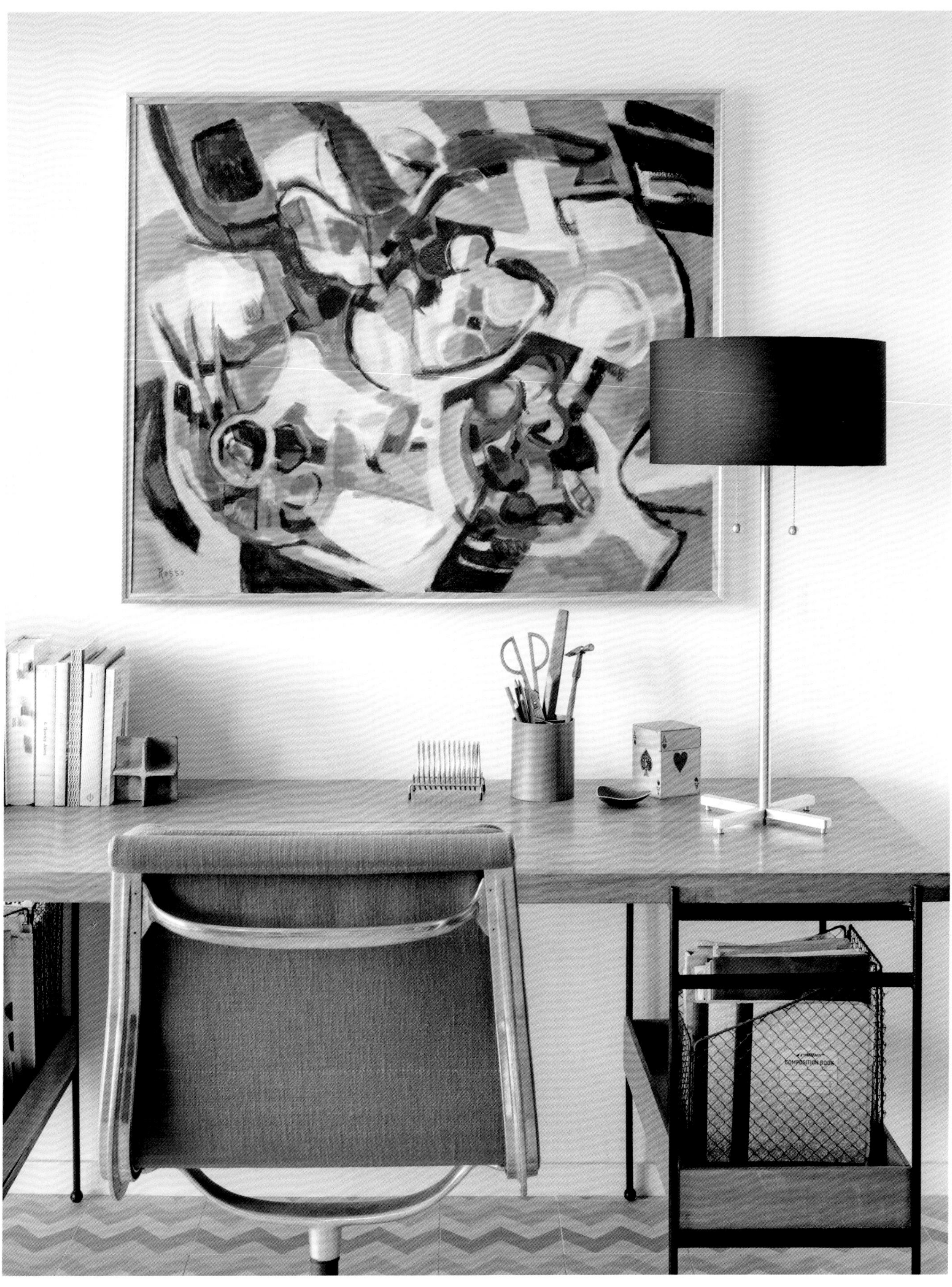
Rosso
COMPOSITION BOOK

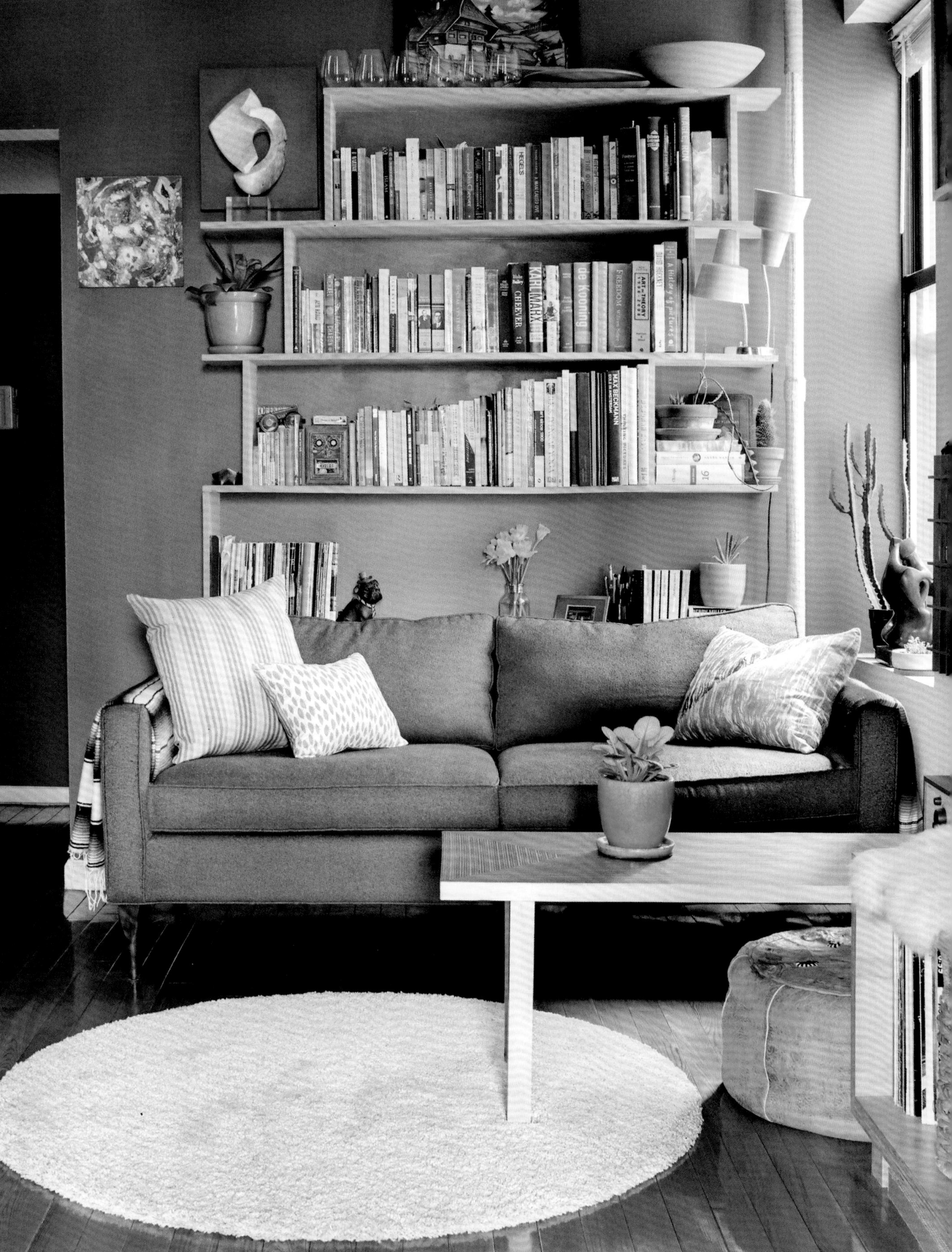
ISLAM
John Cheever
HEGELS
A MAN CALLED OVE
MICHAEL CHABON
CHEEVER
KARL MARX
de Kooning
FREEDOM
ART in THEORY 1900–2000
DAVID HOCKNEY
A history of pictures
MAX BECKMANN
THINKING PICTURES

TREEHOUSE IN THE CITY

CHARLOTTE HALLBERG
ERIC GONZALEZ
Artists

The idea for this Sunset Park, Brooklyn, apartment, home to Charlotte Halberg and her husband, Erik Gonzalez, was to create a pared-down midcentury-modern tree house look. The inspiration for such a dwelling dates back to 2012, when Charlotte had an art show in Philadelphia and visited the gallery where her work would be on display. One of the gallerists lived in a large industrial apartment in which one room, aside from a sofa and coffee table, was entirely filled with plants, floor to ceiling. "The whole room felt green," says Charlotte. She loved that feeling in the middle of a city, where there is often so little green. After that she made a conscious effort to bring more green into her home, in both plant and non-plant form.

Because the living room is the place in the house that gets the least amount of natural light, Charlotte wasn't able to bring in plants, so the green sofa felt like a stand-in for that element of nature. Then, using the sofa as a jumping-off point to anchor their room, they chose analogous accent colors in saturated blues, chromatic greens, and natural warm yellow materials to fill the room around it. Their sofa area is where they read, play music, and watch movies, so they purposely made it a darker, cozier place perfect for curling up and relaxing. Painting the wall a lighter olive color was one way to unify and emphasize that color decision.

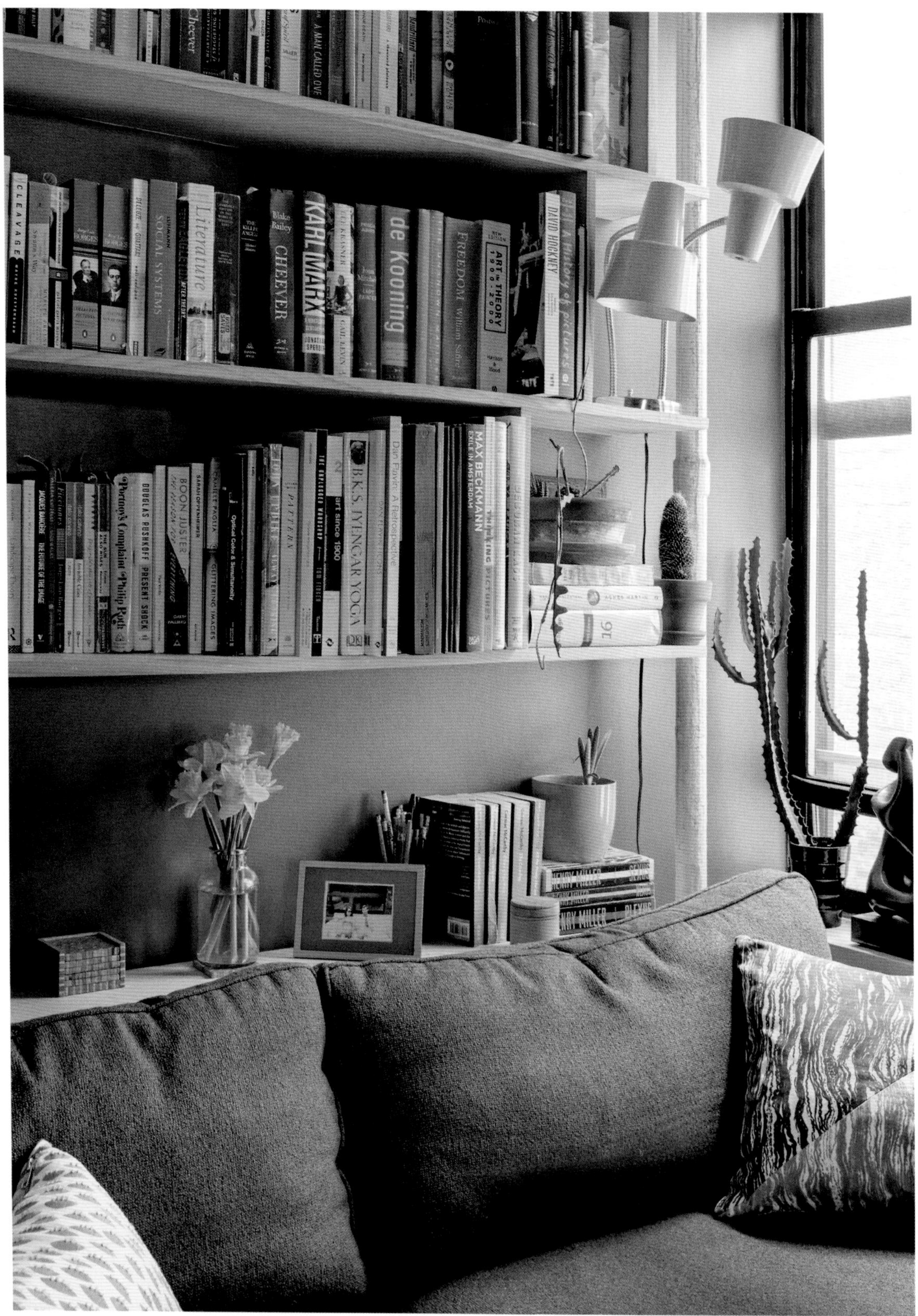
Cheever
A MAN CALLED OVE
CLEAVAGE
SOCIAL SYSTEMS
Literature
Blake Bailey
CHEEVER
KARL MARX
de Kooning
FREEDOM William Safire
ART IN THEORY 1900-2000
DAVID HOCKNEY
A history of pictures
JACQUES RANCIÈRE
THE FUTURE OF THE IMAGE
Portnoy's Complaint Philip Roth
DOUGLAS RUSHKOFF PRESENT SHOCK
BOON JUSTER
CAMILLE PAGLIA
GLITTERING IMAGES
PATTERN
art since 1900
B.K.S. IYENGAR YOGA
Dan Flavin: A Retrospective
MAX BECKMANN
EXILE IN AMSTERDAM
HENRY MILLER
SEXUS
PLEXUS

However, she urges anyone thinking of making such a bold color choice to look at it during different times of day, making sure you see how it changes and love it. While the chartreuse room in the early days of the apartment was an interesting color, it was ultimately challenging. She and her husband woke up, staring at the color every morning. They laughed that the wall was like a chameleon. "Sometimes it would look olive, other times it almost looked orange," jokes Charlotte.

You can see behind the sofa that there is very little storage in their apartment, so nearly everything that's brought in is stored visibly. The objects sit on shelves built specifically for their scale and use, but there's not a lot of clutter. Instead, the space is full of simple and natural materials.

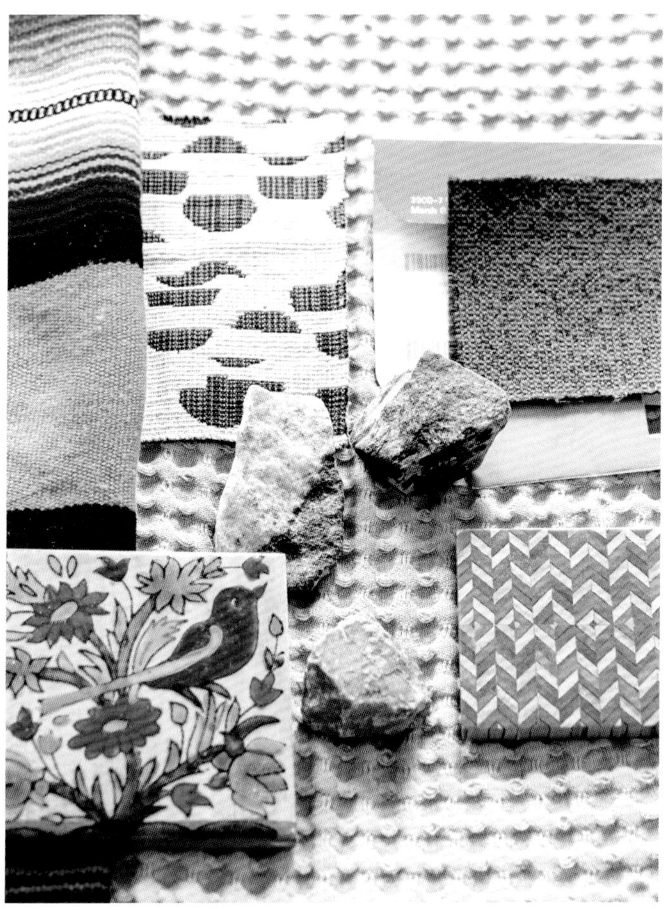

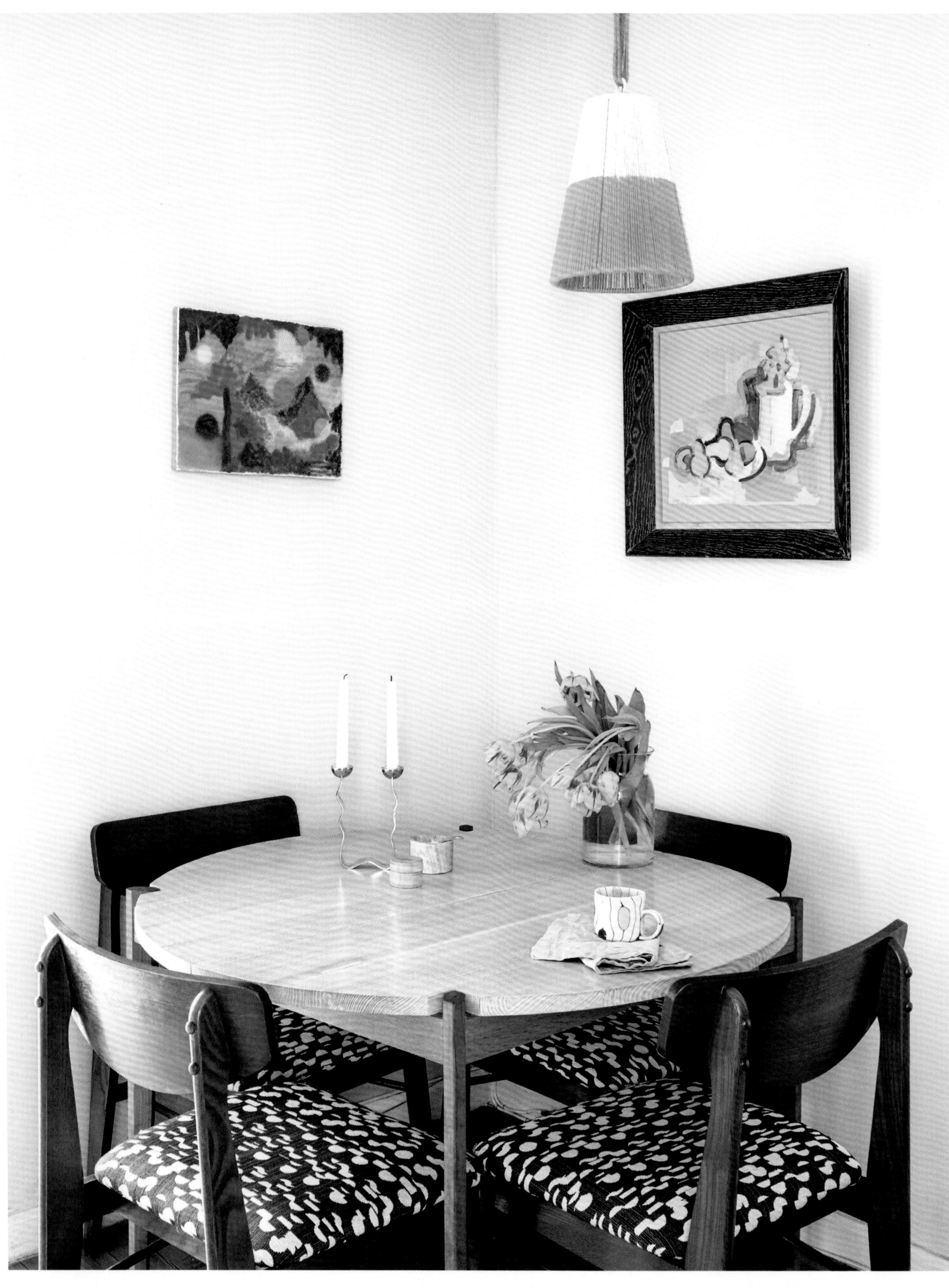

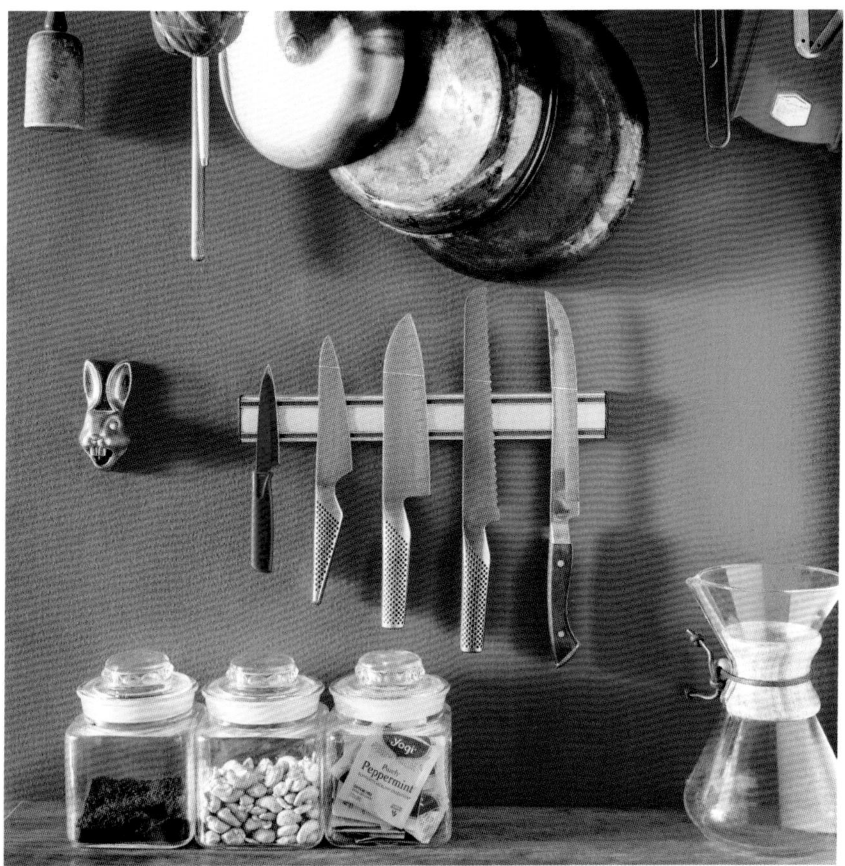

DINING ROOM

Charlotte's husband, Erik, is a fellow artist and furniture designer, and they designed and built most of the furniture in their home. The pieces in the apartment are mostly made from scrap materials, so they didn't cost much to create. For instance, their breakfast table was created from a very beautiful old-growth pine beam that was used in their studio building (originally built in the 1800s).

The other big modification they made to their space is lighting. Charlotte worked in lighting-design studios, and through her work she's acquired an array of lights, even designing a few herself. Swapping out those generic flush-mount lights and adding more than one central fixture made a huge difference to the feel of the space. Their dining corner is directly lit now, so they can see their meals, but it can also be cozy and intimate. Because their space is small, being able to control the lighting in different areas has a big impact on the feel of each room.

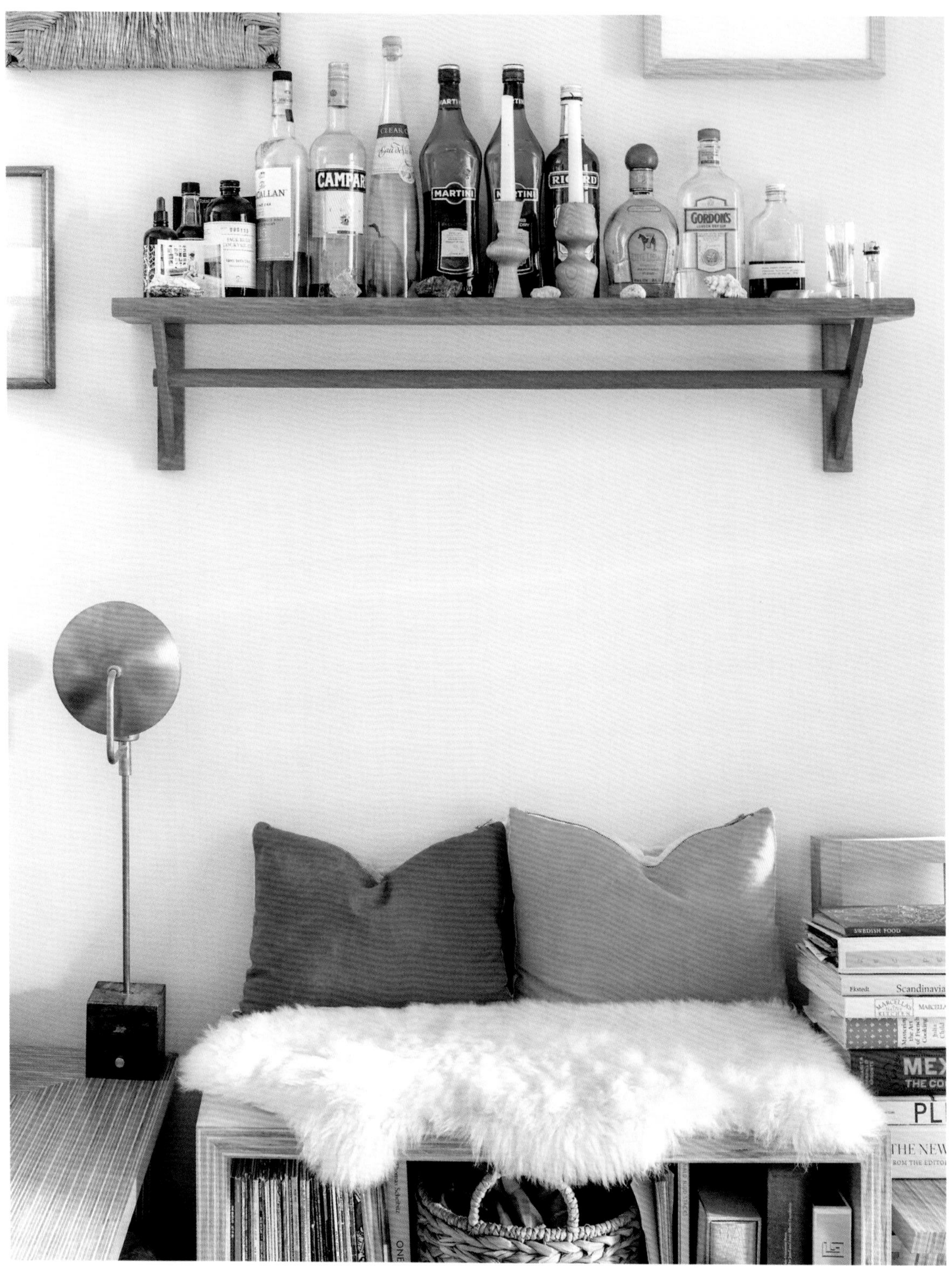
MARTINI
MARTINI
GORDON'S
SWEDISH FOOD

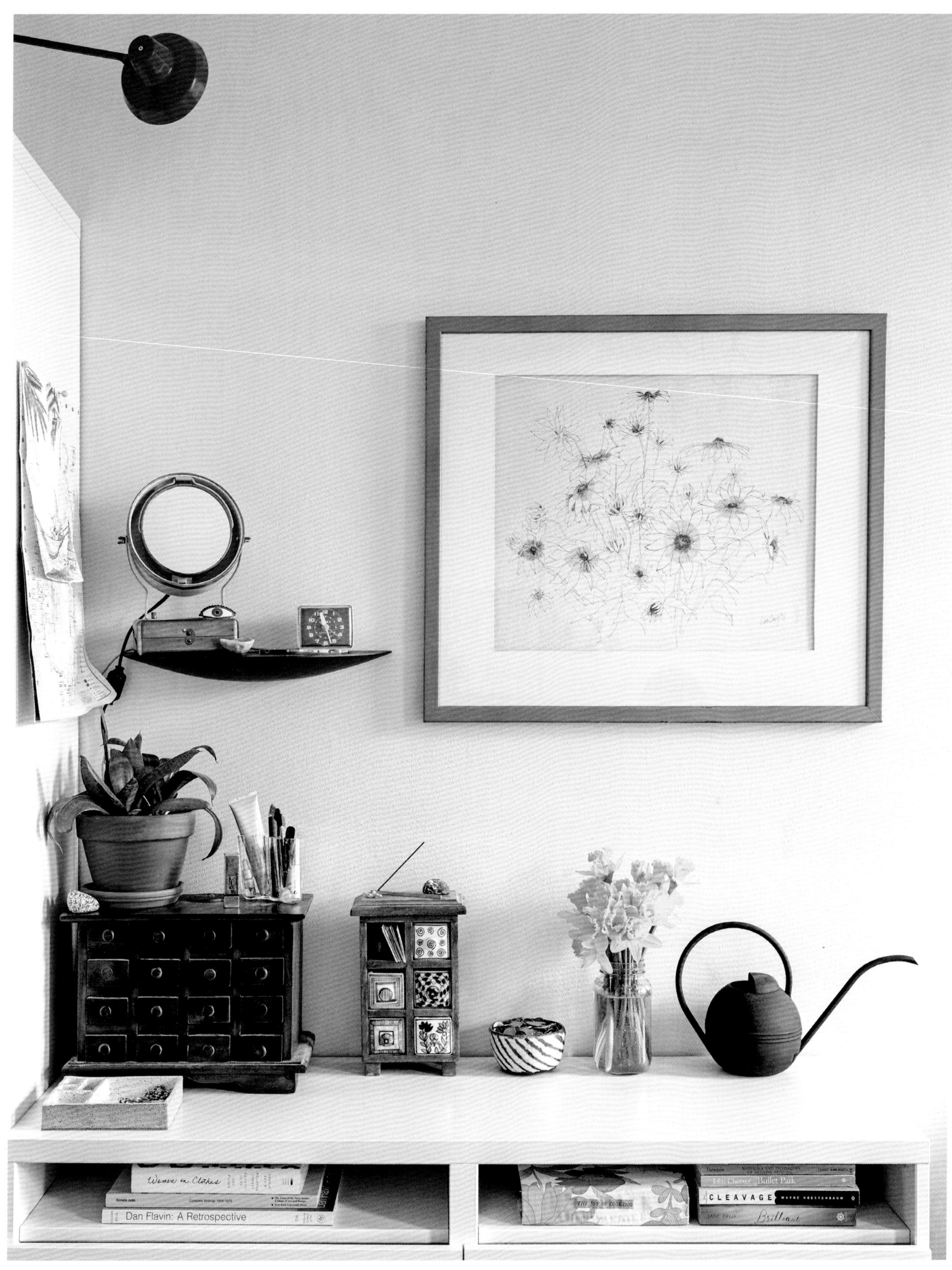

Women in Clothes
Donald Judd
Complete Writings 1959–1975
Dan Flavin: A Retrospective
THE JOY OF COOKING
Bullet Park
CLEAVAGE
WAYNE KOESTENBAUM
Brilliant

BEDROOM

Charlotte loves the natural light in the bedroom, but while it helps her wake up in the morning, she didn't want it to be blinding either. For that reason, she chose a color in the room that feels bright and cool, but not overly bright.

Aside from the functional pieces, you can see that a huge focal point of their home is art, even in the bedroom. They have paintings, drawings, and sculptures from both sets of grandparents and Charlotte's mom, plus works by friends and artists they know and admire, and some of their own works. Charlotte adds, "it's important to us to have a personal relationship with each piece in our home."

Charlotte sees her home as a place to rest and restore, and she simply wanted to make their bedroom, and the home, a place where she was delighted to wake up every day and happy to fall asleep every night.

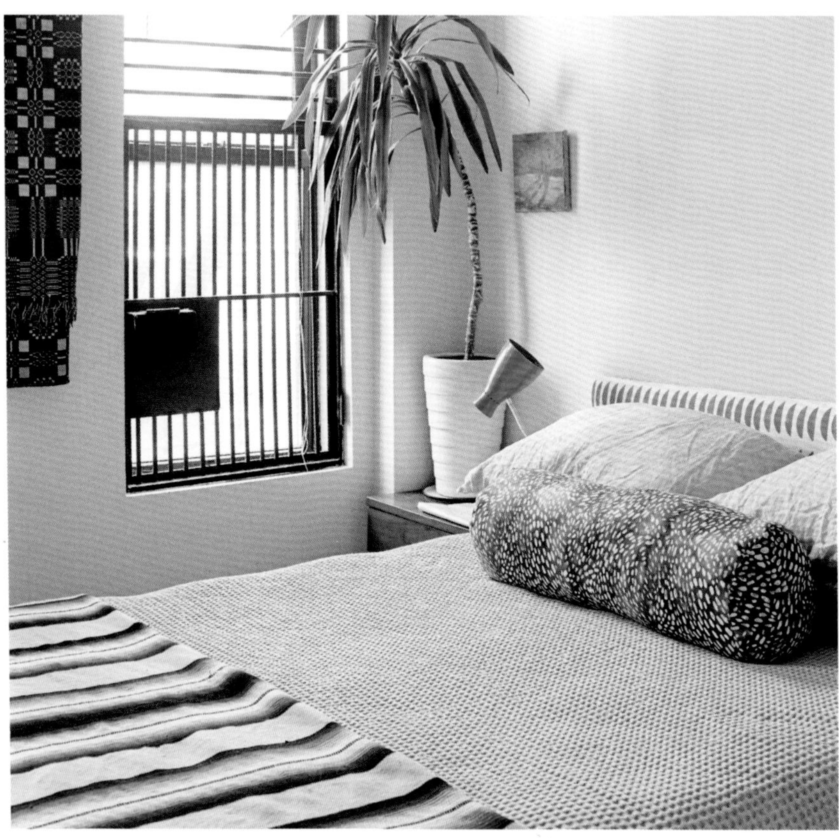

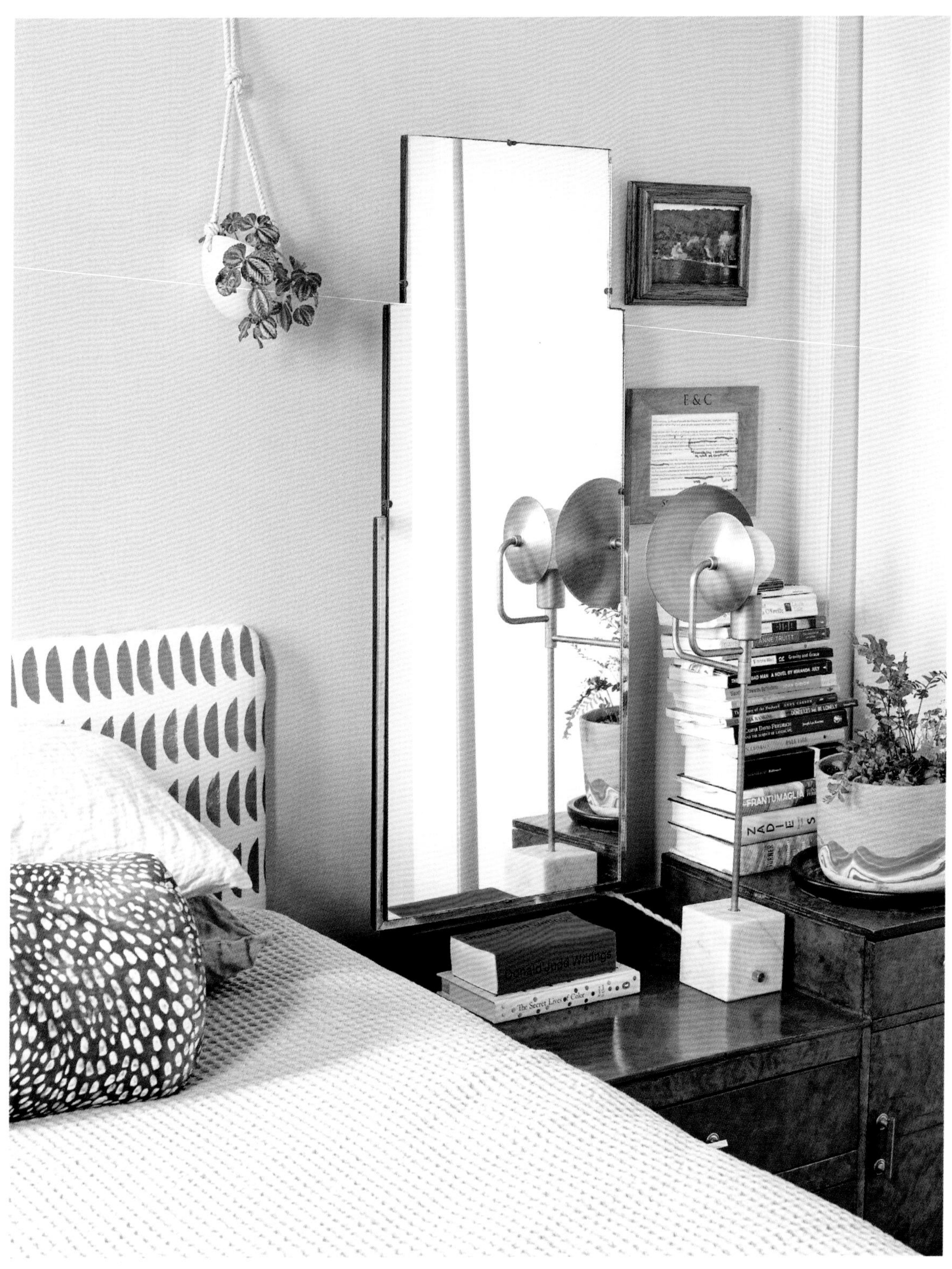
Gravity and Grace
A NOVEL BY MIRANDA JULY
FRANTUMAGLIA
Donald Judd Writings
The Secret Lives of Color

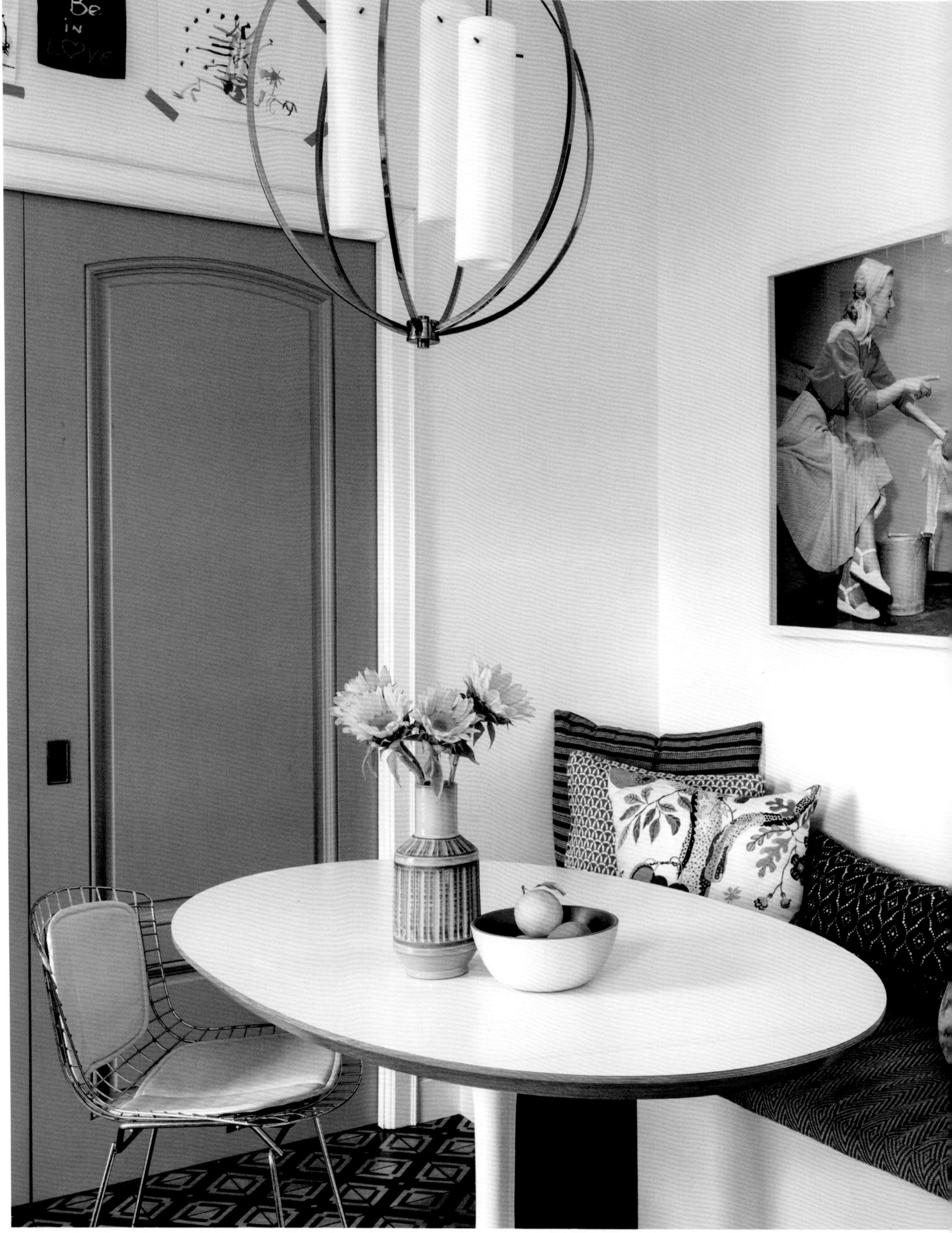
Be
in
L♡VE

A PATCHWORK OF COLOR

KAYLA ALPERT
Screenwriter & Producer

When asked her favorite color, Kayla Alpert will gladly reply, "All of them." Thus she sets the stage for a tour of her 1920s Georgian home in Hancock Park, a leafy residential neighborhood in the heart of Los Angeles. She lives there with her husband, Peter, and their young twin boys. "I've always loved bright colors and patterns," says Kayla. "From the age of three, I insisted on dressing myself in patchwork shirts, flowered skirts, plaid vests, and brightly colored tights—all at the same time. I've toned it down since then, but not much." Both Kayla and her husband were raised in houses in which they were surrounded by antiques, books, family heirlooms, and flea market finds; in other words, according to Kayla, "Minimalism was a foreign concept," which is why Kayla feels free to put all kinds of pieces together without worrying how they play off one another. There's no formal start or end point, and no "decorating" per se, but rather a collection of pieces—a midcentury love seat, a pair of giant brass storks, vintage Josef Frank drapes—that are an amalgamation of different gravitational pulls, each having caught Kayla's eye on her travels.

She wants her home to always feel fun, casual, and vibrant. "Nobody walks in here and feels like they can't touch anything," she says. Looking at her lifestyle, it's clear that Kayla needs a home that feels very lived in and well-worn. Her family likes to host lots of parties, fund-raisers, playdates, and get-togethers. They also want it to feel like a place to cook dinner, watch a movie, and get cozy. "Our home is both a refuge and a perpetually open-door hangout," says Kayla.

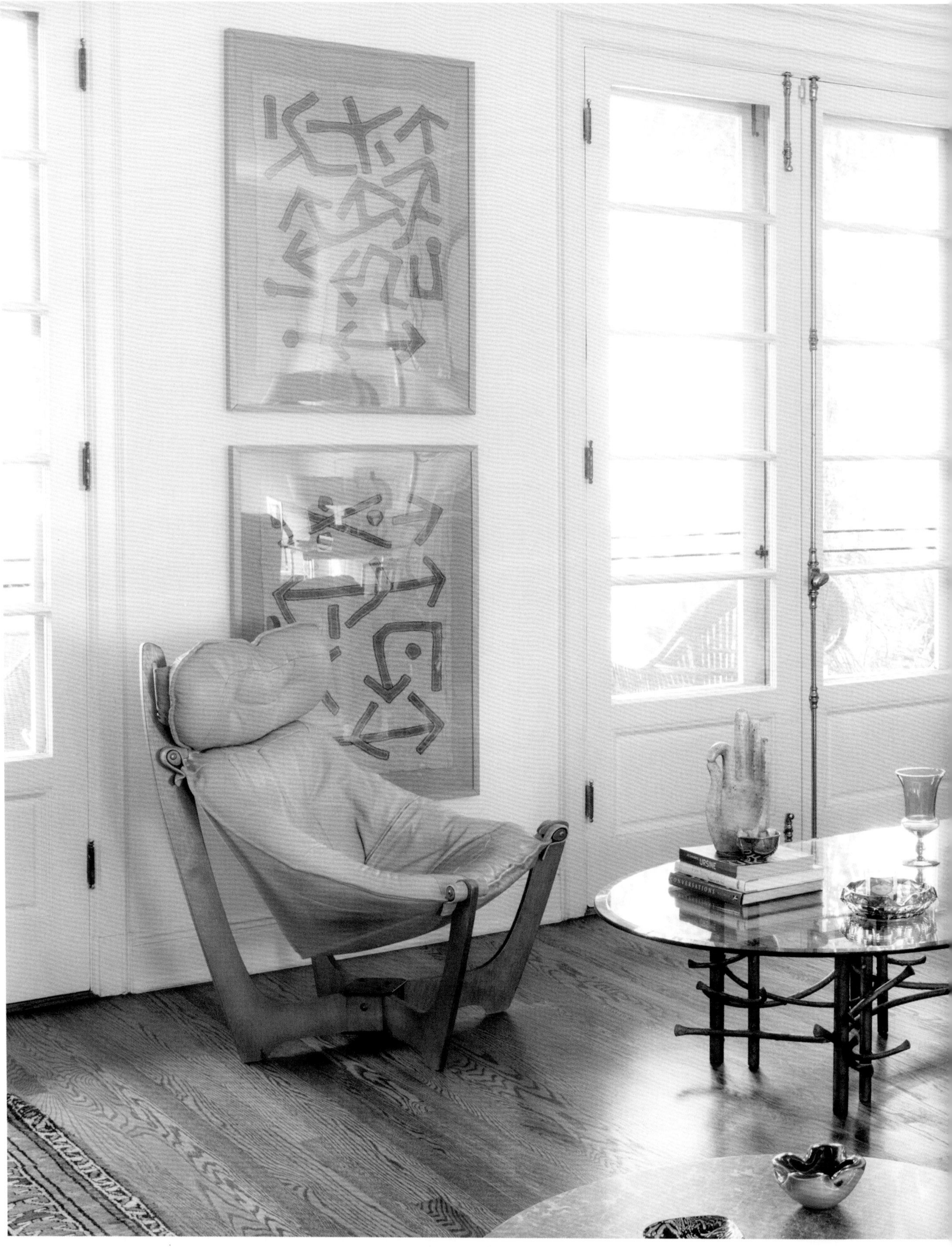
URSINE
CONVERSATIONS

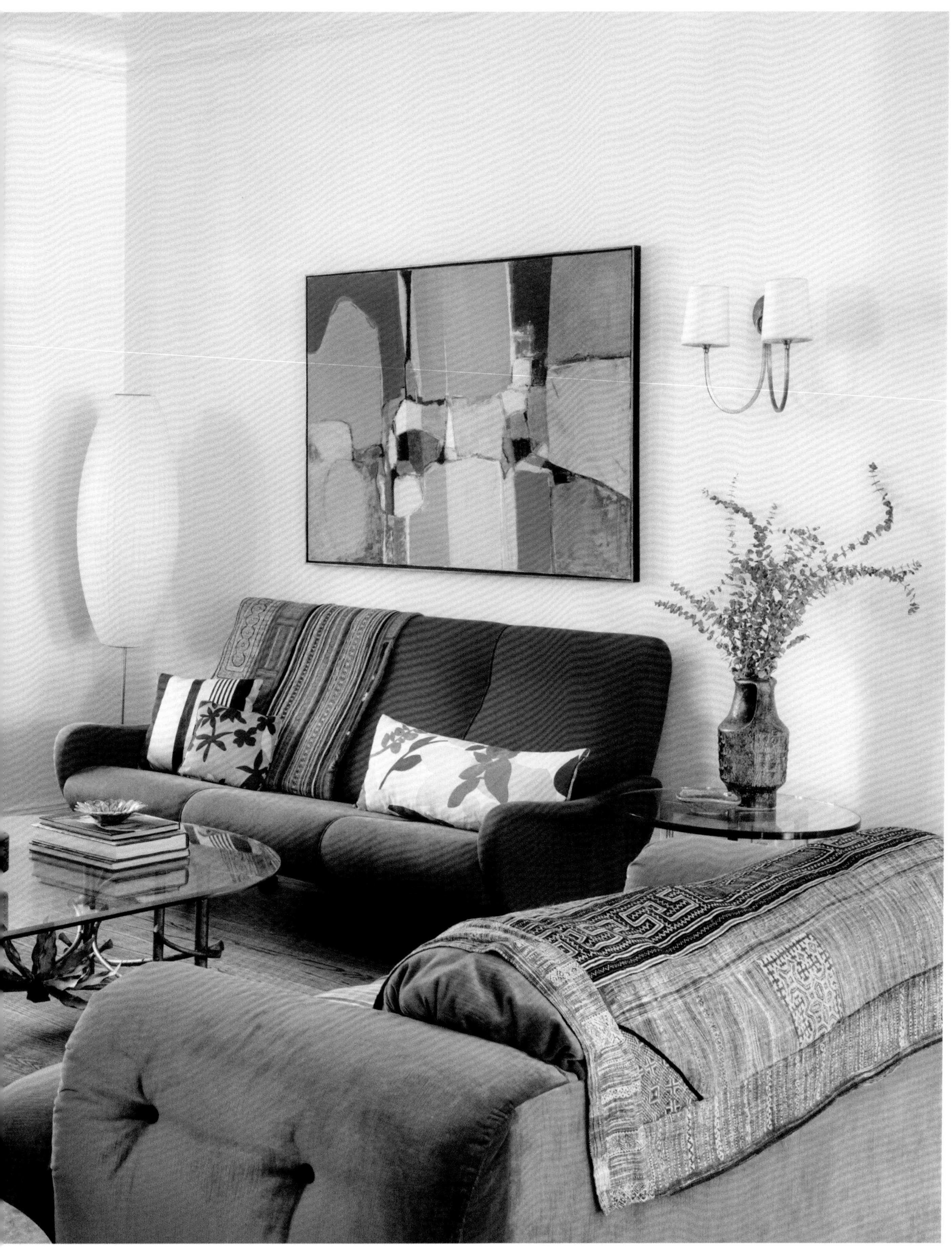

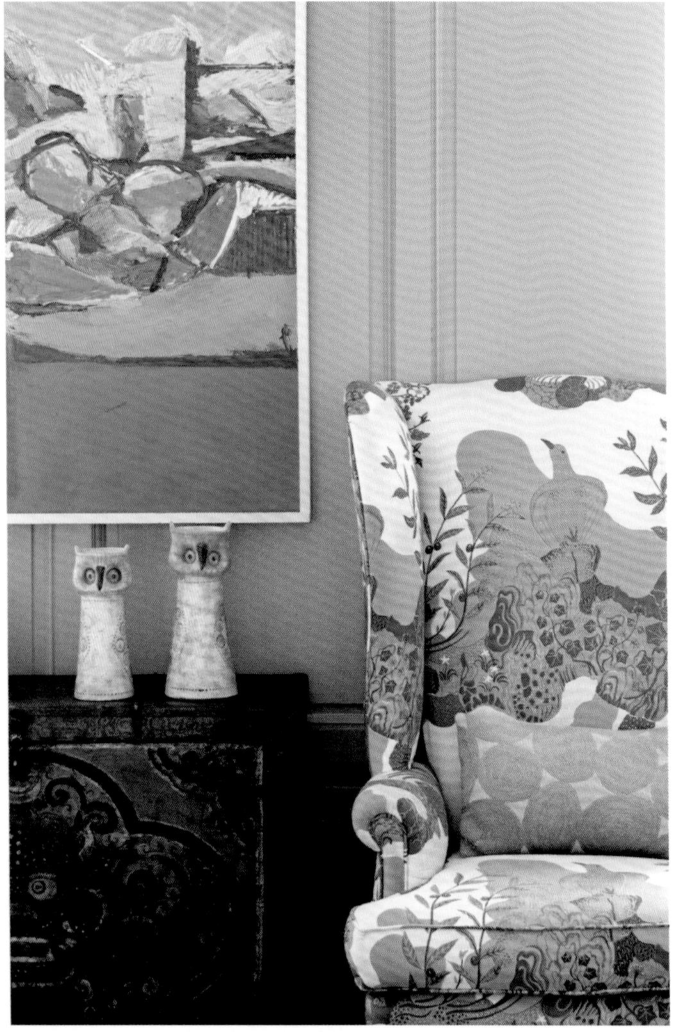

WARM AND COOL LIVING ROOMS

Though there's no unifying color or fabric when Kayla starts, she does begin with white walls, as in the living room, knowing that she'll likely buy a disparate amount of brightly colored and mismatched items and furniture. For starters, she loves Portola Paints & Glazes in Los Angeles. "They have the richest, most unexpected colors and do custom shades, too." The living room is mostly warm colors, like the pink love seat and rich yellow-orange sofa, which lend the room an eclectic feel. Though the space feels like it developed over time, the pieces still clearly show the colors Kayla loves. Her home is a great example of how easy it is to make a room and collect things over time that will work together when you know your colors and how to use them.

The other living room area, with mint-green walls and a deeper green sofa, is so beautiful! I love that monochromatic look of using two shades of one color in a big way in a room. The other colors are layered on top, so it doesn't feel too contrived but instead appears unified. This is the idea of a landscape coming to life, because you usually see more than one shade of a color in the world.

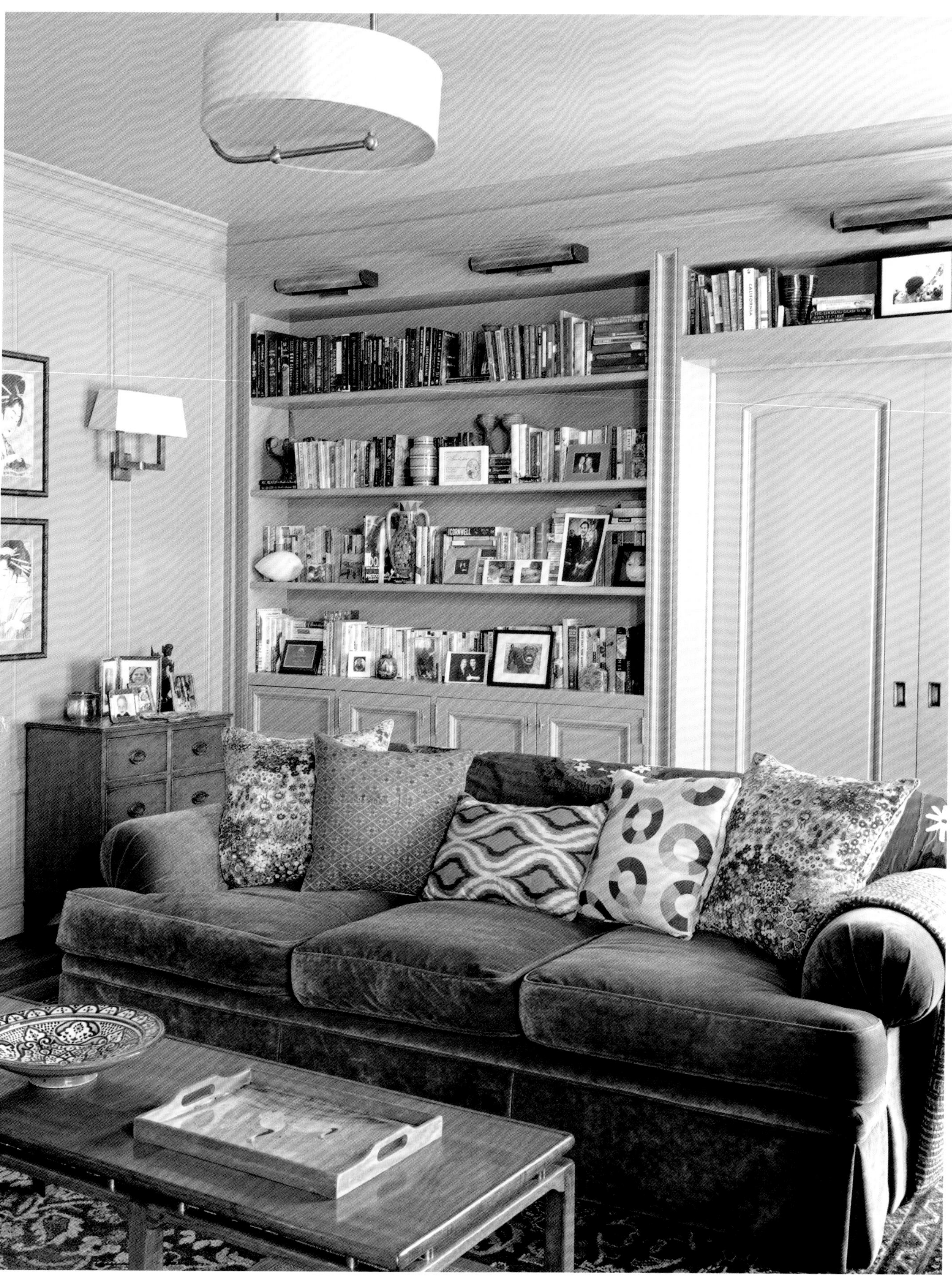
CALIFORNIA
CORNWELL

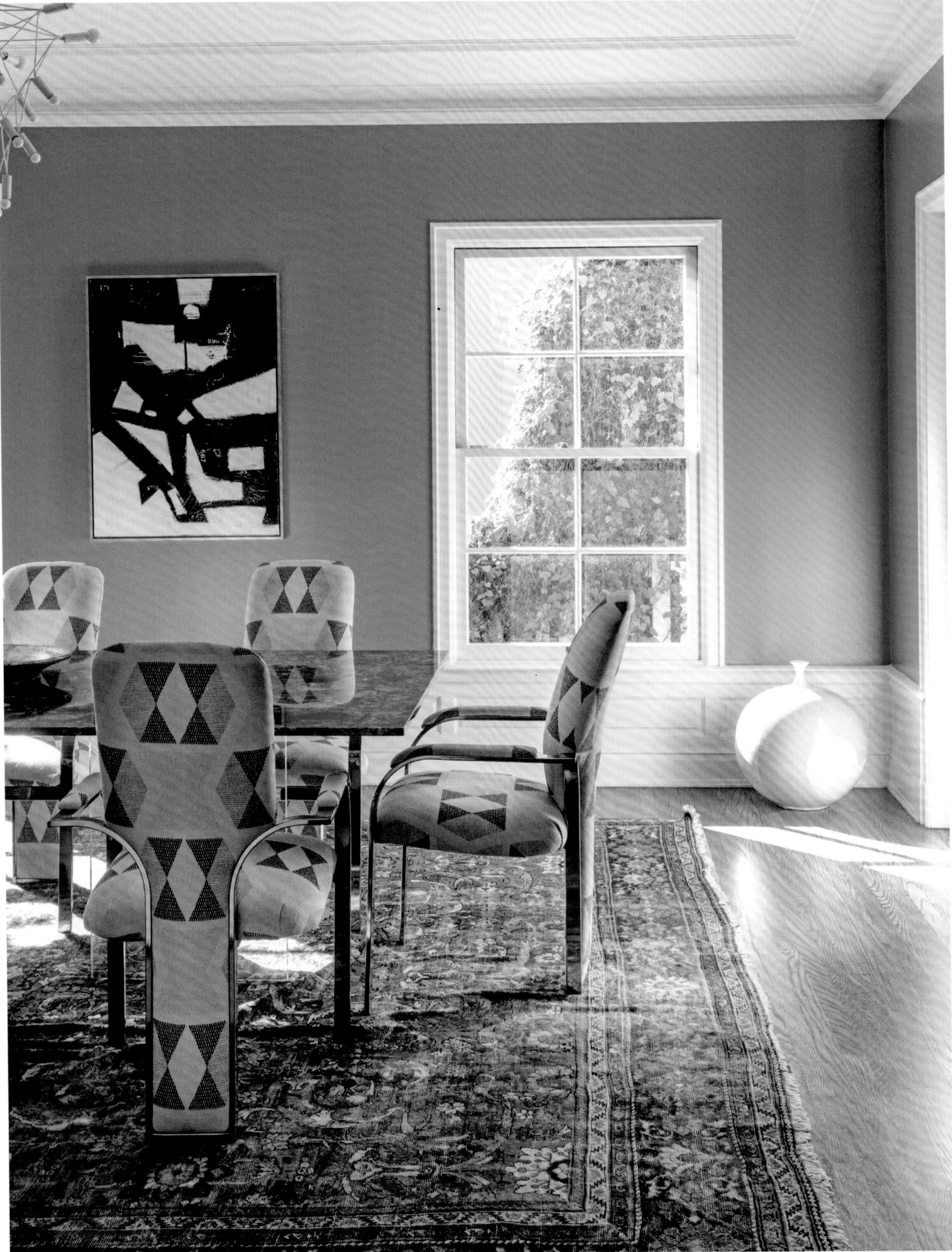

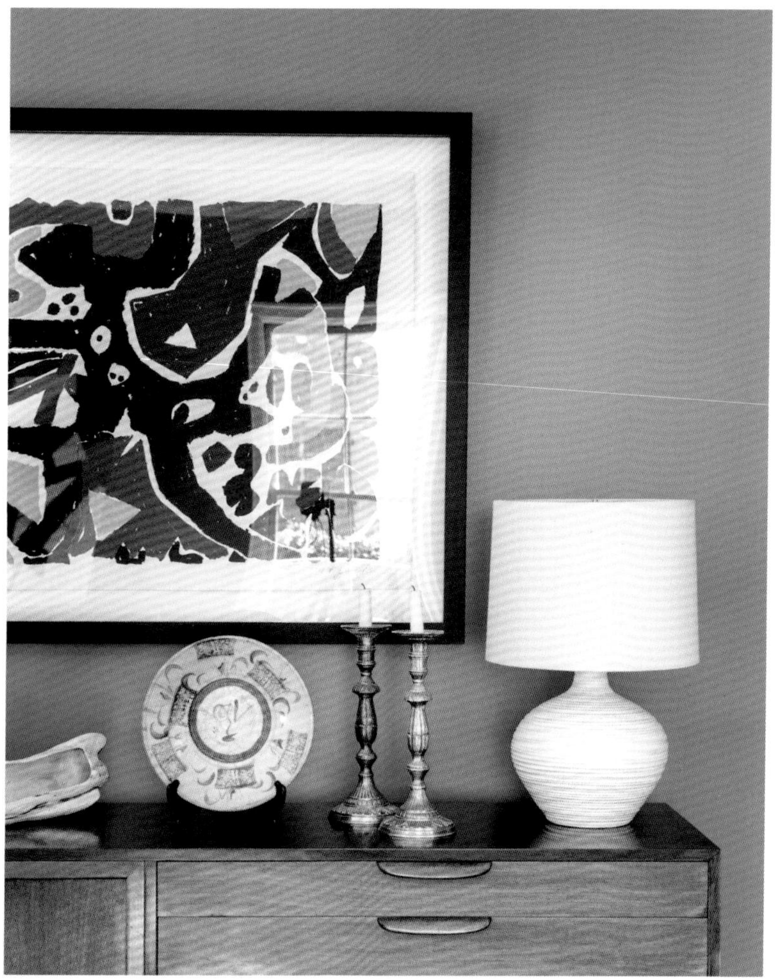

COOL DINING SPACE

This dining space is a wonderful example of bolder use of a cool color that feels alive but not overwhelming. The happy green is balanced by the Oriental rug in deep reds and blues, which grounds the space. A traditional rug, in deep, rich colors that aren't oversaturated, can be a nice counterpoint to brighter colors. When you use a bold color, it's important to find ways to make it feel unified. If everything else were beige and gray, the green would overpower the space. The reds and deep blues become neutrals in this space, even though they are strong colors.

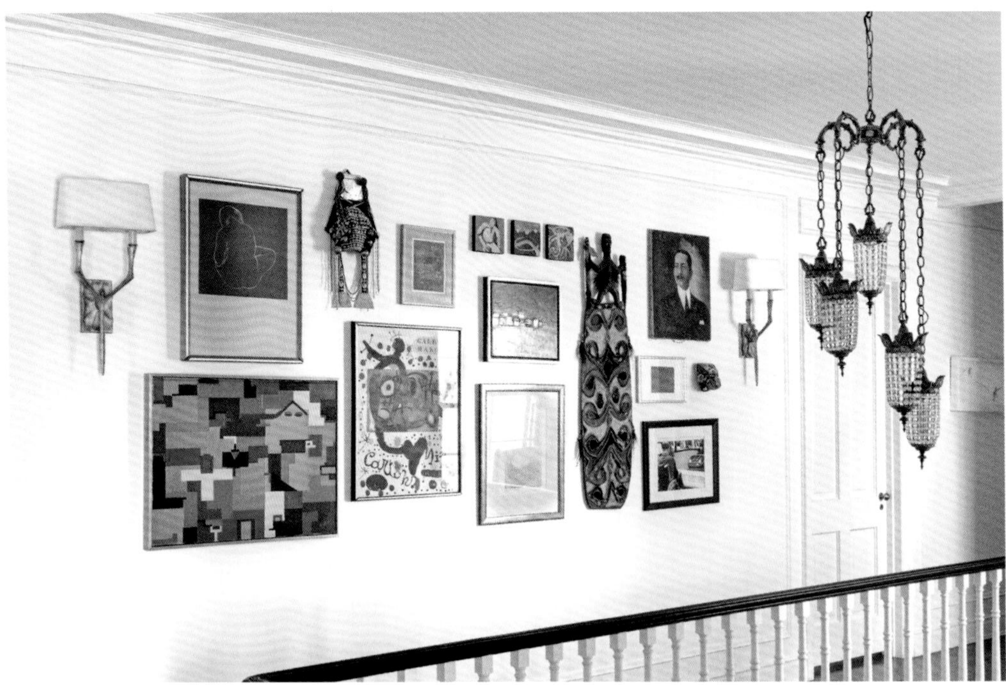

GO FOR WHAT YOU LOVE

Kayla aims to add elements of surprise and humor to each room and has never met a color she doesn't like. She urges anyone working on a new space not to be afraid or to care what "goes together." Instead, she advocates for choosing what you love and colors that look good on you, like the ones in your closet. She adds, "Neutrals looks great in magazine spreads—but if you have kids, dogs, and/or drink wine, you're in for a heap of trouble . . . trust me."

MAKE IT YOUR OWN

- Balance bold colors with bold neutrals.
- Use tonal shades of one color within a space to create a foundation that's interesting but not overpowering.
- Display artwork, pillows, and decorative objects you love. Move them around your home when you want to freshen things up, as a new arrangement can make you see existing pieces in a new light.

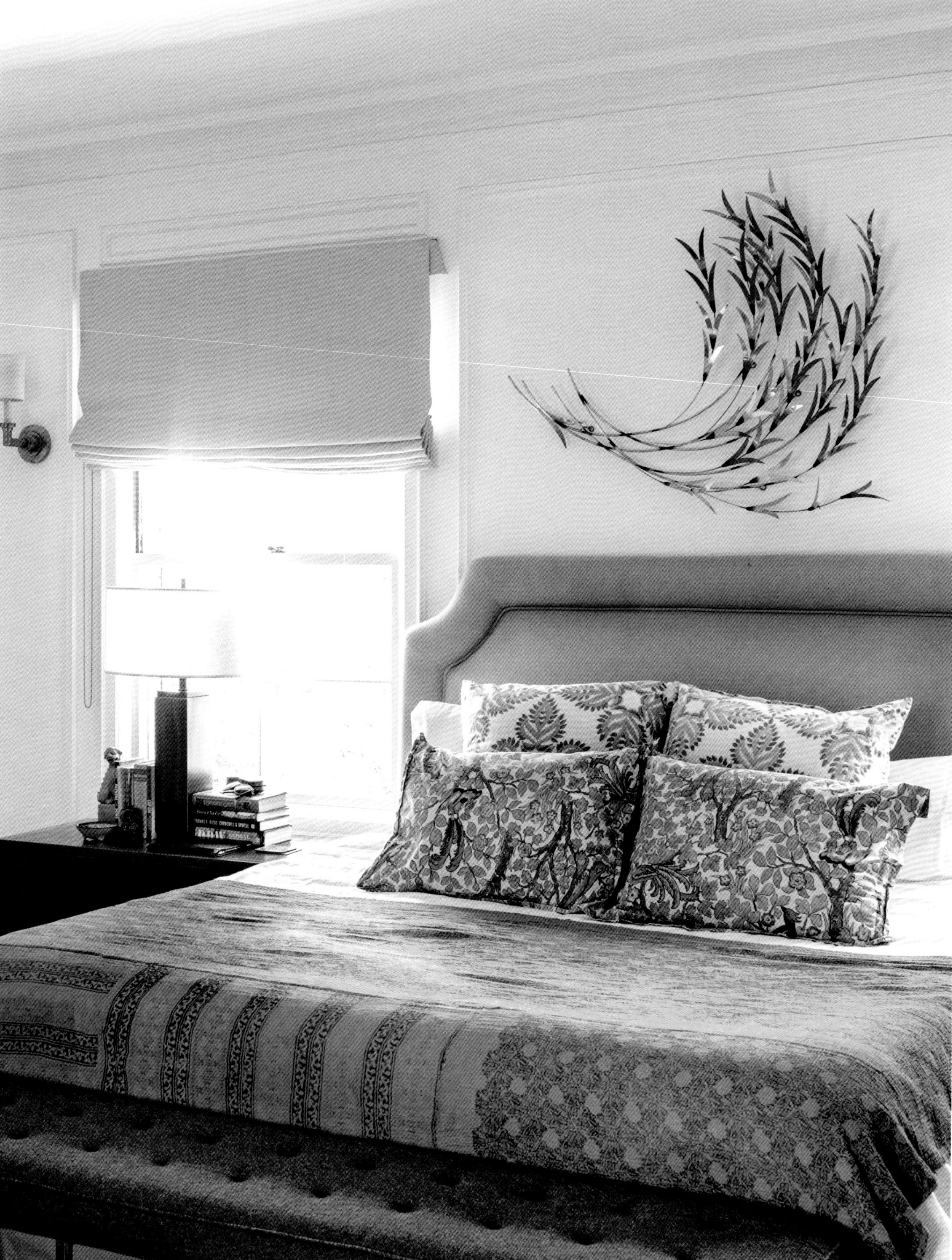

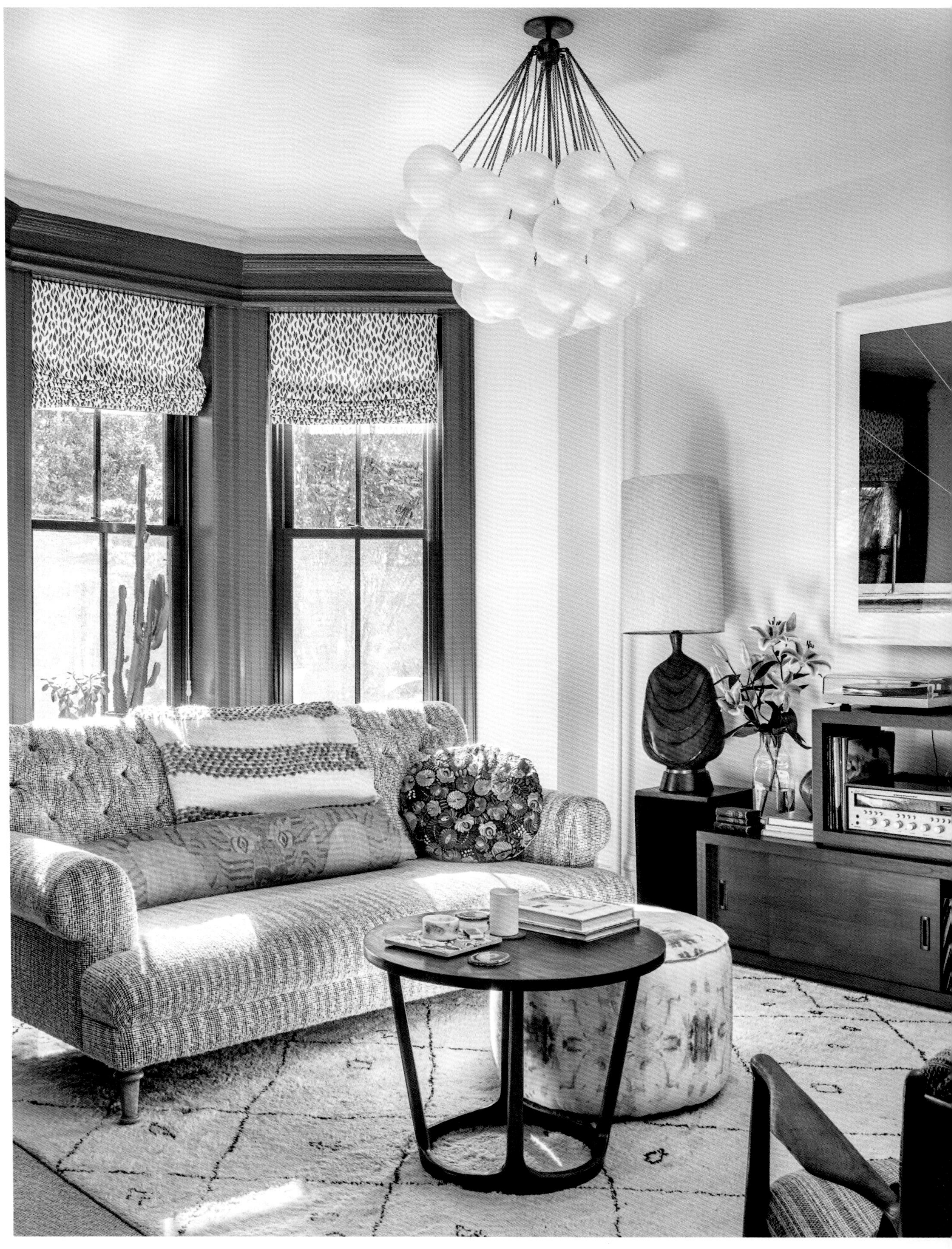

FUN WITH COLOR

KATE TEMPLE REYNOLDS
Co-founder of Studio Four

When you step into the home of Kate Temple Reynolds, you instantly feel how rich it is. While that's partly because Kate herself is warm and caring, it's also her color palette that immediately makes you feel cozy and grounded. She experiments with the way in which different colors give off particular feelings, and she notices that new colors can drastically change a room. "I am constantly amazed by how certain colors play with each other," she says. "Some colors that I really can't stand take on a whole new life when they are paired with the right match."

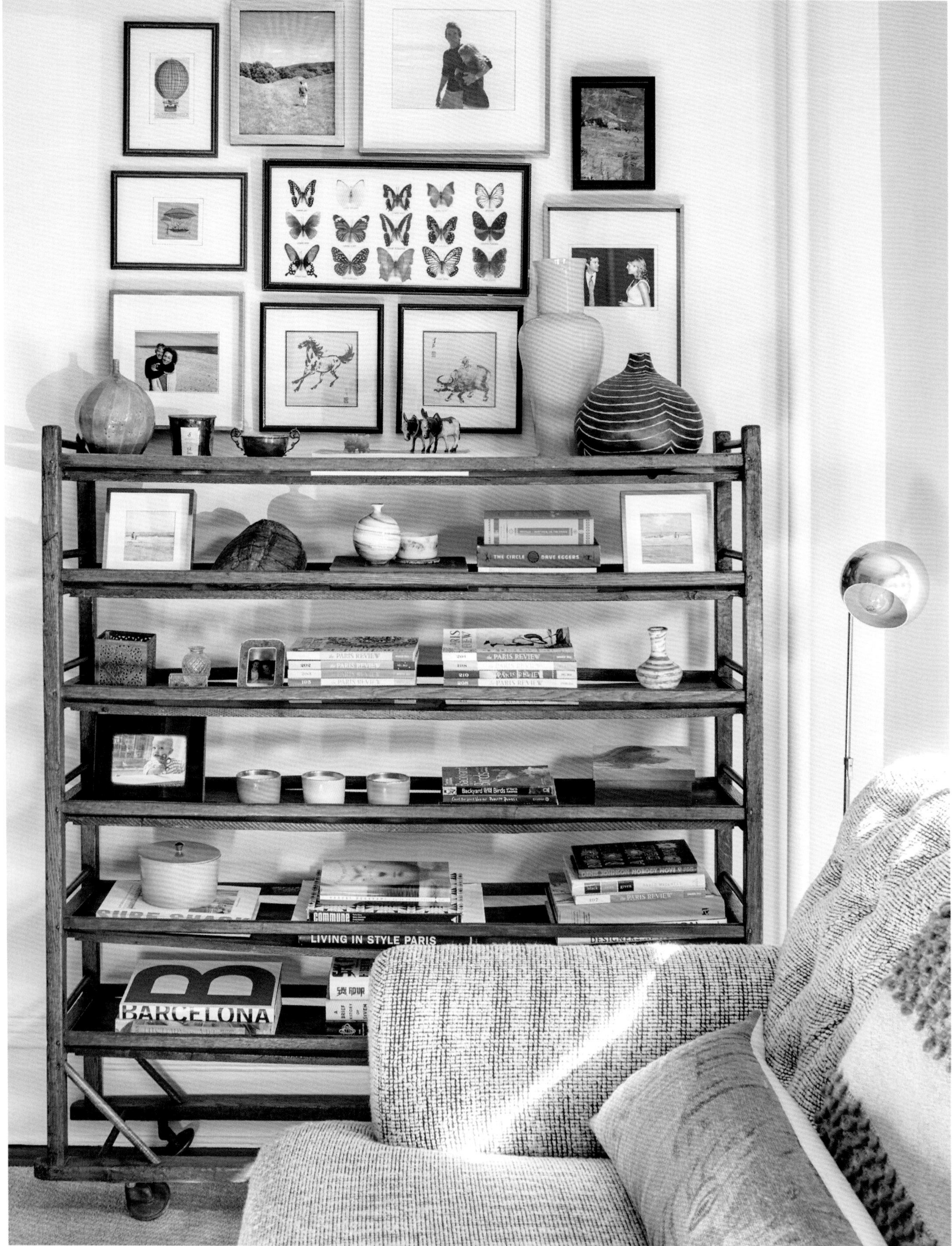
THE CIRCLE DAVE EGGERS
THE PARIS REVIEW
Backyard Birds
DENIS JOHNSON NOBODY MOVE
COMMUNE
LIVING IN STYLE PARIS
BARCELONA

ADDING IN LAYERS

Kate's design approach is to start with a favorite piece and then build upon it through layers. Sometimes it's something big, like an area rug, but other times it is smaller, like a decorative item that inspires her. For instance, the downstairs of her house is largely based on a handwoven fabric her friend Soraya Shah made, and Kate knew she wanted to use it on the sofa in her living room. This fabric influenced other art decisions, and Kate began layering in a broader palette featuring similar textiles and rich plum colors. The result is a great example of using jewel tones and earth tones together. Kate uses purple in a way that feels grounded and natural, not too feminine or opulent, which is how we often think of purple. She advises those recently initiated into the world of color to start testing out new hues with design items that are easy to change. "You might not want to jump straight into a purple upholstered sofa," she says, "but maybe get a purple throw and see how it makes you feel."

PAINT TIPS

Kate urges testing paint on a wall and making sure to look at it during various times of the day before you paint, so you can see how the color is affected by your home's natural light. She once made the mistake of choosing a white paint for the downstairs of her house because she wanted it to feel like there was a consistent flow, but when she walked in the day they were painting it, she knew it was the wrong decision. "Somehow it looked yellow, like a banana split!" she says. Luckily, they made a quick change, but it was a lesson for her about striking a balance between going for it completely and testing things out before jumping. "Go with your gut," she says. "If you feel weird about a color or you are trying too hard to make it work, then it just might not be right for you. But also don't be afraid to try things!"

ALL CONNECTED

Kate's dining room area connects the living room and the kitchen. Since it's open to both spaces, it's important that the color palette flows easily. The charcoal, wood tones, taupe, and purple feature prominently in this space and feel like an extension of the living room. The eat-in kitchen is brighter and airier, but it shares a purple accent.

FAMILY SPACE

This relationship to color is apparent in the décor of her early-twentieth-century attached Brooklyn town house, where she currently lives with her husband, Rem, and their two boys. At home, one of her favorite things is to paint watercolors with her sons. "It's fun to see the mixes they put together, especially when we do abstract pattern painting. My six-year-old is really into painting patterns with shapes," she says.

Though Kate hails from Columbia, South Carolina, she feels her style is less traditional than the Southern homes of her childhood. Her mother, who is an interior designer, was always thinking outside the box when it came to décor, and that had a big impact on Kate's aesthetic. For this reason, she prefers mixing and matching a lot of color and pattern, leaning toward a less "decorated" overall look and feel. As a result, her home is filled with amazing textiles, wall coverings, and rugs.

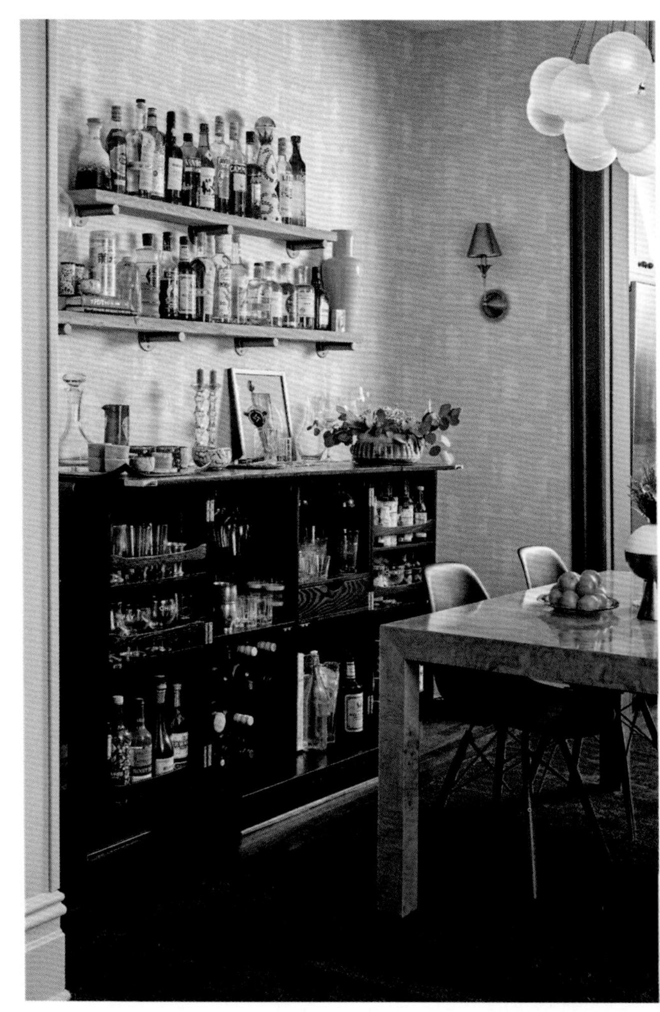

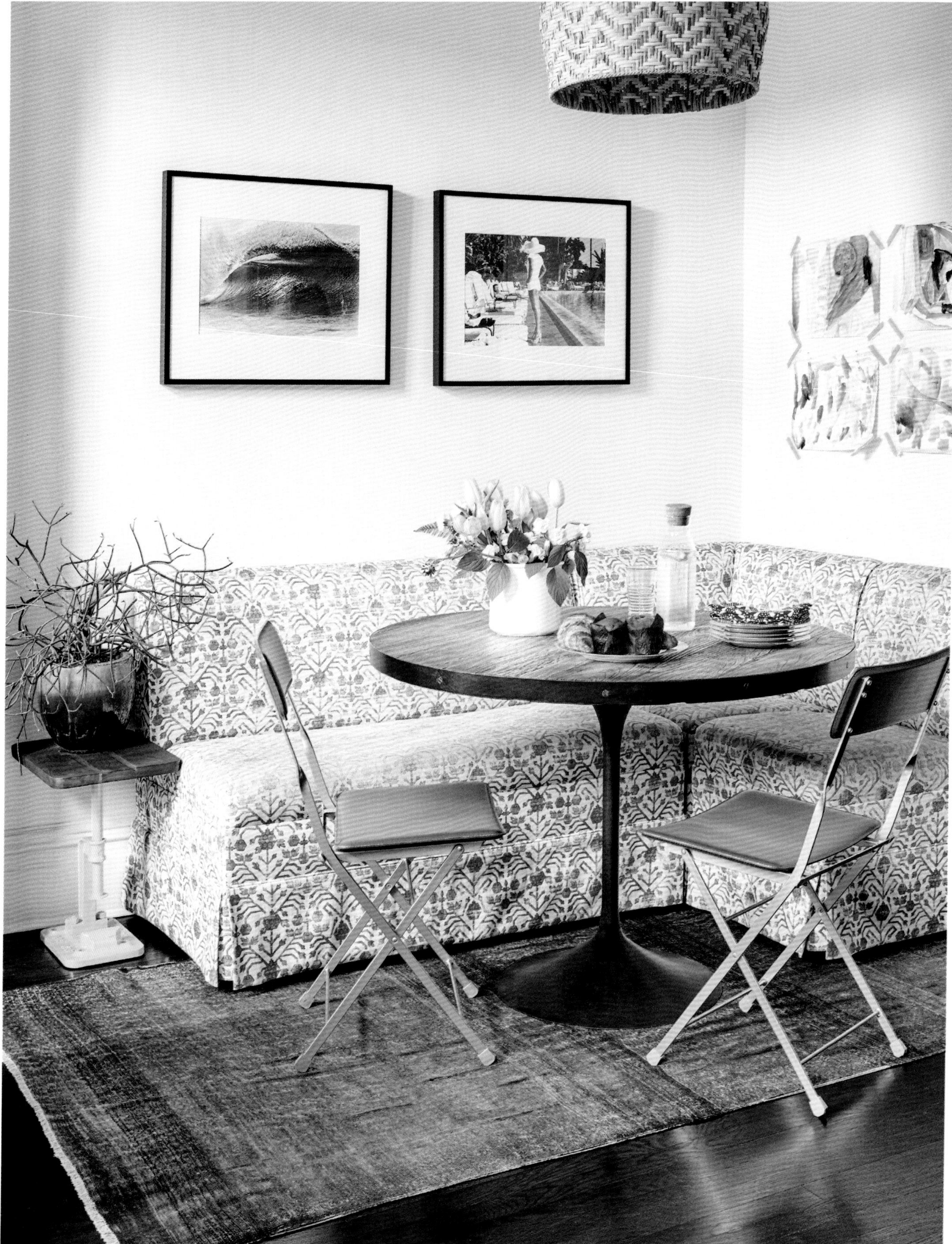

COZY AND COLORFUL

The master bedroom has a cozy, colorful vibe. The soft green-gray walls feel less stark than white would. The bolder hues—golden yellow, red, and blue—are less obtrusive when brought in through the textiles. Using them in smaller proportions than the soft wall color keeps the space calm.

Though her upstairs boasts a slightly more traditional palette with lots of white, Kate brought pops of color into her kids' rooms using window treatments and bedding that also play well with the various colors (mostly in the form of toys) throughout the rooms.

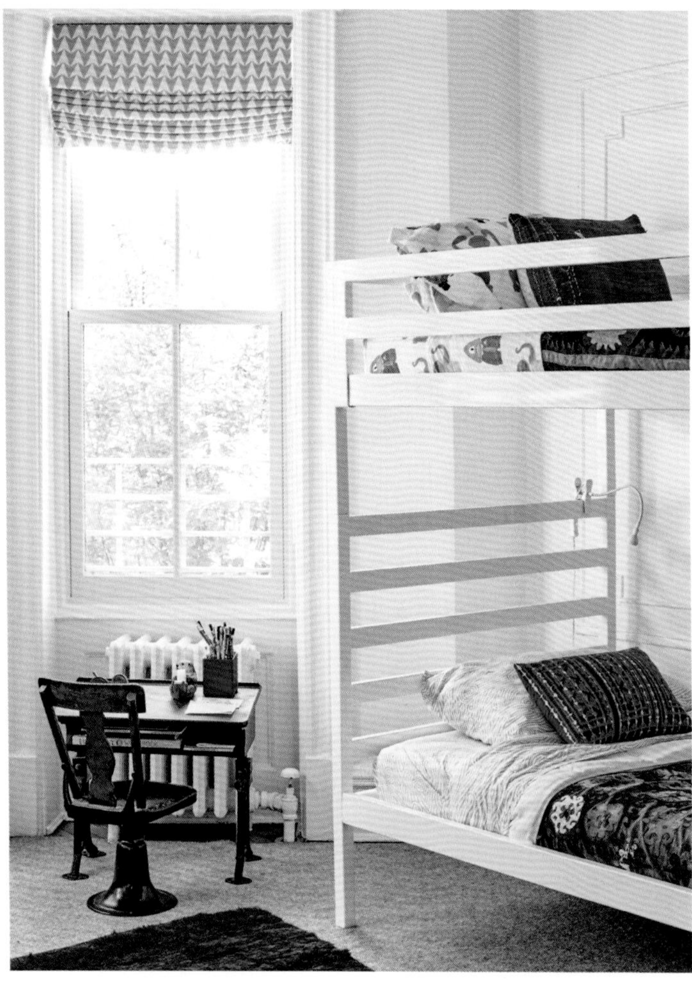

MAKE IT YOUR OWN

- Embrace textiles as a way to add color, pattern, and interest into a space.
- Mix purple (or another jewel tone) with earthier hues like yellow ochre and lots of neutrals.
- Balance bolder colors in a bedroom by using them in smaller proportions.
- Display your collections on shelves. It's also a great way to tie in additional colors.

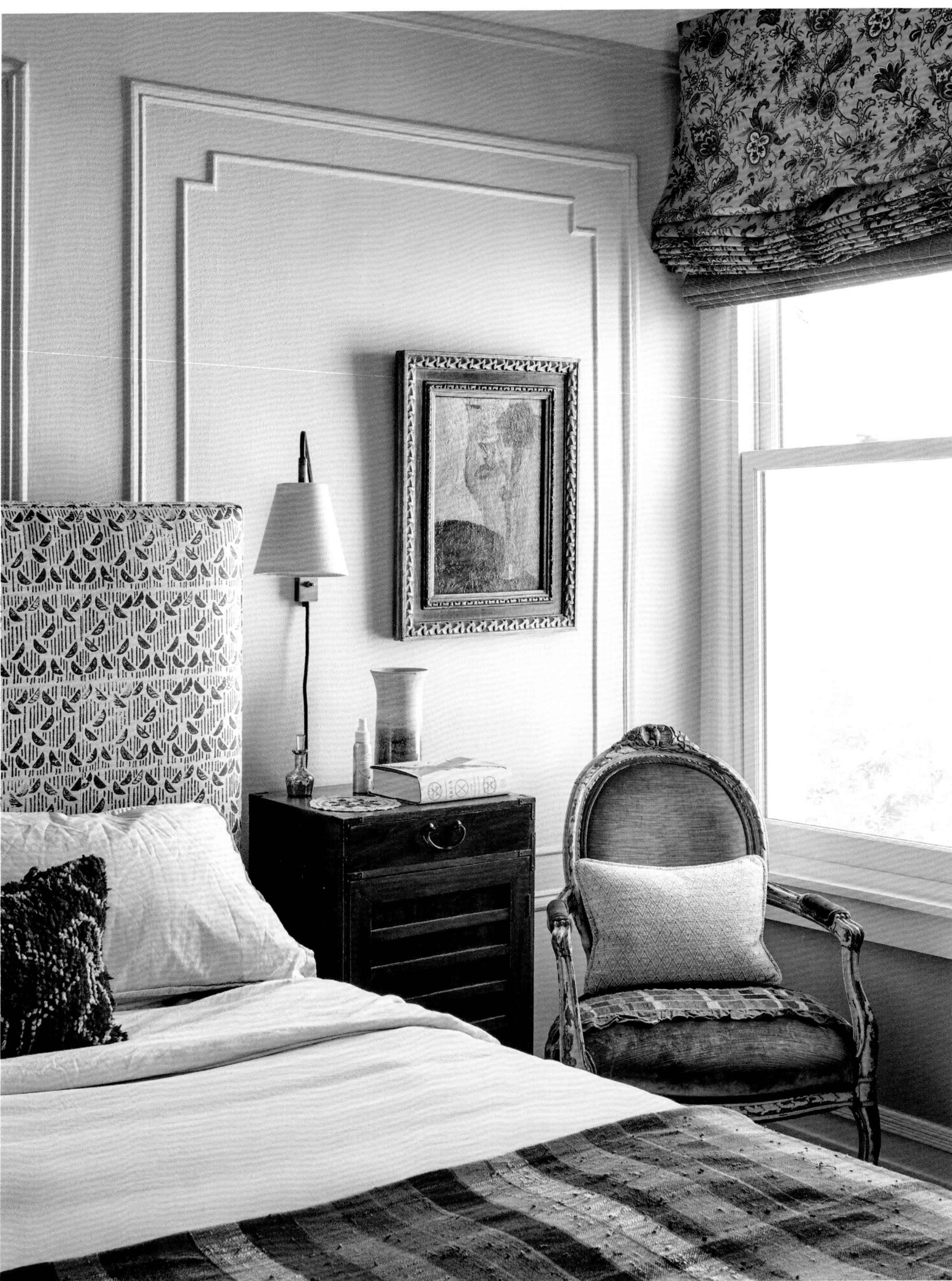

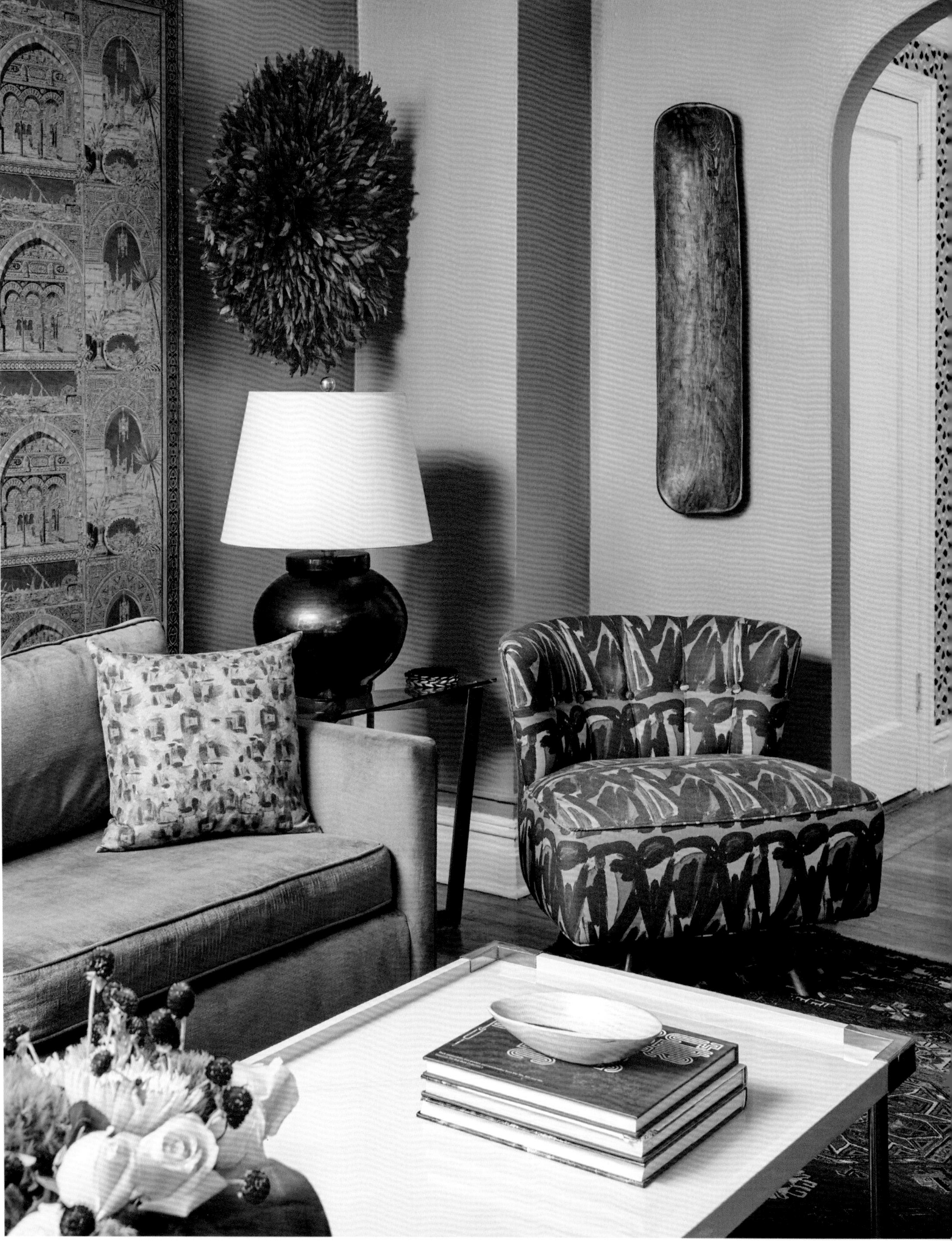

STANDOUT STYLE

ANTHONY GIANACAKOS
Interior Designer,
Textile Designer, Artist

ALISON RUDNICK
Homeowner

Growing up in the Midwest, where safe design was favored, Anthony Gianacakos had a style that stood out. As a kid, he would try wild choices in his bedroom's décor and make design suggestions to his parents, who usually stayed within their color comfort zone, which included subdued taupe, soft yellow, and maroon. He remembers looking forward to a time when he could finally express himself and be more adventurous with color and pattern. Moving to New York and working in interior design finally gave him that opportunity.

That's why when homeowner Alison Rudnick decided she wanted a bold design plan for her Upper West Side apartment, she turned to Anthony. Known for his colorful and livable choices, he was tasked with bringing her space to life.

COLOR AND MOOD

This New York City apartment doesn't get a lot of natural light, so finding a way to warm it up and make it feel comforting and cozy, but also bright and happy, was important. The first thing Anthony did was choose an appropriate color palette. Here he decided to focus on wall color, but other times he uses large upholstery pieces to set the stage. "Color will generate a mood," he says, "and from there, the design process evolves and changes constantly." For those who are skittish about picking a bright paint color, he advises selecting an unusual neutral, like a muddy gray or pinkish taupe. "In neutral colors, you can often find undertones that will give you a little hue of color without using the bold color," he offers.

PRETTY IN PINK

The pièce de résistance of this home is the pink living room. It's a one-bedroom apartment, and most of the homeowner's time is spent in the living area. Pink walls are a bold choice, but the reason they work here is because they are covered in artwork. Anthony believes strongly that artwork changes a room. "Whether you're an art connoisseur or college student doing a DIY art project, you can make a huge impact with it," he explains. "It's an easy way for anyone new to color to incorporate it."

Along the back of the blue-gray sofa, there is a beautiful folding screen that's been hung as artwork. It has golden and black hues with a softer pink accent. This adds an earthiness to the room's bright pink. The artwork also breaks up this strong hue on that wall. At one point, Anthony and Alison tried a teal stripe around the room, but it just didn't work, and they decided to go all in with pink walls. "The great thing about paint," Anthony reminds home decorators, "is that it's not permanent."

On top of that, the other colors in the space are rich and hold their own against the pink, while still letting it be the star of the space. With color, it's all about balance, and this home does that well. If everything in the room were light or white, the pink would appear bolder because it would stand out in stark contrast. But in this room, most of the other colors in the space have similar value (remember, this refers to how light or dark a color is; see page 26) to the pink, or they are darker. The other colors in the palette help the pink feel rich and integrated instead of startling.

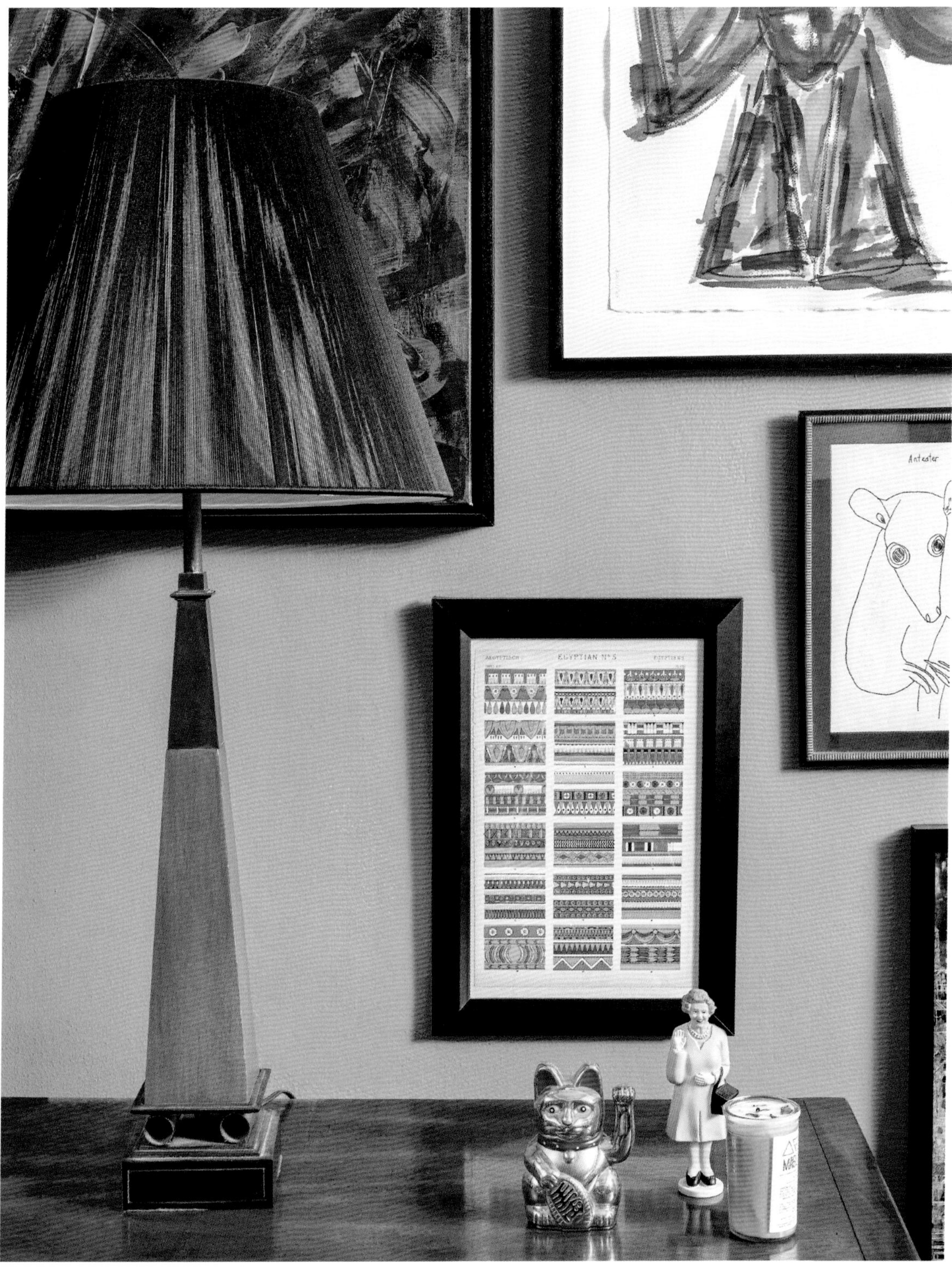
EGYPTIAN N°5
Anteater

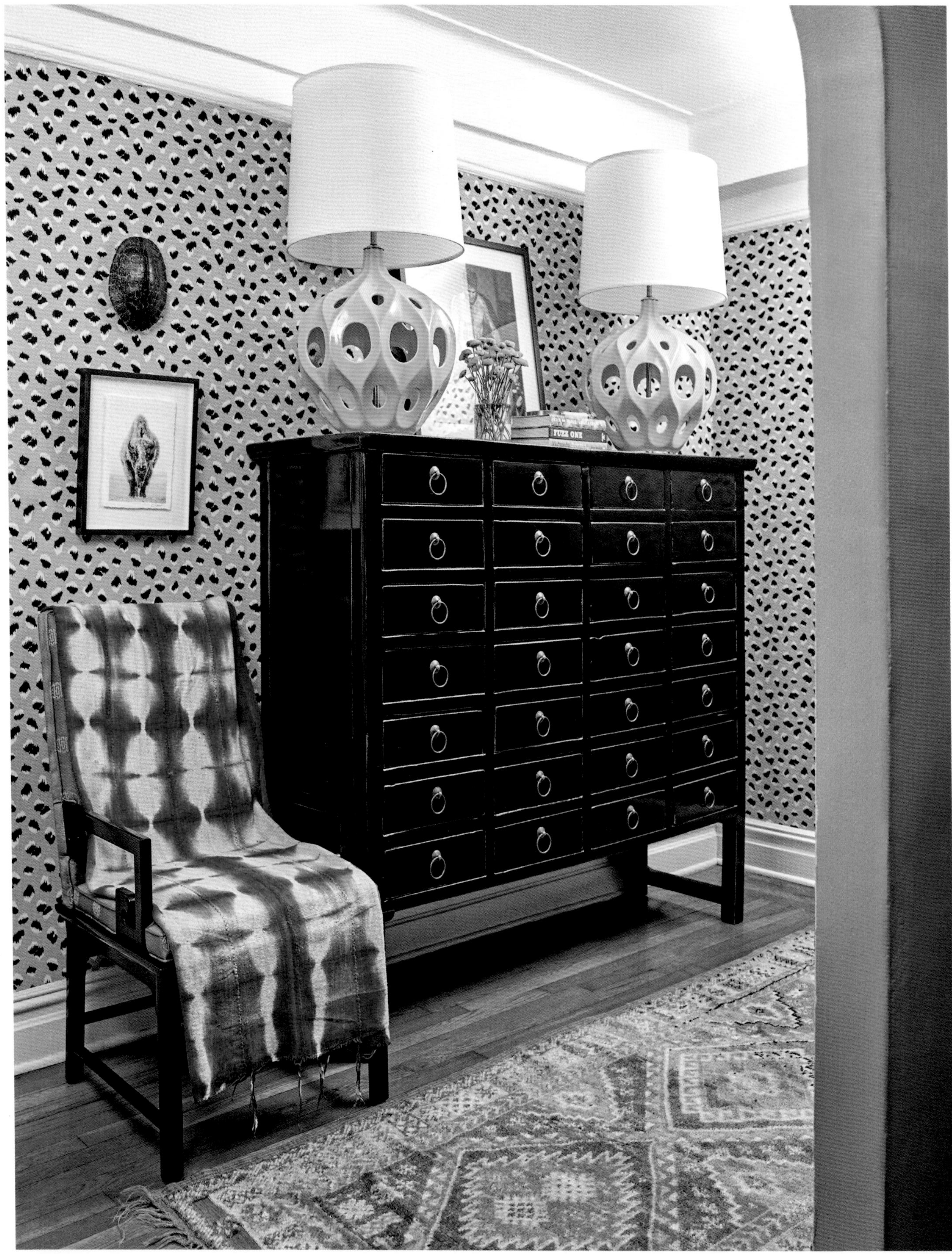

ENTRYWAY STORY

The entryway is more neutral than the rest of the apartment, but it's certainly not boring. The animal-print wallpaper in gray and black, and the golden-yellow carpet, play off of the golden wood tones and make them feel more luxe. And the bright, happy yellow lamps provide a moment of transition, introducing you to the world of color that is in this home before you dive deeper into the palette.

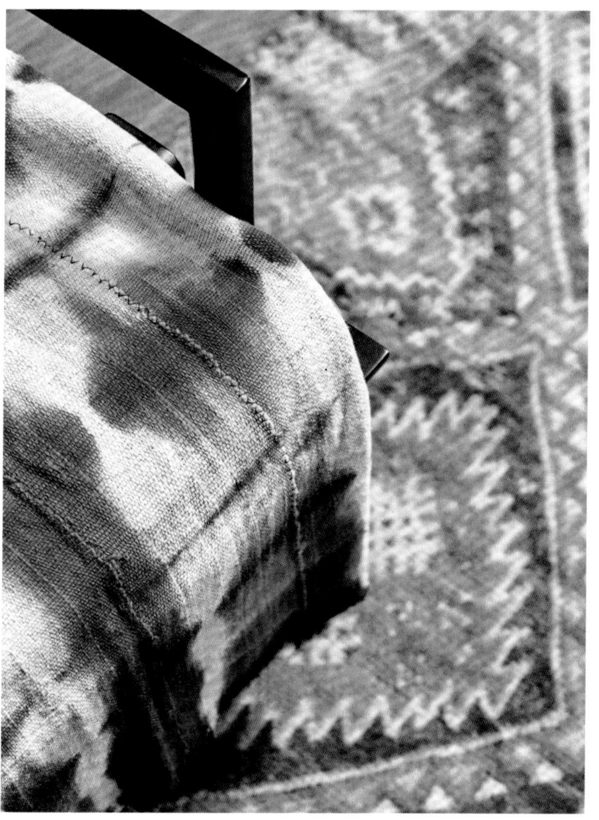

PALETTE INSPIRATION

As a designer, Anthony is always looking to push his boundaries and explore new palettes. He gets his inspirations from traveling, foreign architecture, and home products local to wherever it is he's visiting. At home in New York, he looks for bright pockets of nature amid the concrete jungle, cultivating fresh palette ideas by taking weekly strolls through flower markets. He is also inspired by the city's myriad museums and looks for color in unusual exhibits. He studies the colors found in ancient artifacts at the Metropolitan Museum, and within the Natural History Museum, he's inspired by a host of exhibits, from the colors in the dinosaur bones to the clothing worn by indigenous Mayans.

"I think color gives a space personality," he adds. "Without it you have plain white walls. That doesn't seem very fun. Color in interior design is a way to express yourself, just as in fashion."

BEDROOM REMIX

For bedrooms, Anthony gravitates toward dark, saturated colors, whereas he prefers brighter choices for common living spaces. Here the bedroom has some of the same colors from the living room, but Anthony remixes them. The palette is more limited (it's not as multicolored as the living room), but the colors are used in completely different proportions. In the bedroom, it's all about the teal hue, as opposed to the pink. It's cool and calming instead of rich and vibrant, which makes sense given the purpose of the room. The bed still has pink on it, but it's a much more subdued dusty pink. This is a great example of how you can use colors you're drawn to in very different ways to suit the space you're creating—proportion is key! Reusing color also provides a nod to the other rooms in the house without feeling repetitive or too matching.

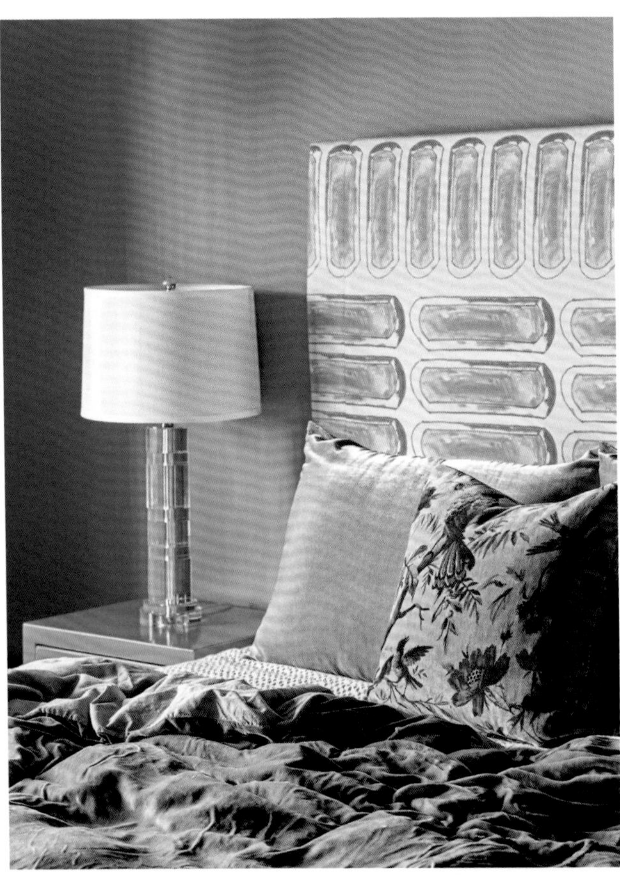

MAKE IT YOUR OWN

- Choose a bold wall color for a dark space that needs life.
- Cover your walls with artwork and larger pieces that will balance out the bold color.
- Make that bold color feel cohesive and integrated by using other colors that have the same range of value. More contrast will make the color feel bolder.
- Take a color palette you love from one room and give it a different mood by playing with proportion.

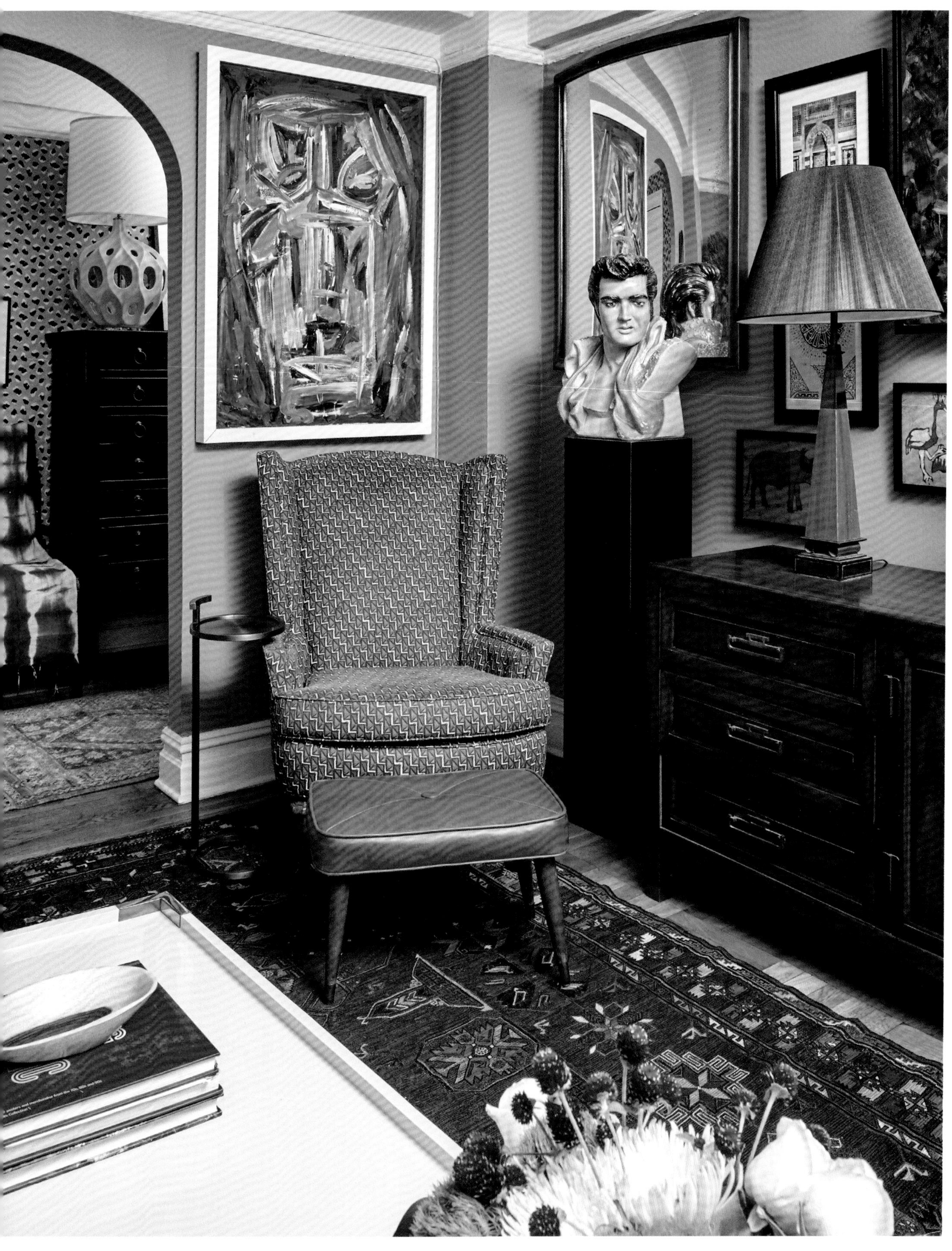

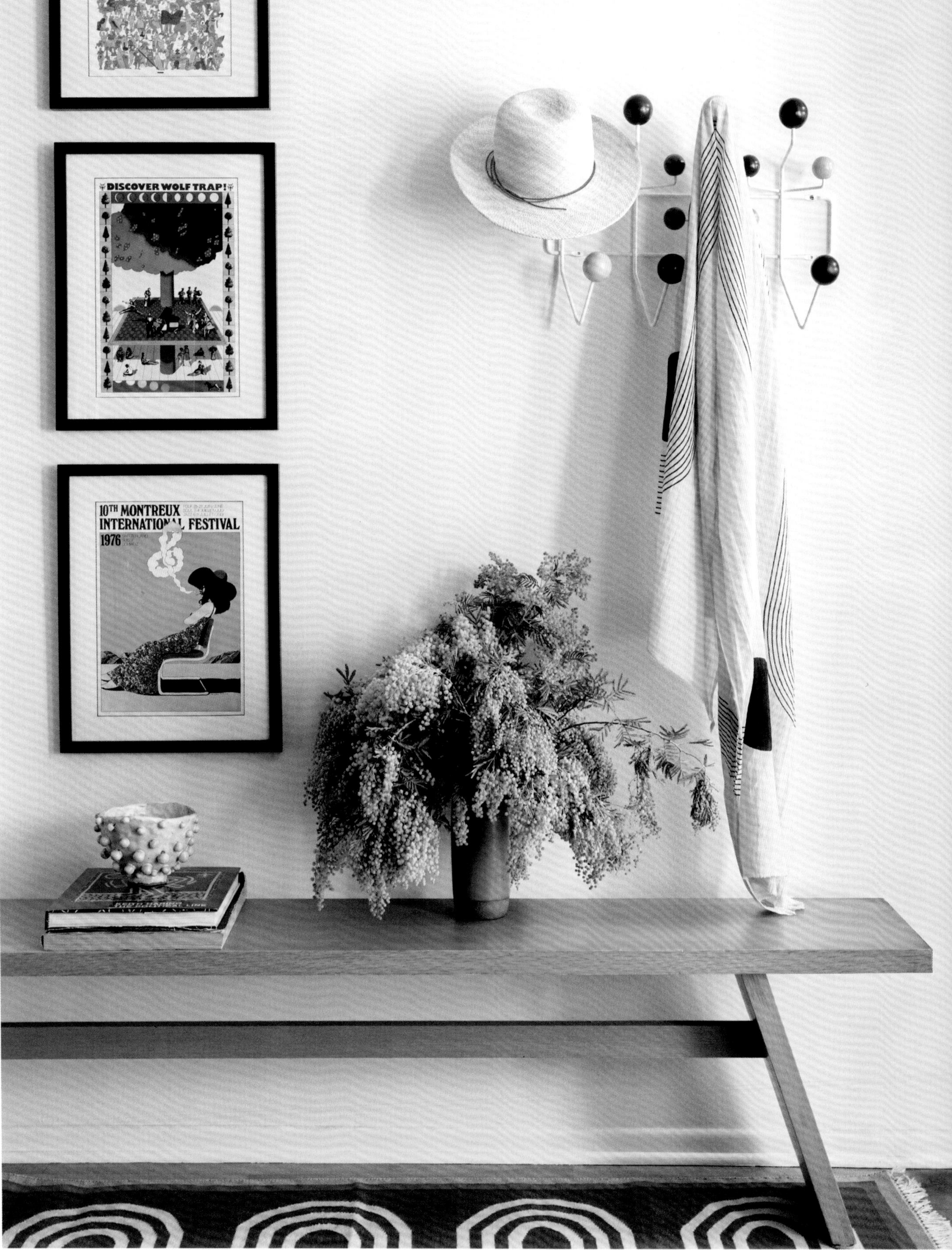
DISCOVER WOLF TRAP!
10TH MONTREUX
INTERNATIONAL FESTIVAL
1976

WORKING WITH QUIRK

HOPIE STOCKMAN
Co-founder of
Block Shop Textiles

It was Hopie Stockman's mother who taught her to design with imagination. When Hopie was growing up, the aesthetic tone of their central New Jersey colonial farmhouse was "anthropomorphic floor-to-ceiling floral chintz and meticulously set tables in an old white barn whose window boxes were stuffed with red geraniums." All this is to say that from a young age, Hopie was exposed to bright colors and bold patterns.

Today, Hopie lives with her husband, David Branson Smith, in what she calls a "true Los Angeles original." A proud home renter, Hopie is fascinated by the design choices of her landlord's architect wife, who built their Southern California–style home in the early 1990s with the help of some friends. The architect's wife designed it for maximum height and light, making use of its western-facing front and shallow lot depth. It also has an open floor plan designed especially to fit the owner's baby grand piano. "The result is a skinny, one-of-a-kind two-bedroom cliff-side house of Tim Burton proportions," Hopie lovingly jokes.

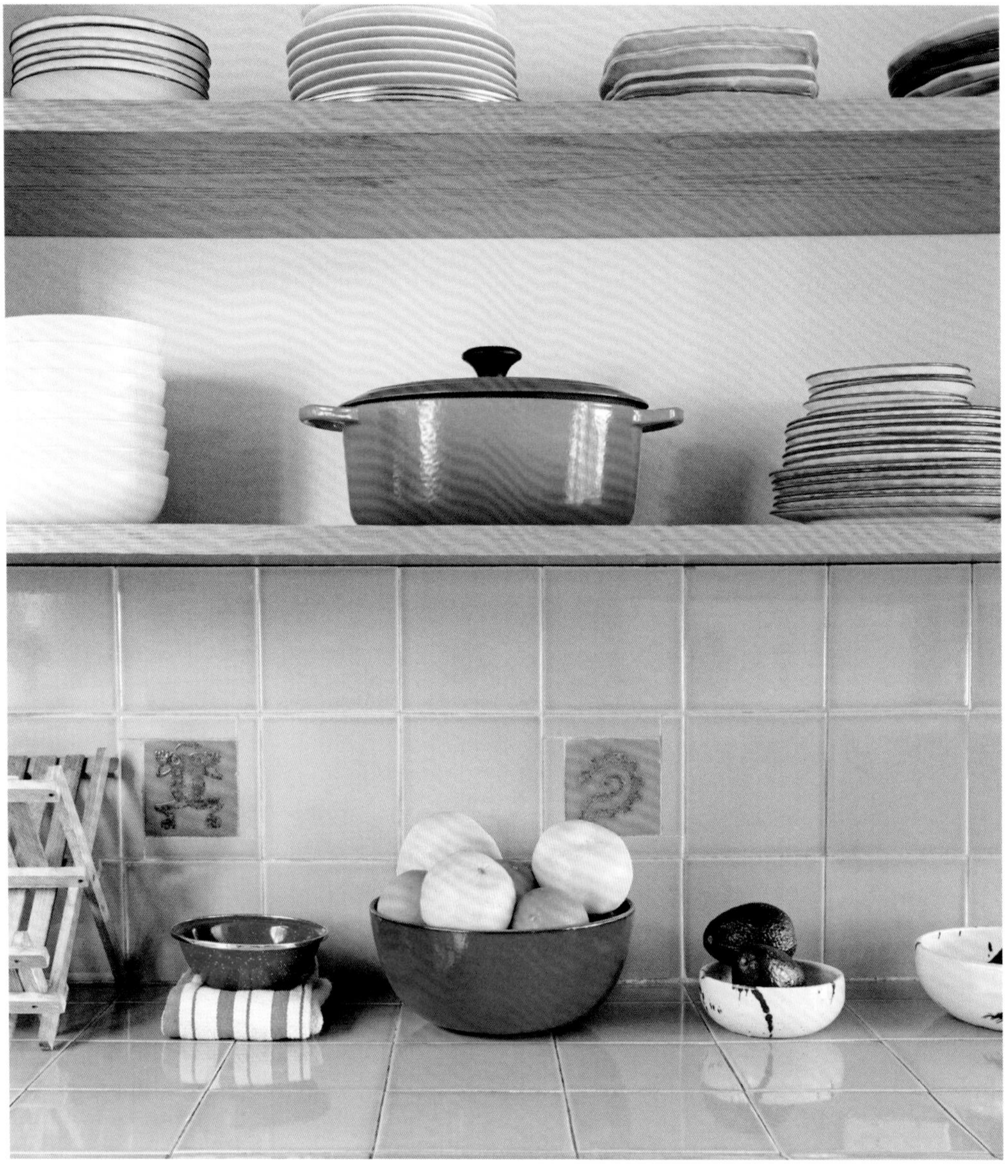

BLUE TILE

Their kitchen is sunny and bright with cheerful blue-green title. Open shelving provides another place to display color, this time through dishes and serving pieces like the happy red-orange cast-iron pot. On the counter, you'll often see a bowl of citrus fruit picked from trees in their yard.

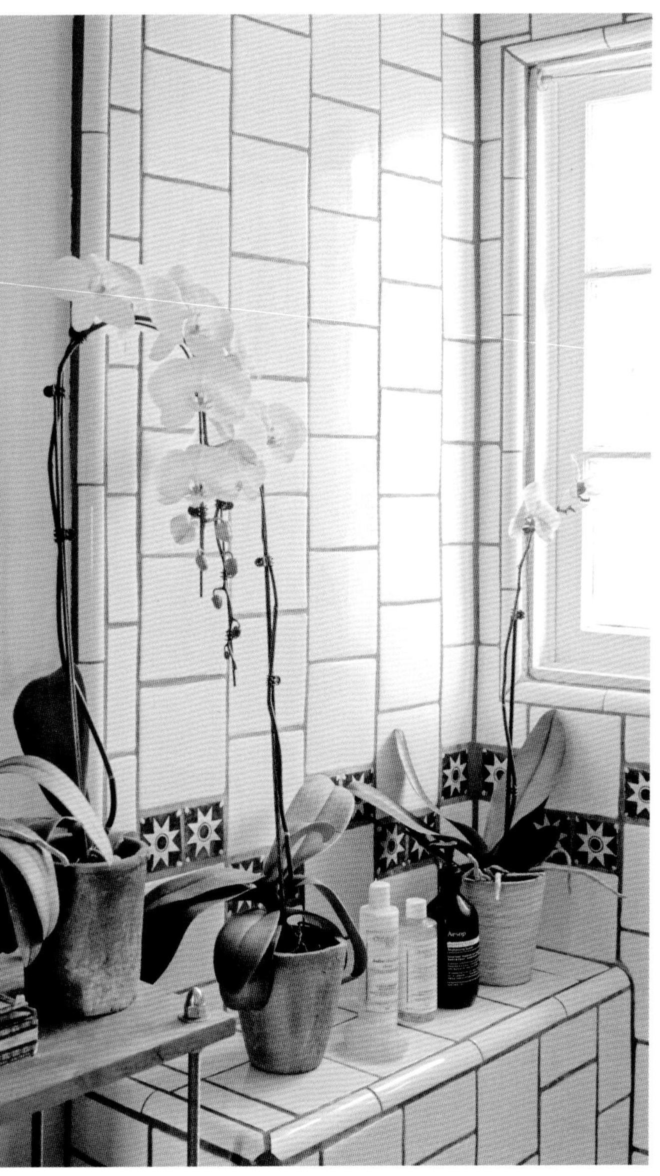

CULTURAL INSPIRATION

As for the bathroom, Hopie simply chose colors that made her happy, and she painted the walls herself, just for fun. Most of the other soft tones in the home are a desert palette of ochre, indigo, peach, and beige, which work well with the mood of the house. Hopie is also constantly inspired by the use of color in the Indian city of Jaipur, and she is enthralled by classic hotels like Diggi Palace or Samode Haveli, which embrace pattern and feature rooms that explode with shades of hibiscus pink, aqua, or pistachio green. One of her favorite interiors is Bar Palladio Jaipur, with its dozens of shades of blue. The psychological effect of all the blue reminds her of artist Anne Truitt, who said that when color is set free, it "sing[s] from the inside. It becomes flesh, it becomes human, it becomes emotion, it becomes alive; it vibrates." Hopie agrees and adds that "having a cocktail in Bar Palladio is like taking a trip into the color blue itself."

BEDROOM COLOR

Though the architecture may be quirky, Hopie likes to abide by the design philosophy of legendary Los Angeles designer Gere Kavanaugh: a room's décor should be informed by its architecture as well as the natural light and outside landscape coming in through the doors or windows. It stems from Gere's idea that design is circular, like a still life painting, never a linear process. For instance, the downstairs bedroom in Hopie's house is at tree level, so she painted it pale green to bring the verdure inside. Likewise, the upstairs bedroom's view is of the Los Angeles skyline, so she painted it pale blue to bring in the sky.

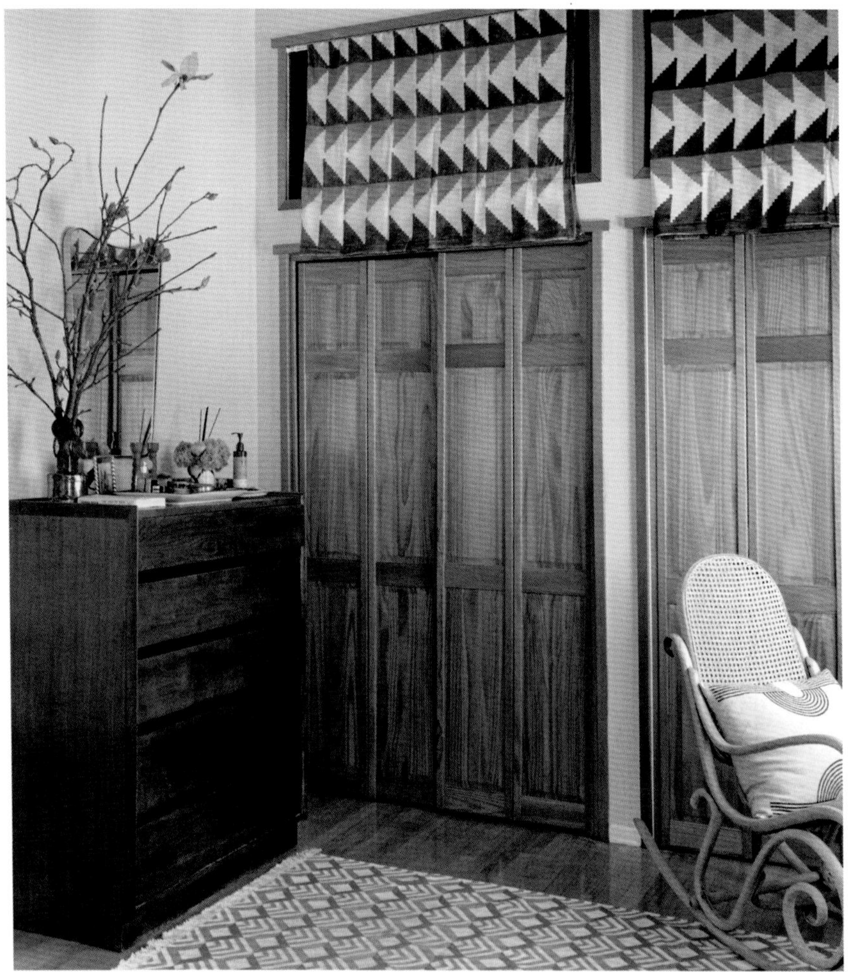

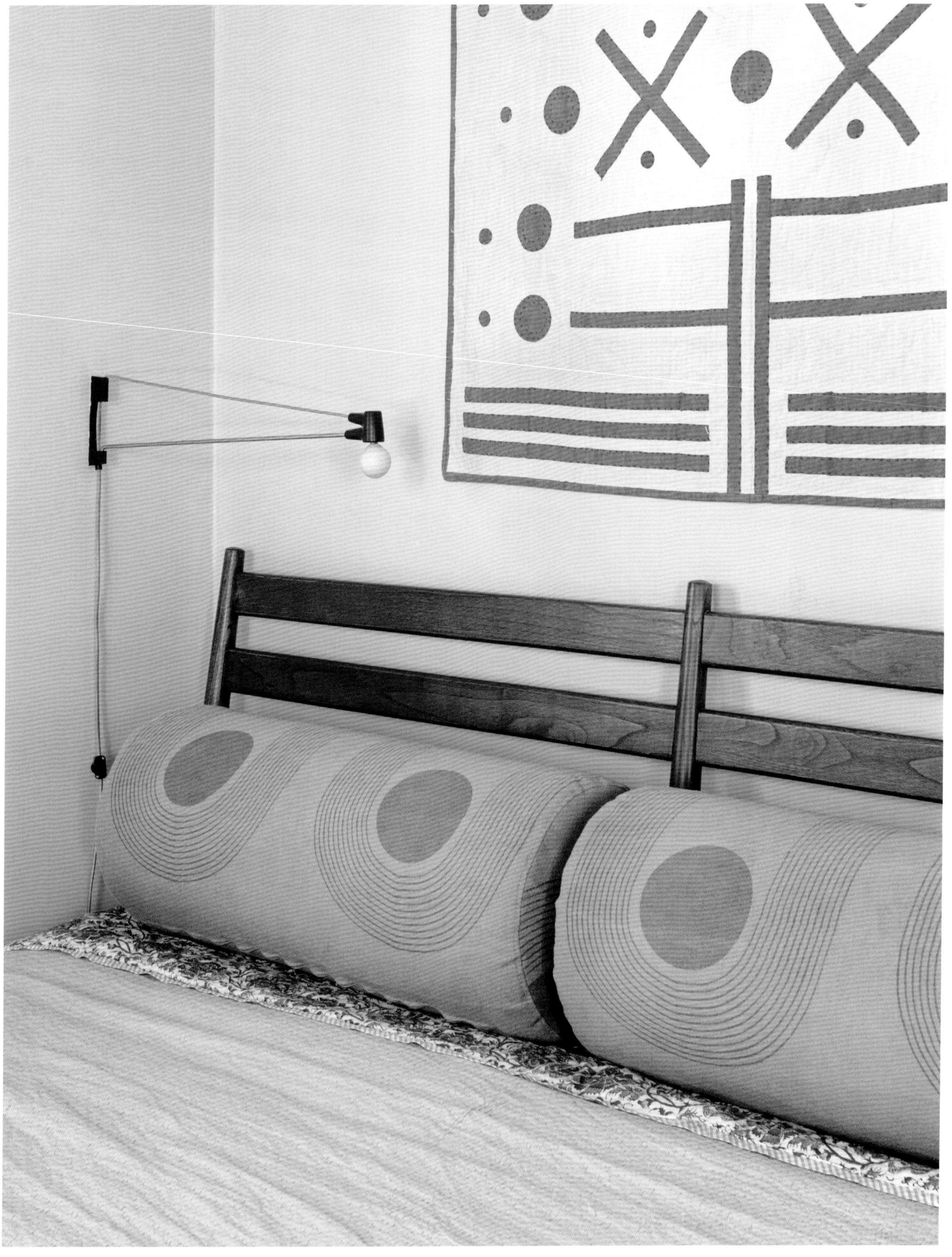

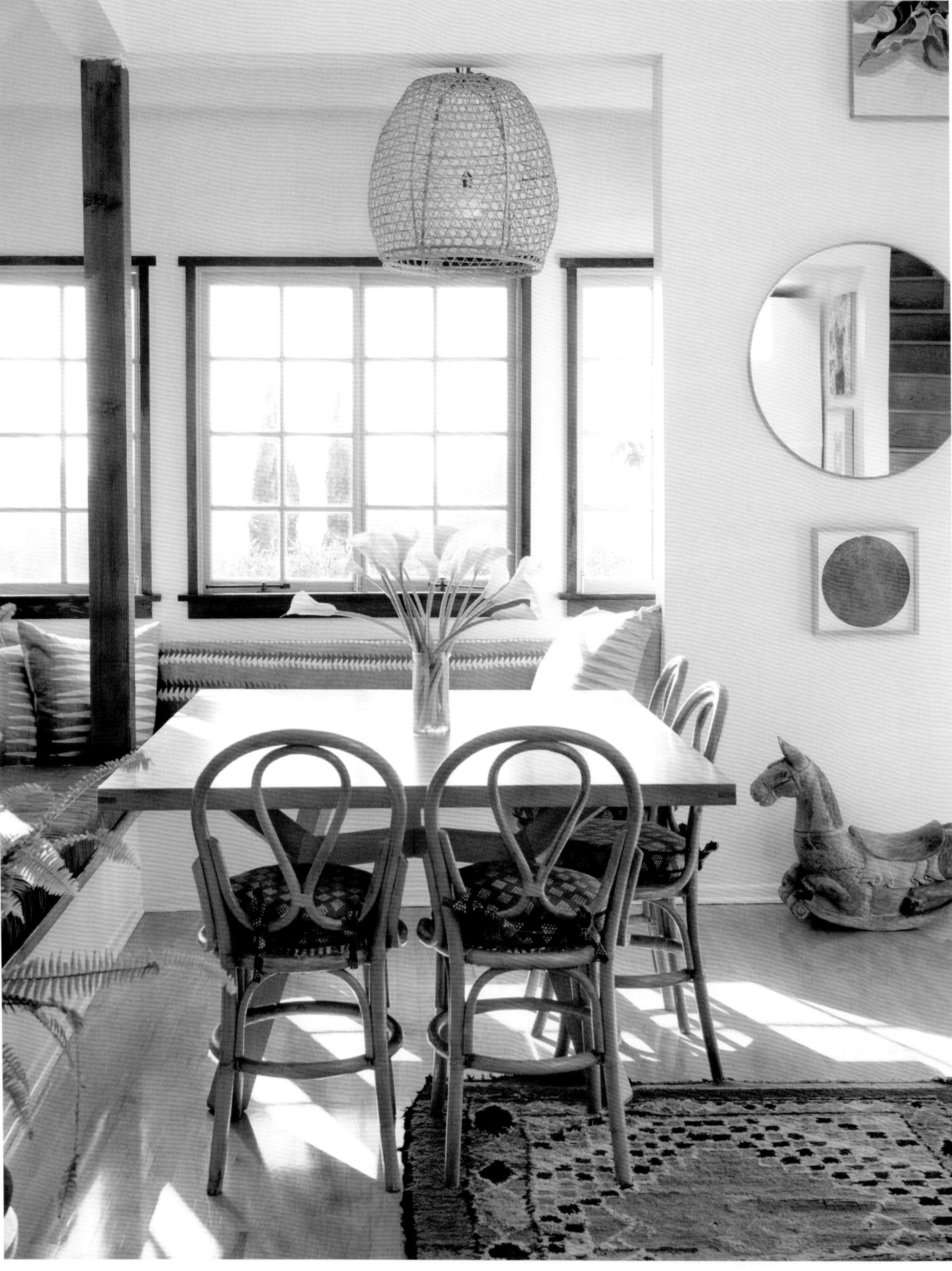

COLOR AND EMOTION

The rest of the house is essentially one large room with rows of windows, so Hopie and David have kept it the same white that their landlords painted it. Their living room is filled with art, framed posters, and colorful textiles. You can tell the space is often changing as they try new things.

It is Hopie's long-held belief that color can lift your mood, inspire ideas, make you hungry, or help you focus. "I love considering those emotional forces when working with color," she explains. She finds it easier to sleep in rooms painted cool colors, like soft greens and blues. She cautions that paint colors are typically richer and darker than they appear on the sample card, so it's usually best to opt for a shade lighter than you think you want. "If you're designing for a small space, keep the walls neutral and go big with color in your accent textiles. Let them provide the pattern and pizazz in a space, and think of them as the room's exclamation points," she advises.

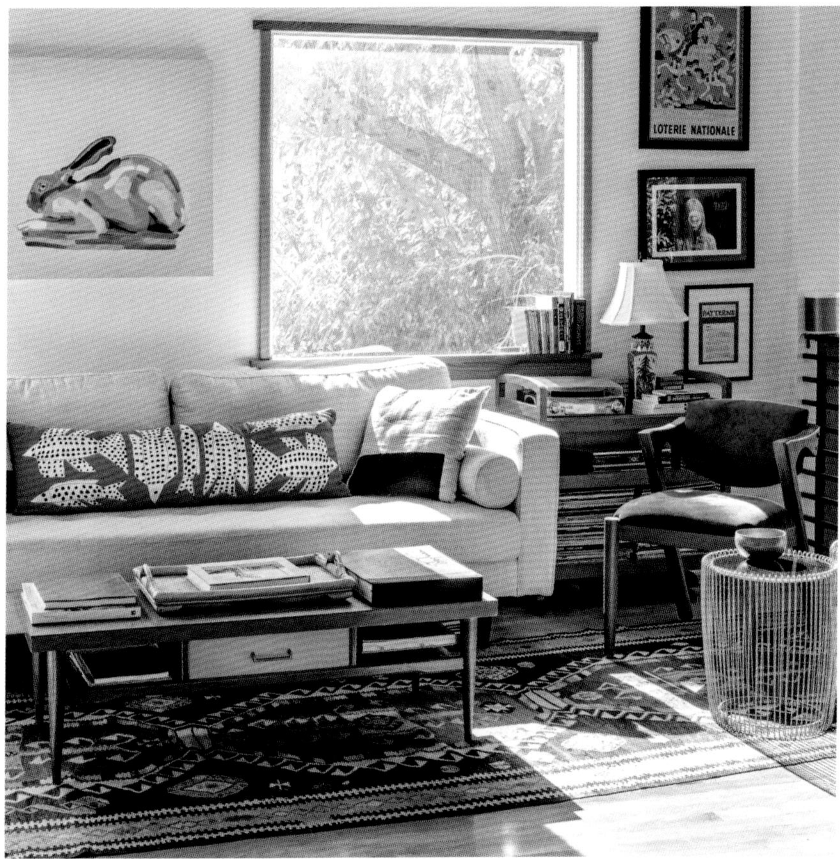

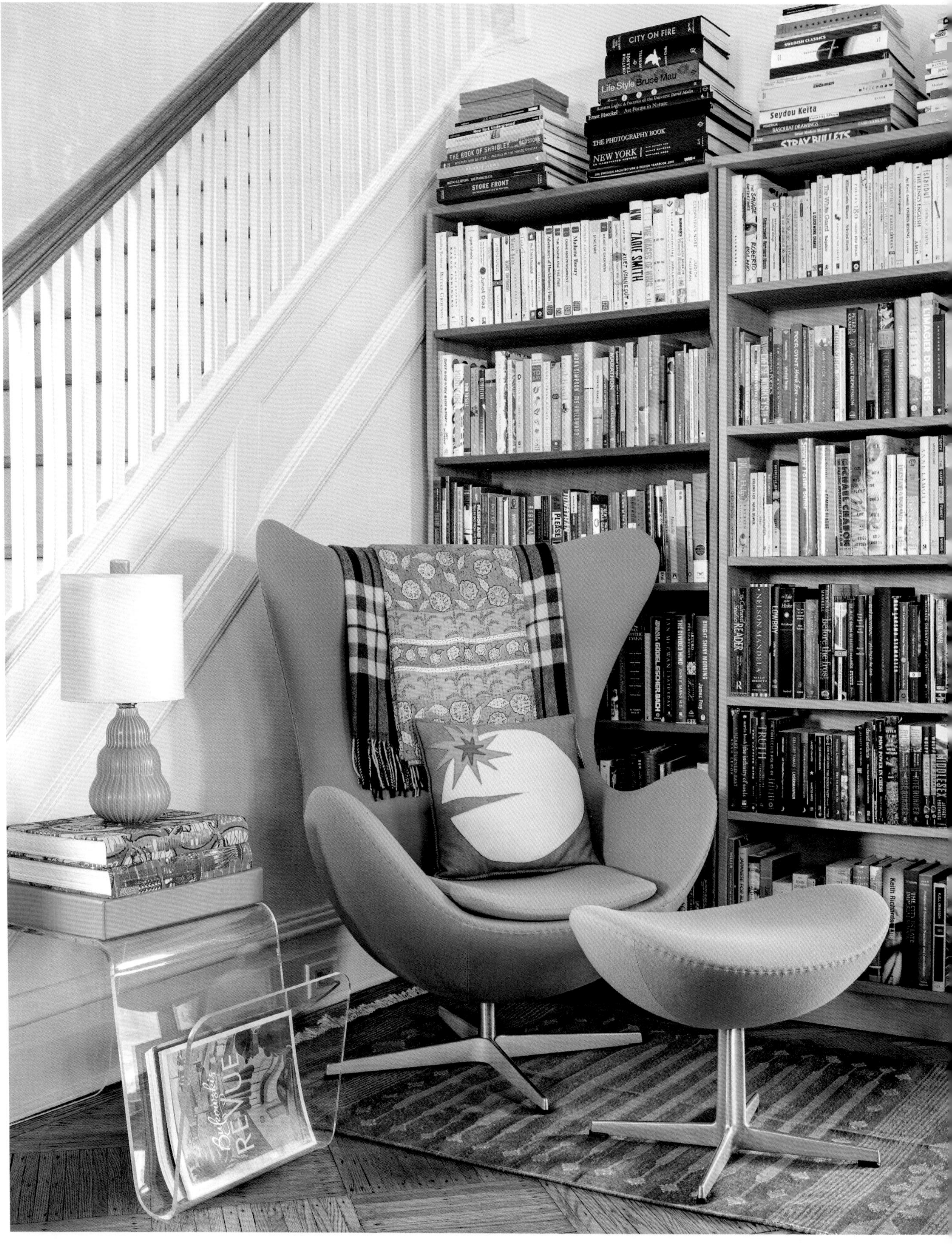

CITY ON FIRE
Life Style Bruce Mau
Ernst Haeckel Art Forms in Nature
THE PHOTOGRAPHY BOOK
NEW YORK
THE BOOK OF SHIRLEY
STORE FRONT
SWEDISH CLASSICS
Seydou Keita
BASQUIAT DRAWINGS
STRAY BULLETS
ZADIE SMITH
KURT VONNEGUT
NELSON MANDELA
LOWBOY
READER
THE DIVIDED MIND
BRIGHT SHINY MORNING
TRUTH
MIDDLESEX
Keith Richards
REVUE

PATTERN PLAY

JEN MANKINS
Owner, Bird Brooklyn

Jen Mankins's Victorian-style home in Ditmas Park evokes the same fresh, midcentury vibe as her stylish stores, Bird Brooklyn. The freestanding three-story house where she lives with her husband (and hamster, Willie Nelson) was originally built in 1910, and the couple purchased it one hundred years later in 2010. It took them a year to renovate, and today it features rich colors and patterns with a fashionable slant. Her husband's Swedish roots and the time they spent together in Sweden also heavily influence their style. "I would definitely say that 'Scandinavian modern meets Mexican color and handicraft' is my look," says Jen. Growing up in Texas, she spent a lot of time in the Southwest and Mexico and fell in love with the colors there.

When you walk into her home, you're welcomed by a colorful corner with a teal armchair, a purple-and-orange area rug, and a rainbow of books. It's clear right away that Jen loves color and isn't afraid to try things out.

When she's purchasing items for her home, she rarely thinks about style and simply goes for what she loves. She's always looking for textiles, rugs, art, and design pieces in vintage stores and online, as well as when she travels. "I think those are the things that make a home very personal and bring all the big furniture pieces together," she says. Her living room mantel is covered in artwork and objects she's collected over time. The warm color of the peach landscape painting over the fireplace sets the mood. Pillows and throw blankets are piled on the sofas and armchairs, providing brightness and warmth.

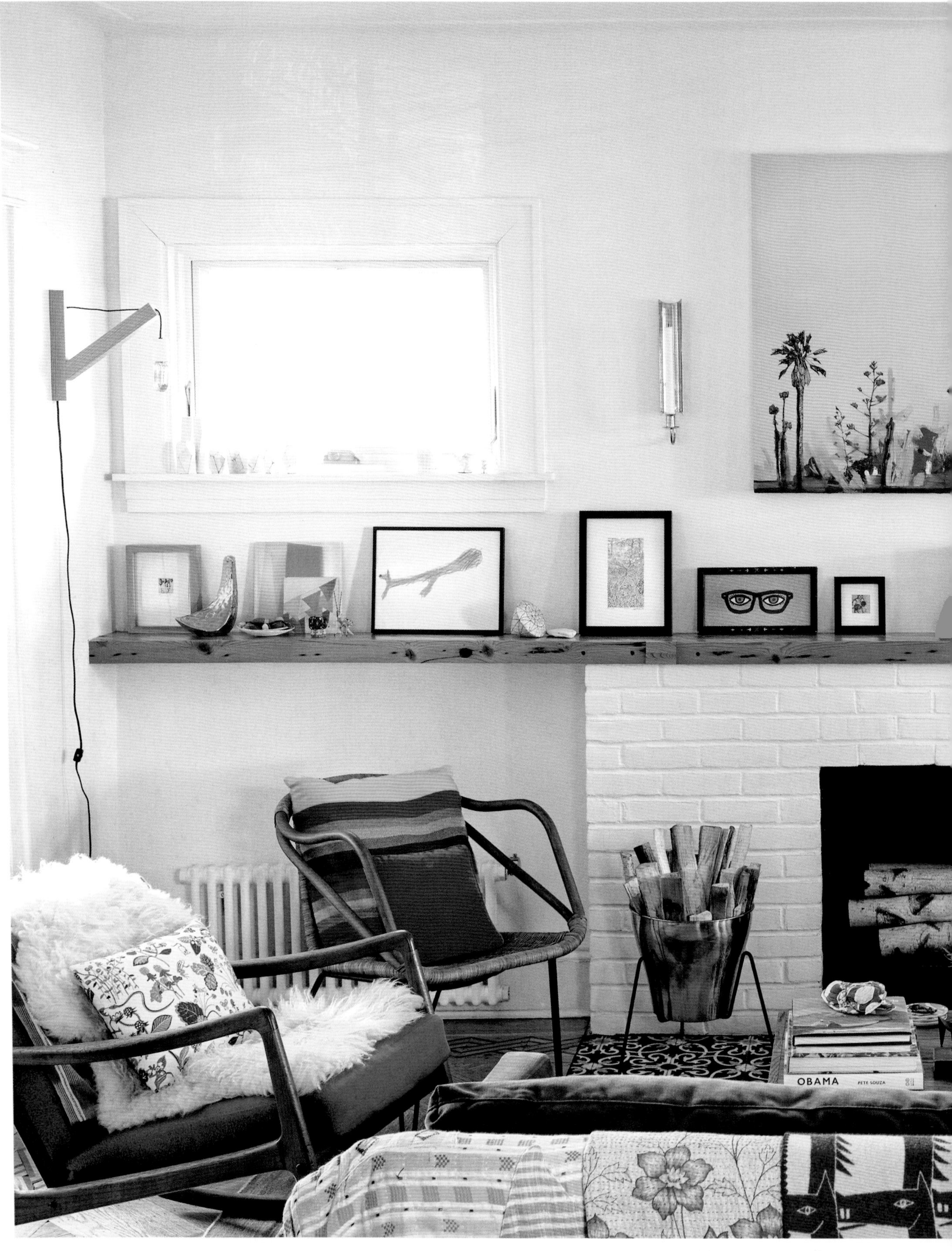
OBAMA
PETE SOUZA

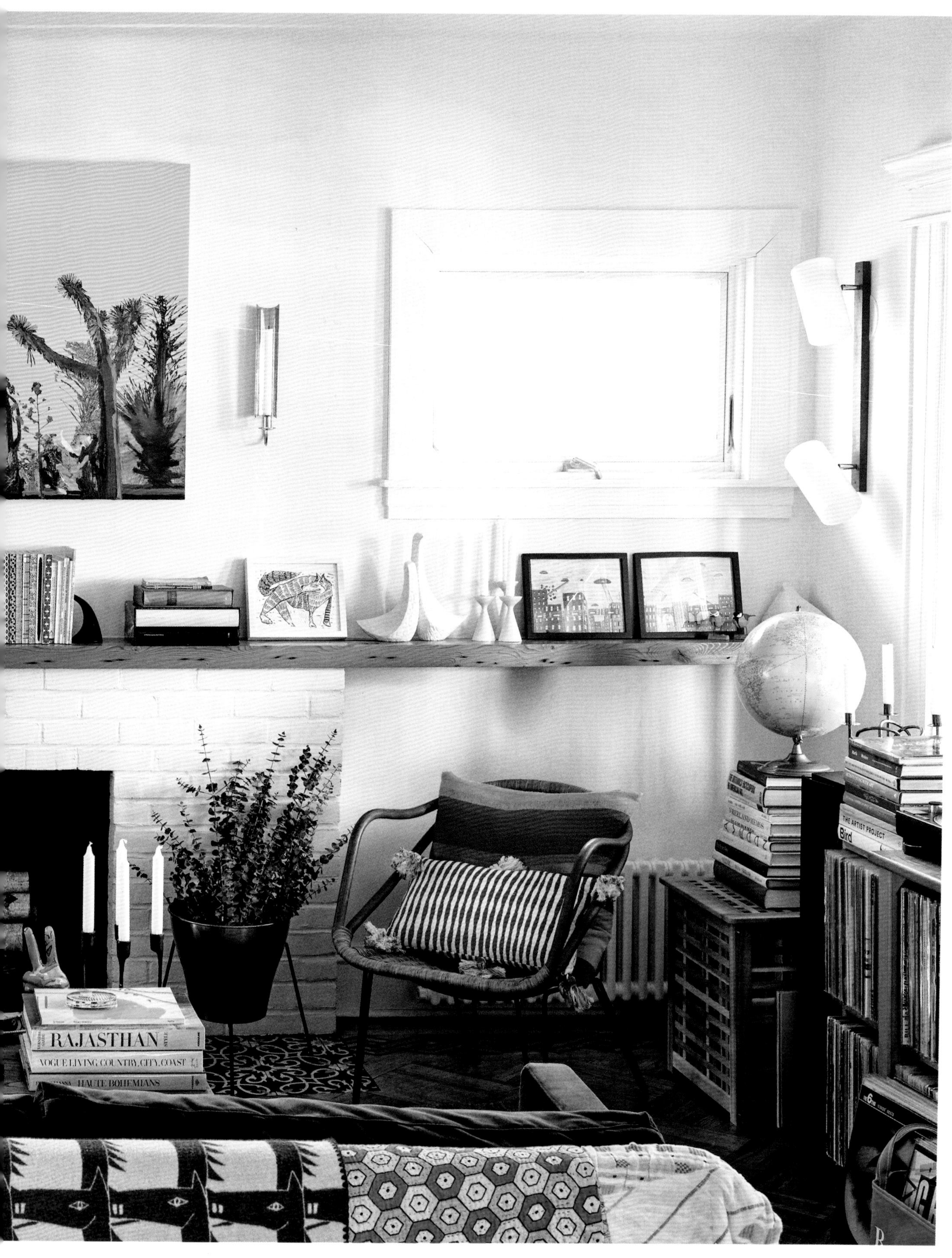
RAJASTHAN
VOGUE LIVING COUNTRY, CITY, COAST
HAUTE BOHEMIANS
VREELAND MEMOS
THE ARTIST PROJECT
Bird

INDOOR GARDEN

The kitchen and dining room are one big space filled with lots of warm wood and plants and accentuated with colorful bursts in the form of chair seats, vases, ceramics, and wallpaper. The wood acts as the primary color in this space, and the lively pieces sprinkled throughout conjure colorful plants in a garden.

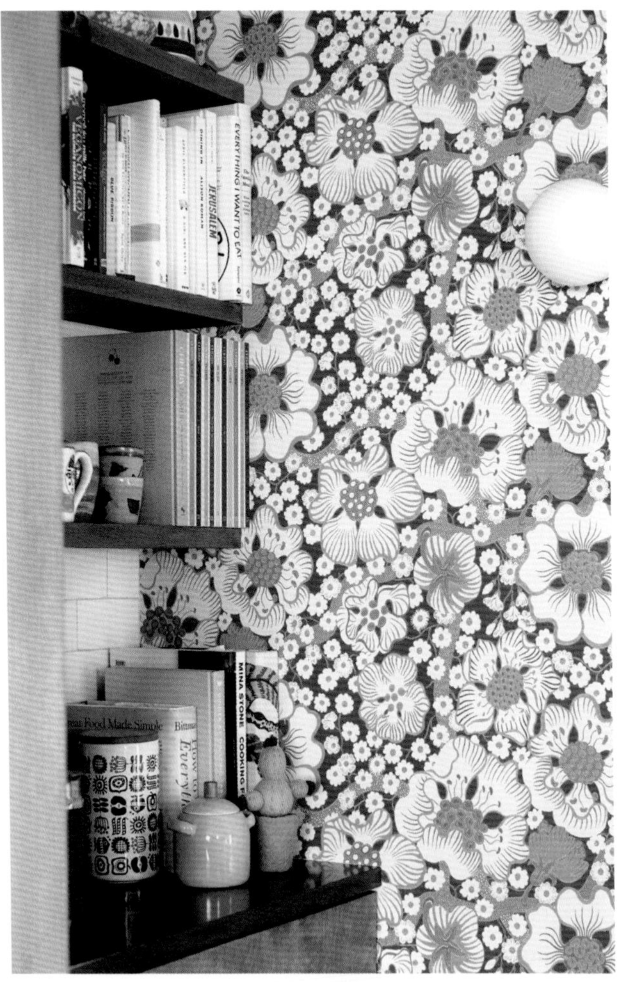

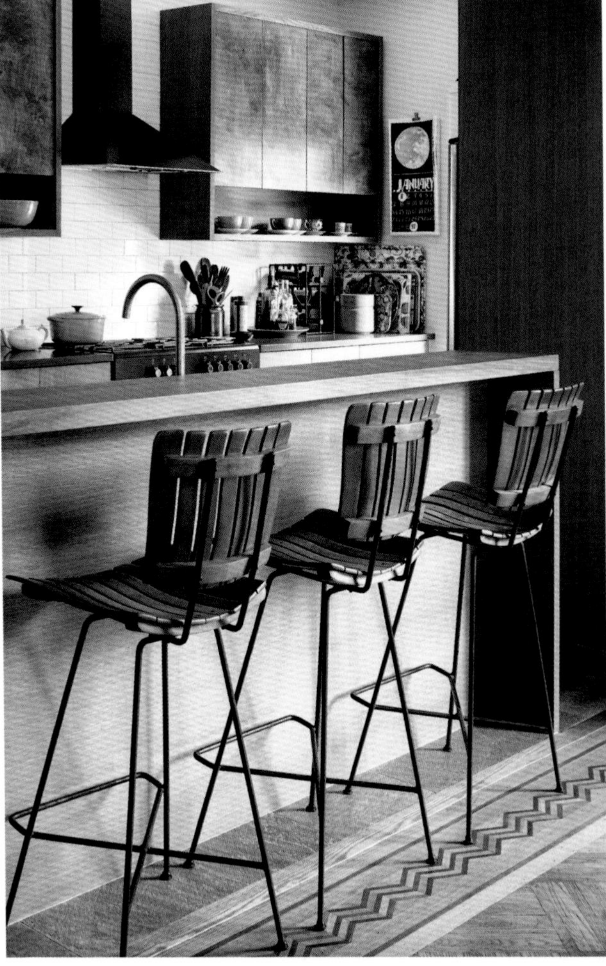

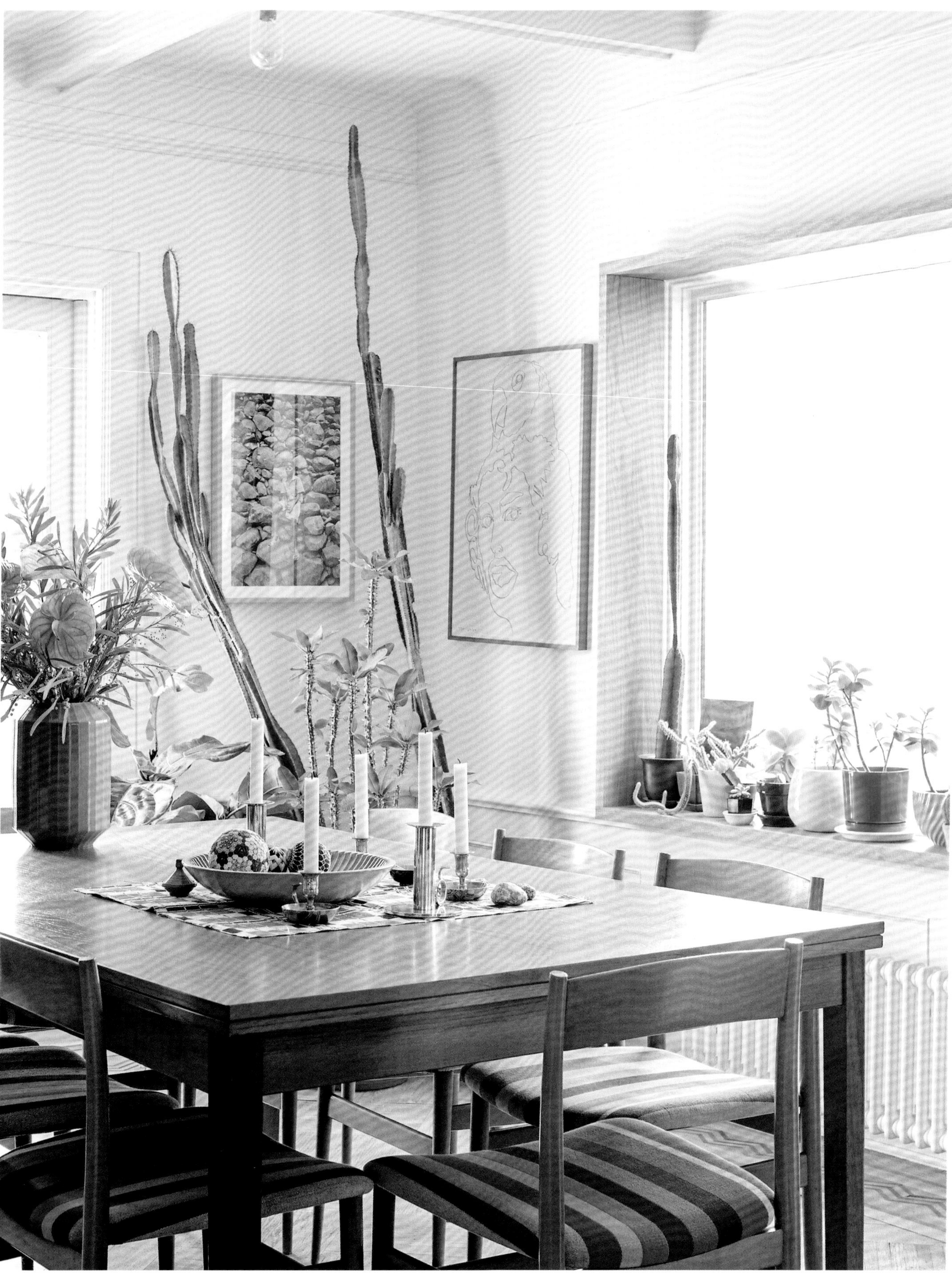

SUNNY YELLOW

Upstairs, it's no surprise that Jen has a room devoted to her closet, since she owns Brooklyn's go-to shop for fashion. A yellow chair adds a punch of color to the space. Yellow is one of Jen's favorite colors, and it makes the room feel cheerful. She displays jewelry and art together on the dresser.

Her home office has a midcentury desk on one side and a pattern-covered couch on the other. The colors in this space are vegetable and garden inspired and are centered around the wallpaper, which was also seen in the kitchen downstairs.

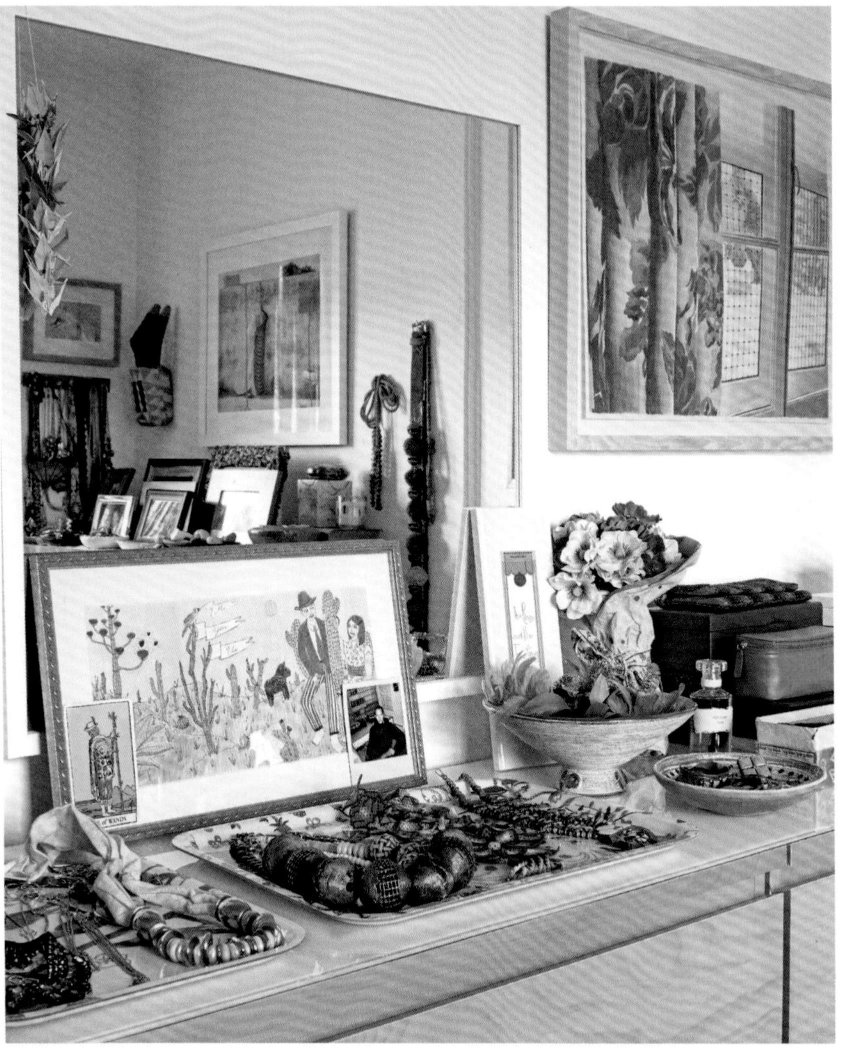

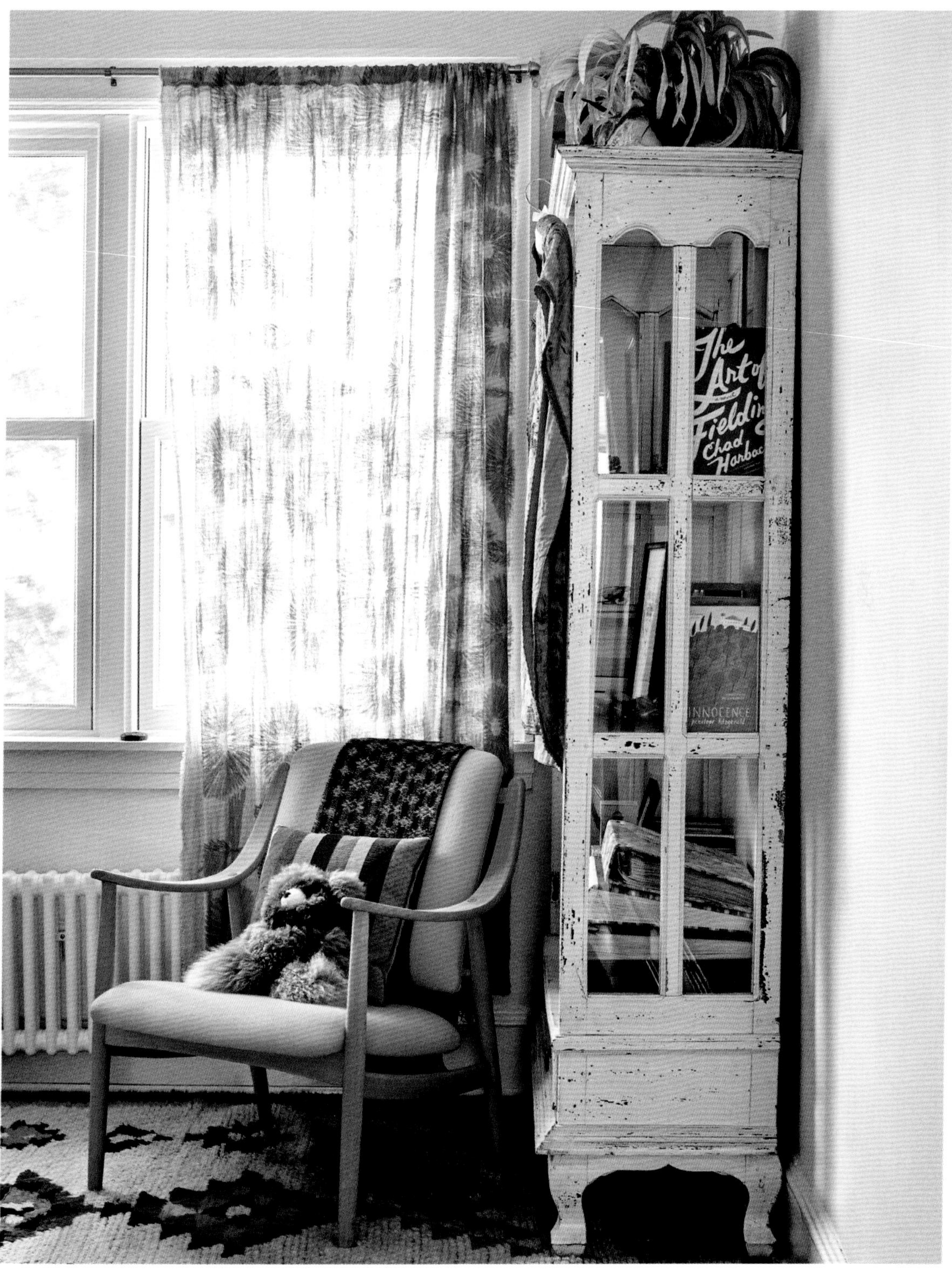
The
Chad
INNOCENCE

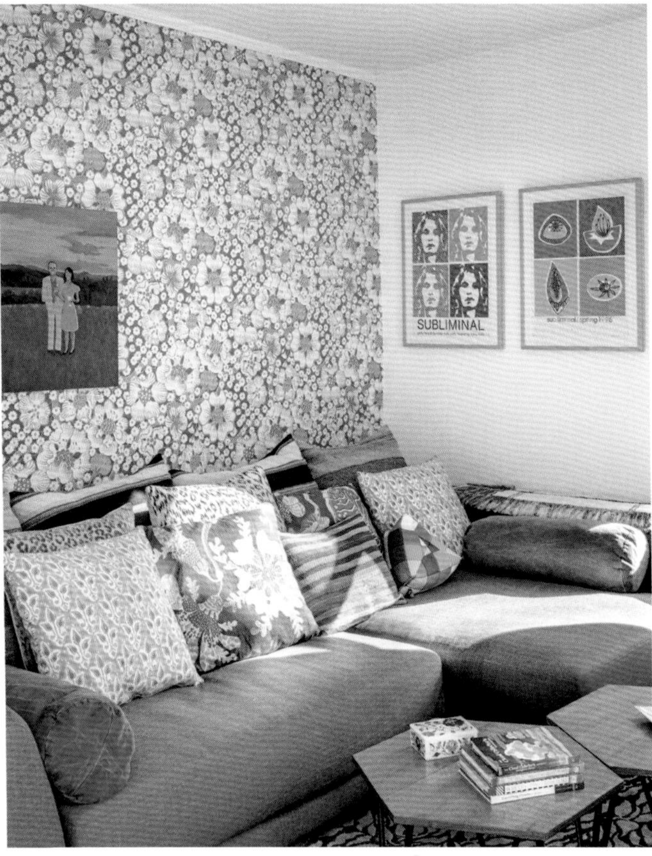

COLOR MOOD

Jen's bedroom is mostly gray with muted accent colors, because she wanted the area to be very relaxing and a place to slow down. She feels that color sets a mood and a tone that can be calming or uplifting, depending on what you want from a certain space. "Color for me has always been linked to nature and fashion," says Jen. "I remember growing up with amazing, vivid pink-and-yellow Texan sunsets and gorgeous pink azaleas, and going down to the beach in Mexico, where the water was bright blue." She's always had white walls, because all of her things are so colorful, but she recently started adding wallpaper and grass cloth, and she's thinking of repainting everything in shades of yellow and pink and blue, having all color everywhere.

MAKE IT YOUR OWN

- Look for patterns inspired by Swedish design, particularly those by Josef Frank.
- Choose midcentury shapes for furniture pieces.
- Use lots of wood! It makes for a welcoming, comforting space.
- Go bold with color and choose warm hues like pink, yellow, and peach.
- Look to the landscape of your childhood or favorite places for palette inspiration.

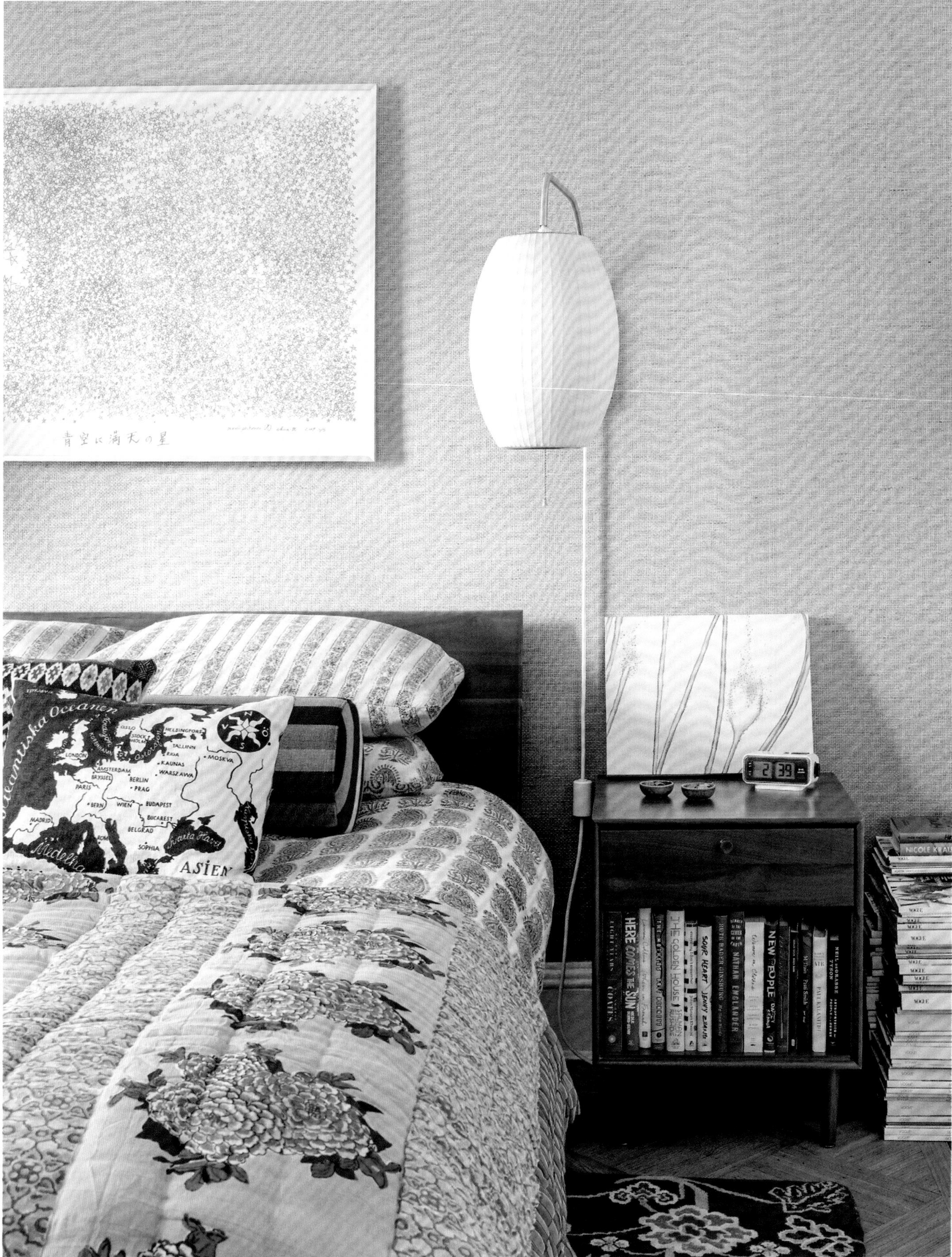
青空に満天の星
Atlantiska Oceanen
OSLO
STOCKHOLM
HELSINGFORS
TALLINN
RIGA
LONDON
MOSKVA
KAUNAS
WARSZAWA
AMSTERDAM
BRYSSEL
BERLIN
PARIS
PRAG
BERN
WIEN
BUDAPEST
MADRID
BUCAREST
BELGRAD
SOPHIA
Svarta Havet
Medelha
ASIEN
N
S
V
Ö
2:39
HERE COMES THE SUN
THE GOLDEN HOUSE
SALMAN RUSHDIE
SOUR HEART
JENNY ZHANG
RUTH BADER GINSBURG
NATHAN ENGLANDER
NEW PEOPLE
DANZY SENNA
PAUL KALANITHI
NEIL DEGRASSE TYSON
NICOLE KRAU

PART FIVE

finding COLOR

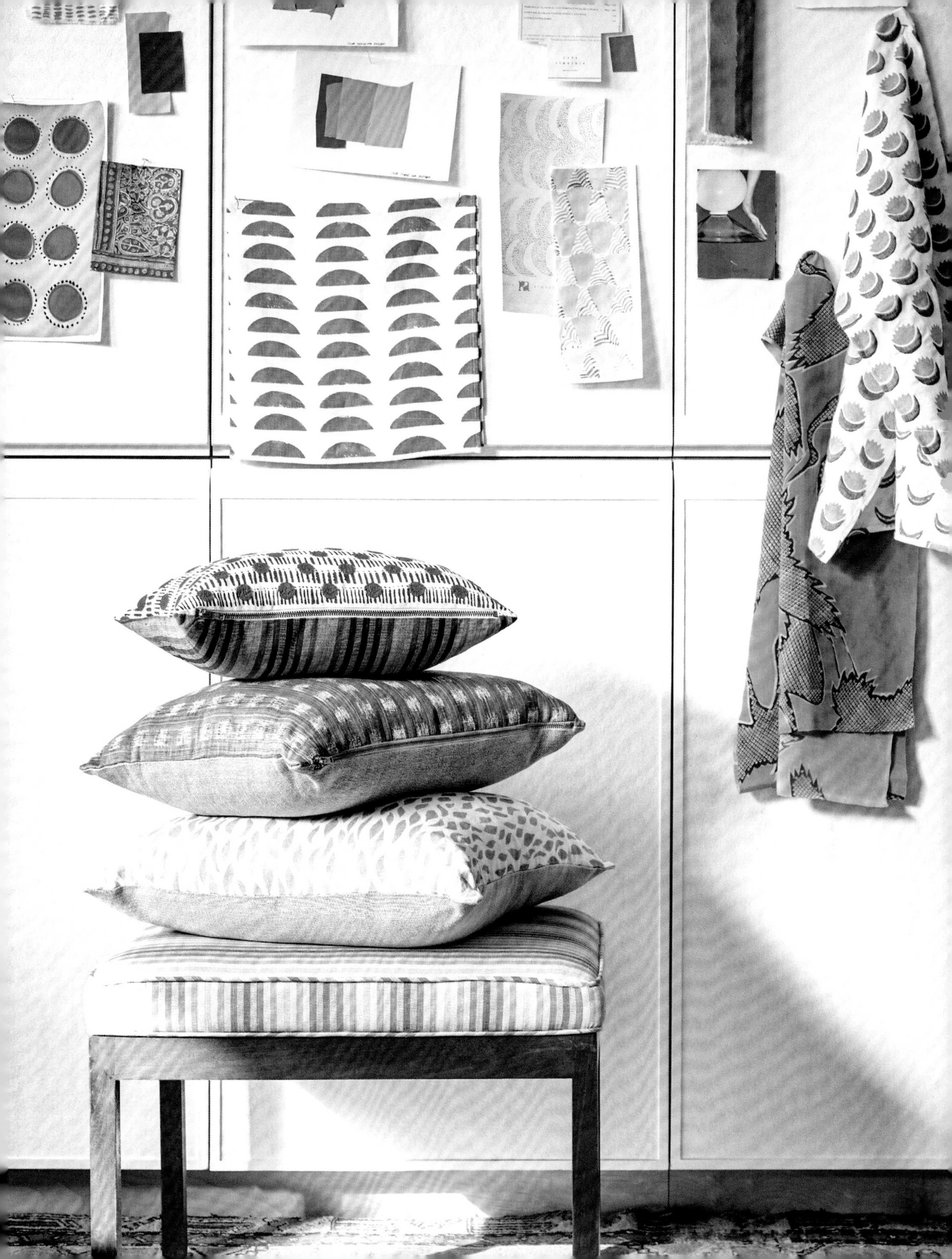

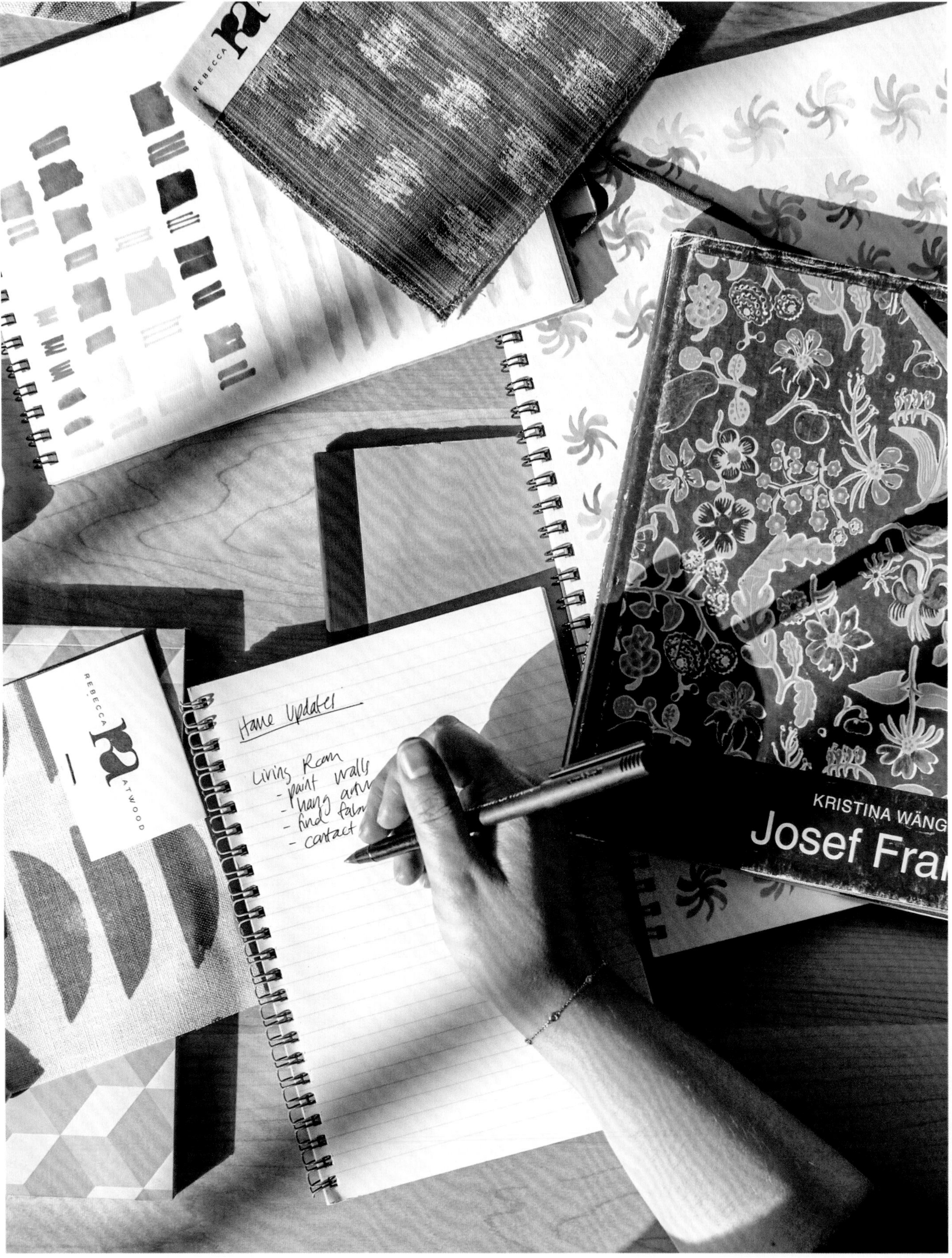
REBECCA
REBECCA
ATWOOD
Home Updates
Living Room
- paint walls
- contact
Josef

After touring the homes in Part Four, I hope you are inspired by the personal process of color selection and have some ideas for incorporating color into your home. The most interesting homes out there are unique to their inhabitants and filled with thoughtful color choices, objects, and patterns that reflect a distinct personality, life, and point of view. While many of us think that the first step to designing a living room is finding a sofa, buying a great rug, or even deciding on a "look" or "concept," the makings of a thoughtful home actually begin with an overall color palette. It can evolve with time, but it's as integral to the process as layout. Now it's time to find *your* colors so you can create a space that makes you feel happy and tells your individual color story.

COLOR SCOUTING

Finding your colors starts with looking at the world. Before you begin decorating your home, or even pulling together color palettes, you need to explore. Go back through your color memories, connect with them, and jot down other color memories that come to mind. Start noticing the subtleties in color you see in everyday life and how they make you feel. Creating a deep connection to your surroundings starts with understanding what you really like. Now that you're familiar with all the variations of tint, tone, hue, and shade for each color of the rainbow, brainstorm about which versions speak to you most. Hopefully, your mind and your eyes are now open to infinite possibilities. I find that this process of gathering inspiration and contemplation allows for discovering color you've never really noticed before and opens the door to making meaningful connections between your life and those colors.

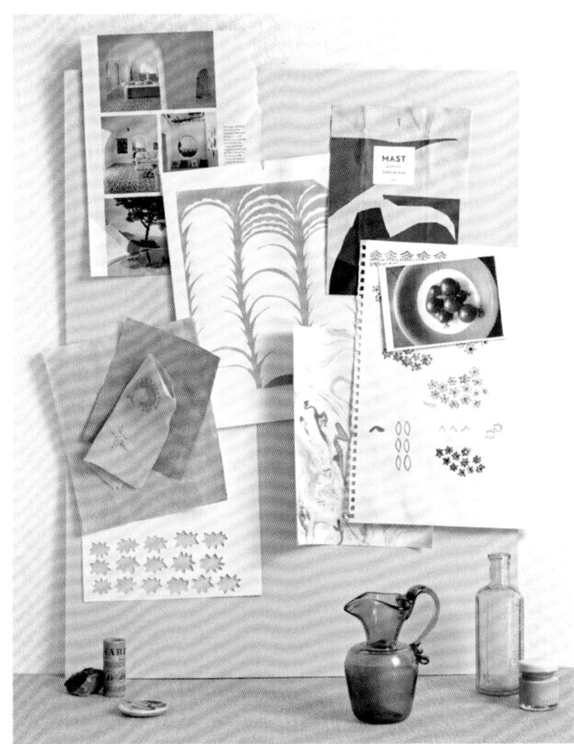

MAKING THE COLOR CONNECTION

Here are a few questions that will help you decide on just the right tint, tone, shade, or finish of a hue. Use these questions for each hue in the color wheel, including neutrals.

When you think about this color. . . .

- What is the softest version of this color you remember? What is the deepest version of this color you remember?
- What happens if you tone the saturation down or up?
- What is a warm version of this color? What is a cool version of this color?
- How does this color change with the time of day? What does it look like in bright light or low light?
- What natural materials are this color?
- How does this color change when it's matte or shiny?
- What objects do you already own that are this color?
- How does this color make you feel?
- What smells do you associate with it?
- What connotations does this color have for you? What does it mean to you?
- What season does it make you think of? Can you think of different versions of this hue for different times of year? Does it feel different in the summer than in the winter?
- Imagine it in a landscape. Is there a place that makes you think about this color?
- What childhood memories do you have with this color?
- Where have you spotted this color recently?
- What foods are this color?
- Are there people in your life you associate with this color?
- Which artists and designers use this color? Which brands?
- Does this color remind you of a certain time in your life or a period of history?
- What places remind you of this color? Have you seen it differently when traveling someplace new?

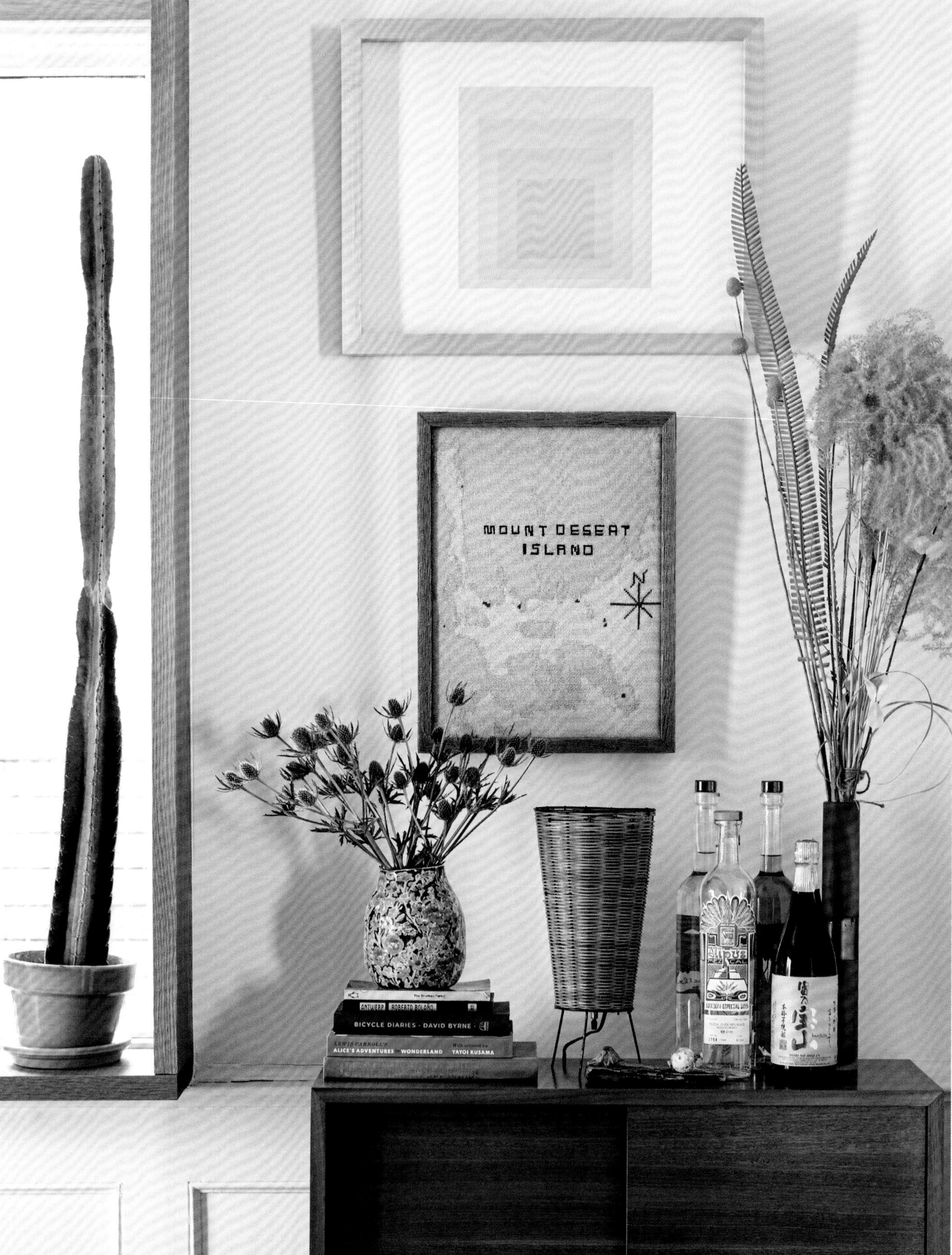
MOUNT DESERT
ISLAND
N
ANTWERP ROBERTO BOLAÑO
BICYCLE DIARIES · DAVID BYRNE
ALICE'S ADVENTURES IN WONDERLAND
YAYOI KUSAMA

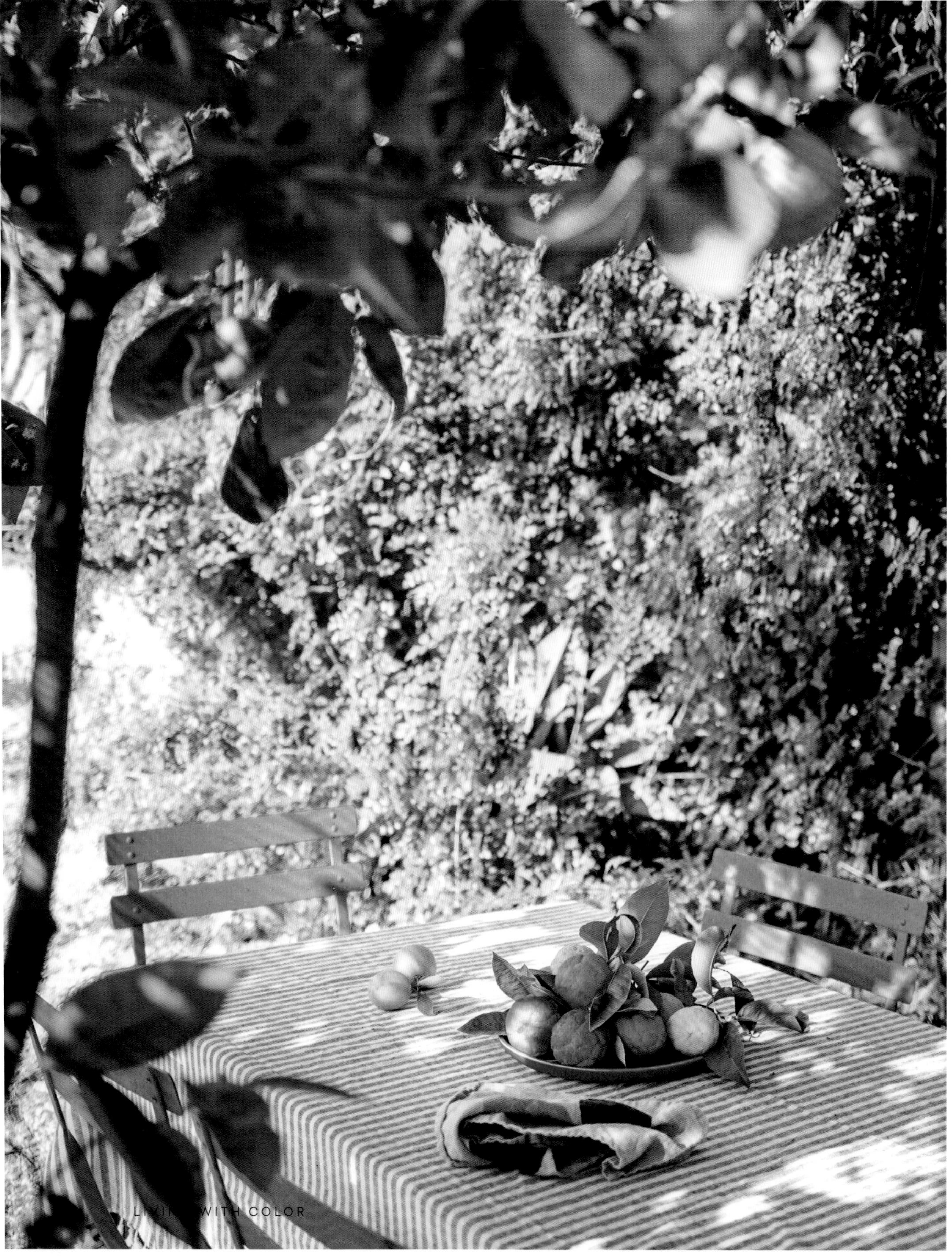

COLOR HUNT

Next, set out on a color hunt. This sort of scouting can become part of your daily routine. Slow down to notice color in the world around you. I like to snap photos of the moments that interest me, because I like to physically gather my inspiration and samples. My photos are abstract and focus on color and composition, as opposed to a scene. They are often up close and cropped. You could also take notes and try to describe the color using words, if you find that more helpful.

DAILY PALETTES

Embrace the newness in every day—every moment, even! Find time here and there and practice slowing down. It's the perfect thing to do when you need a break from your routine or are waiting for the bus or to meet a friend. Look around the spot you're in, and let your eyes wander. Notice the colors, the shapes, the clothes people are wearing, the way the light hits the wall. If you have time, take a walk around the block, or any area you happen to be on a regular basis. Notice the changing colors of the leaves, or drink in a weeknight sunset. You might see an unexpected color pairing that draws you in—like rusted metal against a pink building—or it could be that you start to notice the subtle variations of green within your neighbor's yard. You may not see anything groundbreaking, but sometimes the mundane can take your breath away.

Explore some of your favorite places, but look at them with fresh eyes. Notice the details. This could be your favorite shops (check out the merchandising), a restaurant (look at the color of the menu and the way the food is plated), a garden (take notice of the light), a library (books are so colorful!), or even a friend's home where you love spending time. Seeing how other people pair colors and create a space is eye-opening.

EDIBLE PALETTES

Take a trip around the grocery store and look for color instead of the items on your shopping list. The muted green of an artichoke, the yellow of a Golden Delicious apple, a bright lime, and red-purple endive lettuce are shockingly beautiful when you look at them through your color-hunting lens. Look for interesting packaging. Bring home a few items that speak to you. This color hunt is about exploration and also a chance to think about what colors you might use in certain areas of your home. The colors I find at the grocery store are vibrant, rich, and, of course, food oriented. I might use those in a kitchen or dining space. Start by putting some of what you bought out on your kitchen counter, and see how it makes you feel. It's a safe way to test your reaction to these colors with little commitment.

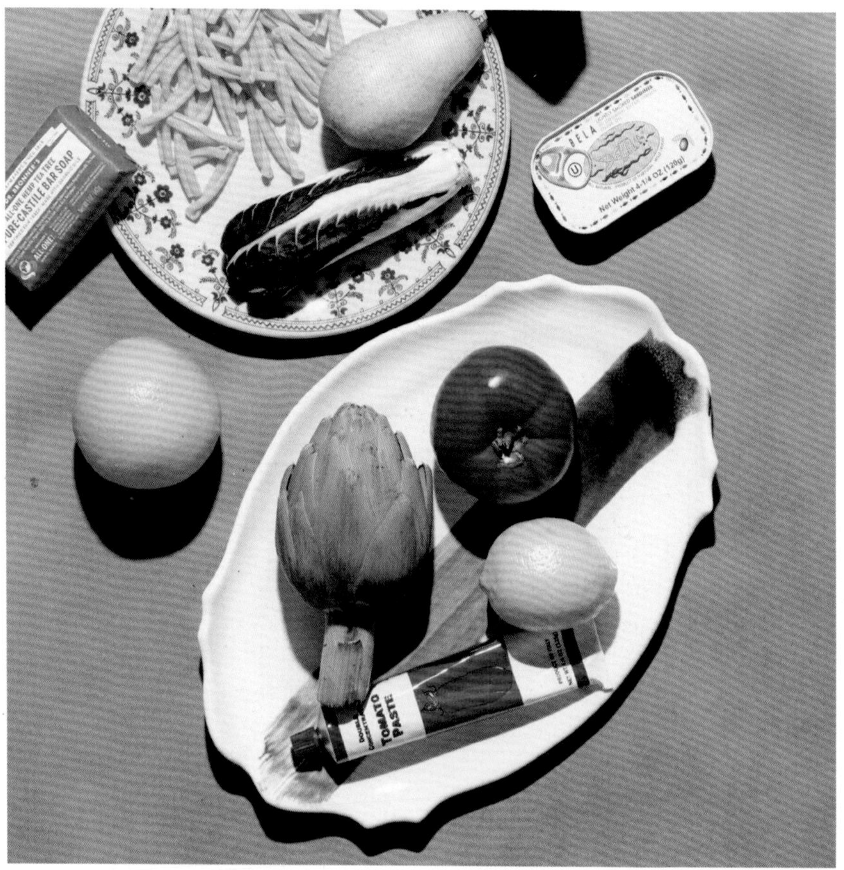

NATURAL PALETTES

Now go out into nature. Take a day trip to the mountains, the beach, the forest, a stream, or the desert. Explore places that are a bit beyond the confines of your daily routine but still close enough to do in a day or weekend. Pick up objects—a leaf, a shell, or a rock. Pay attention to what interests you. Bring home some of those items that you love the most. This is real fieldwork! The more you do it, the more you will notice. Here you can also pay attention to the landscape. Try to gather a whole scene that you want to turn into a room. Remember how it makes you feel, and see how it changes with the time of day.

When you're on vacation, or in a new place, notice how the light may be different than it is at home. Explore how different cultures around the world use color. I always find it's easier to spot inspiration when I'm in a new place. Take it home with you. Create a color story that evokes the feelings you had when you were away.

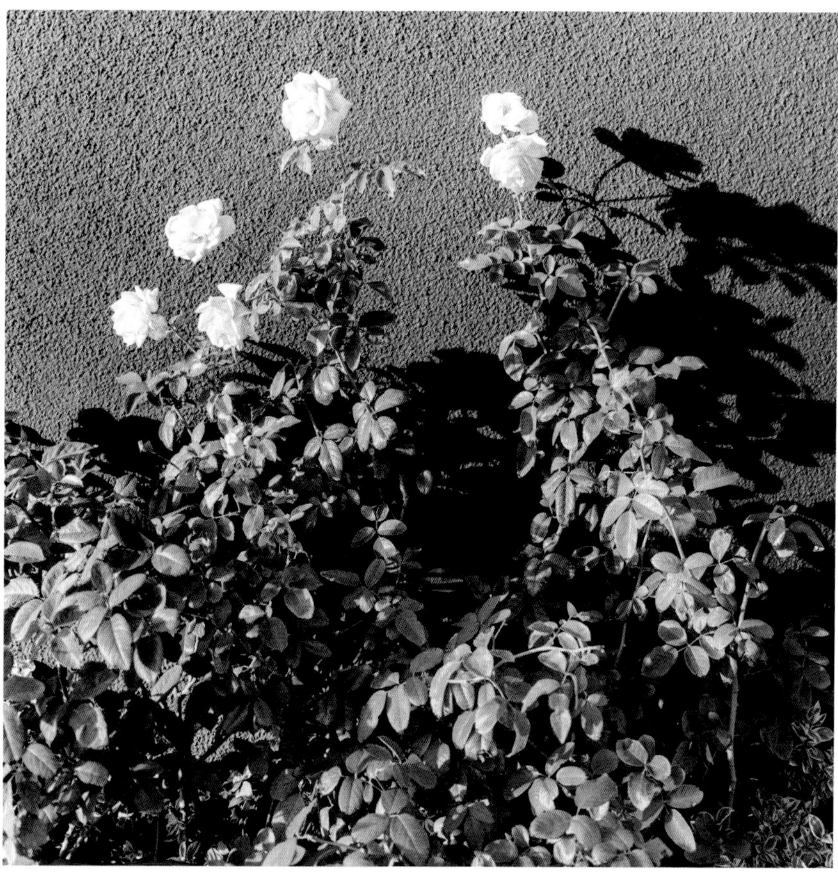

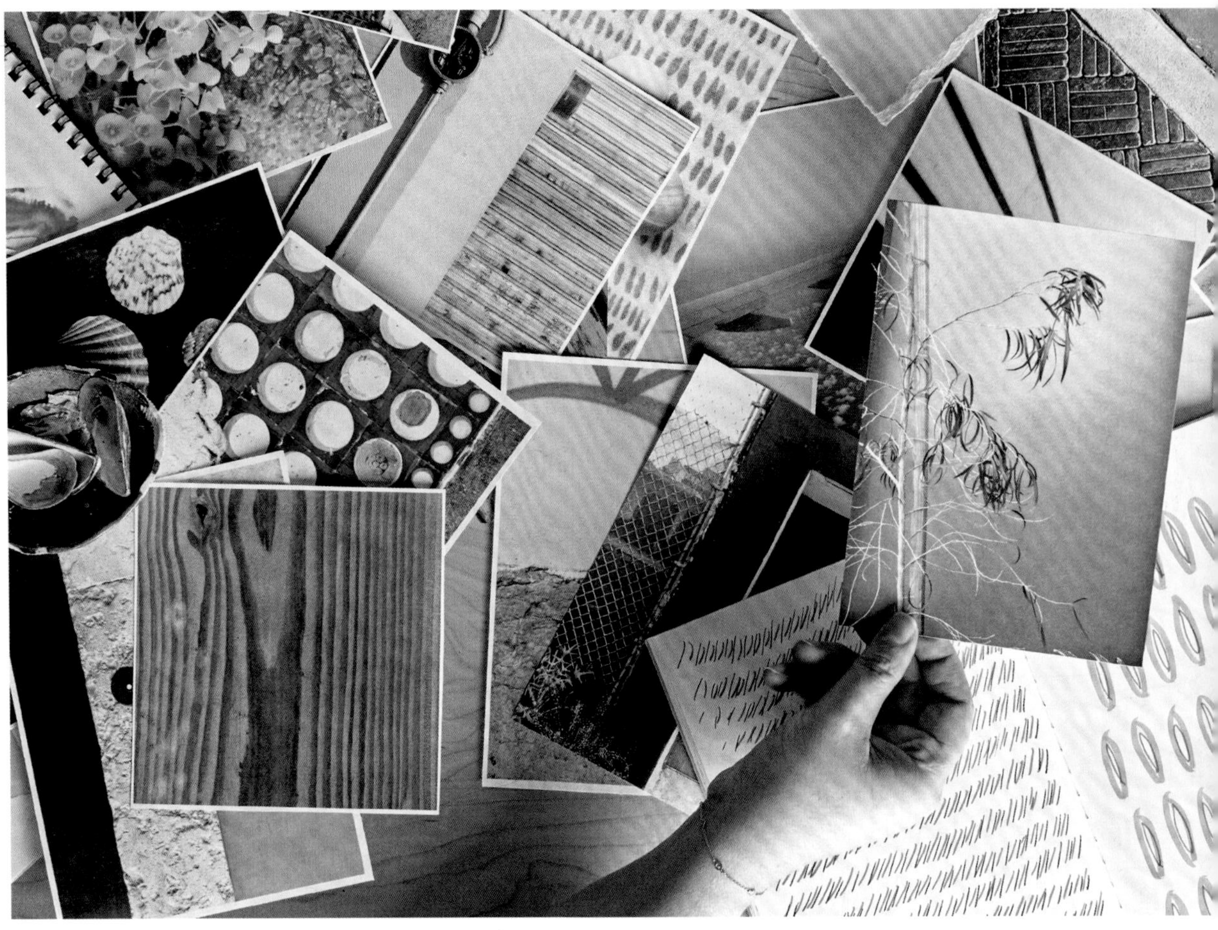

REFLECT

Noticing the colors, patterns, shapes, and beauty around us is one way we can slowly change and grow. It's a practice that can increase and have a big impact on the way you live. Embrace curiosity. Gather all of your color-hunting images, objects, and notes together and keep them in one place so you can take stock of what you're drawn to, and identify any patterns that arise. Maybe you pick the same tomato red over and over again, or you're really feeling shades of green—or perhaps it's more general, such as loving subdued versions of colors. You will continue to grow this collection, but take a moment to reflect after doing this initial color hunt. You're learning to create your own system for inspiration.

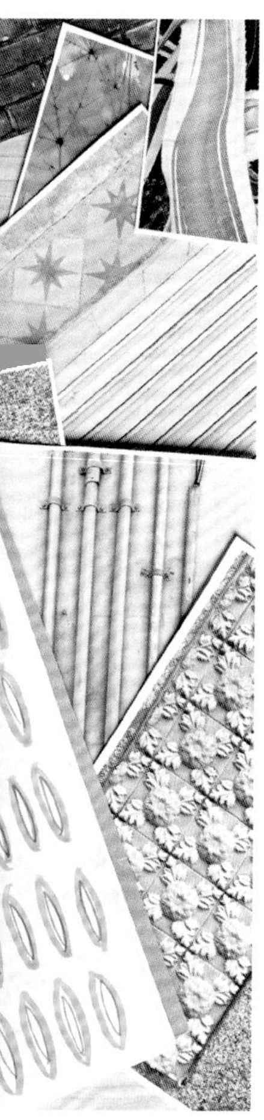

EXPLORE FURTHER

Once you have an initial idea of what you're interested in, delve deeper. Start investigating those patterns even further. Go to a museum exhibit and look at how artists use and pair these colors. Wandering around the museum can give you clues to time periods in art and design that inspire you. You might discover that you love the bright colors in Fauvist paintings or the bold gestures of the Abstract Expressionists. Keep an open mind and don't worry about "figuring out" what the art means; rather, focus on how it makes you feel. Make a note of the pieces and artists who speak to you so you can look up more about them later. Go to the library or bookstore and flip through design and art books and magazines. Pinterest, Google Images, and design blogs are all great places to find more ideas. Embrace this new way of paying attention to the world of color.

COLOR AND LANGUAGE

As you continue your color hunting, consider color language along the way as well. The connection between language and sight is strong. We see colors better when we have a specific word for them, as discussed in a BBC documentary on color and the Himba tribe in southern Africa. While the Himba have names for many different shades of green, they do not have one name for the color blue. When they viewed twelve squares of color—eleven green and one blue—they had a hard time differentiating the "blue" square. However, they can see more shades of green than most Westerners can, with ease, because of their language.

If you give names to the colors you're drawn to, like "lilac blossoms," you will feel more connected to them and see them more distinctively. You might impose your love of these flowers, their scent, and the moment you first picked a fresh bunch for your table onto the color to make it feel more personal. Memories are powerful, and the connection will make you feel happy whenever you look at the chair you upholstered in that color.

This is what I mean by telling your life story through meaningful color. Pick names that speak to places, feelings, memories, or even history. The more personal the name, the stronger its association with good memories, like my "dune-grass green." It reminds me of the movement and varying shades of green at Howes Street Beach, which was just a short walk from my home growing up. It feels comforting, calm, and relaxed, which inspires the places I might want to use that color. I can imagine it in a bedroom or bathroom to remind me of my childhood beach each time I step into those spaces. Open yourself up to new ideas about texture, usage, tint, and shade, and the positive associations that follow will surprise you.

CREATING YOUR SYSTEM

Creating your own process for documenting inspiration, color, and visual ideas takes time and is personal, but it's worth building a system that works for you if your goal is to live in an inspiring and personal space. How deep you go with this research depends on your interests, but always review your inspiration.

In my studio, I have a cabinet devoted to color. I dedicate bins to each major color that are easy to find when I'm working on a project. In my color bins, I'll keep anything that's a solid version of a color—it could be a menu from a restaurant where the paper color was a perfect mint green, an old, ripped silk top that I loved, or paint swatches from the hardware store. This library of colors is a starting point for every collection, and I always have something to react to when I'm designing. I save any colors I made, whether dyeing fabric or painting solid swatches, even if they aren't quite right for the occasion, because they may be just right in the future. When I'm working with a production partner, they need to know exact specifics for the colors. Many companies work with Pantone books, which have become a standard in the industry, but I still prefer to send actual fabrics, colored paper, or, most often, hand-painted swatches. It's more visceral and accurate, like your color wheel will be on page 247.

Once I pick colors for a collection, I refine them based on how they'll be used. The same will be true for you, based on how you specifically implement a color in a space. You may have a green on your wheel that you love, but it might need to be toned down for a wall color or pumped up for an accent lampshade. Think on the context of this color, and you can deepen or soften accordingly. Will it be paint or dyed fabric?

When I pitch colors in the beginning, there's a bit of guesswork and imagination, but then when I get a physical sample of a textile in, I can really see if it looks good. You'll apply this same idea to decorating your home. Bring home samples, move furniture around, create vignettes, and test ideas. There are no wrong answers if you spend the time thinking about what you like and looking at the result. If it doesn't feel right, try something else. If it makes you happy, then you're onto something!

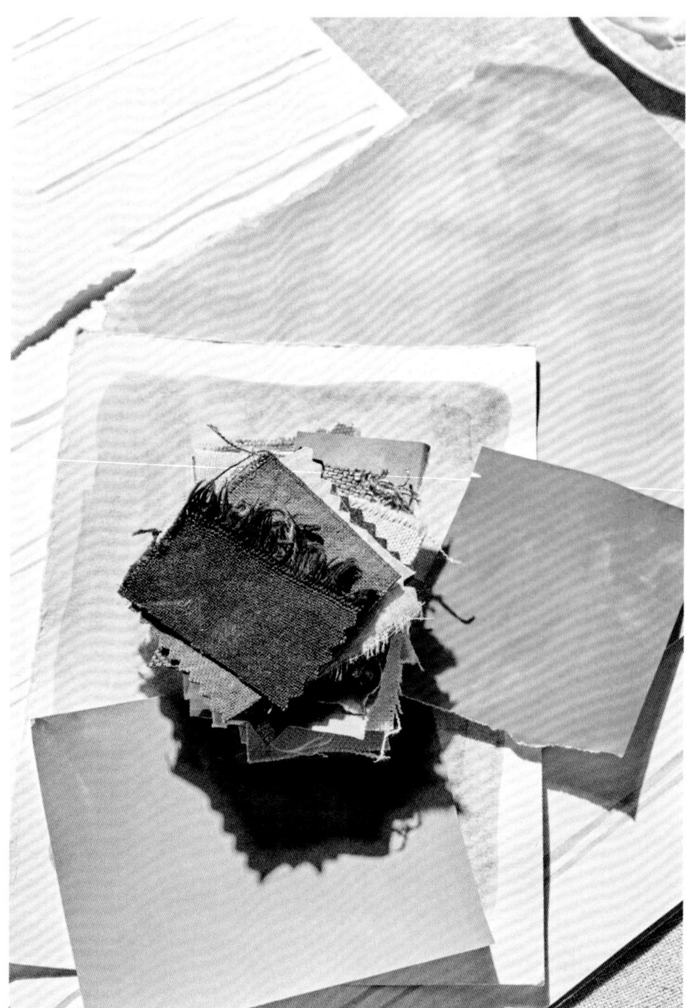

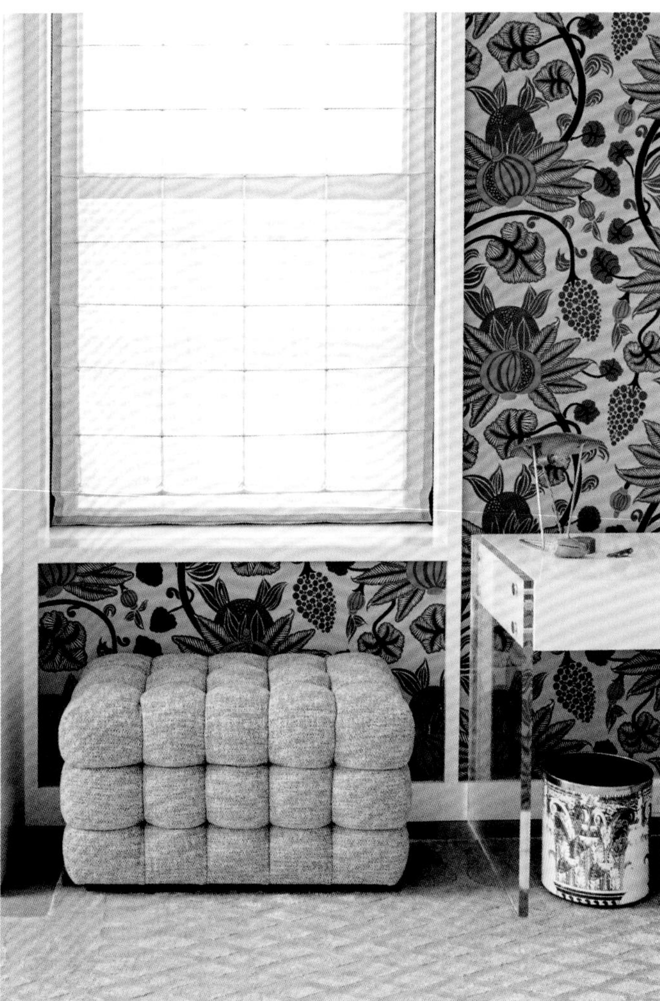

Once you've spent time collecting, documenting, and researching your interests, start organizing them for your own color wheel. I find it helpful to organize the samples by color, so I can start to focus on which versions of the colors I like the most. Let yourself build this over time. You may not have space for bins like I have, but the point is not to shortchange yourself on the gathering process. If you're starting from scratch, give yourself a good amount of time for pulling ideas. The process is artistic, and there's no hurry or right answer.

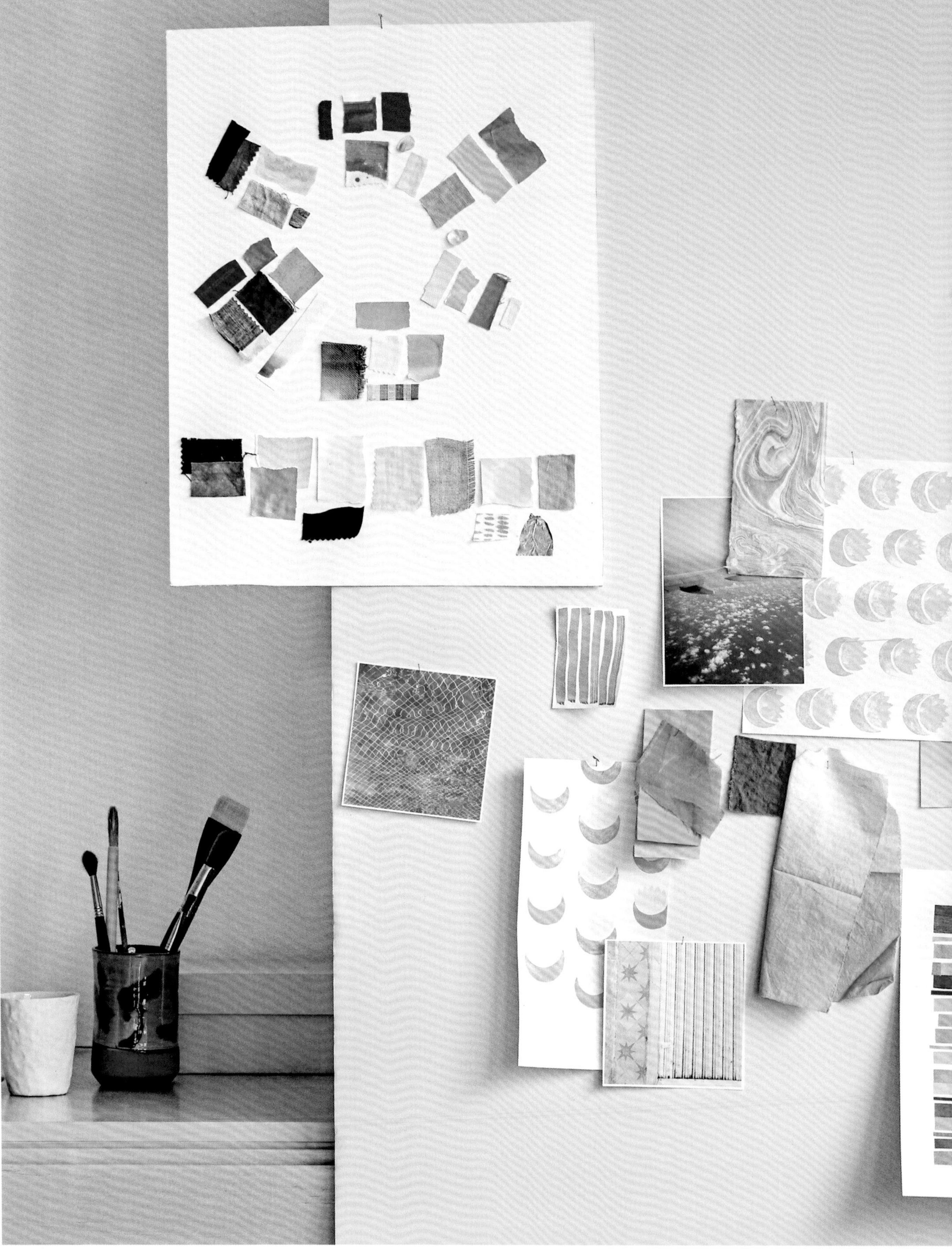

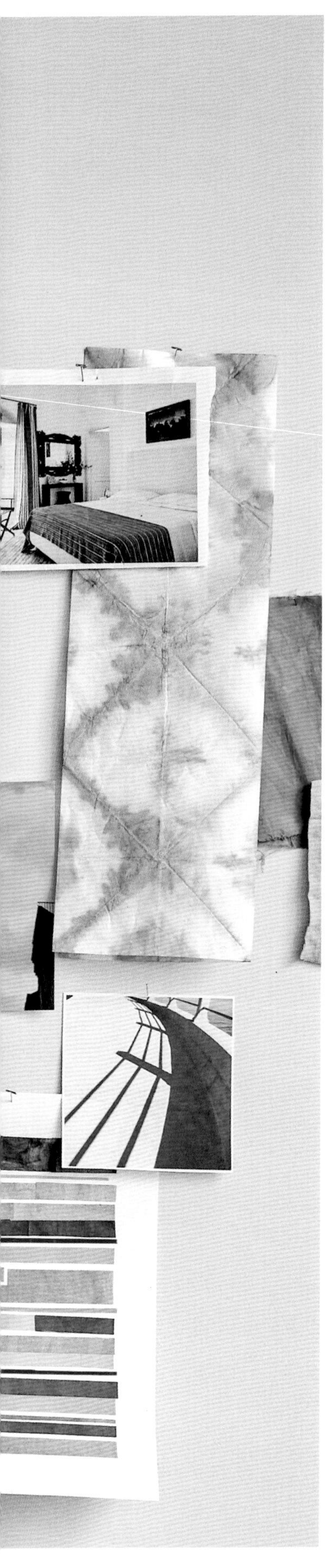

MAKE YOUR OWN COLOR WHEEL

Once you have a solid idea about the particular colors you're drawn to, start to look at how they interact with one another. You can use anything to create your personal color wheel—pieces of paper, paint chips, leaves, packaging, stationery, fabric swatches, photos, shells, broken ceramics, stones—even an eraser! If you find an object that's just the right shade but too big to put on your color wheel, look for it in paper or fabric form, or consider photographing or painting it.

Place the colors in a circle or rectangle, just like a traditional color wheel (see page 19), but using your specific hues. Instead of the traditional Red, Orange, Yellow, Green, Blue, and Purple, you might have Blush, Pumpkin, Ochre, Grass, Navy, and Lilac. You might find you love one color in particular, with several shades represented, but only one shade of a different color. Everyone's color wheel will look different. Try to narrow your choices to just a few tints or shades of one hue so you have to get more specific about your selections.

Don't forget about neutrals! They are important in creating a cohesive room. Include them in your color wheel next to the colors they are closest to, or create a separate section at the bottom.

Notice how finish, texture, and material affect your feelings about the color. Is it the fabric that you love? Or the clay-like texture of the eraser? You may respond differently to the painted version of a color. That's important because it will provide you with valuable information about what form of those colors you'll want to use later.

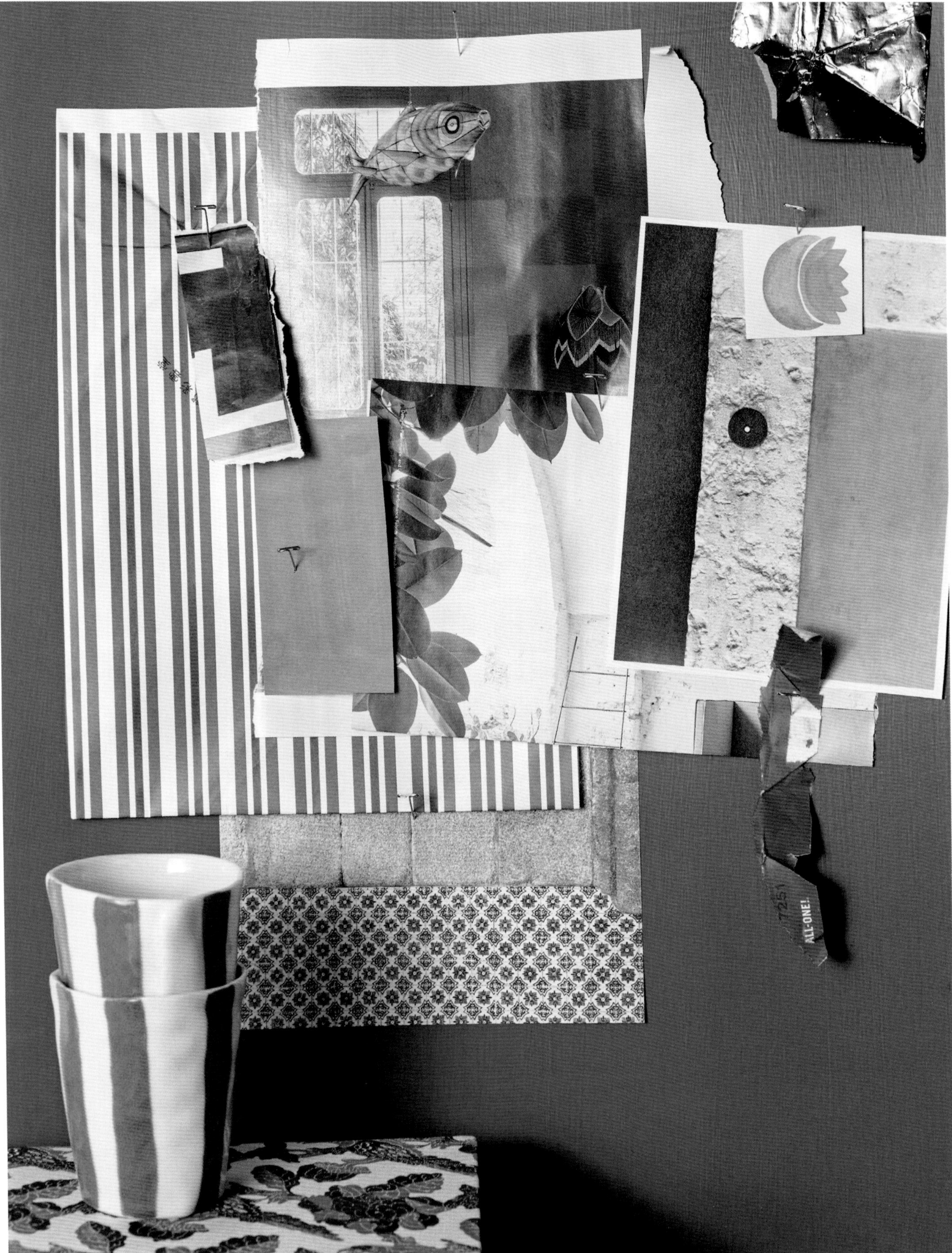
ALL-ONE!
7251

MAKE A COLOR PALETTE

This is where the magic really happens. One color on its own can be dreamy, but colors reacting with one another is what really tugs at your heartstrings.

To start, think of a palette as five hues. Begin with a color that you're most drawn to. Next, add at least two neutrals. (Remember, neutrals can just be less intense versions of a hue.) Think back to tint, tone, and shade (see page 26). Then add a "connector" color—something that bridges the gap between your neutral colors and the anchor you started with. This is what I mean when I talk about a color story. It's a story because there is an inciting incident (your focal-point color) and then there are transitions (your neutrals and connector colors) punctuated with moments of great excitement (accent colors). For example, if you picked tomato red and then added in gray and taupe neutrals, you might want to add in a soft coral-orange color as a connector color. Lastly, add an accent color that will liven up the arrangement. This could be a ribbon or accents of color that will be used only in select areas, or something calmer that enhances the whole mix. While you're doing this, remember what we discussed about proportion playing an important role in your palette on page 64. You can, of course, adjust the formula here and there, creating endless possibilities.

Want to play more? Here are some other color palette formulas to explore.

- For a more monochromatic look, consider analogous colors. Pair three (think purple-blue, blue, and blue-green) with two neutrals.
- Looking for a multicolored palette? Go back to complementary colors (see page 22).
- Or look to your wheel and pull one primary, one secondary, and one tertiary color (see page 19).

Think about color palettes inspired by places, scents, and the seasons. How would you visualize a palette based on the scent of home, the coast, or a favorite memory? Try to break down the individual scents into colors. Which season do you connect with most? Choosing a "season" for your home could help you pull a cohesive palette together. For fall, you could pick richer and deeper colors, like jewel tones and anything autumnal. If your style veers more toward feminine and dreamy, you might want to pick a spring-like palette. For a summer vibe, choose bright, strong, crisp colors. Allow these times of year to inspire you. Look back at the seasonal palettes I created on pages 40–44, but also think about the colors you're drawn to during those times of year. The associations and colors you notice each season may be different from what I notice and am drawn to. What colors do you crave each season?

One last palette suggestion is to look back through the homes in this book (or other inspiration images you've gathered) and pull out the colors from those images.

I suggest making at least five palettes before decorating any one room. Try to create a variety of options and just play. Once you've arranged them, think about how they make you feel; you'll need to know this to help you translate the palette into your home.

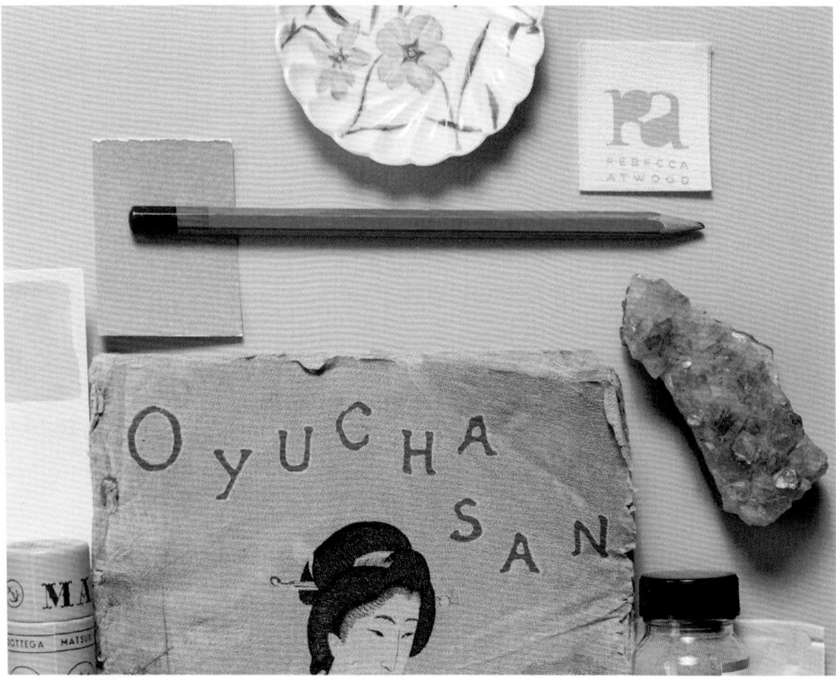

Painting Your Walls

A trip to the paint store is a great way to see the color terms we've discussed in action. A lot of paint brands have color chips that start with the most saturated version of a color, along with its tints, tones, and shades.

1 Don't assume painting is the first thing you need to do when you move in to a new home or you're redecorating. I know many contractors and decorators would disagree with me, but you can always paint later!

2 Choose the mood you want for your space. Then think about the value (lightness-darkness) of a color that will help you achieve it. A new paint color won't actually change the size of a space, but it can change the feeling. While dark colors often make a space feel smaller, a cool dark color like navy can actually feel expansive if it brings to mind memories of star gazing. Light colors can reflect light and feel airy. Mid tones work well in most spaces, especially those that don't get a lot of natural light.

3 Find a piece that sparks the mood you want—it could be a pillow, a painting, an image of a room from a magazine or even a photo of a landscape. Bring this with you to the paint store to see what colors make you feel that way. Give yourself time to play with different ideas; new combinations may surprise you.

4 Bring home trial sizes of paint, apply, and look at them on your wall. Paint in sunny spots and in shadows to see how the value and hue change throughout the day. Some grays and tans turn more purple, green, red, or blue depending on the light. Or paint a board that you can move around to different rooms to see how the color changes. Be sure to live with these paint tests for a few days. It often looks much darker or more saturated on your wall, so you might want to go a shade or two lighter than you think you should.

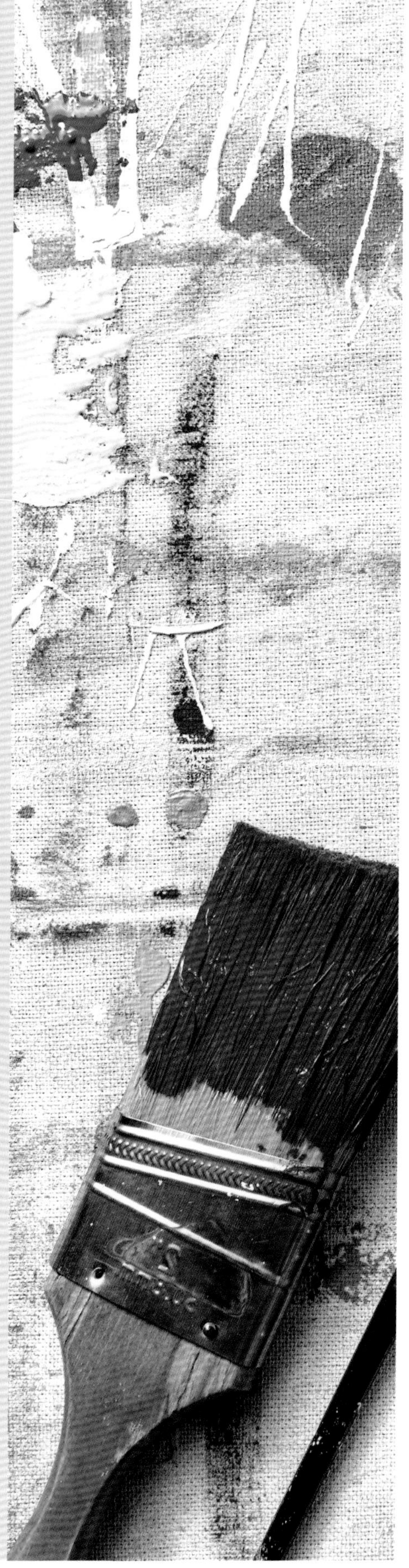

MAKE A MOOD BOARD

Go back to the things you've collected during your color hunt. Pull together the images you found when doing additional research and start to pin those up on a board and see how they relate. Put up your color wheel and a few favorite palettes. Stack the objects you love in front of the board. Figure out which images in particular speak to you. Your color story is informed by images, textures, and patterns. Take the time to gather imagery you love and see how they relate to one another. Live with it for a while, then edit it further. Give yourself time to explore, and don't worry too much about how it's going to translate into a room just yet. This is the time for fun and experimentation!

SKETCH YOUR ROOMS

To get an initial sense of how your mood board and palettes will translate into your home, take time to visualize each room in which you want to add color. You might sketch a few room ideas using your chosen palette. Don't worry about accurately drawing the room; just think about where you would use the colors from your palettes in the room. The drawing could even be abstract, with geometric shapes as reference objects in a room (long rectangle for a sofa, a square for a chair, a floor, or a wall). Or find a black-and-white line drawing of a room online and fill it in with colored pencils to play with some different ideas. If the idea of drawing or painting isn't up your alley, you can also collage, or just look for images online or in magazines that have the colors in your wheel.

This is where your wheel and your palettes will become even more refined. It's an editing process, and you might find you only use half the colors in your palette or only a few from your wheel when you start visualizing living with these colors in larger ways. You can always save the colors you edited out of your palette for smaller items later (accessories are a great place to bring in additional colors that could be smaller accents), but at least you have a road map of what to look for when you layer in more color!

Sometimes you won't know how you feel about something until you give it a try, and that's okay, too. You can always change something if you don't love it!

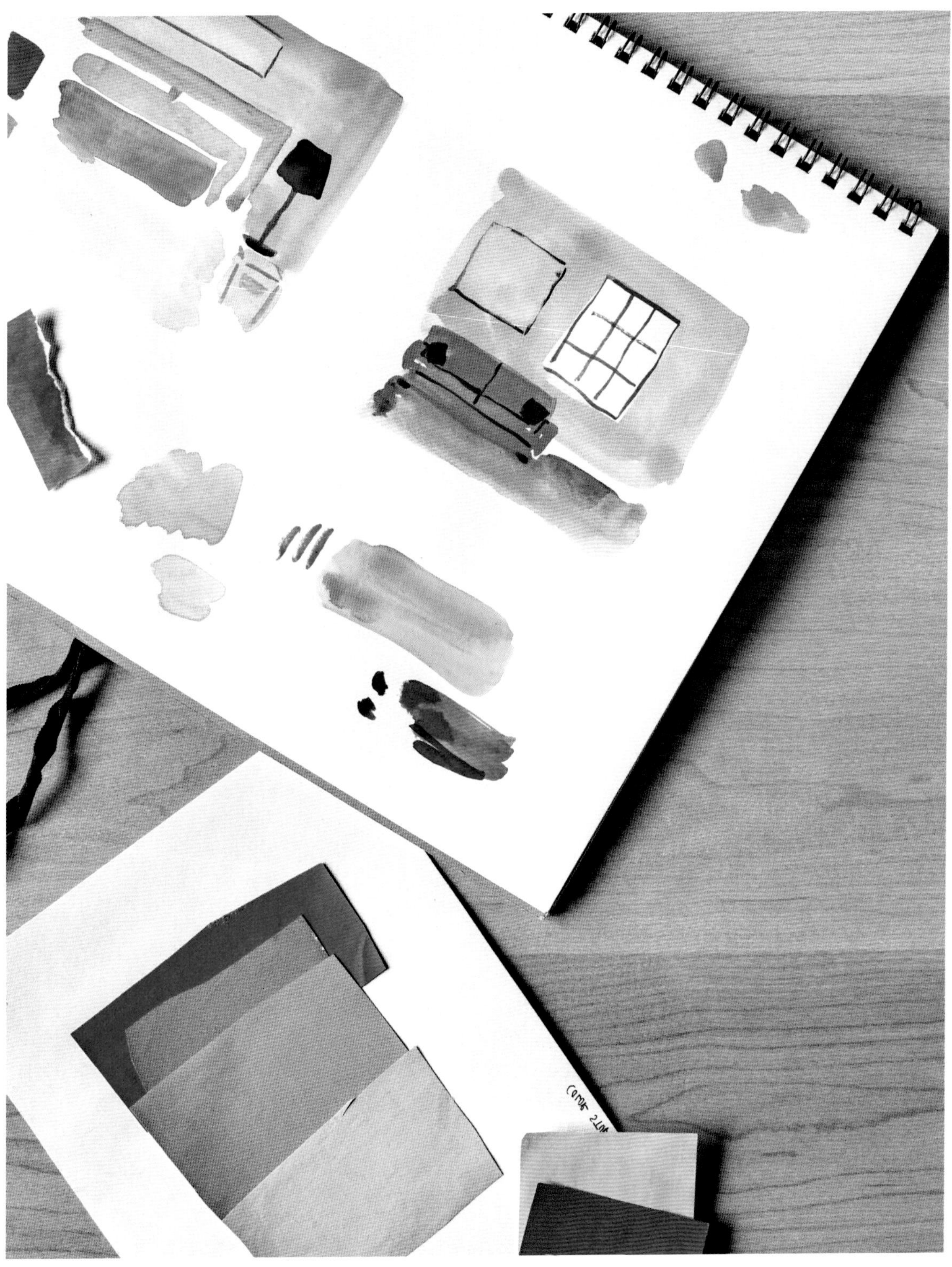

Working with Limited Natural Light

Imagine walking on the beach in the winter; there are soft sandy hues that merge into deeper brown, and golden ochre and soft greens in the dunes, all set against the deep marine hue of the ocean and the crisp blue sky. You might see someone in a red sweater walking along the shore, and a house with blue shutters. Those bright colors pop against the landscape, but they feel cohesive because everything is seen in the same light, and the light is connecting all the colors through shadow and dimension. It is the great unifier, bringing a palette together, which is why the light in a room is the first thing to consider before you start creating your layered canvas.

If your space doesn't get much natural light, the first step is to figure out how to remedy that. Take this step before choosing new colors or making changes, because it will influence everything else. Spaces that don't get a lot of natural light are challenging because the colors you use will look darker overall. In general, each room should have different layers of lighting that break down into three categories: ambient (think overhead), task (think reading lamp, a light over a stove, etc.), or accent (supplementing ambient lighting, used to highlight artwork or other details in a room). Most homes have overhead lighting covered, but consider what else you need to add. If you need to install lights, do so just above seating level to make a room feel cozier.

Now that you have your light sources, consider your lightbulbs. If you love how a color looks with natural light but your lightbulbs make it too yellow at night, find a different bulb. There are many different options these days.

When it comes to picking a paint color for a dark room, renowned designer Emily Henderson has a great tip. Everyone loves white walls, but they can look very dirty in a space that doesn't get a lot of natural light. In that case, you're better off picking a midtone or intentional gray, not a white that ends up looking gray because of the lack of light. Matte-finish paint also reflects light evenly, whereas glossy paint can create a glare.

A décor tip: Add mirrors to reflect light. Use shades of white to help bounce light around the room.

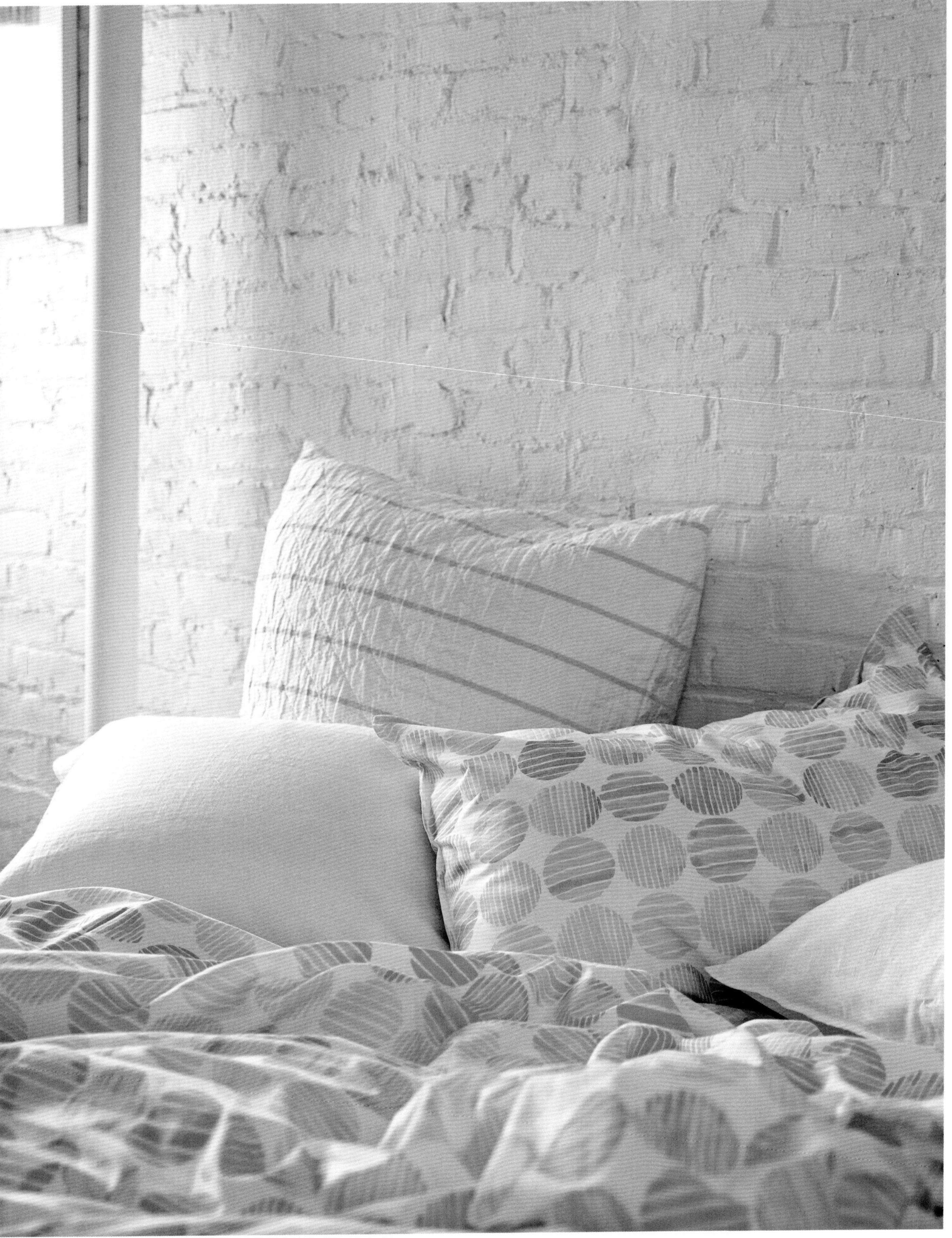

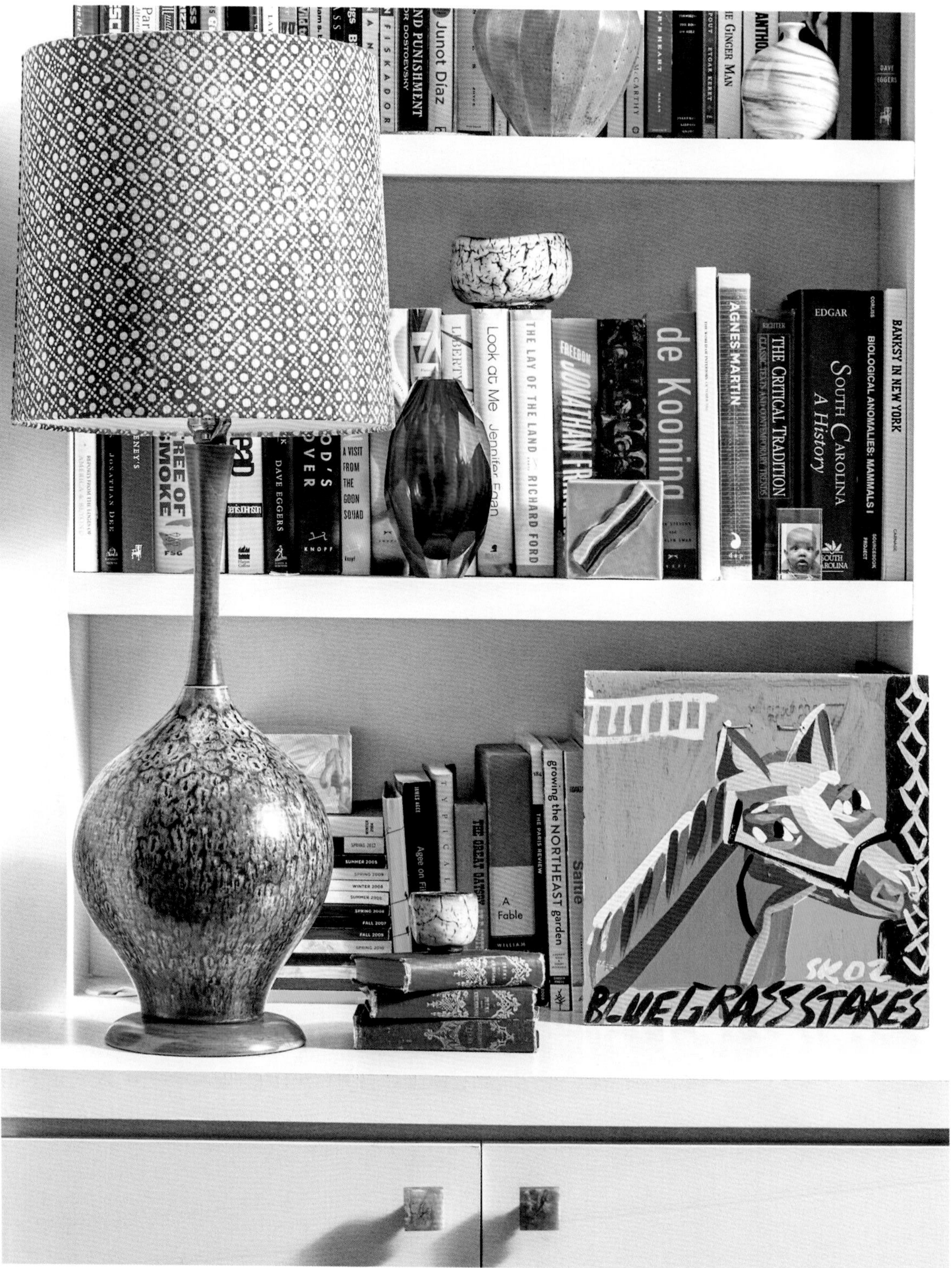
Junot Díaz
Look at Me Jennifer Egan
THE LAY OF THE LAND RICHARD FORD
de Kooning
AGNES MARTIN
THE CRITICAL TRADITION
EDGAR
SOUTH CAROLINA A History
BIOLOGICAL ANOMALIES: MAMMALS I
BANKSY IN NEW YORK
DAVE EGGERS
A VISIT FROM THE GOON SQUAD
JONATHAN DEE
Agee on Film
growing the NORTHEAST garden
THE PARIS REVIEW
A Fable
SKOZ
BLUEGRASS STAKES

ARTFUL ARRANGEMENTS

You've done all of this research—now begin to experiment on a smaller scale with objects you already own. Creating vignettes is a great way to experiment with color relationships and create a story from which to build a room, or just to refresh a space that feels tired. Up until now, we have seen our color story only through two-dimensional projects, but playing with palettes on a three-dimensional level is really important. Colors look different in three-dimensional form than they do on a flat piece of paper because of the way the light hits them. Find objects in your home that reflect the colors you love, or purchase small, inexpensive objects in your colors. Start by creating object groupings like vases, picture frames, or sculptures and see how you like it—even a small artful arrangement can change the vibe of your space and bring freshness to a room!

TRANSLATING IT TO THE HOME

If you're new to introducing color, consider what pieces you're less likely to change and consider the foundation of your room; you may want to opt for neutrals. For example, your sofa is a good place to go neutral, because you're likely to layer color on top. A rug is a great place to add color, even though it's a bigger investment piece in a room. Be sure to work it into the palette in a thoughtful, considered, layered way.

Just because you have your sketches, color wheel, and mood board doesn't mean you have to dive right in with all new furniture. First try draping a throw over the couch in a color from your wheel, and then you can graduate to upholstering it or purchasing a new piece. Another trick: Take a photo of the room, print it out, and then place pieces of colored paper on the furniture or a wall where you're considering changing the color. You could also start by hanging an inspiration painting featuring your palette to slowly inspire you to build with one new piece at a time. The beauty of all the work you've done up until this point is that now you have a plan to slowly and thoughtfully build a room with a gorgeous and unique color story all your own with fewer surprises.

ROOM FLOW

A refined sense of the colors you like will help build a natural relationship between rooms. When you pull from the same overarching color wheel, there will be a connection between the palettes you use in different rooms or spaces in your home, which will help it feel cohesive. Think about the neutrals and connector colors translating across spaces that you can see from one room to another. For example, if you have an open-concept living room and kitchen, you may want to consider using the same neutrals and connector colors within the space. You can then choose palettes that work together but are different for the two spaces to give them their own sense of purpose. You could focus on blues for the kitchen, and a multicolored palette for the living room area that has some of the same blue accents. Perhaps all you can see from one room to the other is a bit of the wall color. Consider, if you like, how those two colors look together.

Remember to think about your home as an entire landscape, and take inspiration from how nature uses color and how that can translate to all of the surfaces and objects within your space. If you're using photos, drawings, or paintings of a scene to inspire your rooms, look at them together and make sure they all speak to one another. Think about the layers you're seeing in each. Think about your walls as the "background" in the scene—it could be the sky or a field at different times of the day and year. Your furniture could be trees, architectural elements, or other big blocks within the landscape. Look at the small accents and elements in the foreground. Think about how the colors connect with one another and how there are many versions of the same hue.

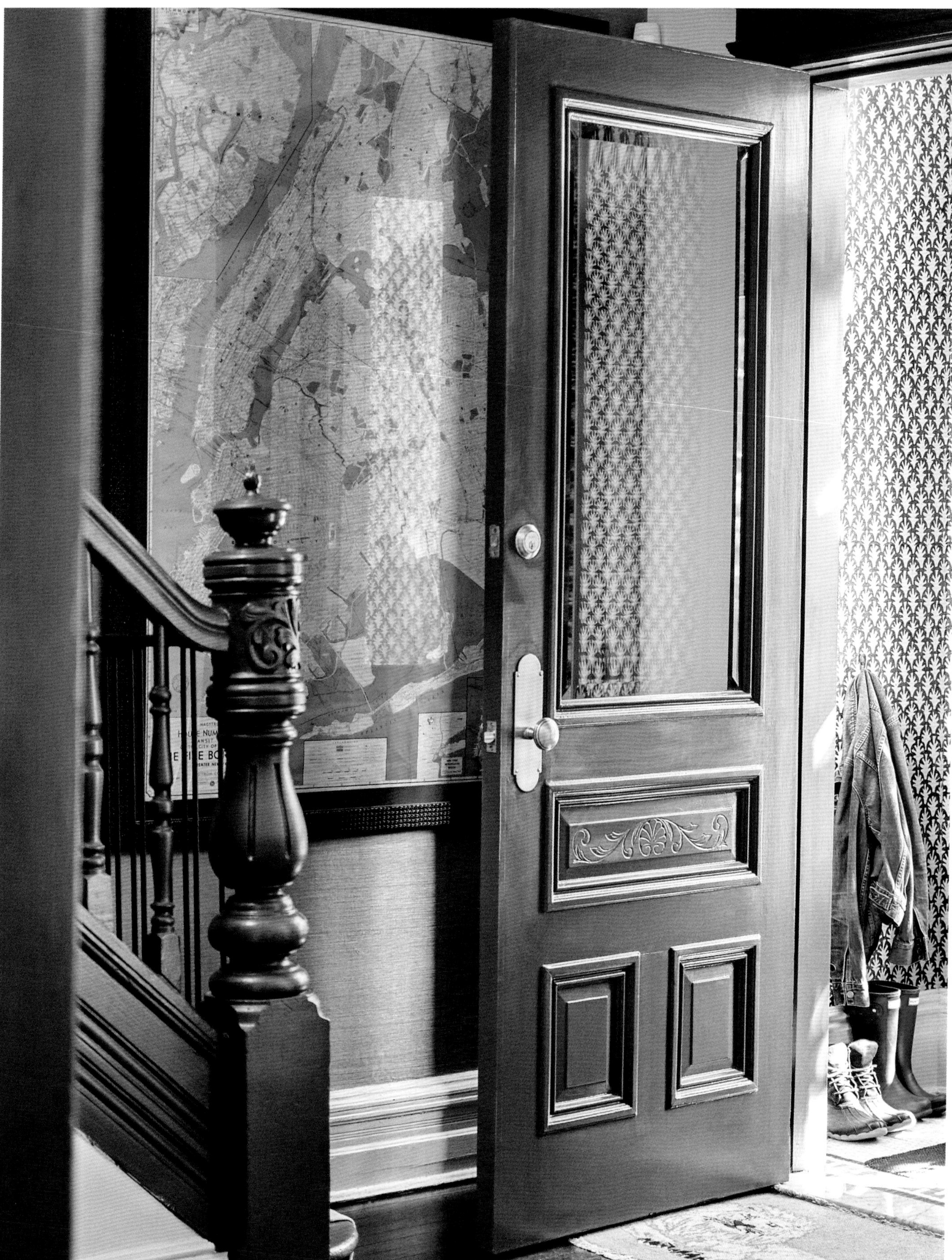

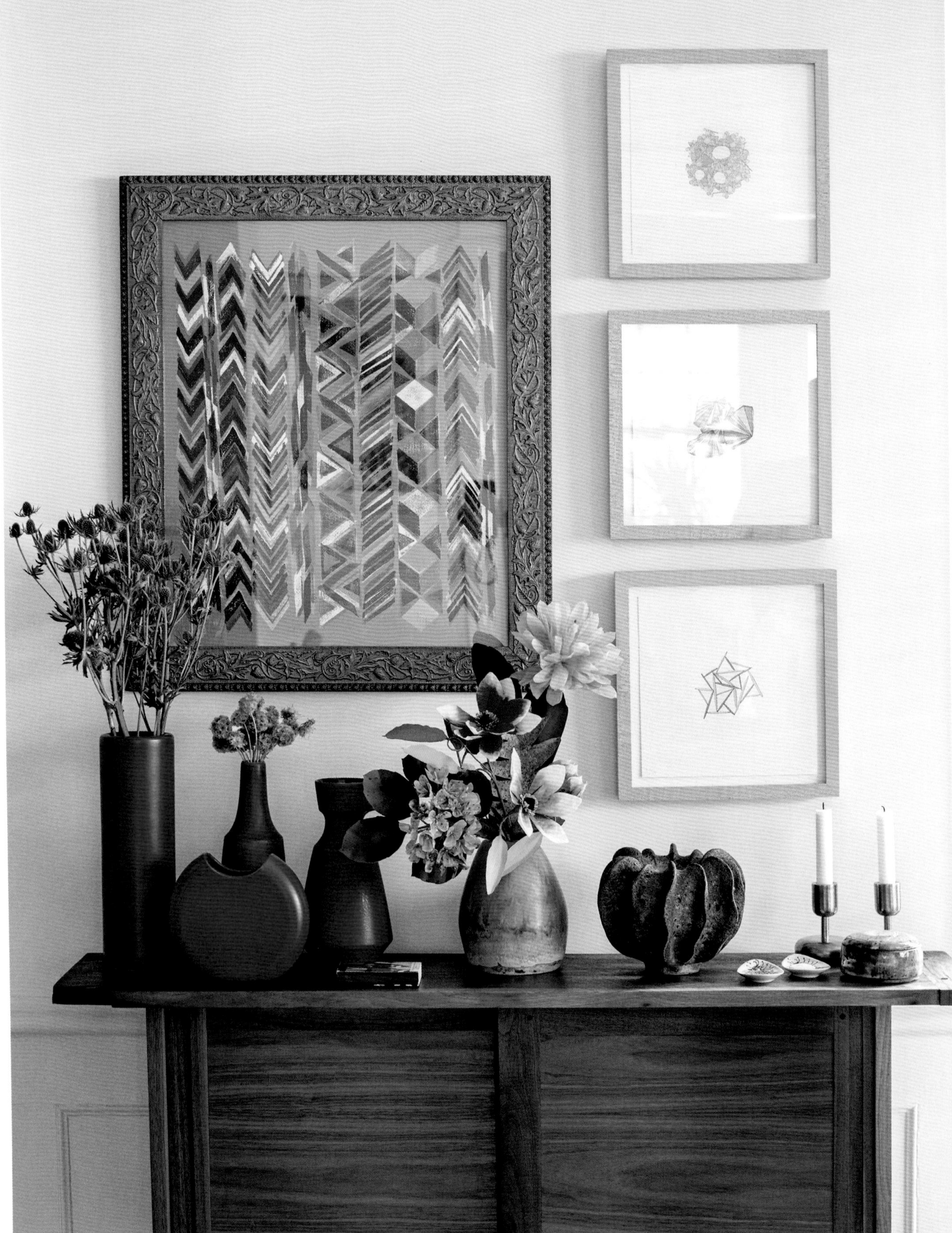

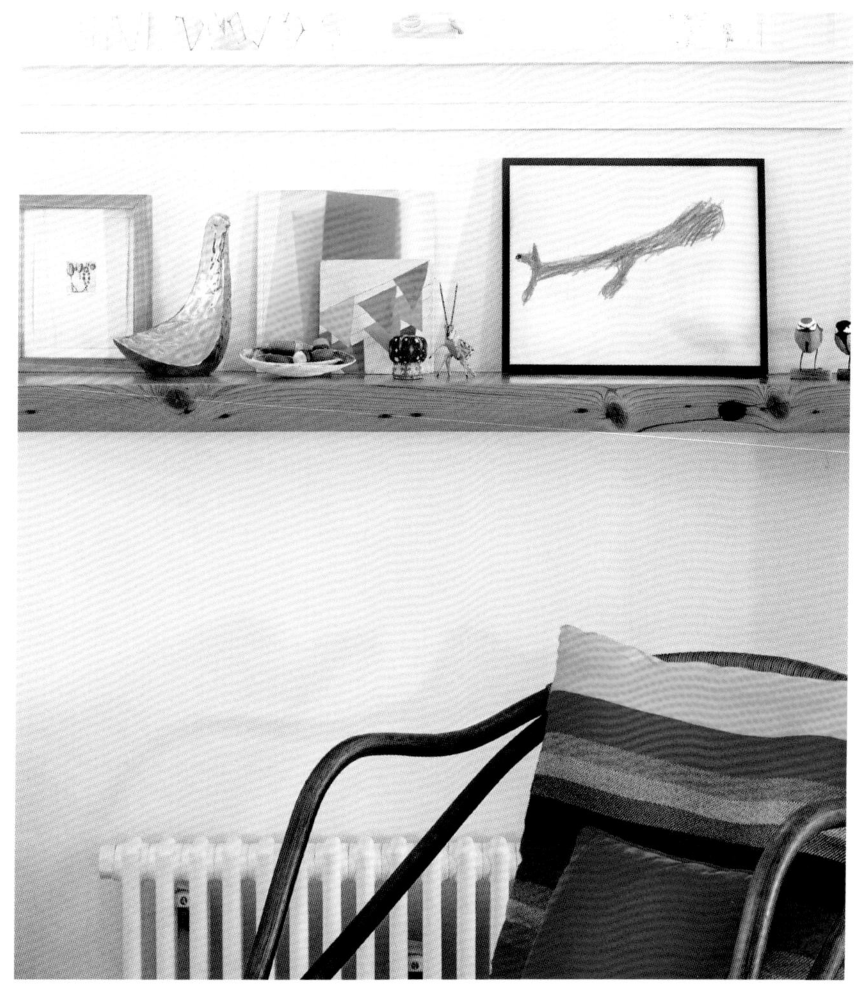

YOUR BRIGHT, COLORFUL LIFE

You've explored, you've played, you've brainstormed, and you've envisioned. Take all of these notions to your home. Remember, it's just a bigger canvas—it's not permanent! You've got all the tools you need to enjoy this journey; tackle a corner, then a whole room, and then the whole house. Reread this book and use it as a reference guide as your color story continues to grow and change along with you, and always remember that you are the author of your own unique color story! You're ready to surround yourself with your colors, create your world, and live in your own magical landscape.

My Top Color Tips

I hope you'll return to this book over time and continue to use it as a reference for different projects you're working on. Here's a reminder of my top tips for using color in your home.

- Figure out what colors you love. Look to your memories. Go on a color hunt. Slow down to notice the subtleties. Ask yourself questions about how these colors make you feel to get specific about just the right tint, tone, shade, or finish of a given hue.
- Consider the mood you want to create. Think about how you want to feel in the space and about places and environments that make you feel that way. Remember, color doesn't need to be loud.
- Build a palette that speaks to that mood. Proportion is an important tool in this! And don't forget connector colors and neutrals when building a palette—they are key for balance.
- Play! Experiment with palettes on paper. Make a mood board.
- Make time to visualize the space. This can be hard, but you're more likely to be happy with how your space turns out if you spend this time up front. It could be a rough drawing, a collage of color and shapes that reference the room, a mood board, or even just a collection of the colors, materials, and finishes you plan to use.
- Start small. Arrange colorful objects in a vignette before tackling a room. Give yourself time to just have fun.
- Think about your room as a landscape, and take inspiration from how nature uses color and how that can translate to all of the surfaces and objects within a space.

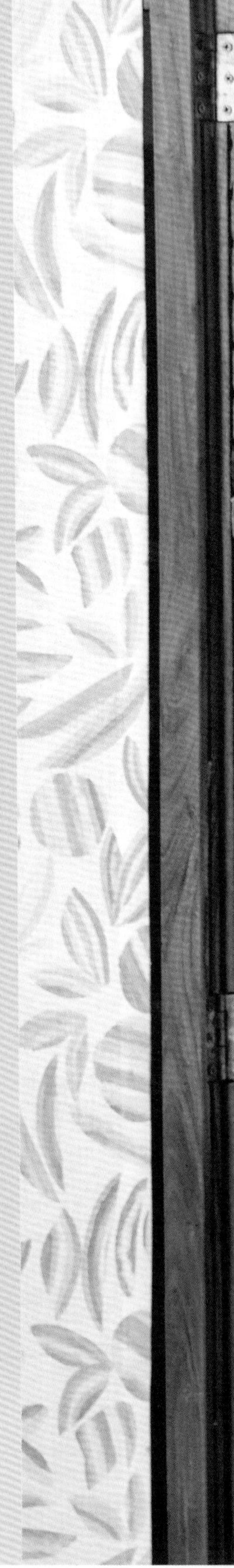

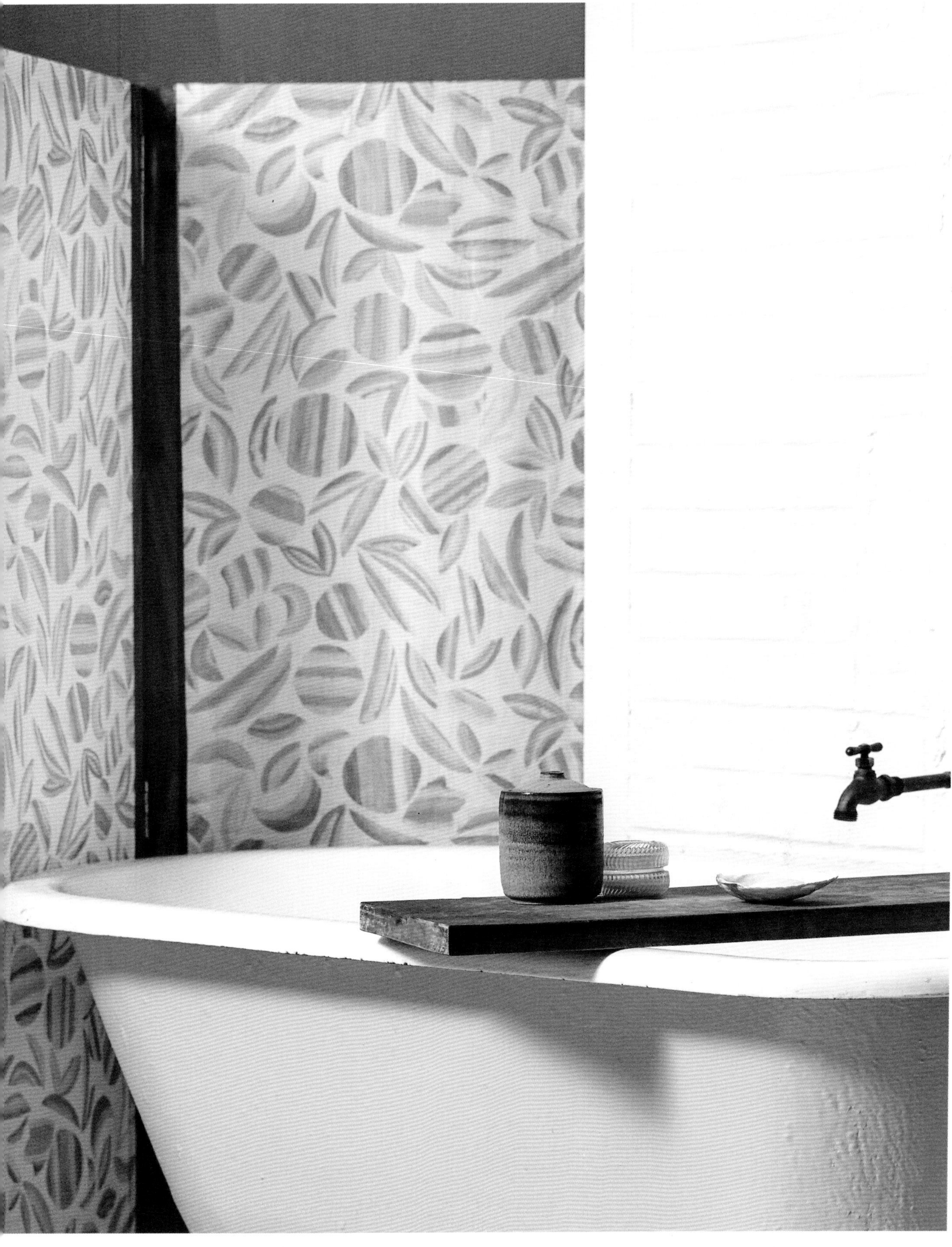

RESOURCES

ADDITIONAL COLOR RESOURCES

Podcasts

Radio Lab, episode on colors
www.radiolab.org/story/211119-colors

Books

The Secret Lives of Color
by Kassia St. Clair

Color Problems
by Emily Noyes Vanderpoel

The History of a Color
series by Michel Pastoureau

Color: A Natural History of the Palette
by Victoria Finlay

Colour: Travels Through the Paintbox
by Victoria Finlay

Interaction of Color
by Josef Albers

On Weaving
by Anni Albers

Ode to Color: The Ten Essential Palettes for Living and Design
by Lori Weitzner

A Colorful Home: Create Lively Palettes for Every Room
by Susan Hable

SHOPS & DESIGNERS FOR COLOR INSPIRATION

Andrew Molleur
Brooklyn, NY
Ceramicist

Artist and Craftsman Supply
Brooklyn, NY
artistcraftsman.com
My favorite local art supply store

Balefire Glass
Portland, OR
Glass artist

Benjamin Moore
benjaminmoore.com
They can custom match colors for you! We did this for the peach wall in our Nolita store.

Bird Brooklyn
Brooklyn, NY, and Los Angeles, CA
birdbrooklyn.com
An inspiring clothing store

Case for Making
San Francisco, CA
www.caseformaking.com
Handmade watercolor paints and workshops

Farrow and Ball
us.farrow-ball.com
Beautiful paint colors make it easier to end up with a color you're happy with.

Heather Taylor Home
Los Angeles, CA
Table linens

Hesperios
New York, NY
Knitwear and more. Their NYC shop is full of beautiful colors.

James Showroom
Austin and Dallas, TX
jamesshowroom.com
A home textile and wallpaper showroom

John Derian
New York, NY
Vintage-inspired decoupage and more

Leigh Forstram
Brooklyn, NY
Ceramicist

Lion Brand Yarn
New York, NY
www.lionbrand.com
Yarns for knitting and more

M&J Trimming
New York, NY
www.mjtrim.com
Trims, ribbons, and much more

Mociun Home
Brooklyn, NY
A favorite home décor shop

Mood Fabrics
New York, NY
www.moodfabrics.com
Fabrics for all sorts of projects

Nicky Rising
Los Angeles, CA
nickyrising.com
A home textile and wallpaper showroom

Oroboro
New York, NY
oroborostore.com
A cool concept store in NYC

Paul+
Atlanta, GA
paulplusatlanta.com
A home textile and wallpaper showroom

Pigment
Tokyo, Japan
pigment.tokyo
Amazing art supply store filled with pigments

Printed Matter
New York, NY
www.printedmatter.org
Art books and inspiration

Rebecca Atwood
New York, NY
Rebeccaatwood.com
Pillows, bedding, fabric, wallpaper, and more

St. Frank
Various locations in California and New York
stfrank.com
Home goods made by artisans around the world

Studio Four
New York, NY
studiofournyc.com
A home textile and wallpaper showroom

Warm
New York, NY
warmny.myshopify.com
A colorful shop for the urban hippie

Workaday Handmade
Brooklyn, NY
Ceramicist

ACKNOWLEDGMENTS

The thoughtful notes from all of you who read my first book, *Living with Pattern*, encouraged me to write this book. I'm grateful to be given the opportunity to work on a project like this that pushes me to learn and grow—and most of all to meet and work with so many amazing people.

First, I must thank my team, Gaby, Nellie, and Karen. I couldn't have done this without you! Gaby, your thoughtful consideration on the photo shoots and visuals was such a great support. Nellie and Karen, thank you for making sure everything ran smoothly while we were shooting and creating this book.

This book also wouldn't be what it is without the talented photographer Sharon Radisch. Sharon, your eye for composition and expertise with light made the spaces come to life. Collaborating with you on this project made me see differently. Your kindness and easygoing nature made the shoots such a pleasure. Thank you as well to Sharon's wonderful assistant, Zack Ahern. Both of you are a dream to work with.

To my agent, Kimberly Perel, thank you for your support and belief in the stories I wanted to tell. Thank you for helping me get all of the ideas in my head down on paper and structured. Without you I never would have written one book, let alone two!

To the whole team at Clarkson Potter who worked so hard to make this book beautiful! Thank you especially to my editor, Amanda Englander, who believed in this book and made it a reality. Thank you to the designer Mia Johnson, who created the beautiful design for this book.

Thank you to my friends and family who have supported me with all of my creative endeavors, and especially to my parents, who always encouraged my love of art. To my husband, Steve, thank you for always being by my side and for believing in me.

CONTRIBUTORS

Homes

Thank you to all of the home owners and designers who opened their spaces to us so that we could share them with you. Your spaces and stories make this book come alive.

KAYLA ALPERT
Los Angeles, CA

EMILY C. BUTLER
Queens, NY
Emilycbutler.com

SHANAN CAMPANARO
Brooklyn, NY
Eskayel.com

GRANT FENNING
Los Angeles, CA
lawsonfenning.com

ANTHONY GIANACAKOS
New York, NY
Anthonygeorgehome.com

CHARLOTTE HALLBERG
Brooklyn, NY
Charlottehallberg.com

LUCY HARRIS
New York, NY
lucyharrisstudio.com

JEN MANKINS
Brooklyn, NY
Birdbrooklyn.com

KATE REYNOLDS
Brooklyn, NY
Studiofour.com

HOPIE STOCKMAN
Los Angeles, CA
Blockshoptextiles.com

STUDIO DB
New York, NY
studiodb.com

MAURI WEAKLEY
Brooklyn, NY
Shopthemansion.com

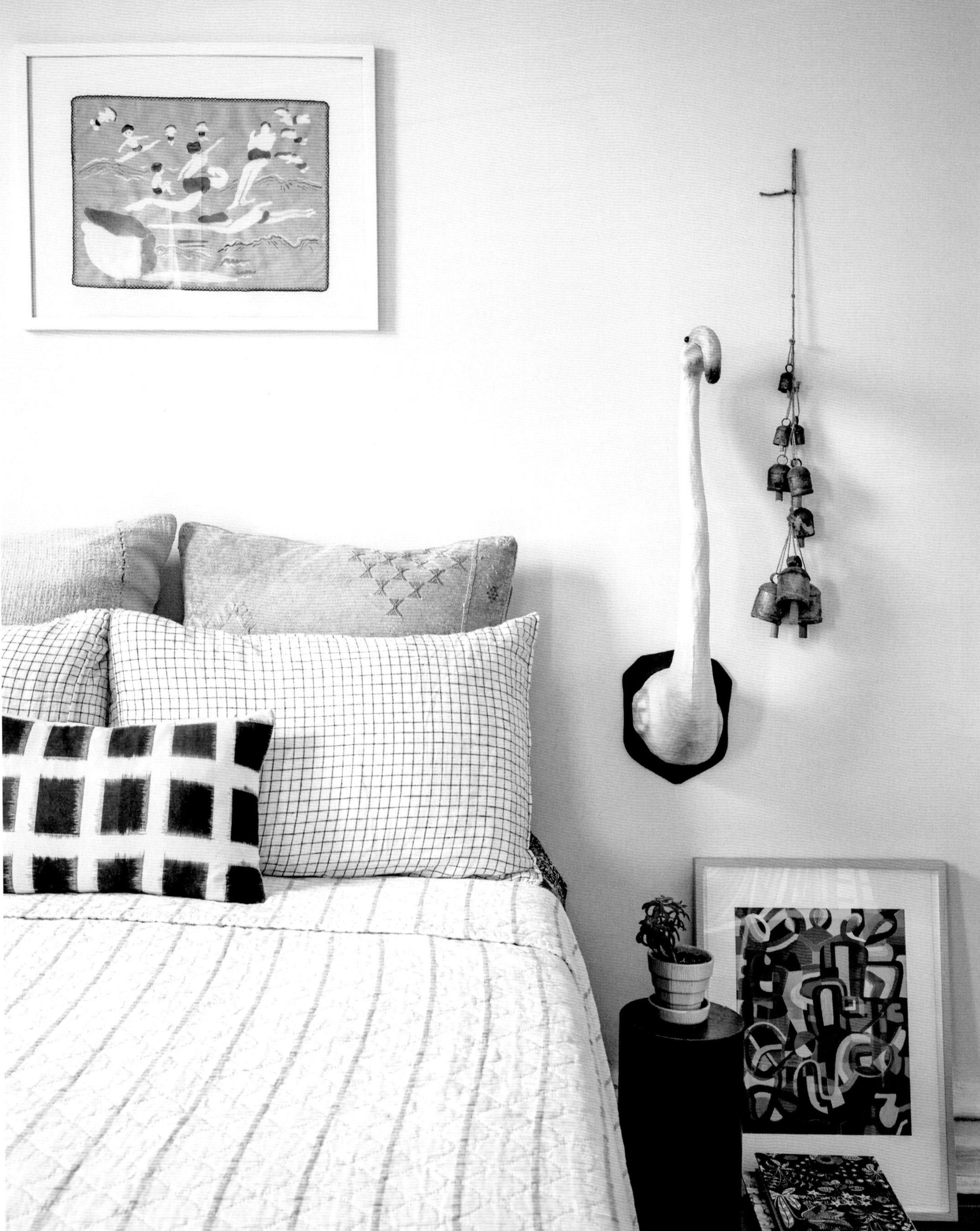

INDEX